YALE UNIVERSITY PUBLICATIONS
IN ANTHROPOLOGY
NUMBER 77

Atopula, Guerrero, and Olmec
Horizons in Mesoamerica

JOHN S. HENDERSON

NEW HAVEN
PUBLISHED BY THE
DEPARTMENT OF ANTHROPOLOGY
YALE UNIVERSITY

1979

LEOPOLD J. POSPISIL
Editor
ANNE F. WILDE
Associate Editor

Copyright © 1979 by Yale University.
All rights reserved. This book may not be reproduced, in whole or in part, in any form (except by reviewers for the public press), without written permission from the publishers.
Library of Congress catalog card number: 79-65060.

PRINTED IN THE UNITED STATES OF AMERICA

CONTENTS

- Rare Pottery Types of the Cacahuananche Phase ... 122
  - Polished Dark Red ... 122
  - Orange ... 122
  - Thin Tan ... 123
  - Red-painted ... 124
- Pottery Types of the Atopula Phase ... 124
  - Tlapala Red ... 124
  - Jiménez Red ... 126
  - Pozo Thin Red ... 131
  - Guamuchil Polished Black ... 136
  - Arana Black-and-White ... 143
  - Pedrusco Polished Gray ... 146
  - Mariposa White ... 149
  - Barranca Smoothed Buff ... 152
  - Bagre Coarse ... 155
- Rare Pottery Types and Trade Sherds of the Atopula Phase ... 156
  - Polished Dark Red ... 156
  - Orange ... 156
  - Red-rimmed ... 157
  - Red-on-White ... 158
  - Orange Lacquer ... 158
- Pottery Types of the Tecolotla Phase ... 159
  - Jiménez Red ... 159
  - Pozo Thin Red ... 164
  - Guamuchil Polished Black ... 167
  - Arana Black-and-White ... 173
  - Pedrusco Polished Gray ... 176
  - Mariposa White ... 177
  - Barranca Smoothed Buff ... 180
  - Bagre Coarse ... 181

3. THE CERAMIC ARTIFACTS OF ATOPULA ... 184
   - Figurines of the Cacahuananche Phase ... 184
     - Solid Torso ... 184
   - Figurines of the Atopula Phase ... 185
     - Solid Helmeted Head ... 185
     - Hollow Body ... 188
     - Solid Torso ... 189
   - Figurines of the Tecolotla Phase ... 190
     - Hollow Olmec Head ... 190
     - Crude Solid Head ... 192
     - Solid Arm ... 192
   - Surface Figurines ... 193
     - Solid D-Type Head ... 193
     - Solid D-Type Face ... 195
     - Solid Crescent-Cap Head ... 196
     - Solid High-Headdress Head ... 197
     - Solid Belted Torso ... 198
     - Solid Leg ... 199
   - Miscellaneous Ceramic Artifacts of the Tecolotla Phase ... 200
     - Sherd Trapezoid ... 200

4. THE STONE ARTIFACTS OF ATOPULA ... 201
   - Ground Stone of the Cacahuananche Phase ... 201

CONTENTS

Preface	xi
1. Introduction	1
2. Excavations at Atopula	8
The Natural Setting	8
The Excavations	12
3. The Preclassic Sequence at Atopula	19
The Cacahuananche Phase	19
The Atopula Phase	27
The Tecolotla Phase	32
4. The Early Preclassic Period and the Olmec Blackware Horizon	35
The Initial Ceramic Period	35
The Initial Early Preclassic Period	37
The Late Early Preclassic Period	42
The Terminal Early Preclassic Period	45
Nonceramic Artifacts	47
"Floating" Assemblages	50
The Tlatilco Problem	51
The Xochipala Problem	56
Settlement Patterns	59
5. The Middle Preclassic Period and the Olmec Whiteware Horizon	66
The Early Middle Preclassic Period	66
Nonceramic Artifacts	70
Settlement Patterns	72
Monumental Art	76
6. Olmec Mesoamerica	83
Olmec Civilization	89

APPENDICES

1. Atopula Ceramics	98
Analysis	98
Type Descriptions	102
Paste and Surface	102
Form Terminology	103
Plastic Decorative Techniques	104
Comparisons	104
2. The Preclassic Pottery of Atopula	105
Pottery Types of the Cacahuananche Phase	105
Tlapala Red	105
Jiménez Red	108
Pozo Thin Red	111
Guamuchil Polished Black	113
Pedrusco Polished Gray	116
Barranca Smoothed Buff	118
Bagre Coarse	120

For Jeanne

CONTENTS

Metates	201
"Palettes"	202
Ground Stone of the Atopula Phase	202
Metates	202
Stone Bowl	202
Ground Stone of the Tecolotla Phase	203
Metates	203
Pestle	203
Mano	204
"Flaker"	205
Discussion	205
Chipped Stone of the Cacahuananche Phase	205
Flakes	205
Blades	205
Chipped Stone of the Atopula Phase	206
Flakes	206
Blades	206
Chipped Stone of the Tecolotla Phase	206
Flakes	206
Blades	207
Discussion	207
Obsidian Hydration Analysis	209
5. THE EL CLARÍN PHASE	212
Ceramics	212
Huisache Red	212
Ratón Black-Brown	214
Pulga Orange	216
Venado Orange-Brown	217
Carrancho Coarse	218
Fine Buff	220
Red-on-White	220
Xilocintla Glaze	221
Stamps	221
Stone	222
Projectile Points	222
Flakes and Blades	222
Beads	222
Ball	222
"Polisher"	222
6. CERRO OTOTAL	223
7. TETIPAN	226
Ceramics	226
White	226
Red-painted Buff	228
Excised Brown-Black	230
Red-Black	231
Polished Orange	234
Red/White	235
White-on-Red	235
Coarse Ware	236
Figurine	236

CONTENTS

8. XOCOHUITE ... 237
   - Ceramics ... 237
     - Red-painted Buff ... 237
     - Polished Orange ... 239
     - White ... 240
     - Excised Brown-Black ... 241
     - Coarse Ware ... 242

REFERENCES ... 243

Figures

1. Preclassic sites in Guerrero. 9
2. Map of Atopula. 13
3. Schematic section through Atopula. 15
4. North-south section of stratigraphic pits 3 and 4. 17
5. Relative frequencies of Preclassic pottery types by phase. 21
6. Relative frequencies of Preclassic vessel forms by phase. 22
7. Relative frequencies of Preclassic vessel forms by type and phase. 23
8. Early and Middle Preclassic chronology of Mesoamerica. 28
9. Hydration readings on obsidian from Atopula and Tetipan. 29
10. Preclassic sites in central and western Mesoamerica. 36
11. Preclassic sites in southeastern Mesoamerica. 38
12. Tlapala Red pottery, Cacahuananche phase. 106
13. Jiménez Red pottery, Cacahuananche phase. 109
14. Pozo Thin Red pottery, Cacahuananche phase. 111
15. Guamuchil Polished Black pottery, Cacahuananche phase. 114
16. Pedrusco Polished Gray pottery, Cacahuananche phase. 117
17. Barranca Smoothed Buff pottery, Cacahuananche phase. 119
18. Bagre Coarse pottery, Cacahuananche phase. 121
19. Rare pottery types, Cacahuananche phase. 123
20. Tlapala Red tecomates, Atopula phase. 124
21. Jiménez Red ollas, Atopula phase. 126
22. Jiménez Red open bowls, Atopula phase. 127
23. Jiménez Red pottery, Atopula phase. 127
24. Jiménez Red pottery, Atopula phase. 128
25. Pozo Thin Red pottery, Atopula phase. 132
26. Pozo Thin Red pottery, Atopula phase. 133
27. Guamuchil Polished Black pottery, Atopula phase. 137
28. Guamuchil Polished Black open bowls, Atopula phase. 138
29. Guamuchil Polished Black pottery, Atopula phase. 139
30. Guamuchil Polished Black pottery, Atopula phase. 140
31. Guamuchil Polished Black beakers, Atopula phase. 141
32. Arana Black-and-White pottery, Atopula phase. 144
33. Pedrusco Polished Gray pottery, Atopula phase. 147
34. Pedrusco Polished Gray pottery, Atopula phase. 148
35. Mariposa White pottery, Atopula phase. 149
36. Barranca Smoothed Buff ollas, Atopula phase. 152
37. Barranca Smoothed Buff pottery, Atopula phase. 153
38. Barranca Smoothed Buff pottery, Atopula phase. 154
39. Bagre Coarse pottery, Atopula phase. 155
40. Rare pottery types and trade sherds, Atopula phase. 157
41. Jiménez Red ollas, Tecolotla phase. 159
42. Jiménez Red open bowls, Tecolotla phase. 160
43. Jiménez Red pottery, Tecolotla phase. 160
44. Jiménez Red pottery, Tecolotla phase. 161
45. Pozo Thin Red pottery, Tecolotla phase. 165
46. Guamuchil Polished Black open bowls, Tecolotla phase. 167
47. Guamuchil Polished Black pottery, Tecolotla phase. 168
48. Guamuchil Polished Black pseudo-grater fondos, Tecolotla phase. 169
49. Guamuchil Polished Black beakers, Tecolotla phase. 170
50. Guamuchil Polished Black pottery, Tecolotla phase. 170

FIGURES AND TABLES

51. Arana Black-and-White pottery, Tecolotla phase. 174
52. Pedrusco Polished Gray convex bowls, Tecolotla phase. 176
53. Mariposa White pottery, Tecolotla phase. 177
54. Barranca Smoothed Buff pottery, Tecolotla phase. 180
55. Bagre Coarse pottery, Tecolotla phase. 181
56. Bagre Coarse pottery, Tecolotla phase. 182
57. Ceramic figurine, Cacahuananche phase. 185
58. Ceramic figurines, Atopula phase. 185
59. Ceramic figurines, Tecolotla phase. 191
60. Ceramic figurines, surface. 194
61. Ceramic figurines, surface. 198
62. Metates, Cacahuananche phase. 201
63. "Palettes," Cacahuananche phase. 202
64. Metates, Atopula phase. 203
65. Stone bowl, Atopula phase. 203
66. Ground stone artifacts, Tecolotla phase. 204
67. Huisache Red pottery, El Clarín phase. 213
68. Ratón Black-Brown ollas, El Clarín phase. 214
69. Ratón Black-Brown pottery, El Clarín phase. 215
70. Pulga Orange pottery, El Clarín phase. 216
71. Pulga Orange pottery, El Clarín phase. 217
72. Venado Orange-Brown pottery, El Clarín phase. 217
73. Carrancho Coarse pottery, El Clarín phase. 218
74. Carrancho Coarse pottery, El Clarín phase. 219
75. Minor pottery types, El Clarín phase. 220
76. Ceramic stamps, El Clarín phase. 221
77. Stone artifacts, El Clarín phase. 222
78. Stone beads, Cerro Ototal (H-16). 223
79. Pottery, Cerro Ototal (H-16). 224
80. Pottery, Cerro Ototal (H-17). 225
81. White pottery, Tetipan. 227
82. Red-painted Buff pottery, Tetipan. 229
83. Red-painted Buff convex bowls, Tetipan. 230
84. Excised Brown-Black pottery, Tetipan. 230
85. Red-Black pottery, Tetipan. 232
86. Red-Black pottery, Tetipan. 233
87. Polished Orange pottery, Tetipan. 234
88. Minor pottery types and figurine fragment, Tetipan. 235
89. Red-painted Buff pottery, Xocohuite. 238
90. Red-painted Buff pottery, Xocohuite. 239
91. Polished Orange pottery, Xocohuite. 240
92. White pottery, Xocohuite. 241
93. Excised Brown-Black pottery, Xocohuite. 242

Tables

1. Distribution of Preclassic Pottery Types by Phase 20
2. Distribution of Preclassic Decorative Modes by Type and Phase 24
3. Atopula Obsidian Hydration Readings 209
4. Tetipan Obsidian Hydration Readings 210
5. Postclassic (El Clarín Phase) Pottery 212

Preface

My chief motive for preparing a new version of my doctoral dissertation (Henderson 1974) is to make basic archaeological data on Guerrero more widely accessible, since Guerrero is still practically *terra incognita* to Mesoamerican archaeologists. In this revised study I have incorporated new data that became available between 1971 and 1977, modified the analysis, and reduced a lengthy discussion of Olmec monumental art to a summary form. The basic conclusions of the original study have changed only slightly. In assessing the relationships of the material from Atopula, I found myself drawn into a full-scale synthesis of the Early and Middle Preclassic periods, which led to the recognition of two distinct Olmec horizons in Mesoamerica. Since these horizons have never been described as such, my analysis and ceramic comparisons are given in detail.

The survey and excavations were carried out under a *Convenio* granted by the Instituto Nacional de Antropología e Historia. Arq. Eduardo Matos M. and Arq. Jorge Angulo V. of I.N.A.H. graciously provided invaluable assistance. I extend my sincere thanks to them and to many municipal officials and residents of Guerrero, too numerous to name. The field work was supported by a Doherty Foundation Fellowship for Advanced Study in Latin America and by a National Science Foundation Dissertation Improvement Grant (GS-03187). The Hull Memorial Publication Fund of Cornell University provided support for publication.

Carol Anzalone and Marjorie L. Ciaschi patiently typed the revised manuscript. Joann Kroll assisted in preparing the illustrations. Irving Rouse, Kwang-chih Chang, and particularly Michael D. Coe of the Department of Anthropology, Yale University, gave me good advice and stimulating ideas. Jeanne J. Henderson shared the field work and contributed in many ways to the analysis and writing. Special thanks go to each of them, but they are in no way responsible for shortcomings.

J.S.H.

Cornell University
Ithaca, New York
December 1978

1. Introduction

The field research on which this monograph is based was carried out during 1970–1971 in the northeastern highlands of the state of Guerrero, Mexico. The project was designed to recover data on the Preclassic period in Guerrero in order to define the archaeological context in which the Olmec style occurs there. The goal was to provide a factual basis for hypotheses that might account for the strong representation of the Olmec style so far from the Gulf-coast Olmec heartland in terms of social and economic factors. The research goals stem from the history of Olmec studies and from the culture-historical questions raised by Olmec material in the highlands—the so-called highland Olmec problem.

Although scattered objects in what is now known as the Olmec style found their way into collections at least as early as the eighteenth century, that style was almost totally unknown until the late nineteenth century. José Melgar y Serrano was the first to publish (in 1869) a description of an Olmec-style object—a colossal head from Tres Zapotes in the Gulf-coast lowlands. During the rest of the nineteenth century and the early years of the twentieth, a few other descriptions of individual Olmec pieces, without specific provenience data, were published.

In *Tribes and Temples*, the report of their expedition to southern Mexico and Guatemala, Blom and LaFarge (1926) provided the first description of the Olmec monument at San Martín Pajápan and, more importantly, an account of the discovery of La Venta. Although they considered La Venta a Maya site, the publication of their report awakened considerable archaeological interest in the Gulf-coast area.

Hermann Beyer, in his review of *Tribes and Temples* (1927), recognized the stylistic affinity between the San Martín Pajápan monument and certain small portable art objects, and applied the term "Olmec" to both. Saville also recognized the relationship and followed Beyer in the use of this term (Stirling 1968; Bernal 1969: 28–32).

Thus in the late 1920s there was a dawning realization of the existence of a distinct art style, embracing both monumental stone sculpture and portable carvings, particularly in jade. As the use of the historic ethnic label Olmec implies, this style was perceived as a lowland phenomenon, localized in the southern Gulf-coast area—the territory of the historic "rubber people."

Vaillant (1932) also recognized the stylistic relationship of the small jade carvings to the monumental sculpture and went farther toward defining a complex of related traits. Although he was the first to discover Olmec objects in an archaeological context in the highlands, Vaillant continued to think of the style as a lowland phenomenon. By the late 1930s there were strong indications that the Olmec-style objects had been produced by an unrecognized civilization—distinct from the Maya—centered in the Gulf-coast lowlands.

The archaeological exploration and excavation that actually established this was begun by Matthew W. Stirling in 1938. In the course of his work at Tres Zapotes and La Venta, Stirling (1942, 1943) became convinced that the Olmec civilization predated that of the Maya.

Similar conclusions were being reached by archaeologists working in the highlands. Vaillant (Vaillant and Vaillant 1934) had found Olmec ceramic figurines in his excavations at Gualupita, a Preclassic site near Cuernavaca, Morelos; and Alfonso Caso (1938) had discovered that traces of the Olmec style appeared in his first phase at Monte Albán.

In 1942 the Sociedad Mexicana de Antropología held a conference at Tuxtla Gutiérrez, Chiapas, to discuss the rapidly accumulating discoveries. One objective of the conference was to assemble an overview of the features associated with the Olmec style, which were being brought to light by excavations, especially those of Stirling. As Stirling (1968: 5) notes, "The concept of the Olmec 'art style' was being changed to that of a culture." The notion that the Olmec style represented one aspect of a distinct culture was certainly a step forward, but it was still conceived as an archaeological culture—basically a collection of material artifacts. The participants were attempting to define a complex of traits, some of which might permit social inferences, but they were not, at that stage, primarily concerned with reconstructing the structural and organizational features of Olmec culture.

The participants in the Tuxtla Gutiérrez conference were generally agreed that the Olmec archaeological culture represented the earliest development of civilization in Mesoamerica, although many Mesoamericanists (particularly Maya scholars) remained unconvinced. Perhaps the staunchest supporter of Olmec temporal priority was Miguel Covarrubias. From his study of the Olmec art style, Covarrubias (1942) concluded not only that the Olmec had preceded the other well-known civilizations of Mesoamerica, but also that they shared an important Olmec heritage. His persistent advocacy of the Olmec civilization as the "mother culture" of Mesoamerica was largely responsible for its wide acceptance.

Covarrubias (1948, 1957) was also the first to emphasize the importance of Olmec material in the highlands of Mexico. Having acquired many Olmec pieces from the Valley of Mexico and Guerrero as well as from the Gulf coast for his personal collection, Covarrubias eventually concluded that Guerrero, or some nearby part of the southern highlands, was the homeland of the Olmec civilization. His position was never widely accepted, but it helped to focus attention on the highlands, particularly Guerrero, as an important locus of objects in the Olmec style.

The 1950s saw continued research in the Gulf-coast Olmec heartland. The highlight of this decade was undoubtedly the work of Drucker, Heizer, and Squier (1959) at La Venta, which produced a series of radiocarbon dates placing Olmec civilization in the early part of the first millennium B.C. There could no longer be serious doubt that the Olmec flourished during the Preclassic period, predating all other civilizations in Mesoamerica.

INTRODUCTION

Interest continued during the 1950s and early 1960s, fueled by the appearance in quantity of Olmec objects looted from scattered highland sites, particularly in Guerrero. Covarrubias (1957) continued to argue for a highland Olmec homeland, as did Piña Chán (1955a). Scattered small-scale archaeological excavations continued.

During the last ten years there has been a considerable itensification of this interest. The preliminary results of Michael Coe's (1968b, 1970) large-scale excavations at San Lorenzo Tenochtitlán have already substantially altered widely held notions about the development of Olmec civilization. Heizer (1968) returned to La Venta for several short seasons of work which resulted in new information and significant revisions of previous conclusions about that site.

Research on the highland Olmec has also burgeoned in the last decade. A renewed interest in monumental Olmec art in the central highlands was stimulated by the discovery of Olmec-style cave paintings and a stela in Guerrero, and of new Olmec reliefs at Chalcatzingo. A great deal of research in the central highlands has been concerned with defining the complex Preclassic sequence there—a prerequisite for establishing the chronological position and archaeological context of the Olmec style in the highlands. The work of Paul Tolstoy and his associates (Tolstoy and Guenette 1965; Tolstoy and Paradis 1970; Tolstoy 1971a) in the Valley of Mexico exemplifies the important work that has been done along these lines.

Much of the recent research has been explicitly framed in terms of the problem: How to account for the abundance of Olmec archaeological materials in the central highlands? The work of David Grove and Kent Flannery illustrates the trend toward the interpretation of highland Olmec archaeological material in terms of social and economic factors—an attempt to use Olmec objects and the pattern of their distribution as clues to the nature of the social and economic institutions of the cultural groups that produced and distributed them.

David Grove's program of extensive surface reconnaissance and excavation in Morelos was aimed at solving some of the problems of Preclassic culture history, particularly those associated with the Olmec presence there. Grove's early (1968b, 1968c) hypothesis explained the distribution of Olmec archaeological materials simply in terms of postulated Preclassic trade routes. Recently (Grove 1974a; Grove et al. 1976) he has begun to reconstruct a much more complex picture of the interaction among highland and Gulf-coast Olmec groups. Kent Flannery (1968), too, has proposed socioeconomic "models" to account for the stylistically Olmec material in the Valley of Oaxaca. The long-term investigations of Flannery (1976) and his colleagues have produced unique contextual data for Olmec material: precise provenience information in terms of internal settlement organization (craft-production zones, house floors, public buildings, and the like). Here for the first time is a substantial archaeological foundation for explanations of cultural interaction during the Early and Middle Preclassic periods.

The period since 1965 has also seen several attempts at broad interpretive synthesis of Olmec archaeological materials. While such efforts have contributed to the understanding of the civilization, there is still no satisfactory synthesis of Olmec culture history, nor even substantial agreement about many of the basic characteristics of the civilization. Consequently, each commentator proceeds from his own, often unstated, definition of Olmec. For some it seems to be purely an art style; for others it is a series of archaeological marker traits; and still others consider only a holistic Olmec civilization. It is not surprising that there has been so little agreement at the interpretive level: generalizations or interpretations generated by analysis of an art style may simply make no sense to a person who thinks of the Olmec in terms of white-rimmed black ware and concave mirrors.

Perhaps a full-scale reconsideration of the archaeology of the Olmec will be feasible when the data from the multidisciplinary San Lorenzo project are available. It would be of tremendous value to know the full range of characteristics of the two major excavated heartland Olmec sites, San Lorenzo and La Venta, and of their several components. Then it should be possible to define the precise chronological and spatial relationships of the components. A detailed archaeological picture of an Olmec site in the heartland—something more than the collection of monuments, ceremonial caches, and features of public architecture that is virtually all we know of La Venta—will provide a far firmer contextual basis for considering Olmec sites and features outside the Gulf-coast lowlands.

In the absence of agreement about the definitive features of Olmec civilization, hypotheses about its institutional and organizational characteristics are bound to be contradictory and unsatisfying—essentially at cross-purposes. A better definition of the Olmec as an archaeological culture is a prerequisite for productive hypotheses. Interpretation of Olmec material outside the heartland is handicapped because crucial questions about the heartland Olmec are not now answerable.

By 1970, when we began the Guerrero project, it had been recognized for many years that the quantity of Olmec-style objects discovered in Guerrero indicated something other than casual contact with the Gulf-coast heartland. More Olmec jades have come from Guerrero than from all the rest of Mexico. Almost without exception, however, these pieces have appeared on the antiquities market without archaeological context.

There was no evidence that could date the Olmec presence in Guerrero directly; too little was (and is) known of the development of the style to permit a stylistic dating of Olmec pieces. The only alternative was extrapolation from the context of Olmec cultural materials elsewhere in the highlands. Data from Guerrero were so scanty that there was no convincing way to tie the Olmec presence there into the chronological framework that could be sketched for the rest of the highlands. The hypotheses that have been offered from time to time were purely speculative.

The primary aim of our Guerrero project was to produce data on the Preclassic archaeology of Guerrero to provide a context for the Olmec material there. In this it was largely successful. Defining the archaeological components in which Olmec-style material occurs, and determining their status within local sequences, is the first step in determining their genetic relationships. The preliminary

INTRODUCTION

definition of Preclassic components in Guerrero presented here permits the proper formulation and initial evaluation of hypotheses about the social and economic factors responsible for the Olmec presence in Guerrero—specifically that of a Preclassic trade network emphasizing exotic raw materials and luxury goods. At every stage the conclusions have considerable relevance for the highland Olmec problem.

The original plan called for investigation of a limited area of the upper Balsas drainage in northeastern Guerrero. Initially, the lower course of the Río Amacuzac seemed particularly promising since it would have been a natural route of communication connecting Olmec sites in Morelos and western Puebla with areas in south-central Guerrero which are rich in Olmec material. There would surely be traces there of any important Preclassic trade route involving Guerrero. Ideally it would have been possible to locate a topographically limited area with several Preclassic sites which would provide data on the intensity and patterning of Olmec archaeological traits. This in turn would permit inferences about the nature of the posited Preclassic trade network.

In the field, extreme difficulty of access made it impractical to concentrate on the area of the Río Amacuzac. Instead, we moved to the Municipio de Huitzuco, to the west. Traces of pre-Hispanic occupation in the immediate area of Huitzuco have been largely obliterated by intensive construction and agricultural activity, so the surface reconnaissance emphasized the area to the south, which is drained by small tributaries of both the Amacuzac and the Tepecoacuilco, another affluent of the Río Balsas (see Fig. 1).

The Río Tepecoacuilco drains a very large portion of northeastern Guerrero, extending nearly to the Morelos border. The Tepecoacuilco is also a natural route of communication between Morelos and central Guerrero: movement from the Amacuzac Valley into the upper Tepecoacuilco drainage is extremely easy.

Several Early and Middle Preclassic sites had already been located in the lower Tepecoacuilco drainage (Fig. 1). Greengo (1967; 1970; personal communication) discovered Figueroa and El Calvario during his brief survey in 1967. Tetipan (App. 7), known to *huaqueros* (looters) for many years as a rich source of Olmec jades, has a substantial Early Middle Preclassic occupation.

We discovered Atopula south of Huitzuco on a small tributary of the Tepecoacuilco, very near the divide between the Tepecoacuilco and Amacuzac drainages. The surface material indicated a primary occupation in the Early Preclassic period; this was confirmed by test excavation, and we decided to concentrate our excavations at this site.

Although there is an artificial platform mound at Atopula, it is a small site and, in comparison with such sites as Chalcatzingo and Salinas La Blanca, it is not particularly rich in artifacts. As Lowe (Green and Lowe 1967: 79) has pointed out, Early Preclassic sites, particularly in highland central Mexico, are typically small and yield relatively few artifacts. These sites, which represent rural and marginal aspects of Early Preclassic Mesoamerican culture, must be taken into account in order to fully understand the period. The preference on the part of archaeologists for large sites with impressive architectural features, monumental art, or elaborate mortuary offerings is easily understood, but if sites with little or no Olmec art are ignored it will be impossible to understand the relationship of the Olmec elite centers with their rural hinterlands, and it will be impossible to discern the existence and nature of contemporary non-Olmec groups.

Besides tending to produce a nuclear or elite bias, the concentration on large rich sites presents severe practical problems: *huaqueros* also have a strong preference for these sites, and most have already been heavily disturbed. The looters are often prepared to adopt extreme measures to eliminate competition for what they perceive as a natural resource with considerable monetary value. At Tetipan, for example, the extreme hostility of local residents of Ahuelicán, who regularly loot the site, effectively prevents controlled digging. Excavation was possible at Atopula only because large-scale prospecting by *huaqueros* had failed to produce marketable artifacts.

The excavations at Atopula did produce Early Preclassic material, much of which can be considered Olmec-related. Olmec material from Guerrero can now be placed in an archaeological context based upon stratigraphy.

Our provisional sequence for the early part of the Preclassic period is an initial step toward a full and reliable archaeological sequence in an area that has been practically unknown archaeologically. Very little field research has been carried out in Guerrero, and much of the work that has been done remains unpublished. Printed reports are limited to brief accounts of reconnaissance projects and cursory descriptions of ceramics from surface collections and small test excavations. Archaeological data for every period are extremely scanty. There is a good deal of information on the Late Postclassic period and the Aztec expansion into Guerrero, but it is based almost exclusively on ethnohistorical sources. For the most part, reconstructions of the culture history of Guerrero have been limited to descriptions of poorly dated local styles of ceramics, portable stone sculptures, and architecture, and to the recognition of external "influences," primarily in ceramic attributes. Not a single Preclassic component has been previously described adequately (Harvey 1971; Lister 1971). In this context the Preclassic sequence based on the Atopula excavations takes on added significance.

The focus below is on the analysis of these Preclassic components in the context of what is known of the Early and Middle Preclassic periods, particularly in neighboring areas of highland central Mexico. Close relationships with complexes from Olmec-related sites in Morelos, the Valley of Mexico, Puebla, and Oaxaca quickly became apparent. In brief, Olmec-related material occurs at Atopula in the Early Preclassic period in the context of a distinct set of features of ceramic manufacture and decoration which appeared suddenly, marking a sharp shift away from the preexisting local ceramic style. The Olmec presence at Atopula was intrusive in the sense that it has the character of a veneer superimposed on the local style, which was not entirely superseded. At the beginning of the Middle Preclassic period, Atopula was abandoned, but the Olmec presence in northeastern Guerrero did not come to an end. Early Middle Preclassic Olmec-

INTRODUCTION

related material—including jade sculpture—occurs at much larger richer sites in the context of a new ceramic style. This pattern of evidence is area-wide; the Olmec presence in central Mexico occurs in the context of two distinct horizons.

The emphasis in this synthesis is on evaluation of the evidence for an Olmec economic network linking various parts of Mesoamerica with one another and with the Gulf-coast lowlands. The evidence bearing on the nature of the network, particularly indications of the possible importance of Olmec secular political power outside the heartland, merits special attention.

A very strong prima facie case can be made for the existence of an economic network emphasizing exotic raw materials and luxury goods, which seems to have been more a procurement system for the Olmec elite groups of the Gulf coast than a trade network linking independent groups of equivalent status and power. A final section briefly places this view of the Olmec in the context of the theoretical literature on the origins of civilization and the nature of pristine civilizations.

2. Excavations at Atopula

The Natural Setting

The archaeological site of Atopula is in northeastern Guerrero, 25 km. southeast of the city of Iguala (Fig. 1) in the Municipio de Huitzuco, midway between the villages of Tlapala and Cacahuananche. During the dry season Atopula can be reached in about 90 minutes by vehicle from the town of Huitzuco, some 10 km. due north. It is not accessible by vehicle during the rainy season.

The Atopula area falls within the upper slopes of the Balsas Depression, the enormous structural basin that trends roughly east–west across Guerrero, separating the central Mexican Plateau and the Cordillera Neovolcánica from the southern sierras of Guerrero and Oaxaca. The entire area is highly dissected with many low hills and, in sharp contrast with nearby central Morelos, there is very little level land (West 1964b: 62–3).

Although the Balsas–Mezcala river system is one of the largest in Mesoamerica, it flows through rugged terrain for most of its length and generally has not produced extensive floodplains that would be ideal for cultivation. The Balsas–Mezcala and its tributaries have always exerted a strong influence on settlement location, however, for precipitation is scant in most of the Balsas Depression. Moisture-bearing winds are intercepted by the plateau escarpments to the north and by the high sierra to the south, and much of the discharge of the Balsas is provided by its extensive tributary system, which drains an enormous highland zone.

The climate of the Balsas Depression is tropical wet-and-dry, with a long and clearly marked dry season. Virtually all precipitation, averaging between 500 and 1000 mm. annually in most areas, falls between May and October (Vivó Escoto 1964). Where the rain-shadow effect is greatest, as in parts of the middle Balsas Valley, the climate becomes more like that of semiarid steppe, with considerably less rainfall and somewhat higher temperatures.

The high evaporation rate, extended dry season, and shallow, often highly calcified stony soils—along with the cumulative effects of long-term human settlement, cultivation, deforestation, and erosion—combine to limit modern vegetation to spiny tropical scrub. Many stream courses and barrancas support a low deciduous seasonal forest, and a thin pine and juniper forest occupies some of the higher slopes.

Mammals, especially large ones, are not numerous in the Balsas Depression, although several species of small rodents are quite common, as are lizards and snakes. The bird life is extremely varied and abundant (Wagner 1964; West 1964a).

Environmentally, the Atopula area is not entirely typical of the Balsas Depression. It is situated in the upper slopes, in a zone of transition between the *tierra*

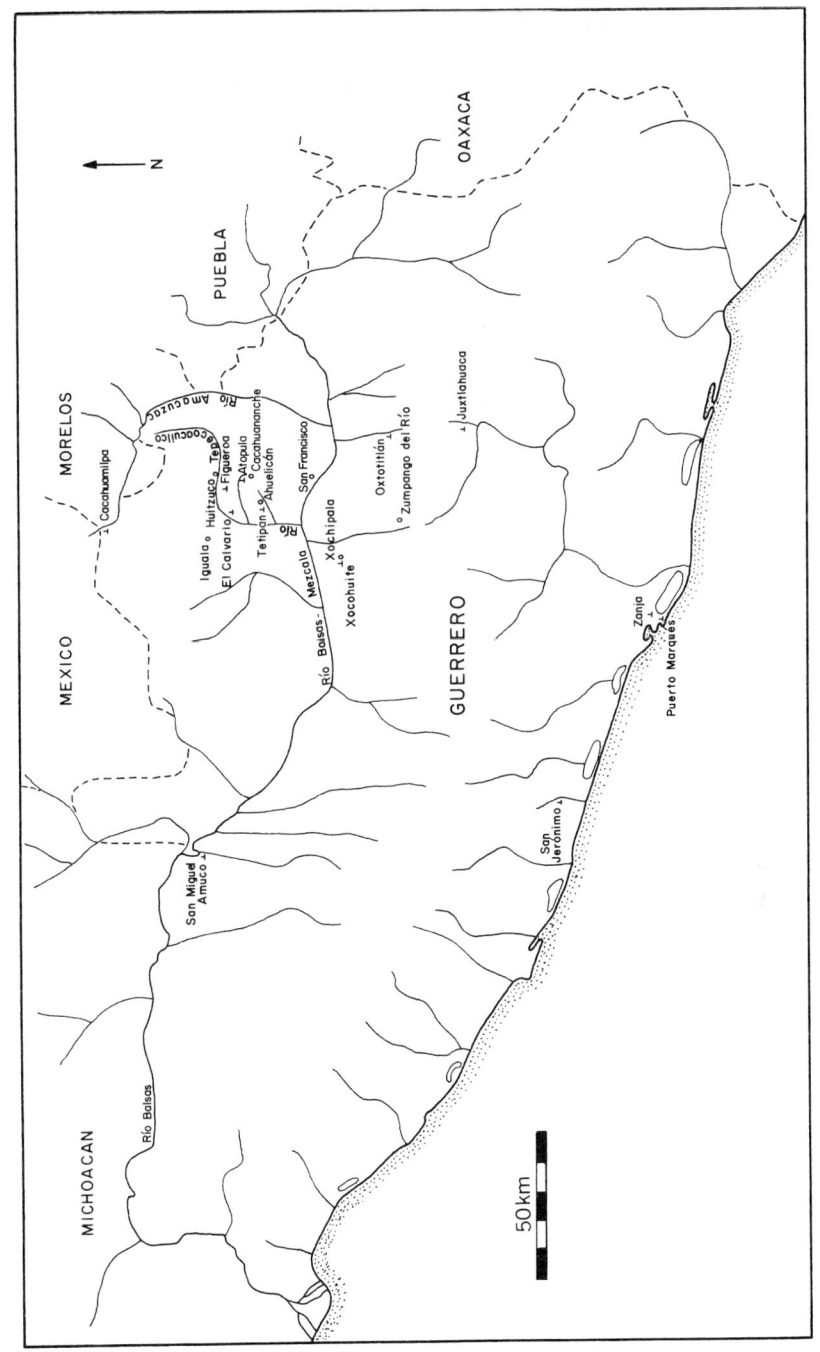

FIG. 1. Preclassic sites in Guerrero.

caliente of the middle Balsas Valley and the fertile, well-watered, volcanic-soil area of the *tierra templada* of central Morelos. Generally, the Atopula area is cooler than the middle Balsas zone to the west, with somewhat more precipitation, although it can certainly be characterized as hot and dry.

The dry season begins at Atopula in October or November, and the vegetation becomes progressively more desiccated until the sudden onset of the rainy season, generally in late May. Annual precipitation averages more than 1000 mm., virtually all of which occurs in the form of afternoon and evening thunderstorms during the rainy season. There is a late maximum in September. The occurrence of a *veranillo*, or respite in the rains, is quite variable, although local residents expect it. Daily temperature variability is quite large; temperatures are high during the day, especially late in the dry season when they may approach 40°C., but nights are quite cool. The mean annual temperature is near 25°C., perhaps slightly higher. The climate would be classified as type Aw in the Koeppen system (Vivó Escoto 1964).

Vegetation in the Atopula area consists principally of a thorn forest, dominated by huisache (*Acacia*), mesquite (*Prospis*), cascalote (*Caesalpina*), palo verde (*Cercidium*), and a large variety of cacti (especially of the columnar *Cereus* group). Stream courses support a much denser low deciduous gallery forest including willow (*Salix*), wild fig (*Ficus*), and Mexican bald cypress (*Taxodium*). A more mesic vegetation featuring guamuchil (*Pithecolobium*) occurs in a few especially favorable localities.

It has often been suggested that this flora represents an extremely impoverished remnant of the original vegetation, devastated by thousands of years of intensive slash-and-burn cultivation and consequent erosion (Miranda 1947; Wagner 1964: 251–2; West 1964a: 381; Paddock 1968: 127).

Large mammals are scarce, although local hunters still regularly take white-tailed deer; large cats, coyotes, and foxes are now rarely seen. Several varieties of rabbits (especially cottontail rabbits, *Sylvilagus*), squirrels, mice, rats, and other rodents are abundant, as are iguanas, other lizards, and snakes. Birds are numerous, particularly hawks, vultures, eagles, and a variety of smaller birds. Streams support turtles, frogs, and a few fish, especially catfish (Stuart 1964; West 1964a: 382–3; Paddock 1968: 127).

The site of Atopula is almost exactly on the divide between the drainage of the Río Tepecoacuilco to the west and that of the Río Amacuzac to the east; both flow south, ultimately emptying into the Balsas–Mezcala (Fig. 1). The small stream flowing past the site is a tributary of the Tepecoacuilco. It flows throughout the year, although its volume is greatly reduced at the height of the dry season in March and April. In a region where a perennial source of water is of extreme concern, the presence of this stream must always have been a powerful factor in settlement location. It flows through the modern village of Cacahuananche, and the fields situated along its course are the most highly prized agricultural plots in the area.

The elevation above sea level at Atopula is 750 m., and the land is relatively flat. This area is separated by only a few low hills from the extensive and well-watered flat region surrounding Huitzuco, which is by far the most productive agricultural land anywhere in the area.

The major cultigens are maize, several varieties of beans and squash, chiles, and tomatoes; peanuts, watermelon, and sesame are important cash crops. A few fruit trees, such as papaya, are cultivated within the towns and villages. The most popular minor crops, especially in the surrounding hill areas, are bottle gourds, maguey, and a tremendous variety of medicinal herbs. Grapes are grown and processed locally into a sweet wine. Small-scale animal husbandry and bee-keeping are common supplements to agriculture.

Intensive irrigation in the Huitzuco area permits at least one dry-season (*de riego*) crop in addition to the rainy-season crop (*the temporal*). At Atopula, agricultural activities are more closely tied to the seasonality of rainfall; a dry-season crop is said to be possible but not sufficiently profitable to be worthwhile. No one attempted to cultivate the area during the 1970–1971 dry season. Even without irrigation, the Llano de Huitzuco, with its larger streams, would undoubtedly always have been a more favorable area for settlement than the Atopula area, from the point of view of agricultural productivity. Unfortunately, long-standing intensive agriculture and the concentration of modern building activities in the vicinity have destroyed or covered virtually all traces of prehistoric settlement.

A range of high hills rises just to the north of Huitzuco and continues into southern Morelos, reaching elevations of nearly 2000 m. The northern tributaries of the Balsas–Mezcala have eroded headward into the southern escarpment of the Cordillera Neovolcánica: the Río Amacuzac and its upper tributaries drain most of western and central Morelos. Similarly, the Río Nexapa drains southeastern Morelos and part of western Puebla; the Atoyac Poblano system drains much of southwestern Puebla; and the Acatlán and Mixteco rivers drain a large zone of the western slopes of the Sierra de Oaxaca in northwestern Oaxaca and southern Puebla.

These river systems, especially the Cuautla–Amacuzac, are natural routes of movement and communication between the central highlands and the Balsas Depression (and from there to the Pacific Ocean). Today, major routes of communication follow the Balsas to its delta, which may have been a terminus for long-distance coastal or seaborne trade with areas as distant as Central America or even, as Weaver (1972: 62) suggests, South America. Alternative routes of communication proceed via the southern tributaries of the Balsas–Mezcala into the Sierra Madre del Sur and down the streams draining its southern slopes to the Pacific.

The metamorphic formations of the Sierra Madre del Sur and Balsas Depression offered some of the richest deposits of metals and minerals in Mesoamerica—gold, copper and its minerals, silver, tin, lead, mercury and its minerals, semiprecious stones, and probably obsidian. These deposits are often exposed by the severe and extensive erosion, although they are scattered, rather than in compact veins. There are indications of prehistoric mining of minerals of copper (azurite, malachite, cuprite) and perhaps cinnabar in Guerrero (Hendrichs Pérez 1940–41; Ochoa Campos 1964: 146–8).

The richness of Guerrero's natural resources, especially exotic raw materials, is reflected in the tribute lists of the Triple Alliance. From the province of Tepecoacuilco—comprising a section of the middle Río Balsas and much of northeastern Guerrero—the Aztecs derived jade (*chalchihuites*), mineral dye (*tlalcozahuitl*), copper and copper artifacts, as well as maize, beans, amaranth (*huauhtli*), chian, honey, chile, jaguars, eagles, copal, pottery, mantles, skirts, blouses, warriors' costumes, and garrison service. Tepecoacuilco was famous as a Colonial mining center. The Atopula area is rich in minerals; until the recent drop in the price of mercury on the world market, a substantial part of the economy of the Municipio de Huitzuco was based upon a large-scale mercury-extraction operation. Two cave sites in the area are, in all probability, prehistoric mines (App. 6).

The coastal province of Cihuatlán provided the Triple Alliance with gold dust, cacao, and red seashells as well as cotton, mantles, and slaves. In the first years after the conquest, the northwestern part of the Costa Grande, near the mouth of the Balsas, was the most important gold-producing area of New Spain. Other provinces of the upper Balsas and Sierra Madre (Quiauteopan and Tlapan) provided copper bells and ax heads, gold, turquoise and other precious stones, and feathers (Barlow 1949; Harvey 1971: 617; Litvak King 1971: 86–97).

Evidence of Preclassic exploitation of these natural resources of Guerrero is not, and cannot be, so conclusive. The Olmecs did reach the Pacific coast, and their remains are abundant along potential routes of communication between the coast and the central highlands. The possible significance of Preclassic exploitation of exotic raw materials—including the most precious of all Mesoamerican raw materials, jade—in connection with the strong Olmec archaeological presence in Guerrero is explored below.

The Excavations

Atopula was located during one of several reconnaissance trips made to the Cacahuananche area in the company of Sr. Anastasio Jiménez, of Huitzuco. It is on the right bank of a small (unnamed) tributary of the Tepecoacuilco, at the foot of Cerro El Clarín, the highest hill in the area (Fig. 2). The unpaved road that runs from Huitzuco through Tecolotla to Cacahuananche passes about 500 m. to the east.

The site lies near a *rancho* belonging to Sr. Jiménez, on the property of Sr. Miguel Benítez of Tlapala, who cultivates maize on it during the rainy season. Permission to excavate was secured with some difficulty, only after Sr. Benítez was repeatedly assured that all pits would be carefully backfilled.

There are two smaller arachaeological sites (H-14 and H-15) in the immediate vicinity, near the same stream course, some 500 and 800 m. downstream from Atopula in the direction of Cacahuananche. Neither site is as rich in surface artifacts as Atopula, and the only indication of possible construction activity is a

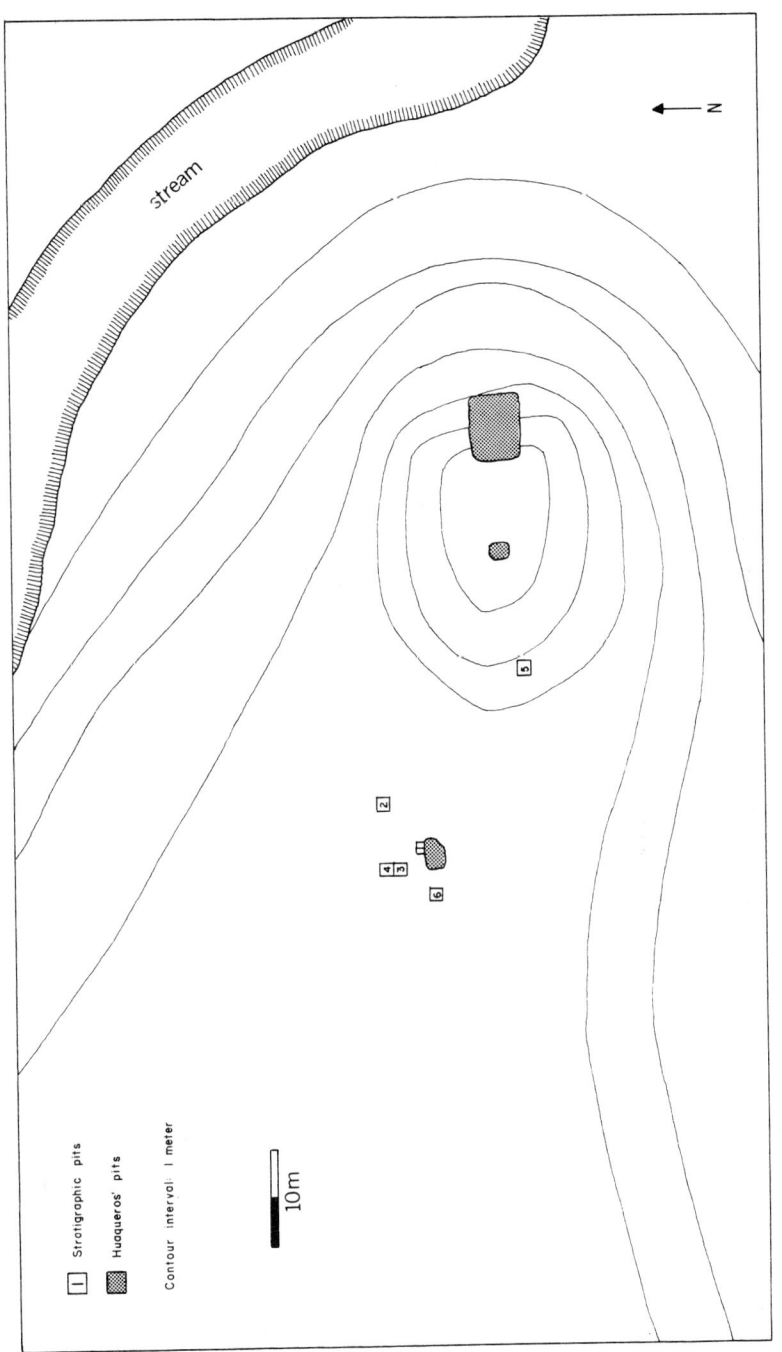

FIG. 2. Map of Atopula.

very low (ca. 1.5 m.) irregular mound at site H-15. Surface ceramics indicate that the main occupation of both sites was in the Postclassic period (El Clarín phase).

The site of Atopula consists of a low circular mound in the angle of a bend in the stream, some 20 to 25 m. from the edge of the arroyo, and a surrounding zone of cultural deposits (Fig. 2). The mound rises very abruptly to a height of 6 to 7 m. above the relatively level ground on the south and southeast. On the east and northeast it rises equally sharply to the same elevation above the edge of the arroyo. The northwest and west slopes of the mound are much more gentle and grade into a relatively flat elevated area, approximately 3 m. higher than the surrounding terrain, which extends 100 m. to the west and northwest.

Just prior to the initial reconnaissance, Atopula had been looted by *huaqueros* who excavated in the mound itself and in its raised flank. The *huaqueros*, from the neighboring town of Pololcingo, have systematically looted archaeological sites throughout the Municipio de Huitzuco. Their operations at Atopula were apparently typical and highlight the difficulties faced by the Morelos–Guerrero branch of I.N.A.H. in attempting to curb illegal excavation in this part of Mexico. The *huaqueros* arrived with a work force of 20 to 25 men, in addition to supervisors and well-armed guards, and thus were able to excavate without the consent of the landowner.

Local witnesses reported that the looters withdrew without having recovered anything of commercial value. These reports are probably accurate: if the local people had been involved in the looting they would be inclined to boast of profits realized. There was no indication that the excavations had uncoverd graves, the most fertile source of salable artifacts, and subsequent stratigraphic excavations produced no indications that marketable antiquities were to be found at Atopula.

Surface artifacts covered the mound and extended for many meters in every direction, particularly toward the west. The greatest concentration of surface material occurred on the raised zone flanking the mound on the west. Examination of the *huaqueros'* excavations confirmed the concentration of artifact-bearing deposits: substantial quantities of pottery remained beside their excavation west of the mound, while the backdirt from the two large pits they had dug in the mound itself was nearly sterile.

Rapid cleaning of the walls of these two pits in the mound permitted a cursory examination and recording of part of the mound stratigraphy. Unfortunately, Sr. Benítez insisted upon refilling the pits before the beginning of our excavations, so that complete advantage could not be taken of the large exposure. Nevertheless, the stratigraphy (Fig. 3) and the virtual absence of cultural material in the backdirt demonstrate that the mound, at least in its upper part, is basically an artificial construction, not a habitation-midden mound. Our stratigraphic pit (SP-5) dug in the west flank of the mound (see below) supported this conclusion.

The surface distribution of artifacts and the *huaqueros'* backdirt seemed to indicate a relatively deep deposit of habitation debris to the west of the mound, overlapping (and perhaps underlying) its western flank. Our initial test pit (SP-1) confirmed this concentration of artifacts and indicated that the cultural deposit

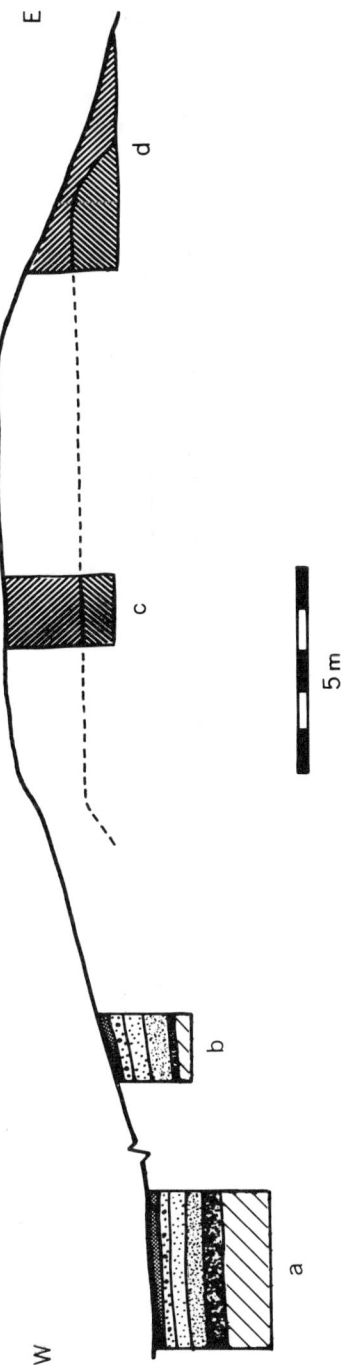

Fig. 3. Schematic section through Atopula: *a*, composite section of stratigraphic pits 1-4 and 6; *b*, section of stratigraphic pit 5; *c*, *d*, sections of *huaqueros'* pits.

reached a depth of at least 1.5 m. in this area. This pit, 1 m. square, was at the north edge of the westernmost *huaqueros'* pit (Fig. 2). It was excavated in arbitrary 20-cm. levels. In subsequent excavations the size of the pits was increased to 1.5 m. square. The uppermost 40 cm. of soil, corresponding to the very highly disturbed plow zone, was removed as a unit; excavation then proceeded in 20-cm. levels as before.

The work force, recruited from the village of Cacahuananche, was quite small, varying between three and five men at any one time. In this way the actual excavation was under constant scrutiny in order to detect traces of construction activity. The surface of the site, including the lower flanks of the mound and the surrounding area, was littered with an extraordinary concentration of relatively large stones, most of which were of a size suitable for construction. It seemed probable from the beginning that these stones represented the remains of prehistoric constructions, perhaps house foundations or walls, and we were anxious to identify them and convert the "telephone booth" test pits to horizontal excavation of structures and features. Accordingly, excavation proceeded very slowly, and every effort was made to detect some pattern in the distribution of stones in the pits. The stones occurred in large numbers in the excavated levels, so that shaving pit walls to make profiles was extremely difficult, and even driving stakes to mark pit corners was a problem. There was, however, no indication of pattern in their distribution, nor was there evidence of intentional shaping of stones.

It is possible that these stones do in fact represent the remains of construction features which were once part of the habitation refuse deposit but, if so, the destruction has been complete. The *huaqueros'* pits, which penetrated deep into the interior of the mound, revealed that the concentration of large stones is not characteristic of the nearly sterile mound fill, in sharp contrast to the refuse deposits to the west.

Since the most pressing research requirement was the establishment of a chronological sequence for the Preclassic period in this part of Guerrero and the recovery of habitation construction and debris, excavation was concentrated in the refuse deposit extending west from the mound. In none of the pits were natural stratigraphic levels clearly marked, although subtle stratigraphic changes were apparent in every case (Fig. 3). Since these changes were extremely gradual, and since they did not correspond to obvious differences in the artifact content of the deposits, the procedure of excavating in arbitrary levels was maintained.

The depositional sequence encountered in pits SP-3 and SP-4 was representative of this part of the site (Fig. 4). The uppermost 5 to 15 cm. in every pit consisted of a very fine gray-brown sandy soil which was converted to clouds of choking dust by every breath of wind. This powdery material gradually gave way to a browner sandy deposit that became progressively more clay-like with greater depth. The sandy deposit extended to a depth of 30 to 40 cm. This entire upper zone had been heavily disturbed in recent times, mainly by cultivation of the soil.

At a depth of approximately 40 cm. there was a zone of transition to an orange-brown sandy clay or clayey sand which became progressively less sandy. Below

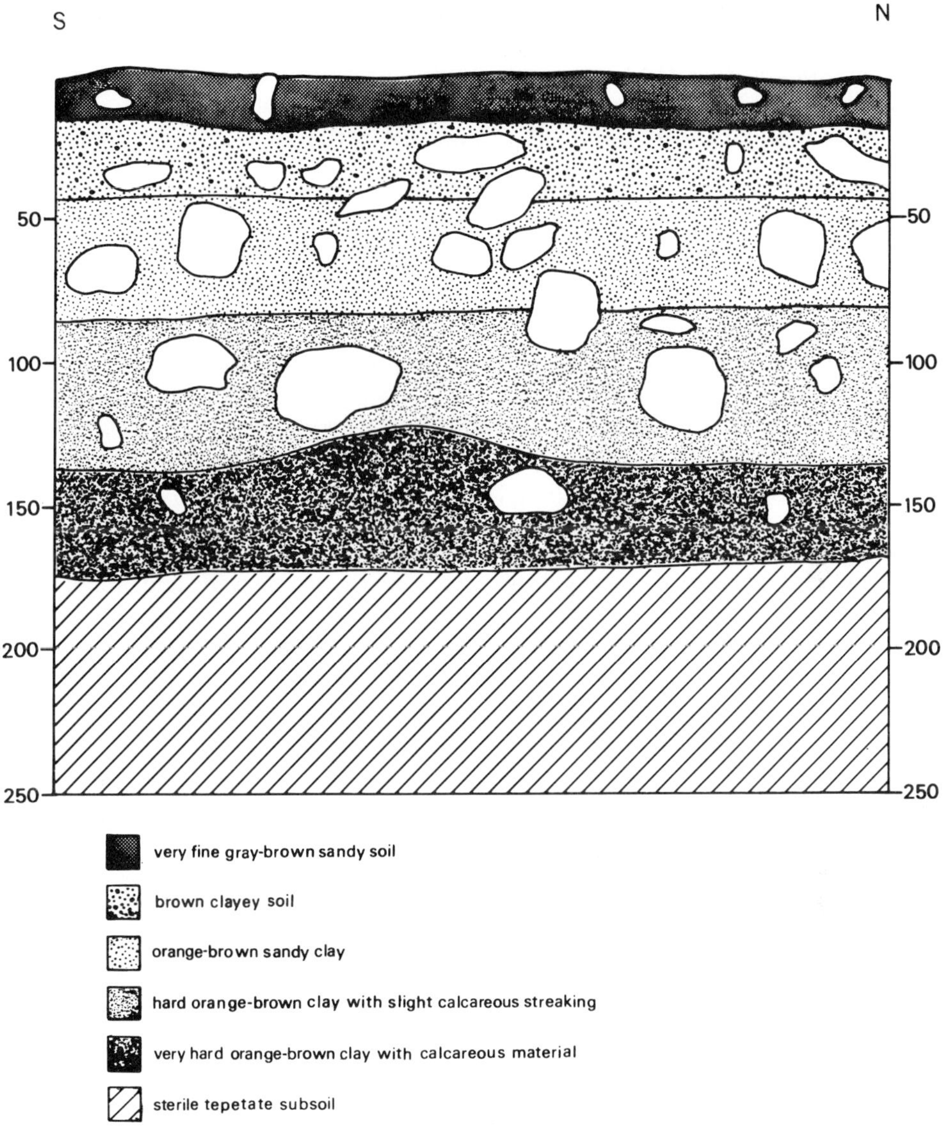

FIG. 4. North–south section of stratigraphic pits 3 and 4.

a second transitional zone at a depth of 85 to 90 cm., a similar but much harder and denser orange-brown clay continued and was streaked with a white gritty calcareous substance. The streaks of white *tepetate*-like material became denser in the lower levels.

At a depth of approximately 140 to 150 cm. (somewhat higher in a few spots), there was a third zone of transition below which the orange-brown clay became even harder and denser and the white streaks became even more concentrated. Between 170 and 180 cm. the white material almost entirely replaced the clay, forming solid *tepetate*, the hard, sterile, calcareous subsoil common to the region. Excavation was terminated at approximately 1 m. into the *tepetate* when it was clear that it was indeed sterile subsoil and not a thin sterile interval between levels of cultural deposition. These stratigraphic differences correspond closely to changes in the artifactual material which were later defined by the ceramic analysis (see below).

The information about the nature of the deposits derived from the stratigraphic pits and from the *huaqueros*' pits suggests that the original occupation was located on the flank of a low natural elevation to the west of its summit. The highest part of the mound as it exists today is an eroded remnant of the second, enlarged stage of an artificial platform which was built at the eastern edge of the habitation zone, on the highest part of the natural elevation. The surfaces of the initial platform construction appear in the rough profiles of the northern faces of the two large looters' pits (Fig. 3).

The deposits were carefully examined and passed through a fine screen in the hope of recovering vegetable remains and bone fragments as well as small artifacts. Unfortunately, no vegetable material was preserved, and almost no bone—only a few splinters of long bone, unidentifiable even as to genus.

A column of soil, extending from the surface to sterile subsoil, was removed from a scraped face of one of the stratigraphic pits (SP-4). The column was divided into samples so that each excavation level was represented by two soil samples, one each from upper and lower half. The samples were submitted for palynological analysis to the pollen laboratory at Arizona State University, under the direction of James Schoenwetter.

The results of the analysis were minimal. Although all the samples yielded pollen, the density was too low to permit vegetation reconstruction or reliable paleoecological interpretation. The two samples in which pollen density was sufficient to justify a count, corresponding to the Atopula and El Clarín phases, are very similar in terms of types of pollen represented and their proportions. Pollen representing plants of the Compositae family accounts for slightly more than 50 percent of the total; the next most heavily represented group (10 to 15 percent) is grass pollen. A high proportion (between 10 and 20 percent) of the pollen represents a variety of insect-pollinated plants. There is no significant frequency of pine or oak pollen. Thorn-forest zones of Sonora approximate these features (J. Schoenwetter, personal communication), but the low statistical reliability of the Atopula pollen samples does not justify a reconstruction of the prehistoric vegetation of the area as thorn forest.

The bulk of the artifacts recovered from Atopula consists of ceramics. Flaked stone, especially obsidian, was relatively well represented, most of it in the form of chipping debris. In addition, several ground-stone artifacts, mostly manos and metates, were recovered. The following chapter characterizes the artifact complexes; detailed descriptions appear in the appendices.

3. The Preclassic Sequence at Atopula

The Cacahuananche Phase

The deepest artifact-bearing deposits at Atopula represent the Cacahuananche phase, which corresponds to a natural depositional unit, although its distinctive features were so subtle that it could not be used as a unit of excavation. In the zone of habitation refuse west of the mound, Cacahuananche deposits consist of a layer of hard orange-brown clay heavily streaked with a white gritty calcareous material (Figs. 3, 4), resting directly upon the sterile *tepetate* subsoil.

Some 30 to 50 cm. above the *tepetate*, this deposit gives way to a layer of similar, slightly softer orange-brown clay with progressively less calcareous streaking, which contains material of the subsequent Atopula phase. The transition is quite gradual, occupying a zone some 10 cm. thick. The contrast in artifact content between the Cacahuananche phase and the Atopula phase is clearly marked, although there is continuity.

Tlapala Red, represented only by tecomate and deep tecomate forms, is the most distinctive marker for the Cacahuananche phase, although it is never the most common type. The frequency of Tlapala Red declines rapidly toward the end of the Cacahuananche phase; it is present in very minor quantities in early levels of the Atopula phase, and then disappears altogether (Fig. 5, Table 1).

Jiménez Red first appears in small quantities in upper levels of the Cacahuananche phase and increases in frequency as Tlapala Red decreases. Barranca Smoothed Buff has its greatest proportional representation early in the Cacahuananche phase, declining gradually and progressively throughout the Preclassic sequence. Pozo Thin Red and Guamuchil Polished Black occur in all levels of the Cacahuananche phase. The proportion of Pozo Thin Red progressively increases, and by the end of the phase it replaces Guamuchil Polished Black as the most frequent type. Pedrusco Polished Gray shows little change in relative frequency until after the end of the Cacahuananche phase. Arana Black-and-White and Mariposa White, distinctive types of the Atopula and Tecolotla phases, are entirely absent from Cacahuananche-phase levels. Polished Dark Red and Orange, rare minor types, occur throughout the Cacahuananche phase and continue into the first part of the Atopula phase. The Red-painted and Thin Tan aberrants or imports occur as isolated specimens in the Cacahuananche phase only.

Vessel forms and their relative frequencies also distinguish the Cacahuananche phase. The most distinctive shape is the deep tecomate, which is restricted to this phase and to Tlapala Red (Figs. 6, 7). Tecomates are the second most frequent form and are far more common than in later levels. The olla is the most popular shape in the Cacahuananche phase, although it loses this position in subsequent phases. Open bowls have their lowest relative frequency in the

TABLE 1. DISTRIBUTION OF PRECLASSIC POTTERY TYPES BY PHASE

Type	Sherd Count			
	Cacahuananche Phase	Atopula Phase	Tecolotla Phase	Totals
Major Types				
Tlapala Red	55	22		77
Jiménez Red	17	137	125	279
Barranca Smoothed Buff	119	254	73	446
Pozo Thin Red	260	853	462	1575
Guamuchil Polished Black	234	577	374	1185
Pedrusco Polished Gray	62	224	64	350
Arana Black-and-White		13	15	28
Mariposa White		15	13	28
Bagre Coarse*	463	2119	2059	4641
Rare Types and Imports				
Polished Dark Red	9	8		17
Orange	3	5		8
Red-painted	1			1
Thin Tan	1			1
Red-rimmed		6		6
Red-on-White		1		1
Totals	1224	4234	3185	8643

* Residual category

Cacahuananche phase and, in sharp contrast to the following phases, occur only in Guamuchil Polished Black and Barranca Smoothed Buff. Flaring and incurved-rim bowls are similarly less popular and occur in fewer types than in the Atopula phase. Four distinctive vessel forms of the Atopula and Tecolotla phases—beakers, bottles, molcajetes, and composite-silhouette bowls—are absent altogether from the Cacahuananche phase.

The Cacahuananche ceramic complex is distinctive in several decorative features. Polishing is noticeably less prominent than in the following Preclassic phases. The major polished types—Pozo Thin Red, Guamuchil Polished Black, and Pedrusco Polished Gray—are less popular in the Cacahuananche than in the Atopula phase. Even in these types, especially Guamuchil Polished Black, polishing is less careful or proficient and is not evident on every sherd in the Cacahuananche sample.

Rocker-stamping is the only distinctive decorative trait that is unique to the Cacahuananche phase (Table 2). It is very rare there but is absent altogether from Atopula and Tecolotla. Much more striking are the Atopula- and Tecolotla-phase decorative modes, which are missing from the Cacahuananche: grooves encircling vessel exteriors, vertical grooving, the multiple-line-break motif, complex incised designs, the use of red pigment in incision and excision, and pseudo-grater fondos.

The Cacahuananche-phase deposits produced only a single figurine fragment. It shows fewer and less precise affinities with figurines from elsewhere in Mesoamerica than do the figurines of the later phases.

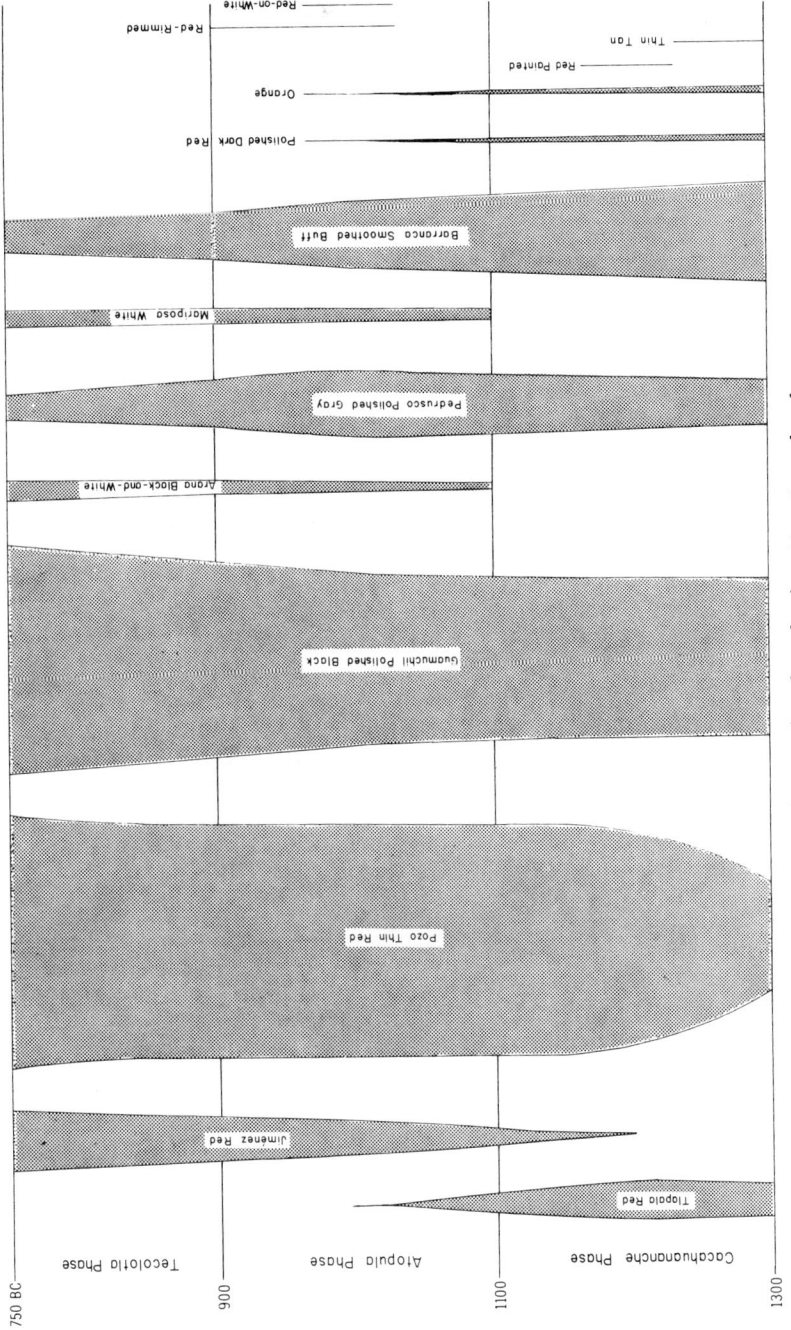

FIG. 5. Relative frequencies of preclassic pottery types by phase.

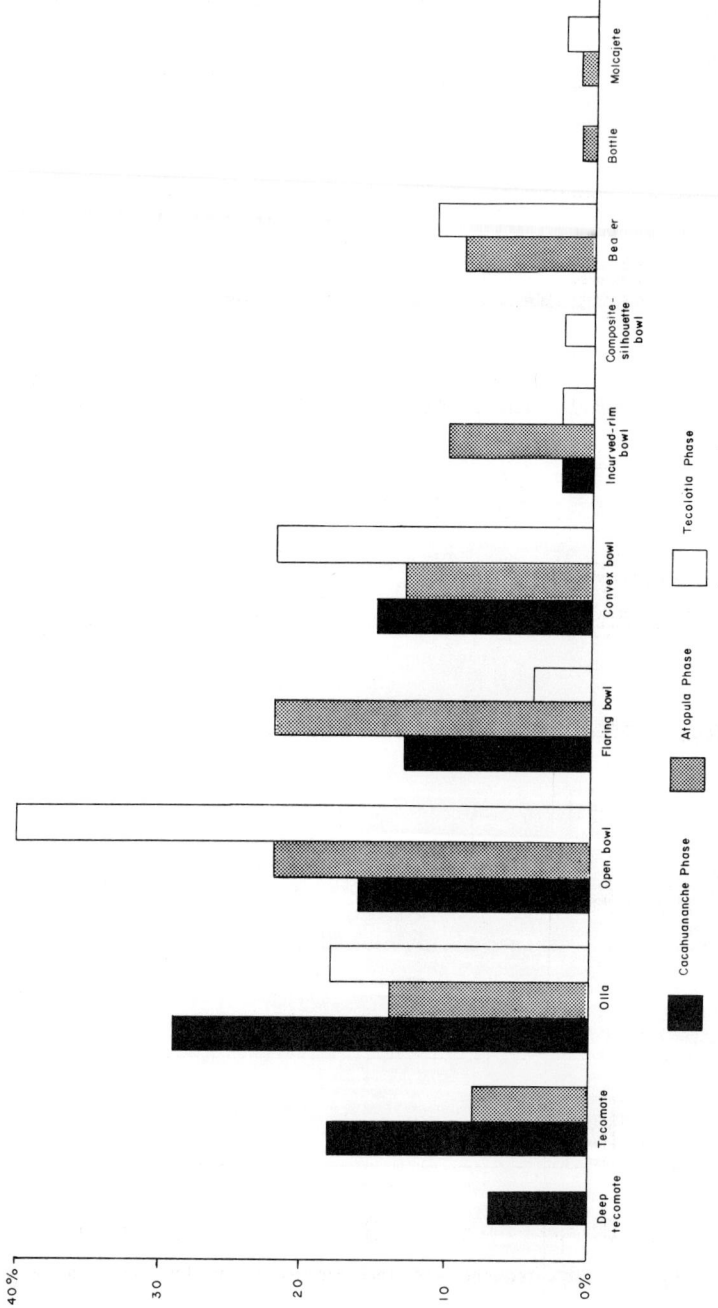

FIG. 6. Relative frequencies of preclassic vessel forms by phase.

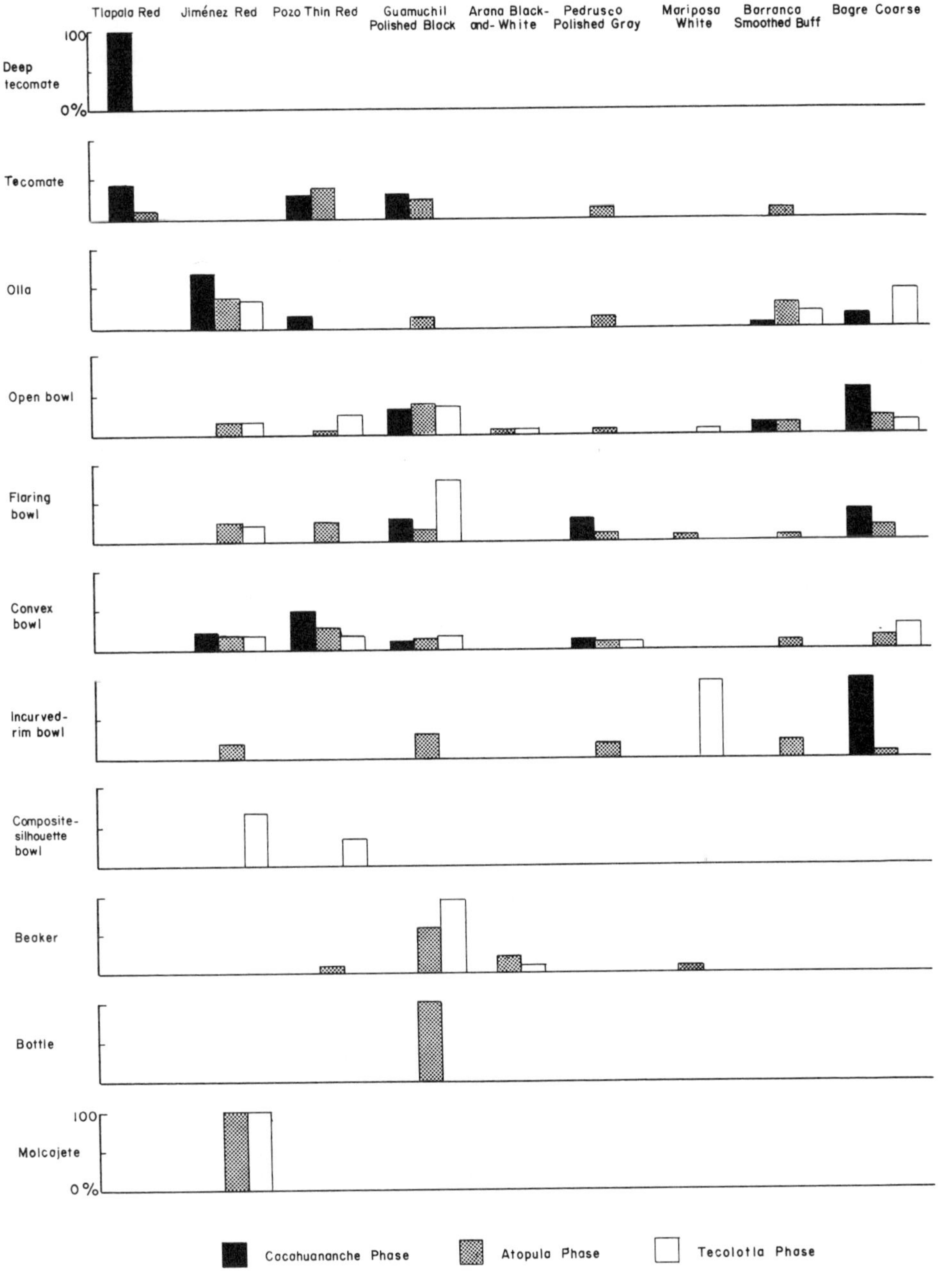

FIG. 7. Relative frequencies of preclassic vessel forms by type and phase.

TABLE 2. DISTRIBUTION OF PRECLASSIC DECORATIVE MODES BY TYPE AND PHASE

Mode	Type	Cacahua-nanche Phase	Atopula Phase	Tecolotla Phase
	Grooving			
One line encircling exterior	Jiménez Red		1	3
	Pozo Thin Red			1
	Guamuchil Polished Black		1	1
	Bagre Coarse			1
	Red-on-White		1	
One line encircling interior	Jiménez Red	1	2	2
Two lines encircling exterior	Jiménez Red			1
Oblique lines, exterior	Tlapala Red	1		
	Guamuchil Polished Black		1	1
	Mariposa White			1
Parallel vertical lines, exterior	Guamuchil Polished Black		1	
	Arana Black-and-White		1	
	Incision			
One line encircling exterior	Tlapala Red	2		
	Jiménez Red			1
	Pozo Thin Red		1	4
	Guamuchil Polished Black		3	7
	Arana Black-and-White		1	
	Pedrusco Polished Gray		1	2
	Mariposa White			1
One line encircling interior	Pozo Thin Red	2	1	
	Guamuchil Polished Black	2	1	3
	Barranca Smoothed Buff	1		
	Bagre Coarse		3	
Single-line-break	Guamuchil Polished Black			2
	Arana Black-and-White			1
Two lines encircling exterior	Tlapala Red	1		
	Pozo Thin Red		1	1
	Guamuchil Polished Black		1	4
	Arana Black-and-White			1
Two lines encircling interior	Pozo Thin Red	2		
	Guamuchil Polished Black			1
	Arana Black-and-White			2
Double-line-break	Guamuchil Polished Black			1
Three lines encircling exterior	Guamuchil Polished Black		2	3
	Arana Black-and-White			1
Triple-line-break	Arana Black-and-White			1
Four lines encircling exterior	Guamuchil Polished Black			1
Oblique lines, exnterior	Pozo Thin Red	1	3	2
	Guamuchil Polished Black	1	3	6
Oblique lines, interior	Guamuchil Polished Black			1
	Arana Black-and-White			1
Intersecting lines, exterior	Guamuchil Polished Black	1	1	7
Intersecting lines, interior	Guamuchil Polished Black			1

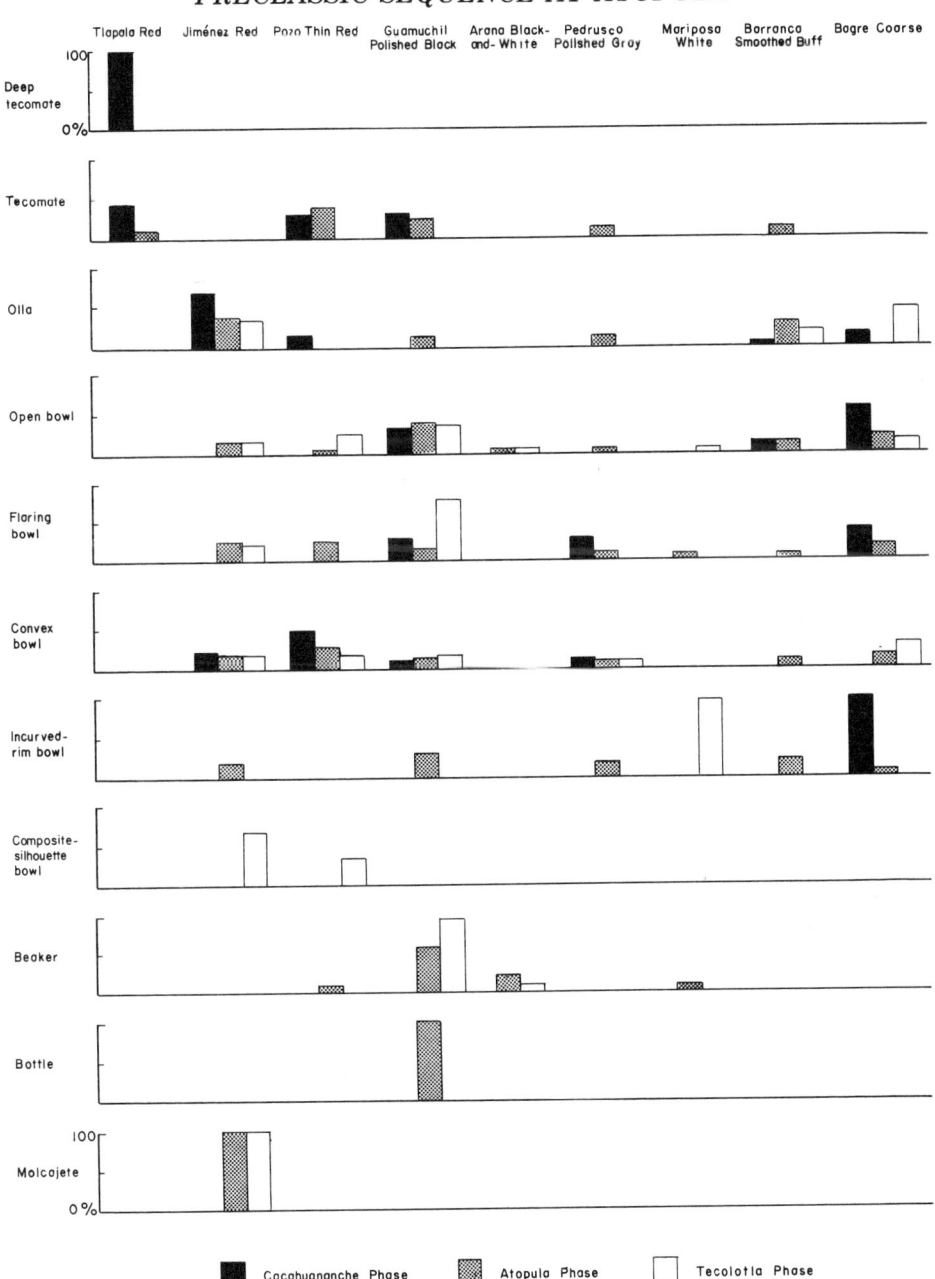

FIG. 7. Relative frequencies of preclassic vessel forms by type and phase.

TABLE 2. DISTRIBUTION OF PRECLASSIC DECORATIVE MODES BY TYPE AND PHASE

Mode	Type	Cacahua-nanche Phase	Atopula Phase	Tecolotla Phase
Grooving				
One line encircling exterior	Jiménez Red		1	3
	Pozo Thin Red			1
	Guamuchil Polished Black		1	1
	Bagre Coarse			1
	Red-on-White		1	
One line encircling interior	Jiménez Red	1	2	2
Two lines encircling exterior	Jiménez Red			1
Oblique lines, exterior	Tlapala Red	1		
	Guamuchil Polished Black		1	1
	Mariposa White			1
Parallel vertical lines, exterior	Guamuchil Polished Black		1	
	Arana Black-and-White		1	
Incision				
One line encircling exterior	Tlapala Red	2		
	Jiménez Red			1
	Pozo Thin Red		1	4
	Guamuchil Polished Black		3	7
	Arana Black-and-White		1	
	Pedrusco Polished Gray		1	2
	Mariposa White			1
One line encircling interior	Pozo Thin Red	2	1	
	Guamuchil Polished Black	2	1	3
	Barranca Smoothed Buff	1		
	Bagre Coarse		3	
Single-line-break	Guamuchil Polished Black			2
	Arana Black-and-White			1
Two lines encircling exterior	Tlapala Red	1		
	Pozo Thin Red		1	1
	Guamuchil Polished Black		1	4
	Arana Black-and-White			1
Two lines encircling interior	Pozo Thin Red	2		
	Guamuchil Polished Black			1
	Arana Black-and-White			2
Double-line-break	Guamuchil Polished Black			1
Three lines encircling exterior	Guamuchil Polished Black		2	3
	Arana Black-and-White			1
Triple-line-break	Arana Black-and-White			1
Four lines encircling exterior	Guamuchil Polished Black			1
Oblique lines, exnterior	Pozo Thin Red	1	3	2
	Guamuchil Polished Black	1	3	6
Oblique lines, interior	Guamuchil Polished Black			1
	Arana Black-and-White			1
Intersecting lines, exterior	Guamuchil Polished Black	1	1	7
Intersecting lines, interior	Guamuchil Polished Black			1

TABLE 2.—Continued

Mode	Type	Cacahuananche Phase	Atopula Phase	Tecolotla Phase
Zoned cross-hatching, exterior	Guamuchil Polished Black		1	
Complex design	Guamuchil Polished Black			2
	Arana Black-and-White			1
Parallel vertical lines, exterior	Bagre Coarse			1
Oblique lines across lip	Pozo Thin Red		1	
Red pigment in incision	Guamuchil Polished Black			3
	Arana Black-and-White			2
Pseudo-grater Fondo				
Parallel straight lines	Pozo Thin Red		1	3
	Guamuchil Polished Black			7
Arcs	Pozo Thin Red		1	1
	Guamuchil Polished Black			6
"Sunburst"	Guamuchil Polished Black			2
Molcajete Base				
Parallel oblique lines on bowl wall	Jiménez Red		2	1
	Guamuchil Polished Black	1	1	
	Bagre Coarse			1
Parallel straight lines	Jiménez Red		2	4
	Pozo Thin Red		1	3
	Bagre Coarse		4	2
Arcs	Bagre Coarse			2
"Sunburst"	Jiménez Red		1	1
Other				
Excised bands	Guamuchil Polished Black			1
Rocker-stamping	Guamuchil Polished Black	1		
Row of punctations, exterior	Pozo Thin Red		1	
Notched or punctate rim	Guamuchil Polished Black			2
	Arana Black-and-White			1
	Bagre Coarse			1
Eccentric or "tabbed" rim	Bagre Coarse			1
Flange encircling exterior	Guamuchil Polished Black			1
	Pedrusco Polished Gray			1
	Mariposa White			1
	Barranca Smoothed Buff		2	
Sharp "ridge" encircling exterior	Jiménez Red		1	

Cacahuananche-phase metates, in contrast to Atopula and Tecolotla, are simple and slab-like with nearly flat grinding surfaces; little care went into their shaping. Small "palettes" or grinding tablets occur only in this phase.

The flaked-stone complex of the Cacahuananche phase is most distinctive in its low proportion of obsidian; the bulk of the raw material consists of an off-white cryptocrystalline variety of quartz. Blades, which become very prominent toward the end of the Atopula phase, are essentially absent: only two fragments were from Cacahuananche levels, and they are probably intrusive from higher levels. Most of the chipped stone fragments recovered are unmodified flakes; even usage flaking is quite rare.

Ceramic types and modes provide the clearest indications of the external relationships and chronological alignments of the three Preclassic components. Samples of nonceramic artifacts are considerably smaller, and these materials generally receive less attention so that the distribution and chronological significance of nonceramic artifact types and modes are difficult to determine.

The importance of the tecomate shape (especially with an all-over red slip) and plain rocker-stamping on polished black vessels, combined with the absence of such sensitive chronological indicators as white-slipped wares, differential white-black firing, and prismatic obsidian blades, indicate a placement in the early to middle part of the Early Preclassic period, certainly prior to 1000 B.C.

Comparison of Cacahuananche-phase modes, mode combinations, and types with those of other Preclassic components, particularly with those of multicomponent phases within well-established regional sequences, provides more precise chronological indications. These detailed comparisons are set out in the type descriptions.

The Tehuacán Valley is the nearest region for which a chronological sequence has been worked out and published in detail. The Cacahuananche component is clearly allied with the Ajalpan phase. Unfortunately, the Early Ajalpan/Late Ajalpan transition does not seem to correspond to the phase divisions that have been established elsewhere in Mesoamerica: several Early Preclassic phases seem to overlap both Early and Late Ajalpan (Coe and Flannery 1967: 66–70; MacNeish et al. 1970: 286–7). Unrecognized subdivisions within the Ajalpan phase are likely, or it may even be that an occupation is missing from the sequence. In any event, the Cacahuananche phase is best aligned with latest Early Ajalpan and the earlier part of Late Ajalpan.

Although the distance from Atopula is considerable and affinities are naturally much less distinct, the chronological precision of the Early Preclassic sequence from Soconusco, particularly coastal Guatemala, makes it extremely useful for comparison. Cacahuananche is most similar to the Ocós phase, although affinities with the Cuadros phase are apparent as well. This alignment is consistent with the Ajalpan correlation (Coe and Flannery 1967: 70; MacNeish et al. 1970: 286–7).

The Chiapa I (Cotorra) phase represents the entire Early Preclassic period in the Chiapa de Corzo sequence, and may eventually be subdivided. There are clear affinities between Cacahuananche and some part of Cotorra. An alignment of Cacahuananche with the earlier portion of Cotorra is consistent with the Ajalpan and Ocós alignments (Coe and Flannery 1967: 69).

Unfortunately, the Preclassic sequence for nearby Morelos has not yet been worked out in detail, but there are close relationships with the Atopula components. Cacahuananche exhibits its closest affinities with the San Pablo A (Middle

Nexpa) phase, although it also has similarities to La Juana (Early Nexpa), perhaps indicating some temporal overlap (Grove 1972, 1974a). A few similarities to early material from Chalcatzingo (Piña Chán 1955a; Grove et al. 1976) suggest the possibility of some overlap with the Chalcatzingo A occupation.

The sequence for nearby coastal Guerrero is even less securely established. Cacahuananche seems to fit best with some part of the Uala period.

Similarities to other Early Preclassic components from Mesoamerica are less obvious but are consistent with these indications of chronological placement. In the Valley of Mexico, Cacahuananche shows some resemblances to Ayotla and Justo subphase material and a few similarities with material from Tlatilco and Tlapacoya graves. (Tolstoy has recently revised his analysis of Early and Middle Preclassic chronology in the Valley of Mexico [Grove 1974b: 50]. The Justo subphase, formerly paired with the Ayotla subphase in the Ixtapaluca phase [Tolstoy and Paradis 1970], has been combined with the Bomba subphase into a Manantial phase. In this report Ayotla, Justo, and Bomba are treated as distinct subphases.) The affinity is not strong, and these subphases seem best correlated with the subsequent Atopula phase. This is consistent with Grove's (1972) alignment of them with the San Pablo B (Late Nexpa) phase of Morelos. The possibility of some overlap with Cacahuananche cannot, however, be ruled out.

There are similarities—although not very strong—with both the Tierras Largas and San José phase in the Valley of Oaxaca. Cacahuananche is best aligned with terminal Tierras Largas, overlapping the beginning of the San José phase.

In northern Veracruz the similarities of Cacahuananche are with both the Pavón and Ponce phases, again suggesting overlap. In central Veracruz, its affinities are with the earlier part of the Trapiche I phase of El Trapiche and Chalahuite. In southern Veracruz and Tabasco, Cacahuananche is best aligned with Chicharras, perhaps overlapping with San Lorenzo A. There are also a few resemblances to the poorly known but apparently contemporaneous "pre-Complex A" material from La Venta.

These comparisons all place Cacahuananche in the middle range of the Early Preclassic period, between 1300/1250 and 1100/1050 B.C. (Fig. 8). This is consistent with the indications of the obsidian hydration analysis (Fig. 9; and Table 3, App. 4), although slightly later than that would have been predicted by the analysis alone.

The Atopula Phase

The excavation levels that yielded artifacts of the Atopula phase correspond closely to a layer of dense orange-brown clay streaked with calcareous material (Figs. 3, 4). Although this layer is stratigraphically distinct, the transitions to the deposits above and below it were so gradual and subtle that it was not feasible to excavate it as as a natural unit. These gradual stratigraphic transitions are matched by the considerable continuity in artifact content from Cacahuananche to Atopula, and especially from Atopula to Tecolotla.

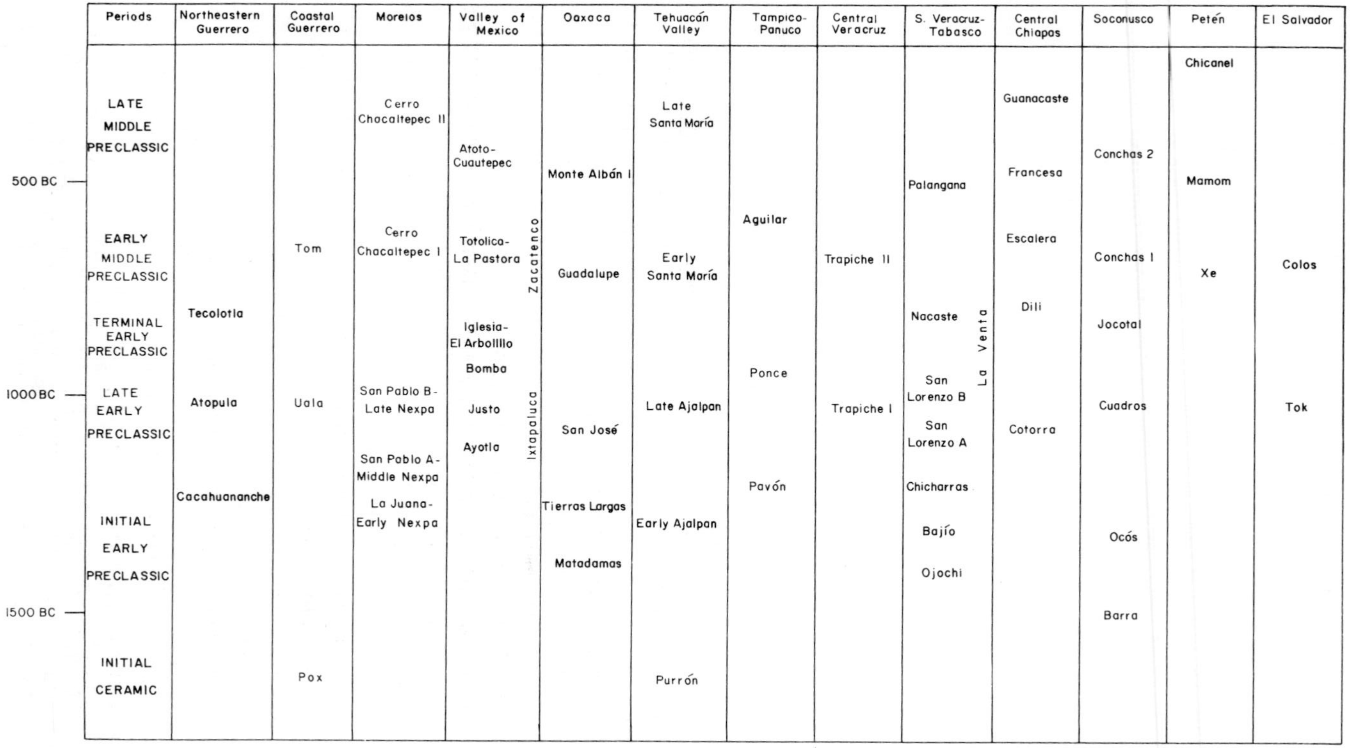

Periods	Northeastern Guerrero	Coastal Guerrero	Morelos	Valley of Mexico	Oaxaca	Tehuacán Valley	Tampico-Panuco	Central Veracruz	S. Veracruz-Tabasco	Central Chiapas	Soconusco	Petén	El Salvador
LATE MIDDLE PRECLASSIC			Cerro Chacaltepec II	Atoto-Cuautepec	Monte Albán I	Late Santa María	Aguilar		Palangana	Guanacaste		Chicanel	
EARLY MIDDLE PRECLASSIC	Tecolotla	Tom	Cerro Chacaltepec I	Totolica-La Pastora	Guadalupe	Early Santa María		Trapiche II		Francesca	Conchas 2		Colos
TERMINAL EARLY PRECLASSIC				Zacatenco									
LATE EARLY PRECLASSIC	Atopula	Uala	San Pablo B-Late Nexpa	Iglesia-El Arbolillo Bomba	San José	Late Ajalpan	Ponce	Trapiche I	Nacoste	Escalera	Conchas 1	Mamom	Tok
				Ixtapaluca					San Lorenzo B	Dili	Jocotal	Xe	
	Cacahuananche		San Pablo A-Middle Nexpa	Justo	Tierras Largas	Early Ajalpan	Pavón		San Lorenzo A / La Venta				
INITIAL EARLY PRECLASSIC			La Juana-Early Nexpa	Ayotla	Matadamos				Chicharras	Cotorra	Cuadros		
									Bajío		Ocós		
INITIAL CERAMIC		Pox				Purrón			Ojochi		Barra		

FIG. 8. Early and Middle Preclassic chronology of Mesoamerica.

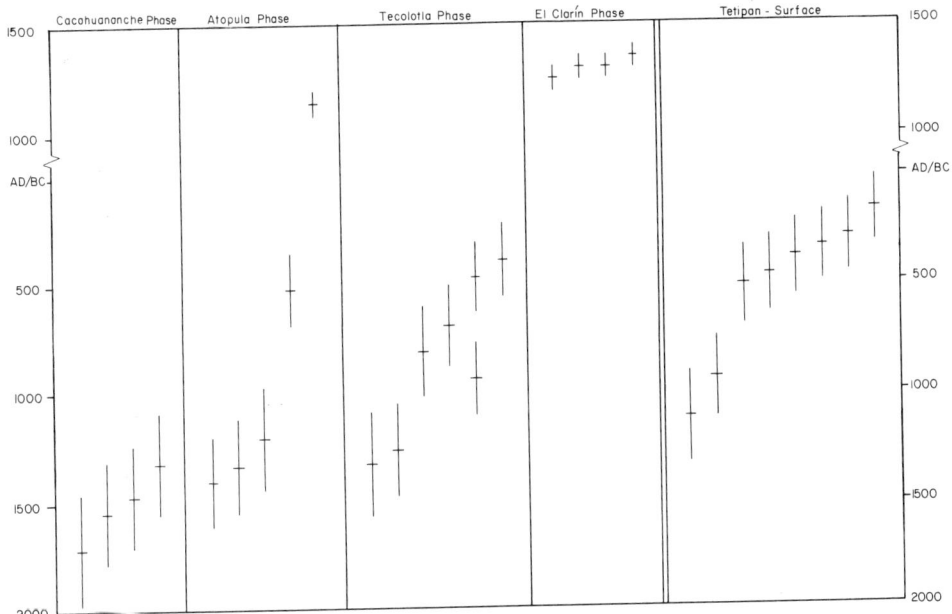

FIG. 9. Hydration readings on obsidian from Atopula and Tetipan.

The most obvious change in pottery types marking the beginning of the Atopula phase is the appearance of two distinctive minority types: Arana Black-and-White and Mariposa White. Both occur throughout the Atopula and Tecolotla phases (Fig. 5, Table 1). Tlapala Red appears in small quantities in early levels of the Atopula phase and shortly disappears altogether. At the same time Jiménez Red, which appeared late in the Cacahuananche phase, increases progressively in popularity; in the later part of the Atopula phase it achieves about the same relative frequency that Tlapala Red had in the early Cacahuananche phase. Barranca Smoothed Buff continues its progressive decline throughout the phase. Pozo Thin Red is the most frequent type, maintaining essentially the same relative frequency from the later Cacahuananche phase through the first part of Tecolotla. Guamuchil Polished Black is second in popularity, with a slight, gradual increase in relative frequency throughout the Atopula phase. Pedrusco Polished Gray increases slightly to its peak popularity and then declines somewhat. Polished Dark Red and Orange, rare minor types of the Cacahuananche phase, are represented in the first part of the Atopula phase but disappear thereafter. The Red-rimmed minor type is unique to the late Atopula phase. Red-on-White occurs as an isolated aberrant specimen.

The complete disappearance of the deep tecomate and the appearance of substantial numbers of beakers are the most striking changes in vessel forms (Figs. 6, 7). The beaker shape is typical of Guamuchil Polished Black and occurs also in Arana Black-and-White, Mariposa White, and Pozo Thin Red. In the Atopula phase, the relative frequency of tecomates declines to about half its

Cacahuananche-phase level, but this shape occurs in more types than in the earlier phase. During both phases it is most typical of Pozo Thin Red and Guamuchil Polished Black. The popularity of ollas also declines by about 50 percent, with a similar broadening of its distribution among the types. It continues to be most heavily represented in Jiménez Red, as in the Cacahuananche phase. The same pattern is also typical of the convex-bowl form—decreased (very slightly in this case) relative frequency, a slight increase in the number of types in which it occurs, and no change in the types in which it is most heavily represented (Jiménez Red, Guamuchil Polished Black, and especially Pozo Thin Red). Open and flaring bowls both increase substantially in proportional representation, and both forms occur in a number of new types in the Atopula phase (particularly Jiménez Red and Pozo Thin Red). Open bowls continue to be most heavily represented in Guamuchil Polished Black, while flaring bowls are fairly evenly distributed among the major types. Incurved-rim bowls increase dramatically (fivefold) in popularity and in the number of types in which they occur. Bottles and molcajetes are minor forms that appear for the first time in the Atopula phase; each is restricted to a single type (Guamuchil Polished Black and Jiménez Red, respectively).

The Atopula phase is thus distinguished from the Cacahuananche by changes in popularity of vessel forms as well as by the appearance of new shapes and the disappearance of old ones. A clear trend is for Cacahuananche-phase forms that survive in the Atopula phase to be represented in a greater number of types than previously.

A few modes of decoration are unique to the Atopula phase, including exterior parallel vertical grooving, exterior zoned incised cross-hatching, oblique incisions across vessel lips, exterior encircling punctuations, and encircling raised ridges. In addition, new decorative motifs appear in Atopula and persist into the Tecolotla phase: a single groove encircling vessel exteriors; triple lines incised around vessel exteriors; pseudo-grater fondos with multiple parallel straight lines and arcs; molcajete bases with multiple parallel straight lines, arcs, and so-called "sunburst motifs"; and encircling flanges or bolsters. Several modes of decoration that appear in low frequencies in the Cacahuananche phase show dramatic increases in popularity during the Atopula phase: single or double incised lines encircling vessel exteriors, oblique lines incised on vessel exteriors, molcajete bases with parallel oblique lines incised in convex or incurved-rim bowls. In general, polishing is more common, and more proficient when present, than in the Cacahuananche phase.

Atopula-phase figurines are more closely similar to figurines from other Mesoamerican sites than is the Cacahuananche specimen. The similarities suggest a connection with the Olmec style and with Olmec-related artifact complexes (see below).

Atopula-phase metates are much more concave, trough-like, and more carefully shaped than those of Cacahuananche. The carefully ground and polished thin stone bowl is unique to the Atopula phase.

The Atopula flaked-stone complex is characterized by an increase in the frequency of obsidian and by the appearance of a new variety of obsidian (cloudy or mottled gray). There is also a wider variety of other raw materials, although the total proportion of raw materials other than obsidian declines. The frequency of specimens with usage flaking increases slightly but remains quite low. In upper levels of the Atopula phase, prismatic obsidian blades appear for the first time in significant numbers, foreshadowing their popularity in the subsequent Tecolotla phase. Usage flaking is common on the blades, whereas it is rare on flakes of both the Atopula and Cacahuananche phases.

The most striking traits of the Atopula phase—the appearance (in small quantities) of white-slipped pottery and differential white-black firing; the increased popularity of polished black pottery, especially beakers and bottles; the dramatic increase in the frequency of flat-based open bowls and incised decoration; and the occurrence of Olmec-figurine fragments—demonstrate that Atopula corresponds to the later part of the Early Preclassic period. The external similarities of the Atopula component are much stronger than those of Cacahuananche, indicating an intensified interaction with other parts of Mesoamerica.

In the Tehuacán Valley sequence, Atopula is aligned with the middle to later part of the Late Ajalpan phase. Atopula shows considerable similarity to the Cuadros phase of the Soconusco sequence, which is consistent with the Late Ajalpan correlation (Coe and Flannery 1967: 68–70; MacNeish et al. 1970: 286–7).

There are strong resemblances between Atopula and the Cotorra phase of the Chiapa de Corzo sequence. An alignment of Atopula with the middle portion of the long period represented by Cotorra is consistent with the Cuadros and Late Ajalpan correlations (Coe and Flannery 1967: 69).

Atopula shows very close similarities to the San Pablo B (Late Nexpa) phase of Morelos, although there are resemblances to San Pablo A (Middle Nexpa) as well, suggesting an overlapping alignment. Affinities with Chalcatzingo (late Chalcatzingo A) are much stronger than those of Cacahuananche. There are also similarities to Vaillant's Gualupita I. Atopula is much more closely related to the Ayotla and Justo subphases in the Valley of Mexico, to material from the Tlatilco and Tlapacoya graves and, to a lesser extent, to the Iglesia subphase (early Zacatenco phase) represented in the Tlatilco refuse deposits. An alignment of Atopula with Ayotla–Justo is consistent with Grove's (1972; 1974a) correlation of San Pablo B with these two subphases.

In the valley of Oaxaca the closest resemblances of Atopula are with the San José phase. In northern and central Veracruz they are with Ponce and Trapiche I, respectively. In southern Veracruz, Atopula is best aligned with the San Lorenzo phase. There are also similarities to La Venta material, although Atopula predates the main occupation there. In each case the similarities are closer and more numerous than those of Cacahuananche.

Some of the material from Greengo's (1967; 1970; personal communication) test excavations at the sites of Figueroa and El Calvario in the Tepecoacuilco drainage is apparently related to Atopula and/or Tecolotla. He has recovered Early Middle

Preclassic material, and it is possible that pre-Atopula material is also represented. His radiocarbon dates (ca. 1150 B.C. and 850 B.C.) lend very general support to the dates proposed for the complexes from Atopula. Unfortunately, Greengo's material is not adequately published. In the coastal Guerrero sequence, the Atopula phase correlates best with the later part of the Uala period.

External comparisons place Atopula in the late part of the Early Preclassic period, roughly in the period from 1100/1050 to 900/850 B.C. (Fig. 8). This is reinforced by the appearance in late Atopula levels of a few traits which are typical of the very late Early Preclassic or early Middle Preclassic, such as prismatic obsidian blades and a trade sherd of Morelos Orange Lacquer. Again, this is consistent with the obsidian hydration analysis.

The Tecolotla Phase

The layer of orange-brown sandy clay that lies immediately below the highly disturbed uppermost deposits (Figs. 3, 4) represents the Tecolotla-phase occupations of the site. The transition from the Tecolotla layer to this late, mixed sandy gray-to-brown level is not sudden, but it is sharp in comparison with the gradual transition between the Tecolotla- and Atopula-phase deposits. As with the Atopula- and Cacahuananche-phase layers, it was impossible to follow the natural stratigraphic level as an excavation unit. The subtlety of the transition is consistent with the cultural continuity from the Atopula to the Tecolotla phase.

The beginning of the Tecolotla phase is not marked by the appearance or disappearance of major pottery types (Fig. 5, Table 1). The Polished Dark Red, Orange, and Red-rimmed minor types, however, do not survive the Atopula phase. Pozo Thin Red continues to be the most frequent type, followed closely by Guamuchil Polished Black; both show a slight gradual increase in relative frequency throughout the Tecolotla phase. Jiménez Red, Arana Black-and-White, and Mariposa White also increase slightly in frequency during the Tecolotla phase, continuing the trend begun in the Atopula phase. Barranca Smoothed Buff and Pedrusco Polished Gray continue their gradual decline.

In vessel forms, the most striking changes marking the Tecolotla phase (Figs. 6, 7) are the total disappearance of the tecomate and bottle forms and the appearance of the composite-silhouette bowl (although in very small quantities and restricted to Jiménez Red and Pozo Thin Red). Ollas increase slightly in frequency, although not to the Cacahuananche-phase level; this shape appears in fewer types, although it is still most frequent in Jiménez Red and Barranca Smoothed Buff, as in the Atopula phase. Open bowls show another substantial increase in relative frequency, far exceeding all other forms in popularity; this form continues to have a broad distribution among the types, with its heaviest representation in Guamuchil Polished Black. The flaring-bowl form, which was as popular as the open bowl in the Atopula phase and evenly distributed among the major types, is extremely reduced in popularity and is now restricted to Jiménez Red and Guamuchil Polished Black. Convex bowls increase in relative frequency and continue to be most heavily represented in Jiménez Red, Pozo

Thin Red, and Guamuchil Polished Black. Incurved-rim bowls show a substantial decrease in popularity and are confined to Mariposa White, a type in which this shape previously did not occur. Beakers and molcajetes increase slightly in frequency. Beakers are now restricted to Guamuchil Polished Black and Arana Black-and-White, the types in which they occurred most frequently in the Atopula phase. Molcajetes continue to occur exclusively in Jiménez Red.

Polishing is still extremely proficient and common, perhaps to an even greater extent than in the Atopula phase. The frequency of plastic decoration increases substantially in the Tecolotla phase. Modes of decoration that appear for the first time include the multiple-line-break (single, double, and triple), four incised lines encircling vessel exteriors, oblique or intersecting incised lines on vessel interiors, complex designs of straight incised lines, pseudo-grater fondos with sunburst motifs, and red pigment in incisions or excised bands. All of these occur only on Guamuchil Polished Black and Arana Black-and-White vessels. Other new modes are double grooves encircling vessel exteriors, molcajete bases with incised arcs, multiple parallel vertical incisions, and notched or tabbed rims. Older modes of decoration which increase in popularity in the Tecolotla phase include single grooves encircling vessel exteriors, multiple encircling incised lines, intersecting incised lines on vessel exteriors, pseudo-grater fondos with multiple parallel straight lines or arcs, and flanges. All but the last are largely confined to Guamuchil Polished Black and Arana Black-and-White.

The Tecolotla-phase figurine fragments—two apparently from large hollow Olmecoid/baby-face figurines—indicate a continuation of the Olmec relationship that is visible in the Atopula figurines. The sherd trapezoid, which is unique to the Tecolotla phase, has external counterparts only in the Jocotal phase of Salinas La Blanca.

The Tecolotla-phase ground-stone complex continues the trend of the Cacahuananche and Atopula phases. Metates are even more carefully shaped than in the Atopula phase and the grinding surfaces are even more concave. One circular specimen with a deep grinding surface enclosed by a raised rim could equally well be called a mortar. A loaf-shaped mano was recovered, as well as a grinding stone that appears to have been used more as a pestle than a mano. A spatulate sandstone object is unique and may have functioned as a flaker.

The flaked-stone complex is marked by another increase in the frequency of obsidian, which is now by far the commonest material. Most of the flakes are still unmodified; usage flaking is rare, and retouch is entirely absent. Prismatic obsidian blades increase dramatically in frequency; they are nearly as common as waste flakes. Almost all blade fragments show usage flaking. Several exhibit prepared striking platforms, and two have been retouched into scrapers or piercing tools.

Among the outstanding features of the Tecolotla phase are increased popularity of polished black ware, incised decoration (especially complex designs), and the flat-based open bowl and beaker forms; a slight increase in the frequency of white-slipped and differentially fired pottery; disappearance of the tecomate;

large hollow Olmecoid/baby-face figurines; the appearance of carefully shaped metates with deep grinding surfaces enclosed by rims; substantial numbers of prismatic obsidian blades. Particularly striking are the use of red pigment in incised and excised decoration and the appearance of the multiple-line-break motif and pseudo-grater fondos (especially with the sunburst motif). These indicate that the Tecolotla phase occupies a transitional position between the Terminal Early Preclassic and initial Middle Preclassic periods.

Tecolotla, occupying an overlapping chronological position, shows strong similarities to both the Late Ajalpan and Early Santa María phases of the Tehuacán Valley and with the Cotorra and Dili phases of central Chiapas. The strongest resemblances to the Soconusco sequence are with the brief Jocotal phase, although, as is to be expected, there are also similarities to Cuadros and Conchas I. An alignment with Jocotal is consistent with the Ajalpan/Early Santa María and Cotorra/Dili correlations (Coe and Flannery 1967: 69; MacNeish et al. 1970: 287). Tecolotla seems to fit best with the later Uala and initial Tom periods of Brush's coastal Guerrero sequence.

Like Atopula, Tecolotla shows strong similarities to the San Pablo B (Late Nexpa) and late Chalcatzingo A phases in Morelos; it also resembles Chalcatzingo B and Cerro Chacaltepec I. As Grove (1972: 45; 1974a: fig. 1) notes, the San Pablo B phase may eventually be further subdivided. Some resemblances with Gualupita are still evident. In the Valley of Mexico there are continuing similarities to the Ayotla and Justo subphases and to material from the Tlatilco and Tlapacoya graves. Resemblances to the later Bomba subphase at Ayotla (Tlapacoya), the Iglesia subphase at Tlatilco, and the El Arbolillo subphase at Zacatenco and El Arbolillo are also strong. A correlation of Tecolotla with terminal San Pablo B and Bomba seems most probable and would be consistent with Grove's (1972; 1974a) equation of San Pablo B with Ayotla and Justo. These comparisons emphasize the transitional nature of the Tecolotla phase.

Tecolotla shows similarities to both San José and Guadalupe in the Valley of Oaxaca; with both Ponce and Aguilar in northern Veracruz; and with Trapiche I and II in central Veracruz. In southern Veracruz, Tecolotla seems to resemble the Nacaste component of San Lorenzo Tenochtitlán most closely, although similarities to the San Lorenzo phase are still evident. Tecolotla has stronger affinities with material from La Venta than the Atopula phase has. Finally, there are several similarities with the Xe-sphere complexes of the Petén.

These comparisons indicate the transitional status of Tecolotla between the late Early Preclassic and initial Middle Preclassic periods; Tecolotla is most comfortably placed in the time range from 900 to 800 B.C., or perhaps slightly later (Fig. 8). Certainly Tecolotla does not extend very far into the Middle Preclassic time range. A transitional placement is compatible with the obsidian hydration readings. It is possible, on the other hand, that interaction with external areas was curtailed, causing Atopula to become a cultural backwater characterized by stylistic lag, with Early Preclassic features remaining dominant well into the Middle Preclassic period.

4. The Early Preclassic Period and the Olmec Blackware Horizon

The Initial Ceramic Period

The earliest known Mesoamerican pottery comes from central Mexico (Fig. 10): the Purrón complex of the Tehuacán Valley and Pox-period pottery from coastal Guerrero (C. Brush 1965, 1969; MacNeish et al. 1970). Pottery may have been manufactured in central Mexico before 2000 B.C., but little can be said about these very early ceramic complexes; their precise relationships to each other and with later, better-known ceramic complexes are unclear.

The Purrón complex is represented by two components of a single site; it is defined on the basis of 127 sherds, including only two distinctive types. More excavated material is urgently needed. The excavators date Purrón between 2600 B.C. (on the basis of a radiocarbon date on the latest preceramic component) and the beginning of the Early Ajalpan phase, about 1500 B.C. The mean of two radiocarbon dates associated with the single "pure" Purrón component is 1925 ± 131 B.C. The excavators place the beginning of the Purrón phase about 2300 B.C. (MacNeish et al. 1970: 21; Johnson and MacNeish 1972: 24–5, tables 4, 9).

There are strong continuities between Purrón ceramics and those of the subsequent Early Ajalpan phase: both diagnostic Purrón pottery types occur in substantial numbers in the Ajalpan phase. Almost half the Purrón Coarse sherds were found in post-Purrón contexts, and the vast majority of Purrón Plain sherds were recovered from Ajalpan and Early Santa María components. Sherds representing four characteristic Ajalpan-phase types occur in one of the Purrón components; the mean of four radiocarbon dates associated with it is 1531 ± 91 B.C. (Johnson and MacNeish 1972: 24–5, tables 4, 9). In fact, as the excavators themselves note, this non-"pure" Purrón component could easily represent the initial Early Ajalpan phase (MacNeish et al. 1970: 21, tables 12, 13). As Lowe (1971: 218–9) points out, the significance of Purrón tends to be exaggerated: 127 sherds can hardly represent the full 800-year time span assigned them. They are more comfortably placed toward its end, removing the troublesome Purrón–Early Ajalpan "gap."

Sample size is a problem with Pox pottery too. Fewer than 600 sherds comprise the Pox pottery complex, which includes only five rim sherds of significant size and only two temporally diagnostic features, both of which also occur in the subsequent Uala period (C. Brush 1969: tables 6, 8). Again, there are considerable continuities in the characteristic features of the ceramic complexes from Pox to Uala and Tom, and the very early beginning date (ca. 2400 B.C.) assigned to Pox pottery is based as much upon similarity with the Purrón complex as upon a single radiocarbon date of 2440 ± 140 B.C. (C. Brush 1965). It is possible that the Pox, Uala, and Tom materials do indeed represent the nearly two millennia from

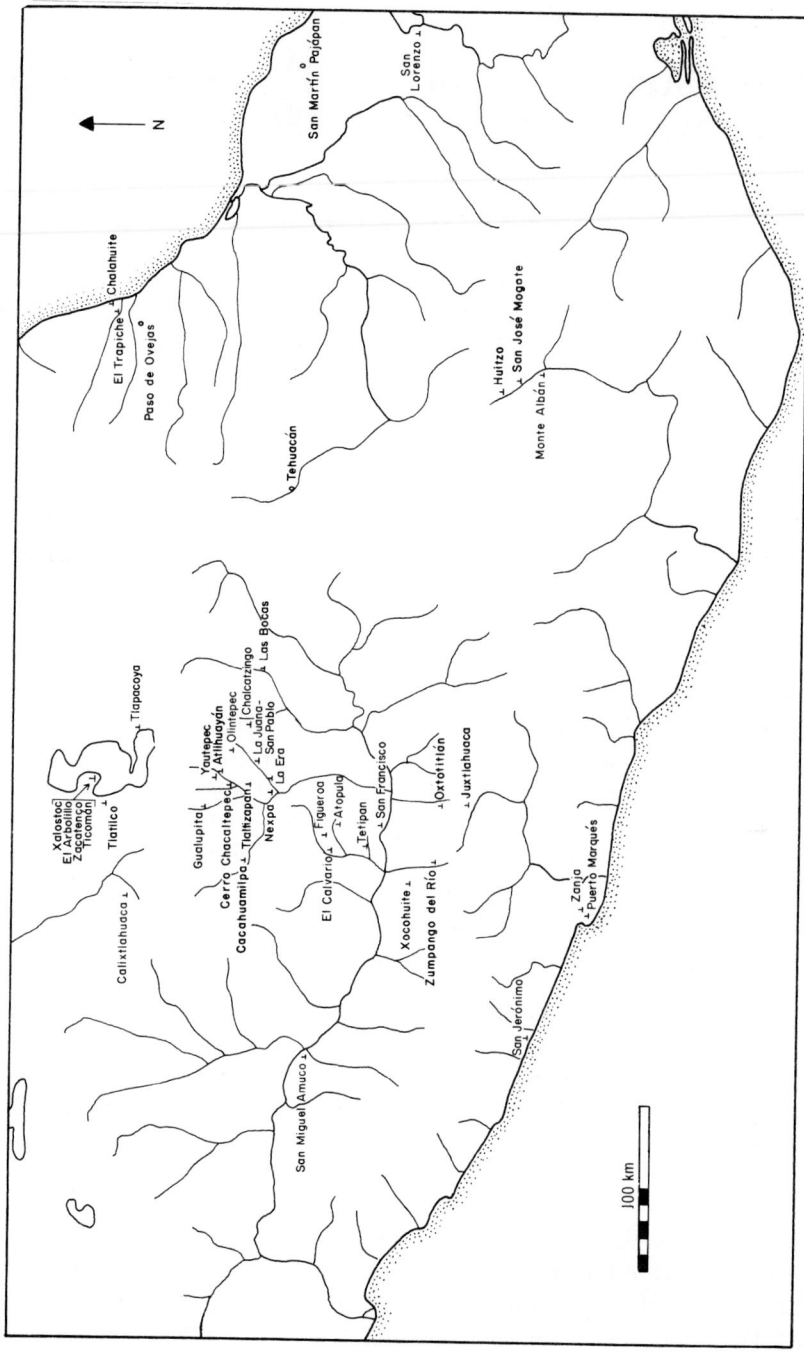

FIG. 10. Preclassic sites in central and western Mesoamerica.

2400 to 500 B.C. (C. Brush 1969: table II). Brush has analyzed the ceramics from the coast of Guerrero in terms of modes rather than types, resulting in descriptions that are difficult to use. Until an adequate description of these ceramic complexes appears, their developmental significance and their relationship to other early ceramics will remain obscure.

Hammond (1977) reports very early radiocarbon dates associated with the newly discovered Swasey ceramic complex from northern Belize. He would place this material between about 2400 and 1300 B.C. Swasey ceramics do not resemble Pox and Purrón pottery; to judge by Hammond's preliminary description, the Swasey material would fit more comfortably at the very end of this range, in the Early Preclassic period. This would imply serious inconsistencies in the interpretation of the radiocarbon dates, a possibility that cannot be evaluated until a detailed report appears. The very poorly known Yarumela I and Yojoa Monochrome ceramic complexes of Honduras (Fig. 11) do show some generalized similarities to Purrón and Pox pottery and may be of comparable antiquity (Strong et al. 1938; Coe 1961: 126–7; Green and Lowe 1967: 62).

In comparison with these problematic "initial ceramic" remains, ceramic complexes representing the period from about 1600 to 400 B.C., the traditional Early and Middle Preclassic periods, are relatively well known and firmly dated. The results of recent research in the Tehuacán Valley, the Valley of Oaxaca, the Valley of Mexico, Morelos, central Chiapas, and the Chiapas-Guatemala coast, have helped to clarify these periods. The excavations and analyses are still in progress and the results have not yet been fully reported so that thorny problems involving the relationships and chronological positions of various components remain. Integrating the results of previous research with the picture presented by recent excavation is especially difficult in some areas. Nevertheless, the Tehuacán Valley sequence can be used as a baseline for a trial synthesis of the ceramic history of the Preclassic period. The ceramic sequence defined at Atopula fits very well with the apparent general trends.

The most widely used scheme of periodization recognizes an Early Preclassic period from 1600/1500 to 900/800 B.C. and a Middle Preclassic period from 900/800 to 400 B.C. (e.g. Tolstoy and Paradis 1970: fig. 1). It is retained in the following discussion because of its familiarity, although it is becoming apparent that these are highly arbitrary points at which to divide the chronological continuum of Mesoamerican culture history. More natural cutting points, marking what seem to be important cultural changes, would be approximately 1200/1100 and 600 B.C. There is a change in cultural pattern in the area around 900/800 B.C., but apparently one of lesser magnitude. Placing the Early/Middle Preclassic period division at this point overemphasizes what seems more like a shift in emphasis than a radical break in pattern.

The Initial Early Preclassic Period

The earliest ceramic complexes of the Early Preclassic period are rather diverse in comparison with ceramic complexes of the period following 1200/1100 B.C. The early part of the Early Preclassic is a period of localized ceramic styles.

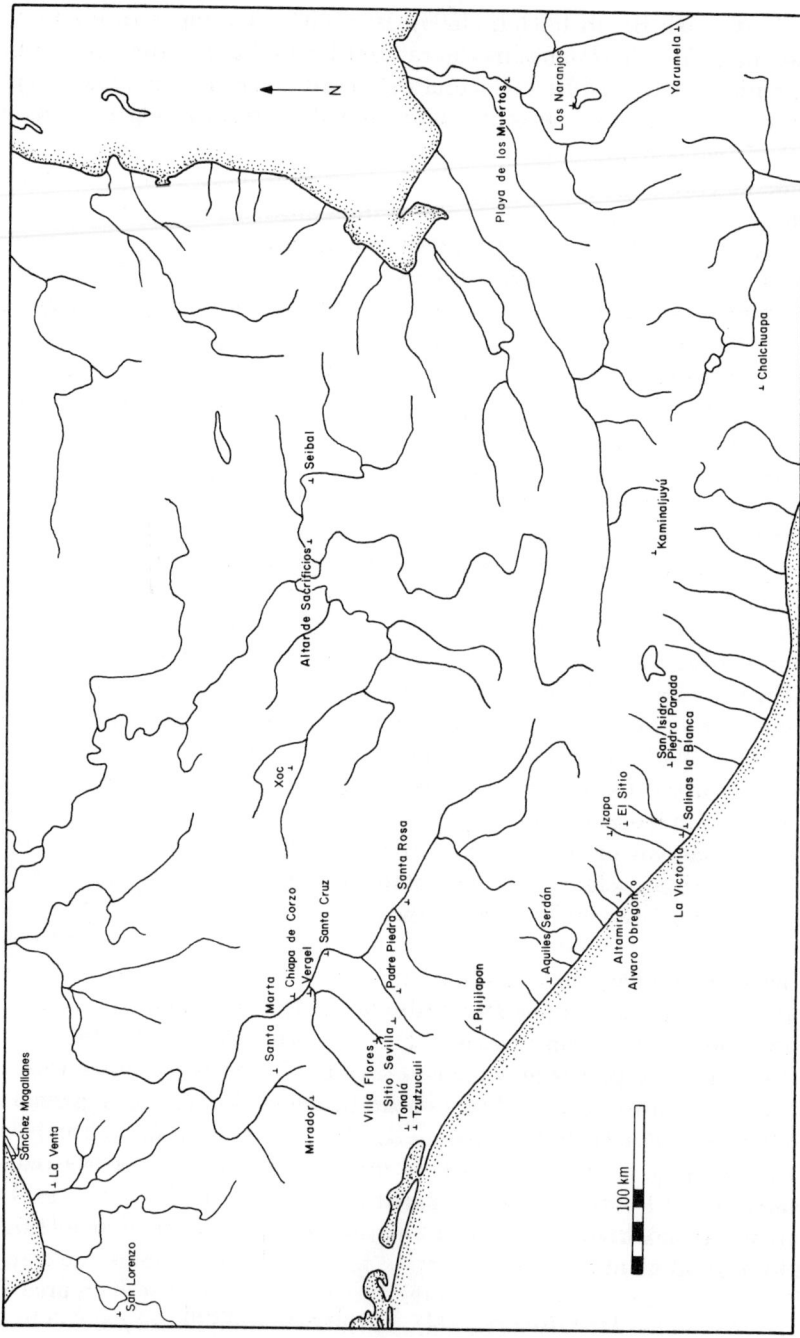

FIG. 11. Preclassic sites in southeastern Mesoamerica.

The Early Ajalpan phase (ca. 1500–1200/1100 B.C.) represents this initial Preclassic period in the Tehuacán Valley. The beginning of Late Ajalpan should probably also be included here. Several radiocarbon dates anchor Early Ajalpan in this time span, but the beginning and ending dates are not firm. The ceramics are typified by tecomate, olla and, to a lesser extent, convex-bowl shapes; flat-based open and flaring bowls are minor forms. Decoration is virtually limited to a red wash or slip, which is sometimes confined to a band at the rim. There is almost no plastic decoration. Few areas in central Mexico have produced contemporary ceramic complexes; the most closely related complex is Tierras Largas, recently discovered in the Valley of Oaxaca. Decoration, vessel forms, and even paste characteristics are very much like those of Early Ajalpan, and several types appear to be shared. Tierras Largas has been tentatively dated to 1400–1150 B.C. (MacNeish et al. 1970: 269–70; Peterson and MacNeish 1972: 25–8, 41–2, table 9; Grove 1972: 46).

In Morelos, nothing so closely related to Early Ajalpan has yet been discovered. The earliest known ceramics, of the early Chalcatzingo A complex, do resemble Tierras Largas and Early Ajalpan, as does Nevada-phase material in the Valley of Mexico (Cyphers 1975; Grove et al. 1976). Grove's (1968b; 1970a; 1970c; 1972) Early Preclassic material from the sites of La Juana-San Pablo (also known as Santa Cruz) and Nexpa has not been described in detail. Substantial modern settlements overlie both sites, and the Early Preclassic stratigraphy at La Juana-San Pablo is further confused by extensive later pre-Hispanic construction. The cemetery areas of these sites, which contain graves with mortuary offerings in both the Olmec and Tlatilco (or Río Cuautla) styles, present additional problems. Correlating the mortuary offerings with the ceramic stratigraphy from the refuse deposits is extremely problematical.

Present evidence suggests that the Early Nexpa complex is contemporary with some part of Early Ajalpan; it is tentatively dated to 1300–1250 B.C. Grove correlates Early Nexpa with the Chicharras phase at San Lorenzo Tenochtitlán (Coe 1970: 25–6). In contrast with the Tehuacán and Oaxaca complexes, the flat-based flaring bowl is the most prominent vessel form in Early Nexpa, tecomates are relatively rare, and red slipping is absent. Ollas, convex bowls, and incurved-rim bowls also occur (Grove 1972: 6–8, 11–12, 35, 41–2, 45, figs. 14–20).

The La Juana complex from La Juana-San Pablo is contemporary with Early Nexpa; they are subsumed in the La Juana phase (1350–1250 B.C.) (Grove 1972: 42; 1974b). As originally defined (Grove 1970a: 2–3), the La Juana complex was based largely upon mortuary furniture looted by *huaqueros* from the La Juana cemetery zone (one of the two at the La Juana-San Pablo site). It was said to be "without question Olmec." In the light of later work at Nexpa, Grove (1972: 42–4) concluded that most of the stratigraphic levels at La Juana-San Pablo and the majority of the graves in both cemetery zones pertain to the Terminal Early Preclassic San Pablo B phase. The abundance of Madera pottery and cylindrical vessel forms supports the reassignment of the bulk of what was formerly considered La Juana-complex material, including the Olmec elements, to the San Pablo B phase. This is consistent with Grove's (1970a: 2, 9) original comparison of this material with Ayotla and Justo in the Valley of Mexico and San Lorenzo at San Lorenzo Tenochtitlán.

The Middle Nexpa and San Pablo A complexes, collectively referred to as the San Pablo A phase, correlate much more closely with Initial Early Preclassic material in other areas. Red-slipped and red-rimmed pottery appears in significant quantities and the proportion of convex and incurved-rim bowls increases. Grove tentatively dates the San Pablo A phase to 1250–1050 B.C.; on the basis of the radiocarbon dates associated with the Middle Nexpa complex, 1300–1100 B.C. might be more appropriate (Grove 1972: 36, 41–2, 46; 1974a).

Johnson and MacNeish (1972: 42) suggest that Levels 32 and 31 of Puerto Marqués on the Guerrero coast correlate with Early Ajalpan, and that three Early Ajalpan pottery types, including a red-slipped type, are dominant in the ceramics of these levels. No radiocarbon dates are associated with these levels, which Brush (1969: 57, table 8) includes within his Pox period. The Ajalpan correlation would indicate either that there is a long gap in the sequence (which is not suggested by Brush), or that the Pox period (now represented only by Level 33) immediately precedes Early Ajalpan (ca. 1500 B.C.). It is difficult to imagine that Level 33 represents a continuous occupation from 2300 to 1500 B.C.

In southeastern Mesoamerica the earliest known ceramics are those of the Barra complex. It has been surely identified only at Altamira, about 2 km. inland from the sea on the coast of Chiapas not far from the Guatemala border (Green and Lowe 1967). The occupation and the artifact sample are quite small, but the relative chronological position of Barra is established by the overlying deposits containing material of the Ocós phase. The suggested beginning date of 1600 B.C. for Barra is simply intended to reflect its pre-Ocós status. Barra ceramics are dominated by tecomates with incised decoration or a red paint or slip; open and flaring bowls, often with a red slip on the interior surface only, are somewhat less prominent.

The Ocós-phase complexes, which appear shortly after 1500 B.C. and end about 1100 B.C., are much better known and much more widely distributed than Barra. Ocós ceramics continue the Barra emphasis on tecomates, with flat-based open and flaring bowls again less prominent. Plastic decoration in a wide variety of techniques is typical. It occurs most commonly on tecomates, and is often zoned. A red paint or slip is also common. The well-known exotic decoration—iridescent painting that occurs at the type site, La Victoria, on the Guatemala coast and in Ocós components in coastal Chiapas (Coe 1961: 48–9; personal communication)— is not typical of all Ocós complexes.

Barra and Ocós ceramics represent an early local tradition of pottery manufacture which shares several features with the early ceramic complexes of central Mexico, especially tecomates, red paint or slip, and flat-based bowls. On the other hand, there are distinct differences in emphasis. The olla, convex bowl, and incurved-rim bowl are prominent in central Mexico, while the southeastern lowland complexes show a tremendous emphasis on the tecomate. This popularity of tecomates largely accounts for one striking contrast between Early Preclassic sites in the two areas—the much larger ceramic samples recovered from such Pacific coast sites as La Victoria and Salinas La Blanca. If the tremendous quantities of featureless tecomate body sherds are subtracted, the totals are quite comparable to those from typical Early Preclassic sites elsewhere in Mesoamerica (Coe and Flannery 1967: 22, table 11).

In discussing the affinities and possible origins of the earliest ceramics of the southeastern lowland area, Lowe (Green and Lowe 1967: 60-1) emphasizes similarities, sometimes quite striking, to early ceramic complexes from Central America and northwestern South America. Coe (1961: 135-6) and Grove (1971) have also stressed these resemblances. The possible manioc cultivation of the Barra and Ocós phases (see below) is very suggestive in this context, since manioc is usually thought to have been first domesticated somewhere in this area. On the other hand, there are related wild species in Mesoamerica as well (Heiser 1973: 145). The earliest pottery of the southeastern lowlands also shows strong similarities to poorly known early ceramics from several sites in Honduras, particularly to some of the Ulua Bichrome-"phase" material. The very simple and crude pottery of the Yojoa Monochrome and Yarumela I complexes may even be earlier than Ocós. Similarities between the ceramics of the Pacific coastal lowlands and Honduras persist into the Late Early and Early Middle Preclassic periods (Strong et al. 1938; Coe 1961: 126-7; Baudez 1966; 1970; Green and Lowe 1967: 61-2).

The Cacahuananche complex from Atopula shares several features with these Initial Early Preclassic complexes, especially with San Pablo A of nearby Morelos—notably the prominence of tecomate, olla, and convex bowl forms and of red slipping.

In sum, the period from approximately 1600/1500 to 1200/1100 B.C. is now known to be represented by several ceramic complexes: Early Ajalpan; Tierras Largas; Chalcatzingo A, Early Nexpa, and San Pablo A/Middle Nexpa; Nevada; Cacahuananche; Barra and Ocós; and probably later "Pox" levels at Puerto Marqués.

Even the generalized features which these complexes share are not universal. Early Ajalpan and Tierras Largas are very closely related, and the material from Levels 32-31 at Puerto Marqués resembles both, although not so closely. Cacahuananche and the San Pablo A complexes are quite closely related to each other, but they share fewer features with the Tehuacán, Oaxaca, and coastal Guerrero complexes. Cacahuananche, San Pablo A, and perhaps Tierras Largas, are best aligned with "middle" Ajalpan (later Early Ajalpan and initial Late Ajalpan). The Early Nexpa complex of the La Juana phase shows relatively few affinities with any of the other complexes. Barra and Ocós material shows very general similarities to other Initial Early Preclassic complexes.

These Initial Early Preclassic complexes do not constitute a horizon style. In comparison with the degree of similarity among Late Early Preclassic ceramic complexes, they seem quite disparate—a series of localized ceramic styles with very generalized similarities. This is consistent with the hypothesis that they developed in place, essentially independently, from Purrón/Pox-like predecessors.

Data on other material cultural complexes of the Initial Early Preclassic components are scant.

The Late Early Preclassic Period

The ceramic complexes that can be dated to the period between approximately 1200/1100 and 900/800 B.C. show a great deal more similarity among themselves than do those of the Initial Early Preclassic period. Polished black pottery is particularly prominent. Some of the shared modes occur in central Mexican Initial Early Preclassic ceramic complexes, but many are new. As a group they are more widely distributed than were individual modes during the Initial Early Preclassic period. Distinctive nonceramic features are associated with the ceramic marker traits. These attributes constitute a horizon style in its original sense: a set of distinctive features which extends contemporaneously over a wide area (Kroeber 1944; Willey 1945; 1948; Bennett 1948; Rouse 1954; 1972: 130, 279). There is an intimate distributional association between these features and the complex and esoteric Olmec art style, which has its center in the Gulf-coast lowlands; many of the modes and mode combinations of the horizon are also elements of the Olmec style "proper." It is appropriate, therefore, to refer to the components linked by the horizon style as the Olmec Blackware horizon, even though it is possible to argue that the most elaborate representations of the Olmec art style may not be sufficiently widespread to constitute in themselves a horizon style (Coe 1965c: 771; Willey et al. 1967: 292). Evidence that the components in question are contemporaneous is independent of the recognition of the horizon style, so that it is possible to consider the implications of the horizon without circularity (Rouse 1955; Willey and Phillips 1958: 29–43).

The Late Ajalpan phase represents the Late Early Preclassic period in the Tehuacán Valley. On the basis of thirteen radiocarbon determinations, modified by the indications of cross-dating and the beginning date of the Early Santa María phase, Late Ajalpan is placed between approximately 1150 and 850 B.C. (Johnson and MacNeish 1972: 42, table 9).

Because of its position in a long, well-documented and well-reported sequence, Late Ajalpan is crucial to the synthesis of the Olmec Blackware horizon. Its ceramics, though, are not particularly typical of the horizon, which makes a late and diluted appearance in the Tehuacán Valley. Late Ajalpan ceramics show continuities from Early Ajalpan; the tecomate form predominates, and red-painted decoration becomes more prominent. There are also some new features: large hollow figurines; polished black pottery and white-slipped pottery in small quantities; a few "mottled" bottles; and the increased importance of flat-based open and flaring bowls and of incised decoration (MacNeish et al. 1970: 41–57).

In the Valley of Oaxaca, ceramic complexes of the San José phase (1150–850 B.C.) retain some Tierras Largas features, such as tecomates and red-rimmed decoration, but here the new group of traits is much more conspicuous. Affinities with ceramic complexes outside the Valley of Oaxaca are closer, suggesting strong interaction with external areas. The new traits become even more prominent in the later San José phase (1000–850 B.C.). Incised and excised decoration first become common in the San José phase. White-rimmed black ware and polished black- and white-slipped monochrome vessels, including beakers, appear; they sometimes bear excised Olmec motifs—the fire-serpent, kan cross, or U motif. Large hollow figurines and white-slipped Olmecoid/baby-face figurines make their first appearance, as do "mottled" bottles and such exotic features as roller stamps and spouted trays (Flannery 1968: 82–5; MacNeish et al. 1970: 270; Johnson and MacNeish 1972: 42–3, table 9; Flannery 1976).

In Morelos, the San Pablo B phase represented at Nexpa and La Juana-San Pablo has a comparable date; Grove (1972: 42; 1974b) places it between 1050 and 900 B.C. San Pablo B shows many of the features of the Olmec Blackware horizon seen in the San José phase. The slightly later beginning date assigned to San Pablo B may reflect a late arrival of the horizon in Morelos, as in Tehuacán. On the other hand, San Pablo B may begin somewhat earlier than 1050 B.C.—most of the radiocarbon determinations are associated with San Pablo A and would be equally compatible with a beginning date of 1100 or even 1150 B.C. for San Pablo B. San Pablo B is characterized by a sudden increase in the proportion of polished dark brown- and black-slipped pottery and by the appearance in significant numbers of beakers, open and flaring bowls, and incised and excised decoration (including Olmec motifs). Small quantities of white-slipped pottery also appear. In addition, the elaborate mortuary ceramics of the two La Juana-San Pablo cemetery zones include hollow white-slipped Olmecoid/baby-face figurines, solid and hollow K- and D-type figurines, cylinder seals, spouted trays, and a red-on-brown bottle complex with stirrup spouts, belted and composite bottles, and *botellones* (Grove 1970c; 1972: 36–46). The grave goods represent both the Olmec and Tlatilco styles. The problem of the chronological and cultural relationships of the two styles, with each other and with the ceramic complexes recovered from stratified refuse deposits, is extremely complex.

At Chalcatzingo (Cyphers 1975; Grove et al. 1976) Grove's tentative new phases do not coincide perfectly with those defined by his earlier work in Morelos. San Pablo B corresponds in time with late Chalcatzingo A and early Chalcatzingo B. Features of the Olmec Blackware horizon (polished black and brown pottery, white-rimmed black ware, incised or excised Olmec motifs, and pottery possibly imported from San Lorenzo) and of the Tlatilco style (red-on-brown ware and figurines, but not the exotic bottle complex) appear in both phases.

At Tlapacoya in the Valley of Mexico, the Ayotla and Justo complexes (ca. 1150–1000 B.C.) are aligned with these Late Early Preclassic complexes. Ayotla has a radiocarbon date of 1070 ± 80 B.C., and Justo has one of 1030 ± 100 B.C. They are characterized by red-rimmed tecomates, polished black- and white-slipped wares, white-rimmed black ware, "mottled" bottles, open and flaring bowls with bolstered rims, beakers, incised and excised decoration including such Olmec motifs as the St. Andrew's cross, large hollow white-slipped Olmecoid/baby-face figurines, and D- and K-type figurines (MacNeish et al. 1970: 272; Tolstoy and Paradis 1970: 347, fig. 1).

The Olmec material from the Tlatilco graves can be correlated with these Tlapacoya complexes. The Tlatilco-style mortuary ceramics from the Tlatilco graves are also Preclassic, but they are extraordinarily difficult to place chronologically. Their relationships with the Olmec style and with refuse deposits in central Mexico are unclear. This "Tlatilco problem" is discussed below.

The Atopula ceramic complex is aligned with these Late Early Preclassic phases. The strong representation of the Olmec Blackware horizon in the Atopula complex indicates that Atopula participated in the cultural interaction that produced the horizon, to a much greater extent than contemporary settlements in the Tehuacán Valley.

Some of the material from Greengo's (1967; 1970; personal communication) excavations at nearby El Calvario and Figueroa is apparently related, although it is inadequately published. These sites may correlate better with the Tecolotla phase and the Terminal Early Preclassic period.

On the coast of Guerrero, the Uala-period levels (30–27) at Puerto Marqués share some of the same features: large hollow Olmecoid/baby-face figurines; polished black- and brown-slipped incised vessels; and a few white-slipped vessels, including flat-based open and flaring bowls. Tecomates and red-slipping, which are also characteristic of the ceramics of lower levels, seem equally prominent (E. Brush 1968: 58–71; C. Brush 1969: 57–8, tables 1, 3, 8, 9).

In the southeastern lowlands the developmental continuity from Barra through Ocós is broken shortly before 1100 B.C. with the disappearance of Ocós ceramic complexes. Some Ocós features continue during the Late Early Preclassic period, but the new (and newly emphasized) features of the Olmec Blackware horizon are more prominent. The basic features of the horizon are distributed widely throughout the southeastern lowlands, although some of the more elaborate aspects are more limited in their occurrence. In some complexes Olmecoid/baby-face figurines and complex incised and excised decoration are not prominent. There are differences in emphasis; polished black pottery is more common at some sites than others.

The Olmec Blackware horizon is strongly represented in the Cuadros phase at sites in Soconusco—Salinas La Blanca, Izapa, and Altamira (Coe and Flannery 1967; Green and Lowe 1967; Ekholm-Miller 1969). Farther south the Tok complex of Chalchuapa, El Salvador, is closely related (Sharer and Gifford 1970; Sharer 1974: 169). In central Chiapas the horizon is strongly represented at many sites of the Chiapa I (Cotorra) phase, including Padre Piedra and San Isidro. In other Chiapa I ceramic complexes there are variations in emphasis. At Chiapa de Corzo a smudged white ware shows greater prominence, and true white-rimmed black and polished black wares are less abundant; figurines are not common. Continuities with Ocós pottery are more apparent in these complexes (Dixon 1959; Coe and Flannery 1967; Green and Lowe, 1967; Bernal 1971: 46).

To summarize, a group of ceramic modes is widely shared in Mesoamerica during the period from 1200/1100 to 1000/900 B.C. The most striking traits are figurines and incised or excised motifs which are part of the Olmec style, along with more generalized features such as the prominence of polished black beakers and flat-based open and flaring bowls, often with bolstered rims. The elements of this horizon are even more conspicuous at San Lorenzo Tenochtitlán on the Gulf coast, where they are associated with a much wider range of Olmec features. The horizon is in some sense Olmec, and thus "foreign" to central Mexico and the southeastern lowlands.

On the other hand, many of the characteristics of Initial Early Preclassic complexes persist alongside those of the Olmec Blackware horizon. Some of the modes and mode combinations that constitute the horizon even appear in the preceding ceramic complexes. The changes from the Cacahuananche to Atopula complexes illustrate very well the sense in which the horizon may be viewed as a shift in emphasis. Black pottery is well represented in the Cacahuananche phase, but it is rarely decorated, not always polished, and almost never very highly polished. In the Atopula phase its popularity increases, it is more commonly incised, and virtually every sherd shows careful polishing. The red wares and tecomates persist into the Atopula phase, although one red tecomate type (Tlapala Red) does not survive until the end of Atopula. The other red types increase in frequency, but the most popular, Pozo Thin Red, shows the same trends as Guamuchil Polished Black: polishing becomes universal and a good deal more proficient, and both the forms and decoration resemble those of Guamuchil Polished Black. The Olmec features (figurines and decorative motifs) are without precedent in Cacahuananche. Similar continuities can be seen in varying degrees in other contemporary complexes.

The Olmec Blackware horizon is not uniformly prominent in all regions. It is most fully represented in the Gulf coast area. Elsewhere in Mesoamerica it appears with variable intensity along with features of earlier local ceramic styles. The Olmec Blackware horizon is not simply an independent development out of the Initial Early Preclassic complexes of these areas; neither is it exclusively an imported phenomenon.

The Terminal Early Preclassic Period

Short phases immediately following and closely related to Late Early Preclassic occupations are distinguishable in some areas between 950/900 and 850/800 B.C. The Bomba complex at Tlapacoya in the Valley of Mexico retains a number of Ayotla and Justo features. Others are lost, and some of the characteristics of subsequent Early Middle Preclassic ceramic complexes begin to appear. Incised and excised dark brown-to-black-slipped pottery continues to be dominant. Flat-based bowls and differentially fired pottery decline slightly; several earlier figurine types are replaced. New types of white-slipped pottery appear and increase in importance, as do interior base incision and the multiple-line-break motif. Bomba, tentatively dated to 1000/950–850 B.C., has a single radiocarbon date of 940 ± 80 B.C.

The Iglesia complex, based on excavated material from refuse deposits at Tlatilco, is also transitional. Iglesia retains such features as large hollow figurines, Olmecoid/babyface figurines, and polished black pottery with incised and excised designs. It is also marked by the increased importance of white-slipped wares and by the appearance of the multiple-line-break motif and interior base incision, including the sunburst motif. The Iglesia complex is tentatively dated to 950/900–800 B.C., with a radiocarbon date of 810 ± 160 B.C. It departs more from the Olmec Blackware horizon pattern than does Bomba. The El Arbolillo ceramic complexes of El Arbolillo and Zacatenco retain a few features of the horizon, but they are more closely related to Early Middle Preclassic complexes; they are also tentatively assigned to the 900/850–800 B.C. period. Bomba, Iglesia, and El Arbolillo overlap one another in time and show a progressive development away from the Olmec Blackware horizon, with the appearance of some Early Middle Preclassic features. Iglesia and El Arbolillo are referrable to the early part of the valley-wide Zacatenco phase. The status of Bomba is less clear (Tolstoy and Guennette 1965; MacNeish et al. 1970: 277–8; Tolstoy and Paradis 1970: 345–9, fig. 1; Grove 1974b: 50).

The Tecolotla ceramic complex at Atopula shows a similar combination: persistent features of the Olmec Blackware horizon and low frequencies of new modes characteristic of Early Middle Preclassic ceramics. Most of the elements of the horizon continue from the Atopula phase and are even intensified. The Olmec figurine style is still represented. Polished black ware, the "imitative" Pozo Thin Red type, differentially fired white-black ware, and incised decoration all increase in popularity; excised decoration appears. Beakers increase slightly and flat-based bowls maintain their popularity (although there is a sharp shift toward the dominance of open bowls). On the other hand, tecomates and bottles disappear; white-slipped pottery increases slightly in popularity; red pigment is sometimes used to fill incision and excision; the multiple-line-break motif and interior base incision (including pendant arcs and the sunburst motif) appear. Tecolotla, like Bomba, is transitional in that Early Middle Preclassic modes appear, but it shows a much stronger retention of the Olmec Blackware-horizon features; Tecolotla is undoubtedly more closely related to Late Early Preclassic complexes. The intensification of the features of the horizon and the loss of older features such as the tecomate shape at the same time that Early Middle Preclassic modes begin to appear does not necessarily indicate a retarded appearance of the horizon at Atopula. The same phenomenon is observable in the Valley of Mexico and is suggested in other areas.

Corresponding Terminal Early Preclassic transitional phases are not clearly defined elsewhere in central Mexico. Some of the material from Greengo's (1967; 1970; personal communication) excavations at El Calvario and Figueroa may be related to the Tecolotla complex. In the Valley of Oaxaca the features of the Olmec Blackware horizon become more prominent in the later part of the San José phase, again indicating that a Terminal Early Preclassic intensification of the horizon does not signal marginality. In latest Ajalpan, typical Early Middle Preclassic features, including white-slipped pottery, appear. Tehuacán, however, never participated fully in the Olmec Blackware horizon. Flat-based bowls with bolstered rims, mottled bottles, and polished black pottery appear only in small quantities—probably mostly as trade items—at the end of Ajalpan. Several features of the horizon, such as incised and excised Olmec motifs, do not appear until the Early Santa María phase (MacNeish et al. 1970: 270, 282–3).

In Morelos, Grove (1972: 44–5; 1974b) has not subdivided the San Pablo B phase, but his data suggest that further work may disclose a Terminal Early Preclassic phase. Early Chalcatzingo B (Grove 1973b; 1974a; Cyphers 1975; Grove et al. 1976) may occupy this transitional status, correlating with the Bomba complex in the Valley of Mexico.

A Terminal Early Preclassic phase, Jocotal (ca. 900/850–800/750 B.C.) appears at a number of Soconusco sites, including Salinas La Blanca, Izapa, and Altamira. Jocotal pottery is closely related to and develops out of Cuadros ceramics. Some Olmec Blackware-horizon features—black and white-rimmed black beakers and flat-based bowls—are more prominent. New features that become typical of Early Middle Preclassic ceramic complexes appear, particularly white-slipped pottery with the incised multiple-line-break motif. An equivalent transitional phase has not yet been defined in central Chiapas, although the long Chiapa I phase may be subdivided in the future (Coe and Flannery 1967: 23, 32–5, 68–70; Green and Lowe 1967; Ekholm-Miller 1969).

Distinct Terminal Early Preclassic phases, where they are distinguishable, show a continuation, even an intensification, of the Olmec Blackware horizon, along with the appearance in low frequencies of ceramic modes that are characteristic of Early Middle Preclassic complexes. This does not indicate a break with the Late Early Preclassic horizon but foreshadows a second horizon that becomes recognizable in the Early Middle Preclassic period. The significance of the transitional phases is their indication of continuity between the two Olmec horizons. The development is especially clear in the Bomba-Iglesia-El Arbolillo sequence of overlapping subphases in the Valley of Mexico.

Nonceramic Artifacts

In addition to widespread modes of ceramic form and decoration, a set of nonceramic artifacts is associated with the Olmec Blackware horizon. These objects can be identified as Olmec through their exclusive occurrence in association with the Olmec style: with the Olmec Blackware horizon in central Mexico and at the great Olmec ceremonial centers in the Gulf coast region.

The most striking of these are small Olmec-style jade figurines. They have come to be thought of as archetypically Olmec, primarily because of their relative abundance at La Venta. Actually they are extremely rare, perhaps entirely absent, everywhere in Mesoamerica in the Early Preclassic period, even at San Lorenzo Tenochtitlán, as is jade in any form. Olmec jade figurines are rare at all times in central Mexico, except in the Morelos-Guerrero area.

Very few Olmec-style jade and serpentine objects can be associated with the Olmec Blackware horizon; none has been recovered in stratigraphic contexts or controlled excavation. Several Olmec-style jade pieces (and one of onyx) were reportedly recovered from the Las Bocas cemetery, where the ceramic offerings represent almost exclusively the Olmec Blackware horizon. This is hardly firm evidence; the association might be with the Terminal Early Preclassic transitional aspect of the horizon, or even with the initial Middle Preclassic. A bead in the form of a head with some Olmec features apparently was discovered in a grave at Tlapacoya; here the probable association would be with the Terminal Early Preclassic period. Two Olmec jade figurines are said to have come from the Tlatilco graves; unfortunately they were not from controlled excavation (Covarrubias 1943: 43; Coe 1965b: 21, ill. 17; Nicholson 1971a: fig. 2). Since these pieces cannot be associated with particular grave lots they cannot be placed in the context of Tolstoy's seriation of the Tlatilco grave goods. Their chronological position could fall anywhere within the time span of the Tlatilco graves—Late Early Preclassic to initial Middle Preclassic, with a Terminal Early Preclassic placement most probable. The few jade and serpentine beads and earplugs reported from Tlatilco and Gualupita, and perhaps some of those from Tlapocoya, may also date to this period, along with serpentine celts and jade pendants in the form of jaguar teeth from Tlatilco. The latter, however, occur also in the Early Middle Preclassic period at Zacatenco and El Arbolillo (Vaillant 1930; 1935; Barba de Piña Chán 1956: 101, 109, 112; Piña Chán 1958a: 113; 1971: 173–5). At Chalcatzingo, Olmec jade and serpentine (Piña Chán 1955a: 24; Cyphers 1975; Grove et al. 1976) is definitely Middle Preclassic. Jade and serpentine ornaments and a green stone figurine are reported from Xochipala graves, and some of the Xochipala sites have produced ceramics and figurines representing the Olmec Blackware horizon (Gay 1972; see below). A fragment of a jadeite celt from Altamira probably dates to the Terminal Early Preclassic Jocotal phase (Green and Lowe 1967).

The vast majority of Olmec jade pieces are without provenience; some of them may be associated with the Olmec Blackware horizon, but most are associated with the Early Middle Preclassic Olmec Whiteware horizon (see below).

Yuguitos, small concave or domed stone objects, are often considered to be Olmec. A Tlatilco figurine (Bernal 1969: fig. 19, pl. 56) suggests that they may have functioned as hand (or elbow or knee) protectors for ball players. The only established provenience of these objects is Tlatilco, although they are said to occur in Guerrero and even Honduras; they are not known in the Gulf-coast lowlands. The only obvious link between yuguitos and the Olmec Blackware horizon is one specimen from Tlatilco with an Olmec were-jaguar face on the outer surface; other decorated examples do not bear Olmec motifs. On the other hand, it is conceivable that the enigmatic "knuckle dusters" depicted in Olmec art are profile representations of yuguitos worn as hand protectors (Coe 1965b: 21, ills. 13–16; Piña Chán 1971: 175).

Very distinctive iron ore (magnetite, ilmenite, hematite) mirrors are also associated with the Olmec Blackware horizon. The reflecting surfaces are very carefully ground and polished, and concave specimens are parabolic, almost as though they were ground to optical specifications (Gullberg 1959). Their precise function has not been established, although it is possible to use them to start fires and to cast images. Drilled suspension holes and the evidence of figurines indicate that they were often worn as pendants (Gullberg 1959; Bernal 1969: pl. 37a).

Detailed stratigraphic information about these mirrors comes only from the Valley of Oaxaca. The large ceremonial-civic center of San José Mogote contains a residential zone occupied by artisans specializing in the manufacture of ornaments, especially small flat iron-ore mirrors. Mirrors, mirror fragments, unfinished mirrors, and worked and unworked chunks of iron ore are abundant in this section of the site in the late San José phase (1000–850 B.C.). Elaborate pottery and figurines representing the Olmec Blackware horizon are abundant in this workshop zone, which also includes public architecture. Mossbauer spectral analysis indicates that the craftsmen of San José Mogote exploited at least four iron-ore sources in the Valley of Oaxaca. Mirrors and ore fragments from the same sources occur at several contemporary sites—in the Nochixtlán Valley to the north, at La Juana-San Pablo in Morelos (San Pablo phase), and at San Lorenzo in Veracruz (Nacaste phase), but they have been found at few other sites in the Valley of Oaxaca. Nacaste-phase mirrors at San Lorenzo have also been matched with a source near Niltepec in the Isthmus of Tehuantepec region. Small flat iron-ore mirrors are plainly high-status exchange items associated with the Olmec Blackware horizon (Curtis 1959; Flannery 1968: 85–9; Pires-Ferreira 1975; 1976b).

The large concave iron-ore mirrors, known mainly from La Venta, are primarily Early Middle Preclassic. A small concave mirror was found in Late Early Preclassic mound fill at San Lorenzo. Concave mirrors from the Tlatilco graves, Tlapacoya, and the cemetery sites in the Xochipala zone do not have clear stratigraphic contexts; they may be associated with the Olmec Blackware horizon. Pyrite mirrors from Tlatilco and the Xochipala sites and a polished "stone reflector" from Altamira (probably Jocotal phase) may also be contemporary (Drucker et al. 1959; Barba de Piña Chán 1956: 124, foto 18; Piña Chán 1958a: 113; 1971: 175; Lorenzo 1965: 48–9, fig. 67; Green and Lowe 1967; Gay 1972: 50–1, figs. 37, 38; Pires-Ferreira 1975; 1976b).

Shell was also exchanged over long distances during the Late Early Preclassic period. In the Valley of Oaxaca, shell was imported from the Pacific coast and the Atlantic drainage. Atlantic-drainage shell also occurs in the Valley of Mexico and Morelos. It is abundant in the ornament-manufacturing zone of San José Mogote, along with iron ore and other exotic raw materials but is much more broadly distributed. Every Early Preclassic house at San José Mogote contains some shell and usually evidence of shell-working, and shell is common at several smaller Early Preclassic sites in the Valley of Oaxaca. Shell ornaments do not mark high status as clearly as iron-ore mirrors, but elaborate shell ornaments are associated with the Olmec Blackware horizon. A shell pendant from San José Mogote is decorated with an Olmec "hand-paw-wing" motif (Pires-Ferreira 1975; 1976b).

Obsidian, probably the commonest item of long-distance exchange, is plainly not a high-status commodity. It occurs at virtually every Late Early Preclassic site and in low-status as well as elite residences (Cobean et al. 1971; Pires-Ferreira 1976a), but the exchange networks that distributed obsidian may well have been associated with the Olmec Blackware horizon. Shell, pottery, and exotic commodities such as iron-ore mirrors, turtle-shell drums, shark teeth, and stingray spines may have sometimes moved along these networks (Pires-Ferreira 1976b).

"Floating" Assemblages

Several assemblages that lack clear-cut chronological placement because they were not excavated under controlled conditions—particularly mortuary offerings looted from cemeteries—can be associated with the Olmec Blackware horizon. The mortuary furniture from Las Bocas (Caballo Pintado) in western Puebla is a nearly pure representation of the Olmec Blackware horizon. It is known almost exclusively from pieces that have appeared on the antiquities market. The Las Bocas material includes large hollow and small solid white-slipped Olmecoid/baby-face figurines; polished black (and occasionally white-rimmed black) bottles, beakers, flat-based bowls, and incurved-rim bowls with excised Olmec designs rubbed with red pigment (Coe's "dark Channeled" ware); some white wares; effigy vessels; and "exotic" elements such as spouted trays, roller stamps, and clay masks (Coe 1965b; Grove 1968b: 180; 1972: 50).

Except for a few red-on-brown bottles, including a stirrup-spout bottle, the Tlatilco style, which often occurs in central Mexican cemeteries along with offerings representing the Olmec Blackware horizon, is unrepresented in the known Las Bocas mortuary furniture. Spouted trays may also be part of the Tlatilco style (Grove 1972: 50). Piña Chán's brief, unpublished excavations at Las Bocas produced ceramics resembling Late Ajalpan. This may strengthen the suggestion that the most elaborate features of the Olmec Blackware horizon reflect partial functional specialization as elite mortuary furniture. K-type figurines and ceramics from surface collections show some resemblances to Early Middle Preclassic Cerro Chacaltepec I material from Morelos (Grove 1968b: 180-2; 1972: 50).

At Tlapacoya in the Valley of Mexico, another looted cemetery has produced closely related mortuary offerings representing the Olmec Blackware horizon. Figurines include large hollow and small solid white-slipped Olmecoid/baby-face types. Polished black-to brown-slipped vessels are incised and excised with Olmec motifs (the St. Andrew's cross, U-motif, and were-jaguar-dragon profile); the decorations are often filled with red pigment. White-slipped pottery includes both Calixtlahuaca-ware beakers with incised were-jaguar profiles and flat-based open bowls with incised multiple-line-breaks and pseudo-grater fondos (including the sunburst motif). Differentially fired white-black pottery and exotic elements— animal-effigy vessels, roller seals with carved Olmec motifs, ceramic masks, and several unusual solid figurine types—also occur. The Tlatilco style is entirely unrepresented in the mortuary material from Tlapacoya. The relative prominence of white pottery, the use of red pigment in incision and excision, the extreme prominence of the beaker form, and the absence of bottles suggest a correlation with the Terminal Early Preclassic Bomba complex of the refuse deposits. At the same time, the possibility of overlap with the earlier Ayotla and Justo complexes cannot be eliminated (Coe 1965b; Weaver 1967; Grove 1968b: 178-9; Tolstoy and

Paradis 1970: 347). Barba de Piña Chán's (1956: 62–70) excavations in another part of the extensive Tlapacoya site produced primarily Late Preclassic material, although a small proportion of the material from her lowest levels may represent the Early Middle Preclassic period.

Calixtlahuaca ware—white-slipped beakers with incised Olmec were-jaguar profiles—was first reported by García Payón (1941) from the site of Calixtlahuaca in the Toluca Valley in association with white-slipped vessels with incised multiple-line-breaks and pseudo-grater fondos. This suggests an association with the Early Middle Preclassic Olmec Whiteware horizon. The beaker shape suggests an earlier alignment with the Terminal Early Preclassic transitional aspect of the Olmec Blackware horizon, as does the occurrence of Calixtlahuaca ware at Tlapacoya. Calixtlahuaca ware also occurs in Morelos, but not at Tlatilco and Las Bocas (García Payón 1941: 215–6, láms. I, II; Coe 1965b: 21; Grove 1968b: 185–6; 1972: 50).

Vaillant's Gualupita sequence is not precise enough to permit a reliable assessment of the relationship of the occupations there with other Central Mexican Preclassic complexes. Further excavation would be required to refine the sequence and to demonstrate the relationship between the burials and refuse deposits. Excavations attempted since the construction of a hotel on the site have proved futile. Plainly, some part of the occupation at Gualupita falls in the Late to Terminal Early Preclassic time range. The large hollow white-slipped Olmecoid/baby-face figurine, incised black-to-brown-slipped bowls and bottles, and white-slipped incised bowls and beakers indicate an association with the Olmec Blackware horizon. The Tlatilco style is hardly represented at Gualupita: stirrup-spouts and belted bottles are absent, although fluted red-on-brown bottles do occur in the graves. There are also D- and K-type figurines, spouted trays, and a few "horned" or spouted figurines which resemble specimens from Tlatilco and La Juana-San Pablo. There are indications that the site was abandoned at the end of Gualupita I. Gualupita II is best aligned with Late Preclassic complexes—Cerro Chacaltepec II and Ticomán (Vaillant and Vaillant 1934; Grove 1968b: 148–53; 1972: 48).

Atlihuayán (Iglesia Vieja) in central Morelos has produced a large hollow Olmec figurine, polished black excised beakers, white-slipped pottery incised with multiple-line-break motifs, and D- and K-type figurines, as well as red-on-brown bottles. Recent excavations (Grennes-Ravitz 1974) suggest that both the Tlatilco style and the Olmec Blackware horizon material are Late and Terminal Early Preclassic. A firm conclusion is difficult since the material has not been adequately described. Stirrup-spout bottles are reported from Yautepec, just to the north (Piña Chán and López 1952; Coe 1965b: 105, n. 53; Grove 1968b: 155–6; 1972: 69).

La Era in southern Morelos, known only from a surface reconnaissance and a few vessels in private collections, has produced both a polished black vessel with an excised Olmec motif and a Tlatilco style bottle (Grove 1968b: 159).

The Tlatilco problem. The best known of the "floating" Preclassic assemblages is the Tlatilco grave material. Tolstoy's (1971a) work confirms that the Tlatilco mortuary offerings span at least the Late Early Preclassic to initial Middle

Preclassic. The entire Tlatilco mortuary complex has often been called Olmec; it is not. A substantial portion of the Tlatilco mortuary furniture does represent the Olmec Blackware horizon; Olmec graves at Tlatilco are extremely similar to those at Tlapacoya and Las Bocas. Offerings in these graves are allied with the Ayotla and Justo complexes which were probably once represented in the refuse deposits at Tlatilco (MacNeish et al. 1970: 278). Radiocarbon dates associated with Tlatilco grave lots (982 ± 250, 1140 ± 100, and 1230 ± 120 B.C.) support this correlation. The offerings include large hollow and small solid white-slipped Olmecoid/baby-face figurines, as well as D- and K-types. Highly polished black-to-brown-slipped pottery, especially convex bowls and flat-based bowls with bolstered rims, often has red-filled incised and excised decoration, including Olmec motifs (the hand-paw-wing, St. Andrew's cross, and jaguar-dragon profiles).

Incised white-slipped pottery, animal-effigy vessels, spouted trays, roller seals, and ceramic masks also occur. Incised multiple-line-breaks and pseudo-grater fondos (including the sunburst motif) on white-slipped and dark polished vessels suggest that the Terminal Early Preclassic transitional aspect of the horizon, equivalent to the Iglesia complex in the Tlatilco refuse deposits, is strongly represented in the Tlatilco burials. The burials may continue into the initial Middle Preclassic period. The prominence of polished dark wares in the mortuary material (ca. 46 percent, compared with 5 percent white-slipped pottery in Piña Chán's [1958a] sample) indicates that the Olmec Whiteware horizon is not strongly represented in the Tlatilco graves. The low frequencies of incised white ware indicate fewer Early Middle Preclassic interments, but Zacatenco-phase ceramic complexes also suggest a weak representation of the late horizon in the Valley of Mexico generally. In any case, the Olmec Blackware horizon is strongly represented in the Tlatilco graves (Porter 1953: 35; Piña Chán 1958a; Coe 1965b; Grove 1968b; Tolstoy and Paradis 1970).

A substantial proportion of the Tlatilco mortuary ceramics cannot be characterized as Olmec and does not closely resemble any of the ceramic complexes from Early and Middle Preclassic refuse deposits in the Valley of Mexico. This material constitutes the "Tlatilco/Río Cuautla" style recognized by Grove: an elaborate bottle complex (stirrup spouts, belted bottles, composite bottles) often decorated in red-on-brown; hollow spouted figurines; D-K figurines and a variety of unusual solid types (D-4, ball players, two-headed and masked figurines); a series of human- and animal-effigy vessels, including "acrobats"; house models; and whistles (Coe 1965b; Grove 1968b: 161–75; 1970c; Tolstoy and Paradis 1970). Ceramics representing the Olmec Blackware horizon and those of the Tlatilco style do not occur in the same graves, although gadrooned bottles and roller seals have apparently been found in burials representing both styles.

The debate about the affiliations of the Tlatilco style has been framed in terms of function, chronology, and cultural relationships. Three alternatives have commonly been recognized: (1) the Tlatilco style is a specialized mortuary style associated with one of the cultural units already defined in refuse deposits; (2) it represents synchronic cultural variation, a distinct group, contemporary with one of those represented in refuse deposits, whose habitation refuse has not yet been encountered; or (3) it represents a distinct chronological period and cultural unit, with no known representation in refuse deposits.

Variants of the third explanation are most popular (e.g. Tolstoy and Paradis 1970: 349), although the fact that the Tlatilco style is known from several other cemetery sites strengthens the functional-specialization hypothesis.

Tolstoy (1971a: 25–6), in a recent seriation of the Tlatilco grave lots, identifies four groups. One, probably the earliest, is characterized by features of the Olmec Blackware horizon and is clearly affiliated with the Ayotla and Justo refuse deposits at Tlapacoya. Another, probably the latest, represents the Tlatilco style; this group should be correlated, he feels, with the latest Justo material on the basis of such cross-ties as a possible stirrup-spout fragment. The other two groups are intermediate stylistically and chronologically.

Tolstoy indicates a chronological distinction between the peaks of the two styles, but he also recognizes considerable continuity or overlap: some elements associated with the Tlatilco style (gadrooned bottles, red-on-brown decoration) occur throughout the seriated grave sequence and the Tlapacoya refuse sequence. Tolstoy's studies also indicate some degree of functional specialization in the Tlatilco mortuary offerings, since many attributes are not matched in the refuse deposits.

The Tlatilco style occurs in mortuary contexts at several other sites in central Mexico. Some of these have also produced mortuary ceramics representing the Olmec Blackware horizon; others have not. There are also cemetery sites that have produced only Olmec Blackware-horizon ceramics.

The few known vessels from Xalostoc, just north of Mexico City, represent only the Tlatilco style: red-on-brown stirrup spouts, belted bottles, and composite bottles (Porter 1953: 45; Grove 1968b: 174–5). At Las Bocas, on the other hand, where the Olmec Blackware horizon is so prominent, the Tlatilco style is represented only by a few red-on-brown bottles (including a stirrup spout) and spouted trays (Grove 1972: 50).

Morelos has been a rich source of Tlatilco-style material for *huaqueros* but, until recently, direct evidence from stratigraphic excavation was no more plentiful than in the Valley of Mexico. Grove's excavations provide a basis for a tentative chronological alignment of the Tlatilco material in Morelos.

Vaillant's excavations at Gualupita produced very little Tlatilco-style material. The full bottle complex is absent, although a few red-on-brown gadrooned bottles, spouted or "horned" figurines, and spouted trays do occur in Gualupita I (Vaillant and Vaillant 1934; Grove 1972: 48). The red-on-brown bottle complex is represented at Atlihuayán, Olintepec, and Tlaltizapan in central Morelos; all have been excavated but none has been fully reported (Grove 1970c: 69; 1972: 49; Grennes-Ravitz 1974). Stirrup-spout bottles also occur at Yautepec, just north of Atlihuayán, and a single Tlatilco bottle was found at La Era in southern Morelos (Porter 1953: 45; Grove, 1968b: 155–9).

In 1971 Jorge Angulo and Jaime Litvak King excavated a series of graves at

Cacahuamilpa in northern Guerrero, recovering Tlatilco-style offerings: composite, belted, and fluted bottles; a double-chambered spouted bottle; spouted trays; roller stamps; solid K-type figurines; hollow "horned" figurines; and a spouted four-footed jaguar figure almost identical with a specimen from Tlatilco (Covarrubias 1943: 41). The offerings include no Olmec Blackware-horizon elements.

Huaqueros have recovered burial offerings representing both the Olmec Blackware horizon and the Tlatilco style from the two cemetery areas at La Juana-San Pablo and from a cemetery at Nexpa, both in southern Morelos. Grove's stratigraphic excavations at these two sites afford the first direct evidence of the chronological and cultural relationships between the two styles.

At Nexpa, the burial offerings encountered in stratigraphic excavation do not represent the full range of the Tlatilco style, and they include very little that can be assigned to the polished Blackware horizon. Two Nexpa grave lots—one excavated by Grove and one by *huaqueros* (but examined as a unit by Grove and with a relatively secure provenience)—do appear to be weakly related to the horizon. They include a differentially fired wide-necked bottle; flat-based flaring bowls with zoned rocker-stamping; roller stamps; an animal effigy with a bowl on its back; and a shell pectoral with animal figures in relief, one of which has a polished iron-ore inset representing the eye. No Tlatilco-style bottles occurred in these two graves. The other graves, though lacking the most prominent Tlatilco-style features (stirrup spouts and belted bottles), do contain red-on-brown globular jars, *botellones,* and composite bottles. At least one of these burials overlies the excavated Olmec Blackware-horizon burial, and is therefore later. There is also an apparent difference in orientation. Although the ceramic offerings in the burials are not precisely matched in the refuse complexes, the later Tlatilco-style burials appear to correlate with the Late Nexpa (San Pablo B) complex, and perhaps with the Middle Nexpa (San Pablo A) complex (Grove 1972: 20–40, figs. 7, 10–12).

At La Juana-San Pablo, the full Tlatilco-style bottle complex is represented in both cemetery areas—La Juana, also known to collectors as Santa Cruz, and the San Pablo Pantheon mound. Only the La Juana burials contain Blackware-horizon offerings. Grove argues convincingly that the refuse deposits at San Pablo, which are almost entirely of the San Pablo B phase, represent the settlement that produced both cemeteries, and that the Tlatilco style in the La Juana-San Pablo graves, and elsewhere in Morelos, dates to this Terminal Early Preclassic period (Grove 1970c; 1972: 42–4).

On the other hand, Grove (1970c: 71) has also suggested that the graves with Olmec Blackware ceramics at La Juana are considerably earlier, dating to his La Juana phase (1300–1250 B.C.), which is not represented in the refuse deposits. He argues that during the San Pablo B phase, interments with identical offerings were made in both cemetery areas, but that those within the San Pablo Pantheon mound were of higher status. Prestige marked by burial location but not by differences in associated offerings would be highly unusual. Grove's more recent work indicates a reassignment of the Olmec Blackware-horizon material to the

San Pablo B phase. Grove (1970c: 72) formerly argued for a neat chronological succession of the Olmec and Tlatilco styles in highland central Mexico, with the latter representing a localized or provincialized style, reflecting the waning of Olmec influence after 900 B.C. Olmec influence did not everywhere disappear, or even diminish, after 900 B.C. As Grove (1972: 55) recognizes, a reconsideration of the La Juana-San Pablo material in the light of the Nexpa data will not sustain a strict chronological separation between the two styles.

Recent research in West Mexico has begun to reveal an apparently early and widespread ceramic style which shows much closer similarities to the Tlatilco style than any other ceramic complex yet discovered (Grove 1971: 33-4; 1972: 52). At the site of Capacha in Colima, Isabel Kelly recovered a ceramic complex that includes red-on-brown decoration, stirrup spouts, and belted bottles. Ceramics recently excavated from an unlooted shaft tomb at El Opeño, Michoacán, show strong resemblances to the Capacha pottery and to the Tlatilco style; they have an associated radiocarbon date of about 1300 B.C.

These discoveries raise the possibility of a western Mexican origin, or at least affiliation, for the Tlatilco style. Tolstoy (1971a: 26) also recognizes these affinities and adds the observation that later ceramic complexes from extreme western and northern Mesoamerica, such as Chupícuaro, seem to show survivals of the Tlatilco style.

The Tlatilco style cannot be assigned entirely to a brief time period, as has often been suggested (e.g. Grove 1970c: 71). Tolstoy's (1971a) seriation of Taltilco graves, the apparent sequence of burials at Nexpa (Grove 1972: 20-40), and the Tlatilco features that appear in stratified refuse deposits at Tlapacoya, Atlihuayán, and Nexpa (Tolstoy and Paradis 1970; Grove 1972; Grennes-Ravitz 1974) all indicate that the Tlatilco style has a developmental history spanning much of the Early Preclassic period. Red-on-brown decoration and gadrooned or fluted bottles occur in the Late Early Preclassic period, although the full complex seems to appear only in the Terminal Early Preclassic. The peak of the Tlatilco style may postdate the peak of the Olmec Blackware horizon, but there is overlap. The Blackware horizon is contemporaneous with a less specular or developmental aspect of the Tlatilco bottle complex. The differences are not solely chronological, and the two styles reflect cultural or ethnic differences involving the intrusion of a second "foreign" influence, from western Mexico.

The earliest occurrences of the Tlatilco style in central Mexico appear to be in the graves of Tolstoy's intermediate groups from Tlatilco (mainly contemporary with the Ayotla subphase) and in Grove's Middle and Late Nexpa graves in Morelos. The later appearance of the fully developed red-on-brown bottle complex—in the graves of Tolstoy's latest group at Tlatilco and in the La Juana-San Pablo cemeteries (and perhaps at Las Bocas, Yautepec-Atlihuayán, and La Era)—falls in the Late to Terminal Early Preclassic period, possibly continuing into the initial Middle Preclassic. All these cemeteries have also produced burials with offerings of the Olmec Blackware horizon which seem to precede and overlap in time with the fully developed Tlatilco style. The sites at which mortuary furniture is exclusively in the Tlatilco style—Xalostoc, Olintepec, Tlaltizapan, and Cacahuamilpa—have no direct evidence for dating. The Tlatilco-style material at these sites might be contemporaneous with that at the mixed sites, or slightly later. In no case does the full Tlatilco style appear at sites where the Early Middle Preclassic horizon is prominent. This might be taken as support for Grove's suggestion that the climax of the Tlatilco style reflects a waning of Olmec influence, although this could be the case only in a few localized areas. At Chalcatzingo, for example, red-on-brown ceramics (but not the exotic bottle complex) appear in phase A; the Olmec Blackware horizon is represented in phase A and apparently continues in phase B, giving way to Olmec Whiteware-horizon material (Cyphers 1975; Grove et al. 1976). The very close similarity of Tlatilco complexes among themselves suggests the appearance or rise to prominence of an elite group, not a localization or turning inward of mortuary styles.

The Xochipala problem. The undated Xochipala style includes a number of features closely related to the Olmec style along with highly unusual non-Olmec features. No controlled excavation has been carried out in the area in which the Xochipala style is centered; only indirect evidence suggests its dating and cultural affiliations.

The material that is referred to as the Xochipala style, or "complex," has been found only in the region around the village of Xochipala, Guerrero, south of the Río Balsas in the zone known also for the Mezcala style of small stone sculpture. Although a few Xochipala-style pieces have been known for many years, the existence of an important, coherent style has been recognized only in the last decade, with the sudden appearance of many Xochipala objects on the antiquities market. This material, excavated by *huaqueros*, lacks specific provenience data. The location and nature of the sites that have produced Xochipala-style material are known only through accounts given by the looters to archaeologists and collectors who have visited the area.

According to local informants, Xochipala-style material has been found in burials at four sites: (1) El Zacatoso, 10 km. south of the village of Xochipala, where some of the burials are said to have been in round stone-walled and slab-covered shaft tombs; (2) Las Mesas, 7 km. south-southwest of Xochipala, where an artificial mound is flanked by two (formerly six) unworked stone "monoliths"; (3) Las Tejas, 5 km. east of Las Mesas, also with architectural remains, including platforms; and (4) Llano Delgado, on a ridge just north of Xochipala, without known construction features.

During a brief reconnaissance of the Xochipala area in 1971 we visited a fifth site, known locally as Xocohuite, on a hill just west of the village. It is apparently distinct from the Llano Delgado burial area. Xocohuite had been extensively looted, and local *huaqueros* report recovering ceramic figurines and jade objects, although none was then still in their possession. No construction features were visible on the surface at Xocohuite. The surface ceramics are dominated by a buff type decorated with red paint and/or incision (App. 8) which is nearly identical with a type common at Tetipan, near Ahuelicán (App. 7). It does not closely resemble any other ceramic type, although similarities with Red-on-Buff pottery of Grove's (1968b: 57-9, figs. 49, 50; 1970a: 8-9) Cerro Chacaltepec II phase in Morelos (ca. 400-100 B.C.) tentatively suggest a late Middle or Late Preclassic dating. This would be a reasonable placement for at least some part of the Xochipala-style material.

The Xochipala style can be defined on the basis of the ceramic figurines, which are notable for their extreme sophistication, naturalism, and portrait-like quality. They are most unlike the familiar Mesoamerican Preclassic figurine styles. Although there is a considerable range in the degree of naturalism, the finest Xochipala figurines are gracefully posed, with delicately modeled features. Most are nude or nearly nude female or asexual figures. The lips are typically parted and the teeth clearly indicated. The hair is usually a crescentic frame for the face; it is almost always parted in the middle and occasionally it is braided (Gay 1972: figs. 7-11).

These figurines often have a very pronounced deep incision extending from the pubic area to the coccyx. This is reminiscent of the naturalistic female torso from the Atopula phase at Atopula, which also shows the lower end of a hair braid on the shoulder (Fig. 58c). Not all Xochipala figurines are nude. Some have footgear with instep appliqués, recalling a figurine leg from the surface of Atopula (Fig. 61b). A few figurines, perhaps ball players, have elaborate costumes with helmets, boots, heavy arm gear, and what seems to be heavy padding on the torso and legs. Occasional figurines are even more elaborately dressed in long robe-like garments and helmets (Gay 1972: figs. 12-16, 19, 22, 23). Xochipala figurines are typically unslipped, although they sometimes have red and/or yellow painted body decoration; they are almost always solid.

The Olmec style is also represented in the burial offerings from Xochipala-area sites. Small solid white-slipped Olmecoid/baby-face figurines are virtually identical with those from Tlatilco, Tlapacoya, and Las Bocas. Several of these show a blending of the Olmec and Xochipala styles, and some solid Xochipala-style figurines are vaguely Olmecoid with puffy facial features, down-turned mouths, and pudgy, gently rounded bodies. The hollow Xochipala figurines show this "blending" more clearly (Gay 1972: figs. 17, 18, 24-26). They range from hollow versions of solid Xochipala figurines to a few specimens that closely resemble the large hollow Olmecoid/baby-face figurines associated with the Olmec horizons in central Mexico. There are several stylistically intermediate types; like the solid figurines, they are often unslipped, with occasional red and/or yellow painted decoration. The single published specimen with a white slip is strikingly similar to the hollow Olmecoid figurines from Tlapacoya which have D-K-type stylized bodies (Coe 1965b: ill. 187). Typical poses of hollow Olmecoid/baby-face figurines are represented, including thumb-sucking and one hand raised to the head. The "cuts" in the skin, especially at the knees, which so perplex Gay (1972: 36-9) probably represent skin folds, which are naturalistically indicated on some specimens. A small bowl in the shape of a human head with a bird-serpent helmet is also related to the Olmec style.

Ceramic vessels that represent the Olmec Blackware horizon include polished brown-to-black-slipped beakers, incurved-rim bowls, and bottles with excised Olmec motifs—the St. Andrew's cross, hand-paw-wing, and jaguar-dragon profile. These vessels correlate with Ayotla, Justo, and other Late Early Preclassic complexes. There are a few similar gray- and white-ware vessels (Gay 1972: figs. 34, 35).

Additional Olmec elements from Xochipala-area burials include a shell with an incised Olmec were-jaguar profile; concave mirrors of magnetite, ilmenite, and pyrite; jade and serpentine ornaments; and a green stone figurine holding a "torch" (Gay 1972: figs. 37, 38, 40).

The Xochipala mortuary material also includes carefully polished thin vessels made of greenish stone—beakers, convex bowls, and flat-based bowls. The bowls recall the thin polished stone-bowl fragment from the Atopula phase at Atopula (Fig. 65). The Xochipala bowls often have abstract incised and excised designs filled with red pigment, resembling decoration on ceramic vessels of the Olmec Blackware horizon, although the motifs are not always Olmec. Red pigment is also used on many Olmec jade and serpentine celts and figurines. The cemetery sites have produced a variety of other objects: a few solid D- and K-type figurines; highly stylized two-faced figurines without torsos; animal-effigy figures; "wing"- or "bracket"-shaped ceramic objects with basin-shaped depressions (perhaps incense burners); stamp seals with geometric designs very similar to examples found at Tlatilco; ceramic tubes; a carved-bone serpent head; small stone balls; stone figurines; and "ritual implements" (Gay 1972: figs. 33, 39).

Although the Xochipala style is highly concentrated in the vicinity of the village of Xochipala, related material occurs in other parts of Guerrero. Xochipala-style figurines, including ball-player types, have been found at San Francisco, some 30 km. northeast of Xochipala on the Río Balsas. A group of Xochipala stone vessels was reportedly found on the coast of Guerrero. Large hollow Olmecoid/baby-face figurines have been found, along with other Olmec-style objects, in the area of Zumpango del Río, about 20 km. southeast of Xochipala (Covarrubias 1948; Easby and Scott 1970: ill. 20; Gay 1972: 50, 57, figs. 20, 21, 30).

The entire range of Xochipala material, like the heterogeneous Tlatilco mortuary offerings, has been dubbed Olmec because part of it is affiliated with the Olmec style (e.g. Gay 1972). Typical Xochipala figurines are Olmecoid only in the vaguest way. Gay's (1972) single seriation of all the figurines from Xochipala-area sites is untenable, as are his arguments for the origin of the Olmec and D- and K-type figurine traditions in the Xochipala style. There is no evidence to support his suggestion that the Olmec style itself originated in this part of Guerrero (Grove 1973b).

On the other hand, the Olmec style is strongly represented in some Xochipala burials by ceramic vessels, large hollow figurines, concave mirrors, and incised were-jaguar profiles, all associated with the Olmec Blackware horizon. This correlation is reinforced by the thin stone-bowl fragment from the Atopula phase. Although Xochipala figurines show some "blending" of the Olmec and Xochipala styles, the relationship between the two is by no means clear. Vague similarities with a few figurines from Atopula hint that some Xochipala-style figurines may date to the Late Early Preclassic period, contemporaneous with the Olmec Blackware horizon. Only controlled stratigraphic excavation will clarify the chronological position of the Xochipala figurine style and its relation to the Blackware horizon.

These figurines probably represent a considerable time span, and the more stylized specimens do show similarities to the D- and K-type-figurine tradition of central Mexico. The jade objects would indicate an Early Middle Preclassic placement for some of the material (see below). The occurrence of a figurine with vague similarities to the Xochipala style at Ticomán (Vaillant 1931: pl. 54) and the possibility that the Xochipala figurine style may be associated with the ceramics recovered from the surface of Xocohuite also hint that some Xochipala material postdates the Early Preclassic. The very generalized similarity of non-Olmec figurines and stamps from Xochipala and Tlatilco might indicate a relationship with the Tlatilco style and with western Mexico, although the red-on-brown bottle complex is not known to occur in the Xochipala cemetery sites.

Xochipala figurines also show a surprising resemblance to white-slipped figurines from Kaminaljuyú (probably of the Las Charcas phase) and to one from Playa de los Muertos in the Ulúa Valley of Honduras (Kidder 1965: figs. 1, 4; Easby and Scott 1970: ills. 5, 6, 8).

Settlement Patterns

Settlement pattern data for the Early Preclassic period are scant. Inference about the social correlates of the Olmec Blackware horizon is correspondingly difficult. Much of the material associated with this horizon lacks adequate context, having been looted. It is clear that the most elaborate vessels and figurines occur as funerary offerings. There were elite burials, and seemingly elite cemeteries, at Tlatilco, Tlapacoya, Las Bocas, La Juana-San Pablo, and Gualupita. The relationships of these burials to the refuse deposits and construction features at the same sites are not obvious. There is little doubt that the burials represent a segment of the population of prosperous agricultural villages, although there are substantial settlement data only from La Juana-San Pablo. The occupation debris at Tlatilco evidently postdates the majority of the burials there.

Small-scale excavations at Las Bocas, as yet unpublished, apparently encountered little refuse material. Vaillant excavated burials and ceramic refuse at Gualupita but found no evidence of construction activity. At Tlapacoya, the Olmec-style mortuary offerings, known only from *huaqueros'* activities, are contemporary with the Bomba complex, which is defined on the basis of refuse deposits. The pyramid explored by Barba de Piña Chán is later than the burials and Tolstoy's refuse deposits.

Only in the Valley of Oaxaca can the Olmec Blackware horizon be seen in the context of settlement patterns: types of settlements, their topographic and environmental context, and their internal structure (types and arrangements of features within them).

Sites of the San José phase represent the horizon in the Valley of Oaxaca. San José-phase settlements are located in or adjacent to the high water table in the river floodplains. Since the climate of this period was slightly drier than today's, this may reflect use of the high soil moisture to negate the effects of erratic rainfall. There is no evidence of water-control techniques that would permit the effective cultivation of other environmental zones such as the piedmont. Simple water control—diversion of water from the major streams, which are not deeply entrenched, or pot irrigation, utilizing shallow wells scattered throughout the fields—cannot be ruled out. These techniques can permit two or three crops annually in the floodplain zone. Pot irrigation was almost certainly in use in the Early Middle Preclassic period; two shallow wells of the appropriate type have been excavated at Guadalupe-phase sites (Flannery et al. 1967: 450; Flannery 1968: 81, 85; Flannery and Schoenwetter 1970: 147–50).

San José Mogote, a substantial (ca. 20-ha.) village, is the largest and richest San José-phase settlement in the valley. It shows considerable internal functional differentiation. One area of the site is an ordinary residential zone: small wattle-and-daub houses and high frequencies of utilitarian artifacts (chipping debris, ground-stone tools, and simple ceramics). A second area has elaborate pottery representing the Olmec Blackware horizon along with wattle-and-daub houses, but few utilitarian artifacts. It is apparently an elite residential zone. A third zone yielded large quantities of elaborate pottery and exotic raw materials: iron ores (magnetite, ilmenite, and hematite), mica, quartz, and marine shell from the Pacific and Gulf coasts. Nearly 90 percent of the exotic raw materials found at San José Mogote came from this one area. Excavation in this zone revealed a number of large wattle-and-daub structures with whitewashed walls. The floors of these structures yielded extremely few ordinary utilitarian artifacts, but tools for working the exotic raw materials—burins, drills, and quartz and iron-ore polishers—were common. Even more abundant were fragments of magnetite, mica, and shell, representing debris from the manufacture of ornaments: waste material; broken and rejected artifacts; and rare finished specimens, including small flat iron-ore mirrors. Near the artisans' area were large public structures on stone-faced platforms. The erection of such ceremonial or "civic" structures, with a special orientation to 8° west of true north like the construction complexes at La Venta, began in the Tierras Largas phase at San José Mogote. In the San José phase they are associated with ceramics and figurines of the Olmec Blackware horizon (Flannery et al. 1967: 451; Flannery 1968: 85, 86, 89; 1976).

All other San José phase settlements are small villages or hamlets (up to 2 ha.), with little internal differentiation, few exotic raw materials, and (with one exception) no public construction. Barrio del Rosario Huitzo, about 15 km. away, has a low stepped platform with plastered adobe retaining walls. It supported a substantial wattle-and-daub structure, with the precise La Venta directional orientation, which was apparently begun late in the San José phase and enlarged early in the Guadalupe phase. In striking contrast with San José Mogote, exotic raw materials were extremely rare at Huitzo, and magnetite was absent altogether.

Since magnetite sources have been located near both sites, social factors rather than availability must have been responsible for the differential access (Flannery 1968: 87–9; 1976).

These data further demonstrate the elite nature of the Olmec Blackware-horizon material and indicate its association with an exchange network and with incipient craft specialization. This evidence does not resolve the more difficult and more interesting question of the cultural or ethnic associations of the horizon.

Substantial status differentiation, both within and between communities, appears in the Valley of Oaxaca in the Early Preclassic period. High status was most clearly marked by evidence of external connections—interactions with other areas of Mesoamerica. The occurrence of Olmec Blackware-horizon material in elite contexts, and an associated differential access to exotic raw materials and status-marking luxury goods, reflects this. Importation of exotic raw materials and the export of elite goods manufactured from them (as well as from local raw materials) are clearly indicated at San José Mogote. This provides an obvious mechanism for the maintenance of interregional interaction, which contributed to the maintenance and intensification of the status differentiation.

Successful productive agriculture was important in connection with these developments. The ability to support large nucleated communities may not be a precondition for the development of hereditary elites and craft specialization, but in the Valley of Oaxaca all three intensified simultaneously, presumably reinforcing one another. The evidence does not point to intensive agriculture or elaborate water-control techniques as causal factors.

Settlement data for Morelos are not so full. Chalcatzingo, the largest site in its region during the Late Early Preclassic period, was a small farming village. Not until the Chalcatzingo B phase, corresponding to the Terminal Early Preclassic and initial Middle Preclassic, is there clear evidence of large-scale public construction, water control, exploitation of local exotic resources (hematite for pigment, kaolin for white-slipped pottery), and other indications of economic specialization. The extent to which these trends toward growth and differentiation in the region and within Chalcatzingo were under way during the Early Preclassic period is not clear (Grove et al. 1976).

Specialized cemetery areas at La Juana-San Pablo have elite burials marked by offerings representing either the Olmec Blackware horizon or the Tlatilco style. There is no other evidence of internal differentiation in Early Preclassic sites in central Morelos, but there is a clear contrast between La Juana-San Pablo and Nexpa. Nexpa is a small settlement, apparently lacking elaborate cemetery zones, and the Olmec Blackware horizon is not conspicuously represented there, even in burials. In comparison with Chalcatzingo or La Juana-San Pablo, Nexpa is more rural, more exclusively oriented toward agriculture, with less internal specialization and status differentation (Grove 1972: 53). This is comparable to the situation in the Valley of Oaxaca, where the importance of San José Mogote and the high status of groups within the community are marked by the elaborate elements of the Olmec Blackware horizon. Tierras Largas, Fábrica San José, and other smaller sites (Drennan 1976; Flannery 1976) are like Nexpa—more rural in the sense that they did not participate so fully or directly in interregional interaction. At Chalcatzingo and La Juana-San Pablo, interaction with external areas is reflected in the Blackware-horizon material, and iron ore from Valley of Oaxaca sources provides direct evidence of participation in an exchange network. The Olmec Blackware horizon is much less prominent in the refuse material at La Juana-San Pablo; it may be that these deposits represent a low-status residential zone, and that there is an undiscovered elite residential area that corresponds to the elaborate burials.

At Atopula the Blackware horizon is represented only in refuse deposits, and it is much more prominent than in the La Juana-San Pablo refuse. No burials were encountered at Atopula; it has a platform mound, not a mortuary mound like the San Pablo Pantheon mound. Although Atopula is smaller than Chalcatzingo or La Juana-San Pablo, it may well have occupied a similar position of local importance, or even political power, vis-à-vis nearby communities. It occupies the most desirable and productive part of the local area. As at the Morelos sites (Grove 1972: 46), the Olmec Blackware horizon appears at Atopula as a series of new (foreign) and newly emphasized decorative attributes added to the local ceramic repertoire.

Greengo (1967; 1970; personal communication) reports mounds at the Early to Middle Preclassic sites of El Calvario and Figueroa in the Tepecoacuilco drainage (Fig. 1). It is not clear whether they represent artificial constructions.

The Tehuacán Valley provides a good example of an area that participated minimally in the Olmec Blackware horizon. The settlement-pattern data from Early Preclassic sites in Tehuacán indicate an interesting contrast with the sites at which the horizon is strongly represented. There is no evidence in the Late Ajalpan phase of large and prosperous agricultural villages. Simple floodplain or barranca agriculture was an important facet of subsistence, but earlier subsistence strategies persisted, reflected in seasonal hunting and collecting camps. There is no indication of intensive agriculture or of water-control techniques. Agricultural productivity was apparently sufficient to support small semipermanent communities in which at least a part of the population maintained year-round residence. The populations of the hamlets, small clusters of wattle-and-daub dwellings, probably did not exceed 200, and a substantial proportion may not have remained in residence year-round. There is no evidence of significant social stratification or occupational specialization—no elite residences or burials, no areas for the manufacture of luxury goods, no public constructions—and no indication of interaction with other areas. The Olmec Blackware horizon is virtually unrepresented in Tehuacán, and there is little evidence of participation in interregional exchange networks. Few raw materials were imported into Tehuacán, and there is no indication that raw materials or finished products were exported. Even imported pottery and figurines are rare: identifiable imports include about fifty trade sherds, and perhaps a few of the vaguely Olmecoid large hollow figurines.

In the subsequent Early Santa María phase, agriculture is more intensive and involves water control. Permanent agricultural villages are larger and more prosperous, with public constructions. The prominence of the Olmec Whiteware horizon, a sharp increase in imported pottery, and indications of the emergence of elite groups, specialization, and the centralization of political power reflect interaction with other areas. The relationships among these factors are undoubtedly very complex. Perhaps the existence of substantial permanent communities, which usually involves productive agriculture, is a precondition or even a partial catalyst for participation in interregional interaction, which exists in a mutually reinforcing relationship with the development and intensification of specialization, status differentiation, and the centralization of authority and political power (MacNeish 1970; 1972).

In the Late Ajalpan phase the "enabling" developments were absent; the economic situation was not conducive to interregional economic interaction. Tehuacán was marginal and economically backward at this time in comparison with areas like the Valley of Oaxaca. Although Tehuacán may have been precocious in terms of subsistence at an early period, by the Purrón and Ajalpan phases it had become conservative; the pace of change was very slow. The intensification of agriculture and the development of fully sedentary prosperous villages took place earlier in other areas, especially in the coastal lowlands, where a fully sedentary community pattern emerged very early, perhaps with less emphasis on food production (Coe and Flannery 1964a; Flannery and Coe 1968). The apparent conservatism or marginality of Tehuacán in the economic and subsistence sphere in the Early Preclassic period may be due in part to the introduction of a newly intensified pattern of food production, perhaps with new hybridized cultigens, from the coastal lowlands into those highland areas with which they were economically linked. Tehuacán, lacking such highly desirable and exportable natural resources as magnetite, had few external links. In any event, during the Early Preclassic period Tehuacán was marginal in that it participated minimally in such widespread interregional cultural currents as the Olmec Blackware horizon.

Coastal Guerrero was also marginal during the Early Preclassic period. The Olmec Blackware horizon is not prominent, and there are no indications of social stratification, specialization, political centralization, or even of large settlements. As in Tehuacán, external connections increased markedly in the Early Middle Preclassic period; this is reflected in the much greater prominence of the Olmec Whiteware horizon.

Settlement-pattern data from southeastern Mesoamerica show interesting contrasts with the situation in central Mexico. The Barra-phase occupation at Altamira evidently represents a very small agricultural hamlet or village, with no evidence of mound construction or other architectural features. To judge from the nonconformities encountered in the excavations, the successive communities at Altamira were rather mobile; the habitation zone shifted about within the site area through time. Surprisingly, in view of Altamira's proximity to the ocean, there is no evidence of significant exploitation of the rich marine-estuary food resources. Barra, like several Ocós components, is characterized by an abundance of obsidian flakes (not blades) with very little secondary chipping. It has been suggested that these represent the remains of manioc graters, and recent experiments demonstrate that Ocós obsidian flakes were so used (M. D. Coe, personal communication). The cultivation of root crops, particularly manioc, was probably an important facet of Barra subsistence (Green and Lowe 1967: 57–60). An abundance of obsidian flakes and the absence of blades is also typical of central Mexican sites predating the Late Early Preclassic, although an emphasis on root-crop cultivation is much less likely in the highlands. Manioc can, however, be successfully cultivated in relatively arid environments and at elevations up to at least 6000 feet (Heiser 1973: 147).

At least twelve Ocós-phase occupations have been identified along the Pacific coast of Guatemala and Chiapas, extending as far west as the isthmian region near Juchitán on the Oaxacan coast. Besides La Victoria, they include Izapa, Aquiles Serdán, and Altamira. With the notable exception of Altamira, the heavy dependence on marine and estuary food resources (especially fish and shellfish), which was first recognized at La Victoria, is typical of these coastal settlements. Evidence for agriculture is indirect, consisting of crude grinding stones at La Victoria and possible remains of manioc graters at several sites (particularly Altamira and Aquiles Serdán). As the Barra phase, this may imply a reliance on root-crop cultivation. Maize may not yet have become an important cultigen along the Pacific coast. The recently discovered Ocós-phase sites in central Chiapas presumably had a very different subsistence economy. Ocós settlements are small simple hamlets or villages without elaborate architecture. The La Victoria-Ocós component, the best known, has traces of wattle-and-daub houses, perhaps on low platforms, but no indication of more elaborate mound construction. A large pyramid at the nearby site of Villa Angela may represent a public structure; Villa Angela could even have been a ceremonial center for the inhabitants of La Victoria (Coe 1961: 111–16, 147; Green and Lowe 1967: 58–60; Lowe 1971: 223). Changes in subsistence and shifts in settlement location accompany the disappearance of Ocós ceramic complexes shortly before 1100 B.C. Some sites are abandoned (at least temporarily) and many new settlements appear. Substantial cultural disturbance is associated with the appearance of the Olmec Blackware horizon. It may even be accompanied by population shifts.

Along the Pacific coast, metates and manos appear in significant numbers at many sites in the Cuadros phase, at the same time that quantities of obsidian flakes decline abruptly; this may indicate a shift from manioc cultivation to maize agriculture. At Salinas La Blanca, impressions and mineralized fragments of maize plants provide direct evidence of maize agriculture. Fish and shellfish continue to be important food sources (Coe and Flannery 1967: 63–4, 71–2, 82; Green and Lowe 1967: 58–60).

Cuadros settlements are more numerous, but they are comparable to those of the Ocós phase in size and internal complexity. Typically, they are simple agricultural villages with nothing more elaborate in the way of architecture than small wattle-and-daub houses, perhaps on low platforms. There is no evidence of planned arrangement. More elaborate architecture—low clay platform mounds, perhaps ceremonial constructions—occurs only at San Isidro in the middle Grijalva region of central Chiapas (Bernal 1971: 46).

Available data strongly suggest that the Olmec Blackware horizon, and the interregional communication and interaction which it reflects, have an essential economic foundation: a widespread exchange network featuring exotic raw materials and status-marking luxury goods manufactured from them. Undoubtedly the interactions were complex and involved the exchange of other kinds of commodities, presumably including utilitarian artifacts and raw materials for manufacturing them, notably obsidian. Complex social interaction must have accompanied the economic activity—intermarriage, the creation of fictive kinship ties, trading partnerships with associated reciprocal obligations and expectations, and semipermanent or permanent residence of individuals or groups in foreign areas.

Beyond reflecting participation in a widespread economic network, the material of the Olmec Blackware horizon also marks high status. It is most conspicuous in the larger and more prosperous settlements in each area. Within these settlements the more elaborate elements of the horizon are concentrated in what seem to be elite contexts, serving as status markers for persons or groups within the communities. Most frequently, Olmec Blackware-horizon material occurs in high-status burials in elite cemeteries, but it is also prominent in elite residential zones, in association with the manufacture of luxury goods, and sometimes in association with public architecture.

The precise mechanisms by which enhanced status was conferred or conveyed are not obvious. Presumably the processes involved were complex, and not necessarily uniform throughout the area. Although the Olmec Blackware horizon often blends with local stylistic traditions and becomes slightly reworked or reexpressed in local contexts, it maintains the character of something foreign, introduced as a whole from the outside. The high-status aspect may then be the result of identification of the features of the Blackware horizon with a foreign ethnic group which was perceived as sophisticated and prestigious—as constituting an elite. Given the associations of the horizon in the Gulf-coast lowlands, the eliteness of this group may very well have a ritual or ceremonial component. This may lend some validity to the notion of the spread of the Olmec style as a religious phenomenon, although the Olmec Blackware horizon is not strictly a religious manifestation. The importance of exchange and secular aspects of social status is quite obvious.

5. The Middle Preclassic Period and the Olmec Whiteware Horizon

The Early Middle Preclassic Period

Early Middle Preclassic ceramic complexes show even greater uniformity than do those of the Early Preclassic period. Most prominent among the shared features is white-slipped pottery with incised decoration. The most typical motifs are multiple-line-breaks, a series of arcs, and incisions on bowl interiors, especially the sunburst motif. The incised designs are often quite complex, even glyph-like, and represent the Olmec art style. Olmecoid/baby-face figurines continue, along with non-Olmec figurines with large, punched eyes. These are the basic elements of a second Preclassic horizon. The simpler features of the horizon are more widely distributed than its elaborate aspects, and some complexes seem a bit regionalized but, in comparison with the Olmec Blackware horizon, it is more pervasive and more prominent. Although there are continuities between the two horizons, the new features spread rapidly and are very heavily emphasized, indicating an abrupt change which is not simply developmental.

Since this Early Middle Preclassic horizon is closely associated with the Olmec style, including monumental art in many areas, it is convenient to designate it the Olmec Whiteware horizon. Grove (1974a; personal communication) argues that few of its distinctive features are strictly Olmec, but some undeniably are.

In the Tehuacán Valley the Early Santa María phase represents the early part of the Middle Preclassic period. External comparisons and 23 radiocarbon determinations date this well-defined phase to 850/800–500 B.C. (Johnson and MacNeish 1972: 43–5).

The Early Santa María ceramic complex is marked by the sudden appearance and great popularity of Canoas White and other white-slipped ceramics, both locally manufactured types and trade sherds. Flat-based flaring bowls, multiple-line-breaks, and pseudo-grater fondos (especially with the sunburst motif) are common. Other widely distributed features are large hollow and small solid white-slipped Olmecoid/baby-face figurines; excised Olmec motifs (the kan cross and notch or inverted V) on black- or white-slipped pottery; polished black pottery with red-filled incision or excision; and bolstered or thickened rims on bowls, especially flat-based bowls. Some of these features—excised Olmec motifs and bolstered-rim bowls—appear earlier in other areas as part of the Olmec Blackware horizon. Others, particularly the incised white pottery emphasizing flat-based bowls with pseudo-grater fondos and multiple-line-breaks, are elements of the Olmec Whiteware horizon.

The Olmec Blackware horizon consists in large part of widely shared modes of surface treatment and decoration applied to vessels manufactured in basic conformity with local traditions. Pastes are generally the same as those found in preceding ceramic complexes or in contemporary types that continue earlier stylistic traditions and do not bear the markers of the horizon. In the Tehuacán Valley, the Early Middle Preclassic horizon does not follow this pattern. The widely shared ceramic features of the Olmec Whiteware horizon appear only on pottery of the Canoas types (most prominently Canoas White) which are restricted to the Early Santa María phase. These ceramic types are characterized by their carefully selected, fine tempering material. In contrast, pottery of the Río Salado types, which carry local stylistic traditions through several phases in Tehuacán, is unslipped and tempered with coarse, unselected material. Continuities with earlier local ceramics appear in Río Salado types; the widely shared features do not. This extra care in the manufacture of pottery of the Whiteware horizon produces a "finer" appearance, suggesting an elite aspect. Some widely shared traits (red-filled incision or excision) appear in Early Santa María only as trade items, but the most conspicuous feature of the Olmec Whiteware horizon—Canoas White—is locally manufactured. Its prominence in Tehuacán, an area that participated only minimally in the Olmec Blackware horizon, reflects the greater extent and pervasiveness of the later horizon (MacNeish et al. 1970: 58–101).

The Guadalupe phase in the Valley of Oaxaca is dated between 850 and 600 B.C. by ceramic cross-ties. The most characteristic pottery type is white-slipped; it is nearly identical with Canoas White in every respect except that pseudo-grater fondos are rare. Some figurine types (including the large hollow white-slipped Olmecoid/baby-face type) and pottery types and modes (especially the multiple-line-break) are shared by Guadalupe and Early Santa María; the same trade types appear in both. They are as closely related as minor geographical variants of the same phase (Flannery 1968: 89–97; MacNeish et al. 1970: 270–1; Johnson and MacNeish 1972: 44; Drennan 1976; Flannery 1976).

In the Valley of Mexico both the Totolica and El Arbolillo complexes are aligned with Early Santa María and Guadalupe; they too are connected with the Olmec Whiteware horizon. Totolica, represented in the Tlatilco refuse deposits, is tentatively dated between 800/750 and 550/500 B.C.; two radiocarbon dates, 710 ± 50 and 480 ± 60 B.C., are associated with early and terminal Totolica, respectively. The El Arbolillo subphase, represented at El Arbolillo and Zacatenco, falls into the 900/850 to 800 B.C. time range. Both subphases have the most typical elements of the horizon—white-slipped pottery homologous to Canoas White, with incised multiple-line-breaks, and pseudo-grater fondos. The horizon, however, seems to be less strongly represented in the Valley of Mexico than in Tehuacán or the Valley of Oaxaca.

The Iglesia subphase at Tlatilco (ca. 950/900–800 B.C.) shares some of the features of this horizon, but the early Olmec Blackware horizon is also strongly represented in this ceramic complex. It is intermediate between the terminal, transitional subphase of the Blackware horizon (Bomba) and the earliest subphase associated with the Whiteware horizon (El Arbolillo). The La Pastora subphase at El Arbolillo and Zacatenco, which is contemporary with Totolica, seems to have an even more marginal participation in the Olmec Whiteware horizon. It gives the impression of local ceramic style. The relationships between the Valley of Mexico and Tehuacán and the Valley of Oaxaca in Early Middle Preclassic times are reflected in pottery and figurine types found in Early Santa María and Guadalupe sites which were manufactured in the Valley of Mexico (MacNeish et al. 1970: 84, 277–8; Tolstoy and Paradis 1970; Johnson and MacNeish 1972: 45).

A small proportion of the material in the lowest culture-bearing levels of Barba de Piña Chán's (1956: 62–70, 84–90, láms. 2–8, 18, 19, cuadro 1) excavations at Tlapacoya probably also represents the Olmec Whiteware horizon. There are similarities to the Bomba complex (especially in the highly polished black vessels), but the prominence of incised and excised white-slipped pottery with the multiple-line-break and sunburst motifs, the absence of beakers, and rare trade sherds of "amarillenta laca" suggest an initial Middle Preclassic placement.

In central Morelos, the Early Middle Preclassic period is represented by the Cerro Chacaltepec I phase (ca. 900–400 B.C.). One of the two most prominent pottery types at Cerro Chacaltepec (Grove 1968b; 1970a: 6–8) is Las Juntas White, a typical incised white ware with multiple-line-breaks and pseudo-grater fondos; it departs from the norm only in that the commonest vessel form is the composite bowl. The other major type in Cerro Chacaltepec I is a thick buff ware with red-painted designs, which also emphasizes the composite-bowl form. This type could be related to earlier red-on-buff ceramics of Tehuacán and the Valley of Oaxaca, but it is more closely allied with the late Middle Preclassic and Late Preclassic red-on-buff wares of Cerro Chacaltepec II in Morelos and late Zacatenco and Ticomán in the Valley of Mexico. All of these may be related to the Red-painted Buff pottery of Tetipan and Xocohuite (Grove 1970a: 8–9; Tolstoy and Paradis 1970; Apps. 7, 8).

Grove's (1973b; 1974a; Cyphers 1975; Grove et al. 1976) recent excavations at Chalcatzingo confirm the indications of Piña Chán's (1955a) early work there, indicating that the major occupation is Middle Preclassic. Some Chalcatzingo B material strongly resembles the Terminal Early Preclassic Bomba complex of the Valley of Mexico, but the extreme prominence of incised white-slipped flat-based bowls with multiple-line-breaks and pseudo-grater fondos indicates that the Olmec Whiteware horizon is well represented, at least by late Chalcatzingo B (ca. 800–750 B.C.). Olmecoid/baby-face figurines also occur. Chalcatzingo C (750–550 B.C.) also includes some Olmec Whiteware-horizon features, but it is characterized by new ceramic and figurine styles. By this time Chalcatzingo seems to show a distinct trend toward regionalization—away from the Whiteware horizon pattern.

The Tom-period complexes of Puerto Marqués and related sites on the coast of Guerrero (ca. 800–500 B.C.) are part of the Olmec Whiteware horizon. Incised white-slipped open and flaring bowls with multiple-line-breaks and tabbed rims are popular in this period. Large hollow and small solid white-slipped Olmecoid/baby-face figurines also occur in Tom-period refuse. They have the widest distribution of any coastal figurine type, occurring continuously along the southern Costa Grande and northern Costa Chica and sporadically throughout the coastal zone (E. Brush 1968: 56–65, tables II–IV, pls. 2–11; C. Brush 1969: 58, 103, fig. 16, table 11).

The Early Middle Preclassic period is not represented in the stratified refuse deposits at Atopula, but the Olmec Whiteware horizon is very prominent at the nearby site of Tetipan (Fig. 1; App. 7). White-slipped flat-based open and flaring bowls with incised multiple-line-breaks and pseudo-grater fondos are very common and virtually identical with Canoas White and homologous types. Incised polished black-to-brown-slipped pottery with multiple-line-breaks and tabbed rims occurs in very small quantities. The primary occupation is Early Middle Preclassic. Hydration readings obtained on obsidian specimens from Tetipan (Fig. 9, Table 4) support this dating. Fine blue-gray Olmec jade pieces recovered by *huaqueros* from graves at Tetipan also represent the Olmec Whiteware horizon. Although Grove (1973b) suggests that at least one such object attributed to Tetipan is a forgery, Olmec-style mortuary offerings unquestionably exist at the site. There can be little doubt that they are associated with the horizon which is so strongly represented in the ceramics.

A substantial minority of the Tetipan pottery consists of a buff ware with very different modes of incised and red-painted decoration. This pottery is identical with a type that is heavily represented in the surface collection from the site of Xocohuite, on the outskirts of the village of Xochipala, some 30 km. south-southwest of Ahuelicán (App. 7). There are enough resemblances to Cerro Chacaltepec II (ca. 400–100 B.C.) red-on-buff pottery (Grove 1968b: 57–9, figs. 49, 50; 1970a: 8–9) to suggest a late Middle Preclassic or Late Preclassic occupation for both sites. Several sites in the vicinity of Xochipala have yielded Olmec-style figurines and vessels to *huaqueros* (Gay 1972).

Some of the materials from Greengo's (1967; 1970; personal communication) excavations at El Calvario and Figueroa in the Tepecoacuilco drainage near Tetipan are apparently related. The only other site in the immediate area at which the Olmec Whiteware horizon is known to be represented is a cave at Cerro Ototal, near Huitzuco, which may represent a prehistoric mine (App. 6).

The Olmec Whiteware horizon is represented at many Early Middle Preclassic occupations in southeastern Mesoamerica. In central Chiapas they include Chiapa de Corzo, Padre Piedra, San Isidro, and Santa Rosa, among many others. In Soconusco there are substantial Early Middle Preclassic occupations at Izapa, La Victoria, and numerous other sites. Farther south the Colos complex of Chalchuapa—with which Las Victorias reliefs are associated—also represents the horizon (Dixon 1959; Coe 1961; Green and Lowe 1967; Ekholm-Miller 1969; Sharer and Gifford 1970; Bernal 1971: 46; Sharer 1974: 169–70).

Again, early material from Honduras seems to show relationships to the Olmec Whiteware horizon, particularly the Jaral complex at Los Naranjos and some of the Playa de los Muertos and Yarumela II material (Strong et al. 1938; Coe 1961: 127; Baudez and Becquelin 1973).

The Xe ceramic-sphere material from Seibal and Altar de Sacrificios, representing the earliest known occupation of the Petén, bears a close relationship to the Olmec Whiteware horizon. The Xe sphere may be later than most complexes of the horizon and it shows a distinctive regional emphasis (Willey et al. 1967; Willey 1970; R.E.W. Adams 1971).

To summarize, the Early Middle Preclassic period (900/800 to 600/500 B.C.) is marked by a horizon whose most prominent feature is distinctive incised white-slipped pottery. Like the Late Early Preclassic horizon, it is associated with the Olmec art style, represented especially by ceramic figurines and motifs incised or excised on ceramic vessels. It is also associated with Olmec stone sculpture—portable jades and relief carving—and with cave paintings in the Olmec style (see below).

There are clear continuities between the two horizons, although a smooth development from one to the other cannot be demonstrated. Several elements of the Olmec Whiteware horizon (white-slipped pottery, the multiple-line-break, and pseudo-grater fondo) appear in low frequencies in Terminal Early Preclassic phases representing the Olmec Blackware horizon. Olmecoid/baby-face figurines are associated with both horizons, as are Olmec motifs incised or excised on ceramic vessels (although they generally occur on polished black vessels in the earlier period). Some features of the Olmec Blackware horizon occur in association with the later horizon, in Early Santa María complexes in Tehuacán, for example. This may be attributable to stylistic lag in formerly marginal areas. Continuity between the horizons is most clearly reflected by the association of both with elaborate features of the Olmec art style, and to a lesser extent by the persistence of particular elements of the Olmec Blackware horizon.

The most striking difference between the two is the much greater prominence and pervasiveness of the Olmec Whiteware horizon. In general, it appears in the same zones as the Blackware horizon, although this in part simply reflects where archaeological research has been concentrated. In some areas (such as the Valley of Mexico) the later horizon seems less prominent, but its geographic distribution is substantially broader. It is very prominent in areas in which the Blackware horizon was minimally represented and/or retarded in its appearance, the Tehuacán Valley and coastal Guerrero, for example. Still more striking is the great prominence of the Olmec Whiteware horizon within the local components in which it is represented and the greater number and larger size of the settlements at which it occurs (see below).

Nonceramic Artifacts

Jade ornaments and figurines, particularly "were-jaguar" figurines, are prominently associated with the Olmec Whiteware horizon, most obviously in the Gulf-coast area. Jade is absent from the Early Preclassic San Lorenzo phase at San Lorenzo Tenochtitlán, although a few celts and ornaments of serpentine and other imported green stones occur in the Chicharras and San Lorenzo phases. A few green stone objects of the Nacaste and Palangana phases, including a pendant with an incised were-jaguar profile and a serpentine "stiletto" fragment, recall the jade offerings at La Venta. Jade celts, figurines, and ornaments are abundant at La Venta in the Early Middle Preclassic.

Unfortunately, the vast majority of Olmec jades have not come from controlled excavations; most lack even reliable site provenience. This is particularly true of central Mexico, where Olmec jades are relatively rare except in Morelos and Guerrero. The jade figurines and ornaments from Tlatilco could be from Early Middle Preclassic-period graves, although a Terminal Early Preclassic placement seems indicated. Jade and serpentine ornaments and celts from Zacatenco, El Arbolillo, and Tlapacoya (Vaillant 1930: 159, 168, pls. 40, 45; 1935: 244, figs. 25, 27; Barba de Piña Chán 1956: 101, 109, 112, 120–3, lám. 27, foto 19) are almost certainly Middle and Late Preclassic. Several jade and serpentine pieces very much like those from La Venta have been excavated at Chalcatzingo (Piña Chán 1955a: 24; Cyphers 1975; Grove et al. 1976). Jade and jadeite ornaments were found in Early Santa María-phase deposits in the Tehuacán Valley (MacNeish et al. 1967: 132–7).

In contrast with the rest of central Mexico, Guerrero has long been noted for Olmec-style jade objects. Most of them have no more reliable provenience than an alleged origin in Guerrero, but information from *huaqueros* and collectors indicates a few zones in which Olmec jades are particularly abundant. In one case they can be associated with a specific archaeological site.

Covarrubias (1948; 1957) pointed out the high frequency of Olmec jades from the vicinity of San Jerónimo, on the coast northwest of Acapulco, and especially from the Zumpango del Río area. Many Olmec jades, often of an extremely fine-grained blue-gray, have been looted from graves at the site of Tetipan, on the outskirts of the village of Ahuelicán. The incised white-slipped pottery littering the surface of Tetipan (App. 7)—discarded burial offerings, according to local informants—represents the Olmec Whiteware horizon. This is a strong indication that the Ahuelicán Olmec jades are primarily associated with the horizon, a relationship also suggested by other indirect evidence. In the first place, controlled excavation has uncovered significant numbers of Olmec jade and serpentine objects only in Early Middle Preclassic contexts, at La Venta and Chalcatzingo. Olmec jades from Ahuelicán and from the Zumpango del Río zone (and from elsewhere in central Mexico) are very similar to distinctive La Venta jades: "stilettos" or "awls," "clamshell" pendants, pendants representing parts of the body, notched plaques or celts, and figurines representing deformed individuals (Covarrubias 1948; Drucker 1952: pls. 50, 51, 58; Drucker et al. 1959: fig. 34; Bernal 1969: pls. 42, 44, 61). Were-jaguar figurines and other more familiar forms also occur. Olmec-style jade is absent from the Late Early Preclassic components at Atopula, which represent the Olmec Blackware horizon that is generally not associated with jade.

In southeastern Mesoamerica, Olmec jades also occur in Whiteware-horizon complexes, but they are less common. Jadeite ornaments and an ax coated with cinnabar are associated with Jaral burials at Los Naranjos, Honduras (Baudez

1970: 37–8; Baudez and Becquelin 1973). A jade "awl" discovered in a Réal Xe cache at Seibal also strongly recalls La Venta offerings (Willey 1970; R.E.W. Adams 1971).

Taken together, these facts suggest that Olmec jades date primarily to the Early Middle Preclassic period and that they are associated with the Olmec Whiteware horizon, although they are not found in every component representing the horizon.

Iron-ore mirrors continue to be associated with the Olmec Whiteware horizon, though rarely. The parabolic mirrors from La Venta indicate that the magnetite trade continued into the Early Middle Preclassic period, though the Valley of Oaxaca dropped out of the exchange network. Neither mirrors nor iron ores occur in Guadalupe-phase settlements. La Venta and other Gulf-coast centers exploited iron-ore sources outside the Valley of Oaxaca, such as the one near Niltepec in the Isthmus of Tehuantepec region (Pires-Ferreira 1975; 1976b). This partial withdrawal from the interaction sphere represented by the Olmec horizons may be an indication that the Valley of Oaxaca, like Chalcatzingo, developed an early tendency toward regionalization.

Settlement Patterns

Data for settlement patterns for the Early Middle Preclassic are quite limited. One known contrast with the Olmec Blackware horizon, however, is that Olmec Whiteware-horizon material does not consist principally of elite mortuary furniture although it does occur in this context (notably at Tetipan). The most adequate settlement-pattern data again come from the Valley of Oaxaca and from nearby Tehuacán. In the Guadalupe phase the Valley enjoyed a substantial population increase; more and larger settlements are known. This is presumably related to increased agricultural productivity. Pollen profiles suggest a wetter climate during the Guadalupe phase than during the preceding San José phase when conditions seem to have been drier than today. Also, evidence of wells of the type used today for pot irrigation at two sites indicates that simple water-control techniques were in use during the Guadalupe phase. Modern pot irrigation in the Valley of Oaxaca can produce two or even three crops annually. In the later Middle Preclassic (Monte Albán I-A subphase) and the Late Preclassic, the same trends continue and intensify; more and larger sites are known, and they spread into the piedmont zone along permanent tributary streams where small-scale canal irrigation is feasible. Stratification and specialization within and among settlements increase. The earliest direct evidence of canal irrigation (a "fossilized" canal and terrace system at Hierve del Agua) dates to the Late Preclassic period (Flannery et al. 1967: 451–2; Flannery 1968: 89; Flannery and Schoenwetter 1970: 147–51).

Like the Olmec Blackware horizon, the later horizon is most prominent at larger sites and, within these sites, in elite contexts. San José Mogote grew (to 40 ha.) during the Guadalupe phase and large-scale public construction activity continued. The striking settlement hierarchy of the San José phase continued; no other Guadalupe settlement is larger than a small village, although ceremonial-"civic" structures now appear at several sites. At Huitzo, too, the Guadalupe phase was marked by expanded public construction. The San José-phase platform was enlarged, and another platform was constructed with the same orientation—8° west of true north, like Complex A at La Venta. This platform was one of four bordering a rectangular white-surfaced plaza. It supported a large wattle-and-daub house coated with adobe and white plaster, perhaps an elite residence area. Adjacent to the elite residences were smaller and simpler wattle-and-daub houses without platforms or plaster coatings, probably lower-status residences of retainers or dependents (Flannery 1968: 87–8, 94–7; 1976).

This platform-plaza zone is very reminiscent of La Venta in associated ceramics, in some of the construction techniques, and especially in the orientation. In striking contrast to La Venta, however, this complex shows little indication of a ceremonial character. As in the Early Preclassic period, the Olmec Whiteware horizon is associated with high social status and probably "civic" functions, but not obviously with ceremonial functions or religion. There may be a ceremonial or religious component in the elevated social status, and the careful orientation of the platforms does suggest the kind of esoteric knowledge that was associated with astronomy, calendrics, and writing in an intellectual-scientific-priestly context in later Mesoamerica.

The Valley of Oaxaca continued its involvement in interregional exchange in the Guadalupe phase. Shells, stingray and marine fish spines, shark teeth, and turtle-shell drums indicate continuing relationships with the coastal lowlands. Basalt grinding stones and obsidian were imported from a number of areas, mainly in the highlands. There is some evidence that obsidian is now redistributed by a central institution at San José Mogote, perhaps an indication of its growing political power and centralization. Given the abundance of concave iron-ore mirrors at La Venta, there is a surprisingly little evidence of a continuation of the iron-ore mirror industry in the Guadalupe phase. This may indicate incipient regionalization, which eventually culminates in the emergence of the distinctively Oaxacan Monte Albán civilization (Flannery 1968: 116; 1976; Flannery and Schoenwetter 1970: 151; Pires-Ferreira 1975). The context of the Olmec Whiteware horizon in the Valley of Oaxaca—larger, more prosperous settlements associated with more pronounced evidence of status differentiation—seems to reflect an intensification of the Blackware-horizon pattern.

Unlike the earlier one, the Olmec Whiteware horizon is prominent in the Tehuacán Valley in the Early Santa María phase. Participation in interregional interaction is also reflected in trade items from Early Santa María components; there is an increase of more than 600 percent in identifiable trade sherds over the Late Ajalpan phase (MacNeish et al. 1970: tables 22, 31).

Striking changes in settlement pattern are associated with a substantial population increase. Twenty-one Early Santa María components are known, compared with thirteen for all of the Ajalpan phase, and MacNeish estimates a fourfold increase in population density. Agriculture became more intensive and more productive, and there is evidence of irrigation. Associated with these trends is a change in types and locations of settlements. MacNeish characterizes the overall settlement pattern as a Nuclear Village pattern. A few Early Santa María seasonal camps are known, but they were agricultural. Hamlets continue to be the most common settlement type, but they are now clustered into "community groups," each oriented toward a "nuclear" village, a larger settlement distinguished by large-scale public construction—a central plaza, mound, or mound group. Outlying hamlets focus, administratively and/or ceremonially, on the nuclear village. Stone masonry appears along with wattle-and-daub construction, and burials also indicate status distinctions. MacNeish feels that there is also evidence of increased specialization in public works (water control, mound construction, etc.), trade, and perhaps ceremonial activity (MacNeish 1970: 245–6, table VI; 1972: 82).

The striking feature of Early Santa María is the greatly increased participation of Tehuacán in wider Mesoamerican cultural interaction. It is visible in the prominence of the locally manufactured elements of the Olmec Whiteware horizon and in evidence of external economic ties. Early Santa María sites are linked with the Gulf coast, Chiapas, and Soconusco, as well as with other highland areas, particularly the Valley of Mexico (MacNeish et al. 1970: 283–5; MacNeish 1970: 245).

Although MacNeish is inclined to attribute ceremonial functions to some of the public construction features, implicitly assigning an important role in these developments to ceremonial organizations or cults, Tehuacán is comparable to the Valley of Oaxaca. Indications of occupational specialization, social stratification and the emergence of elite groups, and the centralization and concentration of political power are strong. While these trends may have had ceremonial or religious components, and while the high-status groups may have been religious as well as political elites, the evidence for the secular aspects is much more direct. As in the Valley of Oaxaca, the later part of the Middle Preclassic period saw a continuation and intensification of these trends—further population increase, intensification of irrigation agriculture, increased specialization and status differentiation, greater interaction with external areas, and the appearance of new and larger administrative and/or ceremonial centers.

Settlement-pattern data for the Early Middle Preclassic period in Morelos are considerably less complete. Recent excavations at Chalcatzingo (Grove 1973b; 1974a; Cyphers 1975; Grove et al. 1976) indicate that the major occupation falls in the Middle Preclassic period. The Whiteware horizon is prominently represented, apparently in late Chalcatzingo B and early Chalcatzingo C. The enormous quantity of ceramic refuse illustrates what appears to be a typical contrast in Mesoamerica: Early Preclassic sites yield small artifacts assemblages, while the quantities of debris, especially ceramics, at Early Middle Preclassic sites are quite large. Where adequate data are available they reflect a significant change in settlement pattern: Early Middle Preclassic sites are more numerous, and at least some represent a scale of settlement that was unknown in the Early Preclassic period. There is a change in overall settlement pattern and in internal organization of settlements, as well as a substantial population increase.

In the Chalcatzingo region, the number of settlements increases sharply during the Chalcatzingo B phase. Most are small villages or hamlets clustered around Chalcatzingo, now a substantial (20 ha.) nucleated settlement with considerable internal differentiation. It occupies a terraced hillside with an elaborate water-control system to channel runoff. A distinct public quarter contains major ceremonial or "civic" architecture; houses are scattered around this zone in a dispersed pattern. Exploitation of local kaolin and hematite sources and workshop concentrations of obsidian, hematite, and occasionally serpentine suggest that Chalcatzingo was an important processing and exporting center in a widespread economic network. These trends continue into the Chalcatzingo C phase when the site achieves its maximum size and greatest sociopolitical complexity. An elite Chalcatzingo C residence in the public sector of the site contains burials with Olmec jade and serpentine offerings and one with a concave iron-ore mirror. Despite continuing interaction with the Gulf-coast region, Chalcatzingo shows a clear trend toward regionalization in phase C with the emergence of a distinctive local ceramic style.

Chalcatzingo's Olmec monumental sculpture can be assigned mainly to Chalcatzingo B, though some monuments continued in use during Chalcatzingo C. The Olmec Whiteware horizon also appears at Cerro Chacaltepec. Other than the fact that it occupies an elevated location at the confluence of two major streams, no settlement-pattern data are available.

In the Valley of Mexico, the Olmec Whiteware horizon is represented in refuse deposits at El Arbolillo, Zacatenco, Tlatilco, and Tlapacoya. In contrast to the Olmec Blackware horizon, the later horizon is not particularly prominent. The more elaborate features—Olmec symbolic motifs incised or excised on the pottery, jade figurines, and the large hollow white-slipped Olmecoid/baby-face figurines—are conspicuous by their absence. There are few indications of settlement hierarchies or social stratification; the elite cemeteries at Tlatilco and Tlapacoya are primarily Early Preclassic. Settlements appear to be small, simple, undifferentiated farming communities. The traditional contrast between these "village cultures" and the more elaborate Olmec manifestation at Tlatilco and Tlapacoya has some justification, although these particular village cultures do not represent an ancient context into which Olmec influence intruded.

In highland Guerrero, the firmest evidence of the Olmec Whiteware horizon comes from the site of Tetipan. Although controlled excavations have not been carried out, there is little doubt that the ceramics are associated with the many Olmec jade mortuary offerings. The Whiteware horizon appears here in an elite context. In keeping with the trend recognized in other areas, Tetipan is considerably larger than Early Preclassic Atopula. A possible Early Middle Preclassic mine has been located near Huitzuco at Cerro Ototal (App. 6).

On the coast of Guerrero, the Whiteware horizon is better represented than the Blackware horizon, but it is not prominent. It is represented by ceramics and Olmecoid/baby-face figurines; the more elaborate features of the horizon (jade and complex ceramic designs) are missing. There are no settlement-pattern data for Early Middle Preclassic Tom occupations, but they resemble contemporary complexes in the density of ceramics in refuse deposits (more than twice the number of sherds of any other period). There is no evidence of social stratification, site stratification, or hierarchies (C. Brush 1969: 58).

In southeastern Mesoamerica the disappearance of the Olmec Blackware horizon at the end of the Early Preclassic period was accompanied by an even greater cultural disruption than the one that marked its appearance. Considerable occupation relocation took place at this time. Salinas La Blanca and Altamira were abandoned (at least temporarily), while many sites were newly occupied or reoccupied in the Early Middle Preclassic period. In a few cases (as at La Victoria) this took place at the very end of the Jocotal phase, emphasizing its transitional character (Coe and Flannery 1967: 67; Green and Lowe 1967). The area of Mound 1 at Chiapa de Corzo illustrates the disruptive nature of the change: a substantial Chiapa I occupation zone was deliberately removed and dumped in a gigantic clearing operation preceding the Chiapa II occupation (Lowe and Agrinier 1960: 7, 8; Green and Lowe 1967: 69, 70). Jaral, the earliest occupation at Los Naranjos near Lake Yojoa, includes a large "defensive" ditch, clay platform mounds (one of which contains a burial with offerings of jadeite ornaments), and a nearby group of burials associated with a jadeite ax coated with cinnabar. In many ways it is reminiscent of La Venta (Baudez 1970: 37-8; Baudez and Becquelin 1973). In contrast, most Early Middle Preclassic settlements in southeastern Mesoamerica are small villages or hamlets without public architecture.

Elaborate large-scale public construction is associated with the Olmec Whiteware horizon. At San Isidro in central Chiapas, a pyramidal clay mound with offerings of groups of celts, burials surrounded by celts, and a cache with jade earplugs strongly recall La Venta, as does the pottery. San Isidro was apparently a ceremonial center of the Olmec heartland type (Bernal 1971: 46). At Chiapa de Corzo, Chiapa II-phase structures are limited to low, relatively unimpressive platforms (Lowe and Agrinier 1960: 9, 15; Lowe 1962: 58-9). At Izapa, on the other hand, an elaborate complex of superimposed pyramidal temple platforms dates to the contemporary Duende phase (Ekholm-Miller 1969: 13-22, 98-100). At Chalchuapa a platform some 20 m. high was constructed during the Colos phase (Sharer 1974: 167-70).

Monumental Art

Most Olmec monumental art outside the Gulf-coast region is relief carving, although there are a few examples of sculpture in the round and two sets of cave paintings. Some reliefs and free-standing sculptures in related or "Olmecoid" styles pertain to later periods. In central Mexico, monumental Olmec art occurs in a very restricted area of highland Guerrero and nearby Morelos, on the fringes of the Balsas basin.

The reliefs of Chalcatzingo, first reported by Guzmán in 1934, are the most widely known examples. They cannot be dated by direct archaeological evidence, although the "Group B" carvings on detached boulders at the base of the Cerro de la Cantera are in close association with the Early Middle Preclassic occupation zone. Comparative analysis of the style and motifs of the reliefs supports this dating. The Chalcatzingo reliefs show close similarities to the monumental art of La Venta, in specific motifs as well as overall style and theme (Coe 1965c; Gay 1966; 1971; Cook de Leonard 1967; Grove 1968a; 1973b; Joralemon 1971; Clewlow 1974; Grove et al. 1976).

Reliefs I and II, the most complex, show that the canons of La Venta Olmec art were observed in detail at Chalcatzingo. Not only do the same elements appear, they also are combined according to the same rules. Joralemon (1971) even suggests that the same deities are represented. Relief I shows a richly dressed figure seated in a "niche" or enclosure holding a "ceremonial bar" across its breast. This object and the only other definite representation of the ceremonial bar in Olmec art (Coe 1965c: figs. 14, 53), are extremely similar to the ceremonial bars common in Classic Maya relief carving.

"Ceremonial bar" is probably a misnomer: many or most of the richly attired figures on Maya stelae represent not priests but political leaders. The ceremonial bar functions primarily as a marker of high status and a symbol of secular authority; it is not an enigmatic ceremonial object. It is interesting to note in this context that the figure-in-a-niche motif in Classic Maya art is associated with the accession to power of political leaders (Proskouriakoff 1960; 1961). The figure in Relief I at Chalcatzingo is undoubtedly an important personage, and here too the ceremonial bar is a marker of prestige and authority. It may also mark ethnicity or cultural distinctiveness. The bars are homologous to the small, stylized figures commonly held by the personages represented in Olmec art, especially at La Venta (Stirling 1943; 1955; Drucker 1952).

In the Gulf-coast Olmec centers, the small figures would be associated with the elite group, marking high status and secular authority and political power. At Chalcatzingo, the ceremonial bar would be a marker of prestige, authority, and power; as an attribute of the Gulf-coast elite group it would also mark ethnicity—foreignness and cultural distinctiveness.

The traditional interpretation of Relief I in terms of a rain deity and agricultural fertility (e.g. Grove 1968a: 486-7; 1968b: 135-8) is not necessarily invalidated, but secular themes of status and authority are primary.

Relief II at Chalcatzingo has often been interpreted in secular terms. This relief represents another complex scene involving three richly dressed standing figures carrying paddle-shaped objects and a seated figure almost without ornamentation.

The elaborate attire of the three standing figures emphasizes their importance and their "Olmecness." In sharp contrast, the seated figure conspicuously lacks these symbols; he is in some way subordinate, even if he is not a bound captive as Coe (1965b: 18) suggests. The scene conveys the prestige, authority, and power of an elite group vis-à-vis a subordinate group. The paddle-shaped "clubs" carried by the standing figures could easily represent symbols of status and authority rather than offensive weapons. They resemble the objects held by the figures on Stelae 2 and 3 at La Venta (Heizer 1967) which are definitely staffs or scepters, not clubs. They belong to a series of related objects in Olmec art, including several actual scepters as well as representations of them (Navarrete 1971). Scepters, staffs, and clubs are equivalent, and they are similar in function to were-jaguar infants and to ceremonial bars. All are symbolic of an elite group and its prestige, authority, and power. In central Mexico these elements also mark ethnic distinctiveness from the local population (Henderson 1974: 312-14). The overall theme of Relief II emphasizes the same thing.

There are several other reliefs at the base of the Cerro de la Cantera, and Grove's recent excavations uncovered four Olmec stelae and a large stone altar within the occupation area at Chalcatzingo (Cyphers 1975; Grove et al. 1976). The altar is identical in form with those of La Venta, but it is composed of eighteen individual blocks. It was found in a Chalcatzingo C (750-550 B.C.) context, but its incorrect assembly suggests an original phase B (1000-750) date.

The only example of free-standing monumental Olmec stone sculpture from central Mexico—a seated headless figure quite similar to monuments at La Venta (Drucker et al. 1959: pl. 52; Heizer 1968: fig. 12)—also comes from Chalcatzingo.

The only other example of Olmec relief sculpture in central Mexico is the recently discovered stela from San Miguel Amuco, Guerrero (Grove and Paradis 1971). This small stela, now in a private collection in Arcelia, depicts a single standing figure. The general style recalls the reliefs of Chalcatzingo and La Venta, as do specific motifs. The most intriguing similarity is the staff- or bundle-like object cradled diagonally in the left arm. It is held precisely as are many staffs, scepters, and were-jaguar infants, and it is homologous to them. It suggests themes of status, authority, and power, recalling the Aztec *tlaquimilolli,* or sacred bundle, which contained objects connected with the cult of a deity. The *tlaquimilolli* was particularly important in connection with deities who stood in tutelary or patron relationships with particular sociopolitical groups, and who often had totemic or "deified tribal ancestor" status as well. Besides their ceremonial importance, sacred bundles functioned as symbols of group identity—of authority, political power, and sovereignty. They are emphasized in accounts of migrations and of the establishment of important political centers, when they were in the charge of priestly leaders who served as spokesmen of the gods, passing on divine commandments. The capture of the patron deity's *tlaquimilolli* symbolized the conquest of a group as clearly as did the capture of his image or the sack of his temple (Nicholson 1971b: 409-10). Other Mesoamerican groups, including the Maya, had comparable sacred objects and bundles—they may even be a typically Mesoamerican trait (Recinos 1950: 205; Edmonson 1965: 12, 90; 1971: 212-14; Coe 1973: 16). These are precisely the kinds of symbolic functions suggested for the were-jaguar staff or scepter objects in Olmec art. The derivation of power and authority from a tutelary or totemic relationship with a deity figure is the most appealing way to account for the apparent combination of religious or ceremonial and secular themes in Olmec art.

The similarity of the San Miguel Amuco stela to the relief sculptures of Chalcatzingo and La Venta suggests an equivalent chronological placement in the Early Middle Preclassic period. Information from local informants casts some doubt on the reported association of two white-rimmed black-ware vessels with the stela (L. Paradis, personal communication).

The other examples of monumental Olmec art in central Mexico are two groups of cave paintings in the east-central highlands of Guerrero. Oxtotitlán Cave (Grove 1970b) is located about 12 km. northeast of Chilapa, near a tributary of the Río Balsas. The paintings occur near the mouth of the cave. Many of the motifs show close similarities to the Chalcatzingo reliefs and to those at La Venta. The most striking example is Painting Ic, a serpent that is nearly identical with Relief V at Chalcatzingo.

Despite the similarities in motifs and motif combinations, the Oxtotitlán paintings do not seem to be intended to convey quite the same meanings as the Chalcatzingo reliefs. The specific symbols of prestige and authority are missing. Mythical or religious themes seem dominant. The location of the Oxtotitlán paintings, in a much less public and conspicuous setting than the Chalcatzingo rock carvings, is consistent with the different emphasis in their content.

The similarities of the Oxtotitlán paintings to Chalcatzingo and La Venta indicate an Early Middle Preclassic date. This is the placement suggested by Grove, who found a white sherd incised with a double-line-break motif typical of the Olmec Whiteware horizon at a nearby site (Grove 1970b: 28, 32).

Olmec paintings are also found in Juxtlahuaca Cave, some 30 km. south of Oxtotitlán (Gay 1967). Unlike Oxtotitlán, the Juxtlahuaca paintings are more than a kilometer inside the cave. There are some similarities to the Oxtotitlán paintings, and to Chalcatzingo and La Venta.

Interpretation of the Juxtlahuaca paintings is difficult. Like those at Oxtotitlán, they do not seem to deal primarily with secular themes of status and power. This may be related to their exceedingly nonpublic location. Painting 1, with a large figure in an elaborate colorful costume, towering over a much smaller seated figure, does imply the dominance/subordinance theme of Relief II at Chalcatzingo. It is reminiscent of the stela from Padre Piedra, Chiapas, which also can be interpreted in terms of dominance/subordinance.

The Padre Piedra stela, from the Frailesca region of inland Chiapas (Navarrete 1960: 10–12; Green and Lowe 1967), is very similar to La Venta relief carving and to central Mexican monumental Olmec art. The representation of a large figure towering over a much smaller figure seated at his feet conveys a dominance relationship recalling Relief II at Chalcatzingo as well as the Juxtlahuaca Cave paintings.

Padre Piedra was occupied during both the Late Early Preclassic (Chiapa I) and Early Middle Preclassic (Chiapa II) periods, but the Chiapa II occupation was more extensive. In view of this and the stylistic relationships of the stela, an Early Middle Preclassic placement is most probable. Green and Lowe (1967: 67) assign it to the Early Preclassic because identical "knuckle-dusters" appear on San Lorenzo Monument 10 (Stirling 1966: pl. 15), but the knuckle-duster motif also occurs at La Venta (Drucker 1952: fig. 47a; Drucker et al. 1959: fig. 40).

A second Olmec relief from inland Chiapas is the standing figure carved on a rock at Xoc (Batehaton) in the Río Jatate drainage of eastern Chiapas (Cordan 1963: facing p. 72; Ekholm-Miller 1973). Many features have close counterparts at Chalcatzingo and La Venta. The indistinct object held in the right hand has been called a knife but is more likely a scepter; the pointed portion is probably a later embellishment. The figure cradles an oblong object in his left arm, as on the San Miguel Amuco stela from Guerrero. Both mark high status, authority, and perhaps ethnic distinctiveness and political sovereignty.

Surface survey and minor test excavation in the vicinity of Xoc produced Late Middle Preclassic (Chiapa III–IV) pottery, but not in direct association with the relief (Ekholm-Miller 1973: 19–21). The stylistic relationships make a tentative Early Middle Preclassic placement more appropriate.

Other examples of Olmec relief carving are scattered along the Pacific coast and slope from western Chiapas to El Salvador. Petroglyph I at Tonalá (Ferdon 1953) represents a frontal view of a jaguar face with a subtrapezoidal mouth and fangs. It is similar to a number of Olmec representations, particularly celts and monster-masks from La Venta. Several other monuments from Tonalá have been described as Olmec (Navarrete 1960: 11; Bernal 1969: 171, pls. 82, 84), but they are not squarely within the Olmec style.

Although there is no good archaeological evidence based on excavation at Tonalá, the architecture and the bulk of the occupation are certainly later than the Early Middle Preclassic period. However, Navarrete (1959) found Chiapa II-phase pottery at the site of Tzutzuculi, less than a kilometer away. As Lowe and Mason (1965: 199–200, 210) suggest, the Olmec relief might have been moved from there to Tonalá. At least there was an Early Middle Preclassic occupation in the immediate area, and this would be an appropriate date for Petroglyph 1.

A series of Olmec relief carvings at Pijijiapan, southeast of Tonalá on the Chiapas coastal plain (Navarrete 1969), resembles the monuments of Padre Piedra, La Venta, and the central highlands (particularly Chalcatzingo) in the stylistic treatment of figures and in specific motifs. The two scenes at Pijijiapan are difficult to interpret. The central figure on Piedra 2 holds an object cradled in his right arm. It resembles the bundle-like objects held in the same way by the figures on the San Miguel Amuco stela and the Xoc relief. This suggests a similar interpretation as a symbol of prestige, authority, and perhaps of cultural distinctiveness. The central figure is also considerably larger than his two companions.

Navarrete's (1969: 189–93, fig. 5) test excavations at Pijijiapan produced pottery that he assigns to Soconusco types—Guamuchal Brushed and Pampas Black-and-White. On this basis he suggests a Cuadros-phase occupation and a Late Early Preclassic date for the reliefs. Although Guamuchal Brushed is a Cuadros-Jocotal-phase type, Pampas Black-and-White is primarily a Conchas 1 type (Coe and Flannery 1967: fig. 8). Given the stylistic relationships of the reliefs, an Early Middle Preclassic assignment is much more satisfactory.

The boulder carving at San Isidro Piedra Parada, in the Pacific-slope zone of Guatemala, depicts a kneeling Olmec figure whose costume (Thompson 1943) strongly recalls Relief II at Chalcatzingo and various La Venta monuments (especially Altar 5). In the absence of direct archaeological evidence bearing on the date of this relief, an Early Middle Preclassic placement is consistent with its stylistic relationships.

Relief figures on four sides of a boulder at Chalchuapa (Las Victorias) in the Pacific-slope area of El Salvador represent the southernmost known occurrence of Olmec monumental art (Boggs 1950). Again the costumes show strong similarities to the Chalcatzingo reliefs and La Venta monuments. Three figures definitely carry objects cradled under their arms, two of which are rather staff-like; one is thicker, somewhat more like the bundle motif. In each case the object is carried in precisely the same way, and the equivalence with the scepter, staff, and bundle motifs is beyond question.

At El Sitio, on the Pacific slope of Guatemala, Shook (1965: 185, fig. 1) excavated a Late Preclassic burial with offerings which included, besides jade ornaments, a carved stone staff or scepter identical with the object carried by one of the Las Victorias figures. Several other small scepters have been found (Navarrete 1971). The scepter or staff motifs in Olmec art represent actual physical symbols of prestige and authority, which could be carried and displayed. The El Sitio staff was found in a late grave, but there was an occupation at the site, with mound construction, at least as early as the Middle Preclassic (Shook 1965: 185). The staff could have been an heirloom. At least one small Olmec piece has been discovered in the vicinity of El Sitio (Navarrete 1971: fig. 5).

Recent excavations at Chalchuapa revealed an occupation extending back to the Early Preclassic period (Sharer and Gifford 1970; Sharer 1974). The earliest phase (Tok) is closely related to Cuadros at Salinas La Blanca, and to the Olmec Blackware horizon. The subsequent complex (Colos) is affiliated with the Olmec Whiteware horizon and the Xe ceramic sphere of the Petén lowlands. The reliefs are best assigned to the Early Middle Preclassic period.

One indisputable Olmec free-standing stone sculpture was found on the eastern coast of Chiapas, not far from Altamira (Navarrete 1971: 75–8, láms. 4–10). It is a large standing figure with a backswept cleft head and a gigantic pectoral bearing an Olmec face in relief. Many of its features resemble those of La Venta monuments (Heizer 1968: fig. 13).

The Olmec reliefs outside the Gulf-coast region are remarkably uniform. There are many specific similarities in style and motifs, and they have a common theme: the prestige, authority, and ethnic distinctiveness of a dominant elite. The symbols of this status and authority are the scepter or staff and bundle motifs. All Olmec reliefs outside the Gulf coast are best interpreted as visible public statements of the prestige, authority, and dominance of an Olmec elite group, which emphasizes its peculiar attributes to set itself apart from subordinate local groups.

The apparent contrast in subject matter between the relief carvings and the cave paintings at Oxtotitlán and Juxtlahuaca is a matter of emphasis rather than a strict dichotomy. The obvious symbols of status and authority so prominent in the reliefs are not represented in the cave paintings, which are seemingly more concerned with religious or mythical topics. The basic contrast in the intended functions of the two sets of representations is reflected in their placement. The relief carvings, which stress the high status and authority of an Olmec elite, are public—located in accessible and highly visible places, especially at Chalcatzingo. They were intended to impress a culturally distinct populace with the prestige and authority of the foreign Olmec elite, and thus to enhance their power and political control. They are in some sense public statements of the Olmecness of the dominant group and of the immediately surrounding territory. The cave paintings are much less accessible, particularly those at Juxtlahuaca; although prestige and dominance are implied, the privateness of the paintings indicates the importance of ceremonial themes and religious or cult functions (Henderson 1974: 304–20).

6. Olmec Mesoamerica

The Olmec art style appears in Mesoamerica in the context of two horizons during the Late Early and Early Middle Preclassic periods (ca. 1200–600 B.C.). In the Gulf-coast lowlands this style is most intensively represented in the widest range of media (particularly monumental free-standing stone sculpture), and in association with elaborate large-scale public constructions. The key question is the relationship of this area with the rest of Mesoamerica: What social factors and systems can account for the presence of Olmec material outside the Gulf-coast region?

Covarrubias (1957) and Piña Chán (1955a) offered the simplest explanation: that the Olmec originated in the Morelos-Guerrero area and that the elaborate Olmec occupation in the southern Gulf-coast zone is derivative. This does not solve the problem, but only in a sense reverses it—it does not address the question of the cultural and social factors that conditioned the interaction. In any case, there is no convincing evidence in support of this hypothesis.

All available evidence indicates that the fullest and most elaborate representation of the Olmec style and its associated features occurs in southern Veracruz and western Tabasco. Although there is still no satisfactory developmental sequence for the Olmec style in the Gulf coast (or elsewhere), the presumption must remain that this area is the Olmec heartland. It is true that the earliest fully Olmec component, the San Lorenzo phase at San Lorenzo Tenochtitlán, does in some ways appear intrusive—a complex of features which cannot be adequately explained as an obvious developmental transition out of what preceded it. It is also true, however, that some of the features of the San Lorenzo phase are foreshadowed in the earlier occupations.

Ojochi, an Ocós-like occupation with no Olmec traits, is followed by Bajío, a phase with very different, still non-Olmec, ceramics. Bajío figurine fragments show vague hints of the Olmec style, and massive construction activity begins at San Lorenzo in the Bajío phase. Bajío is followed by the brief Chicharras phase, again marked by new ceramics; Chicharras appears to be a simpler version of, and leads directly into, the fully Olmec San Lorenzo phase. Chicharras deposits contained a fragment of a monument, quantities of basalt chips, Olmec-style figurines, and ceramics strongly resembling those of the San Lorenzo phase (Coe 1970). What is missing is a developmental sequence for the Olmec art style itself. This may be beyond archaeological recovery, especially if it was a relatively rapid phenomenon, as the San Lorenzo sequence hints, or if it emphasized representation in a perishable medium. The role of the people of the Bajío phase in the emergence of the Olmec may be crucial, but it remains elusive. The influx of new ceramic complexes at San Lorenzo Tenochtitlán indicates that ideas were exchanged on a fairly wide scale, at least in the Gulf-coast lowlands, and this may have been accompanied by movements of people. All indications are that interaction, communication, and exchange between different areas and groups were crucial in the emergence of the Olmec civilization, as in the emergence of other early complex cultures. The details of this interaction are obscure. Present evidence from San Lorenzo Tenochtitlán suggests the addition of an art style and associated ceramic complex of unknown origins to a social context in which large-scale public construction activity was already emphasized. Although Olmec origins cannot be adequately explained, the Gulf coast was the crucial area.

Hypotheses about the Olmec presence outside the Gulf-coast area commonly treat Olmec material as a unified cultural phenomenon. The possibility that the interaction between these areas and the Gulf-coast Olmec centers changed through time has not been seriously considered. It is now clear that Olmec material occurs in two chronologically and culturally distinct contexts—an earlier Olmec Blackware horizon in the Late Early Preclassic and a later Olmec Whiteware horizon in the Early Middle Preclassic. Hypotheses about the Olmec outside the Gulf coast must take into account the existence of these distinct horizons and the differences between them.

Initial Preclassic ceramic complexes share some general features, but they basically represent local ceramic traditions. In the Late Early Preclassic period, these local traditions are modified and partly supplanted by the Olmec Blackware horizon.

These earliest traces of the Olmec outside the Gulf coast region are strongly Olmec. This material is not "Olmecoid" in any sense, although it does not include the full range of the Olmec style as it is known at San Lorenzo Tenochtitlán. The Olmec Blackware horizon is accompanied by evidence of direct economic interaction of the Gulf coast with the rest of Mesoamerica.

An economic network featuring a wide range of commodities linked Olmec Blackware-horizon sites with San Lorenzo Tenochtitlán. The Valley of Oaxaca supplied San Lorenzo, and presumably contemporary Gulf-coast centers, with iron-ore mirrors and other luxury goods manufactured from locally available exotic raw materials. Obsidian from Pachuca, the Valley of Teotihuacán, El Chayal, and Ixtepeque Volcano was used at San Lorenzo Tenochtitlán in the Chicharras and San Lorenzo phases (Cobean et al. 1971: table 1; Pires-Ferreira 1975; 1976a).

Shell, stingray spines, marine-fish spines, and turtle shell were among the coastal lowland products (Flannery 1976). A variety of perishable commodities was presumably exchanged as well. Cacao, a major product of southeastern Mesoamerica in the Postclassic period, may have been an important Preclassic exchange item; salt is another possibility.

Though the exchange was not one-way, the flow of goods into the Gulf-coast lowlands was very heavy. Iron-ore mirrors, for example, are unknown in southeastern Mesoamerica. In general, luxury goods were not exchanged between central Mexico and southeastern Mesoamerica, nor were they redistributed from the Gulf-coast lowlands. They were procured from both areas for elite groups of the Gulf coast, and they stopped there.

The components of the Olmec Blackware horizon represent substantial periods of time, throughout which the features of the horizon are maintained, and even intensified. There is no regionalization or localization of the Olmec style, no drift out of the orbit of Olmec influence. This implies continued interaction with the Gulf coast, largely through participation in the economic network. The existence of such a network focused on the Gulf coast is certain. Coe (1965b: 122–3; 1968a: 91–103), Grove (1968c), Flannery (1968), and others have proposed explanations of the Olmec outside the Gulf coast in terms of economic factors, but the nature of the interaction which accompanied and conditioned this economic network remains to be explained.

One striking feature of the Olmec Blackware horizon is the extent to which it occurs in elite contexts. The best-known examples are the elaborate graves of Tlatilco, Tlapacoya, Las Bocas, and La Juana-San Pablo. In the Valley of Oaxaca the horizon appears in an elite residential context in association with the manufacture of luxury articles. There is a sharp contrast with lower-status residential zones in the same community and with other communities in which the elements of the horizon are less prominent or absent. At sites like Tlapacoya, where the horizon is prominent in both graves and refuse, and at Atopula, where it occurs only in refuse material, the Blackware and associated features are probably an index of the high prestige of the community as a whole vis-à-vis its neighbors.

The same may be true of southeastern Mesoamerica, where the Olmec Blackware horizon does not often occur in obviously elite contexts. Present evidence is mainly from refuse deposits which do not necessarily represent elite residential areas. There are a few exceptions—including Los Naranjos in Honduras—but in general the elaborate elite burials of the central highlands are not duplicated. Lowe (Green and Lowe 1967: 71) suggests that the greater Isthmus zone and Soconusco were part of the Olmec heartland, an enormous sustaining area for San Lorenzo and other centers. The entire area, essentially a continuous lowland zone, may have been culturally unified.

In central Mexico, at least, the prestige marked by the features of the Olmec Blackware horizon has a foreign aspect, a connotation of ethnic distinctiveness. The elite groups whose high status is marked by this material may have been Olmecs from the Gulf coast or, as Flannery (1968) suggests, local elites who adopted the symbols and status trappings of a more sophisticated group with which they had economic ties, in order to enhance their own prestige and authority.

At sites like Atopula, the Olmec Blackware horizon style does not suddenly replace the preexisting ceramic complexes. Rather, it has the character of a veneer superimposed on the local traditions. Earlier features of the local styles persist; those which are also part of the horizon style are reemphasized and recombined. In other words the local style is reworked and partially superseded but not replaced.

This is consistent with Flannery's notion that local groups or subgroups adopt foreign styles and symbols for their own purposes. At sites like San José Mogote, on the other hand, where the horizon is represented in restricted residential zones, and perhaps at sites like Tlatilco, Tlapacoya, and Las Bocas with elaborate mortuary offerings and refuse so very similar to those at San Lorenzo, the possibility of foreign residents must be taken seriously. With prolonged economic interaction it would be natural for some of the traders or economic specialists from the Olmec heartland—who may have constituted a group not unlike the Aztec *pochteca* (Coe 1965b: 122-3)—to take up residence in the areas that supplied them with valuable goods. This is especially likely in the Terminal Early Preclassic period, with its intensification of Olmec Blackware-horizon features. The argument that *pochteca*-like groups appeared only with the rise of urban civilization in highland central Mexico (e.g. Parsons and Price 1971) is related to the perception of all nonurban lowland cultures as much simpler, with much less specialization, than their highland counterparts. Both views are based on negative evidence and become increasingly less tenable as research sheds more light on the lowland civilizations of Mesoamerica (R.E.W. Adams 1970; Becker 1973).

The Terminal Early Preclassic period foreshadows the Olmec Whiteware horizon. The changes involved in the appearance of this horizon are more far-reaching than a shift in modes of ceramic decoration. A few areas become regionalized and seem to drift out of the Olmec orbit, at least partially. In the Valley of Mexico, for example, the Whiteware horizon is not so prominent as was the earlier horizon. New areas, such as the Tehuacán Valley, begin to participate in the interaction sphere.

In many areas in which both horizons are prominent, such as Morelos, and Guerrero and Chiapas, there are disruptions in settlement pattern. The clearest evidence of disturbance comes from central Chiapas, nearest the Gulf coast. Early Middle Preclassic occupations are more numerous and larger than those of the Olmec Blackware horizon, and there is more evidence of specialization and social stratification. The changes seem least abrupt and disruptive in the Valley of Oaxaca. In the Late Early Preclassic Period, this area shows the strongest indications of the trends that characterize the Early Middle Preclassic—trends toward larger settlements, increasing specialization, and social stratification. Here too are the strongest hints of the residence of a foreign elite group. This suggests that one new feature of the Early Middle Preclassic horizon was the introduction of foreign Olmec people from the Gulf coast, causing considerable disruption in those areas in which they had not formerly been resident or present in force. Such a movement of people might be related to the events responsible for the massive disruption at San Lorenzo Tenochtitlán at the end of the Early Preclassic; large-scale population movements need not have been involved.

In any event, the economic network supplying the Gulf coast continued to function in the Early Middle Preclassic period. La Venta exploited iron-ore sources in the Isthmus of Tehuantepec for its concave mirrors; serpentine and schist were imported from the same area. Obsidian from distant sources, including Pachuca and El Chayal, also traveled to La Venta (Jack and Heizer 1968; Stross et al. 1968; Pires-Ferreira 1975; 1976b). Chalcatzingo became an important center for the manufacture and distribution of obsidian, iron ore, kaolin, and perhaps serpentine products (Grove et al. 1976). Again, perishable products were probably important. Cacao is a prime possibility; it was very important in Soconusco and the Pacific slope in Postclassic times. Cacao was also an important product in parts of the southern Gulf coast at the time of the Spanish conquest, particularly in Tabasco on the eastern fringe of the Olmec heartland. With the exception of highland areas, the distribution of Olmec monumental art corresponds closely to important cacao-producing zones. Salt is another possible export from Soconusco (Thompson 1956; Coe 1961: 15–19; Bergmann 1969; Parsons and Price 1971).

A new and extremely important component of the exchange network is jade, which was as highly prized by the Olmecs as by later Mesoamerican peoples. An Olmec jade source was probably located in the highlands of Guerrero, most likely in the Middle Balsas region. Central Mexican Olmec monumental art occurs only around the Balsas basin in Guerrero and Morelos, and more Olmec jade objects have been found in Guerrero than in all the rest of Mexico. In the Balsas region, particularly the Teloloapan-Iguala zone, antiquities forgers today use the very blue-green and blue-gray jade favored by the Olmecs. Isolated Olmec jades have been found in the southeastern lowlands, but the jade trade was not nearly so significant as in central Mexico. A minor jade route may have linked the Gulf coast and southeastern lowlands with Costa Rica. Unworked jade, waste material from the working of blue-green jade, and finished Olmec jades have been found in northern Costa Rica (Balser 1964; Stirling 1964; Easby 1968; Haberland 1969: 358; Parsons and Price 1971).

The relationship between the Gulf coast and the rest of Mesoamerica intensifies during the Early Middle Preclassic period. The Olmec Whiteware horizon is more uniform, more pervasive, and more prominent. More specifically Olmec stylistic features are associated with it—ceramics and associated luxury goods including jade ornaments and figurines, monumental Olmec art, and aspects of Gulf-coast ceremonialism. The Early Middle Preclassic upsurge in temple platform construction at Izapa and Chalchuapa, and especially the pyramids and jade offerings at San Isidro and Los Naranjos, suggest a sharing of Gulf-coast Olmec ceremonial patterns.

The mound and plaza complexes in the Valley of Oaxaca have precisely the same orientation as the ceremonial complex of La Venta, suggesting an extraordinarily close relationship. The two areas shared not just items of material culture, but also patterns of esoteric knowledge and ceremonial symbolism. This is more than the imitation of status trappings, and it is almost impossible to escape the conclusion that Olmecs, people intimately identified with the La Venta elite group, people from the Gulf coast, were living in parts of the central highlands. The first constructions with this orientation appear in the late San José phase, reinforcing the suggestion that this pattern began earlier in the Valley of Oaxaca than elsewhere, in the Terminal Early Preclassic period.

Olmec monumental art outside the Gulf coast leads irresistibly to the same conclusion. It not only represents the style of La Venta Olmec art but also follows precisely the same canons of attribute combination. The similarities are so close that Joralemon (1971) feels able to identify, on the basis of attribute clusters, the same deities in the Olmec art of La Venta. This complex system, a symbolic language, is probably the best indicator of cultural unity, other than a true writing system, that can be preserved in the archaeological record.

The content of monumental Olmec art supports the same conclusion. Relief carvings emphasize secular themes—Olmec identity coupled with prestige and authority. It is difficult to avoid the conclusion that they are public statements of the political power and cultural distinctiveness of a dominant foreign elite group. The cave paintings at Juxtlahuaca and Oxtotitlán echo the dominance/subordinance theme, although less emphatically, and they also suggest shared aspects of Olmec ceremonialism. Both Proskouriakoff (1971: 148) and Clewlow (1974: 139–41, table 20) have reached very similar conclusions about the stylistic similarities, secular content, and dating of these Olmec reliefs.

There is a fascinating ethnographic parallel to this emphasis on ethnic identity among traders in Africa (Cohen 1969). The Hausa operate an elaborate long-distance economic network centered on cattle and kola nuts, which involves their residence in enclaves among the Yoruba. The key to the operation of the network, in the absence of sophisticated banking and credit mechanisms, is an extreme emphasis by the Hausa traders on their ethnic identity and their distinctiveness from the Yoruba, which is marked both outwardly and privately, by dress and religious observances for example. It facilitates the movement of goods over long distances on the basis of trust stemming from group membership.

These several lines of evidence suggest that an Olmec group, involved in extensive exchange relations, enjoyed great prestige. The Olmec apparently resided in a number of regions outside the Gulf coast; in at least a few areas they acquired political power and exercised authority. The Aztec *pochteca,* with whom Olmec merchants have been compared, played political as well as economic roles. They sometimes served as agents for the Triple Alliance, facilitating the extension of Aztec political control in the areas in which they did business, transforming trade into tribute. Aztec "colonists" often resided in and partly controlled trade enclaves (Chapman 1957; Sahagún 1959; Coe 1965b: 122–3). Most of the commodities of the Olmec economic network for which there is direct evidence flowed *into* the Gulf coast zone, although undoubtedly many items have left no trace in the archaeological record. The distribution of the most elaborate manifestations of the Olmec Whiteware horizon corresponds remarkably well with areas in which valuable raw materials were available, especially Morelos and the Balsas basin (jade, iron ores, kaolin).

The validity of this analogy does not depend upon the existence of an Olmec empire comparable to the Aztec empire. The possibility of an Olmec empire based upon military force has been raised (Caso 1965; Coe 1965c: 771), but there is no evidence of wholesale military conquest by Olmecs from the Gulf coast. In only a few areas are there indications of some political control by a foreign Olmec group. In areas where the Olmec Whiteware horizon is not so prominent, such as coastal Guerrero, Flannery's foreign-imitation hypothesis is the most plausible, as it is for most Olmec Blackware-horizon occupations.

Nevertheless, militarism or force may have played a role in the establishment of enclaves of Olmec political power. The disruption that marked the appearance of the Whiteware horizon, as well as the pervasiveness and uniformity of the horizon, do suggest coercion. The possibility that militarism was a factor in the Olmec economic network in the Early Middle Preclassic period, as it was in connection with Postclassic trade and commerce, cannot be eliminated.

Olmec political domination of localized areas, in connection with a network for the procurement of valuable commodities available only in restricted areas outside the Gulf-coast heartland, recalls strategies for the control of natural resources in the Andes. Such strategies, which Murra (1968; 1972) has discussed in terms of "verticality," typically involve transhumance or "archipelagos," in which small groups reside away from their home communities to exploit locally available resources or to take advantage of different climatic conditions to raise desired crops. In large-scale political entities such as the Lupaqa kingdom, verticality operated on a vast scale; the kingdom consisted of a central core and an archipelago of enclaves in distant areas (up to 250 km.), all of which were thought of as integral parts of Lupaqa territory and were settled by Lupaqa from the core area. These islands or oases functioned successfully as colonies despite their distance from the political center and despite the necessity to traverse intervening areas not under Lupaqa control, which may even have been hostile.

This is not entirely different from Mesoamerican "ports of trade" enclaves, in some of which Aztec colonists exercised a degree of political control. Some such zones were annexed to the Aztec territorial state through the machinations of the *pochteca,* who operated outside the normal Aztec market system, procuring luxury goods and exotic raw materials for the use of, and redistribution by, the emperor. This might even represent a survival from an early period, when nonmarket redistributive systems were more important in Mesoamerica, as they always were in the Andes (Chapman 1957; Sahagún 1959; Coe 1965b: 122–3).

The archipelago pattern was very widespread in the Andes. The Lupaqa example demonstrates that a large-scale political entity can successfully control distant local areas with valuable resources, inhabited by people from the core area, without maintaining a territorially continuous empire by military force. The basic features of the Lupaqa pattern are remarkably consistent with the Mesoamerican pattern of evidence indicating enclaves of Olmec political control, in which at least a dominant group from the Gulf coast resided, and which served as nodes in an economic network for the procurement of valuable commodities for Gulf-coast centers.

Olmec Civilization

The emergence of the great Olmec centers at San Lorenzo Tenochtitlán and La Venta and the spread of the Olmec horizons far beyond the Gulf-coast lowlands herald the appearance of the first truly complex culture in Mesoamerica. Whether or not the scale and complexity of Olmec culture make it a civilization is a question that has provoked continuing sometimes acrimonious debate. Many of the important features of Olmec culture, and what can be reconstructed of the complex processes involved in its emergence, are comparable to those associated with pristine civilizations in other parts of the world. This is particularly true of the pattern of evidence associated with the spread of the Olmec outside the core area, and the implications of this pattern for the structure and organization of Olmec society. The scale, complexity, and early chronological position of Olmec culture require that it be taken into account in any consideration of the emergence of complex society in Mesoamerica.

In the evolutionary view, Olmec culture is often said to represent a chiefdom level of sociopolitical organization. In contrast to civilizations, chiefdoms are characterized by ranking rather than true social stratification, by the absence of clearly defined social classes, and by leaders who lack "formal delineation of power and coercive techniques of political control" (Fried 1960; Service 1962; Sanders and Price 1968: 42–5, 53, 139). Much of the discussion of the emergence of complex culture in Mesoamerica revolves around this civilization/chiefdom contrast.

Since chiefdoms are nearly as complex as civilizations and represent the immediately preceding evolutionary stage, even those who are convinced of the reality of the distinction find it difficult to make in practice (Sanders and Price 1968: 53, 115–16). Olmec culture qualifies as a civilization, even according to the criteria suggested by Sanders and Price (1968: 43, 52–3, 140), who set out to show that it is a chiefdom. Olmec centers in the heartland have monumental architecture (broadly defined, to include all large-scale public construction projects), which Sanders and Price consider the best indicator of social complexity. The scale of this construction activity implies "formal delineation of power and coercive techniques of political control." There are definite contrasts in scale and complexity among Olmec sites: the settlement pattern shows considerable site stratification, which is taken to indicate "true" social stratification. Differential access to and control of strategic resources on the part of the elite group—whether precious exotic raw materials and luxury goods or perhaps such crucial resources as the most productive agricultural land—typifies Olmec settlements (Coe 1969: 20; Flannery and Coe 1968: 282). This is another indicator of "true" social stratification, not a characteristic of chiefdoms. The procurement of valuable commodities involved a far-flung economic network, which emphasizes the organizational expertise and the prestige and authority and political power of the Olmec elite group.

The chiefdom/civilization contrast as outlined by Sanders and Price (1968) does not clarify the emergence of complex cultures in Mesoamerica and it is not helpful in comparing them with other pristine civilizations. It is impossible to make the crucial distinctions on the basis of archaeological evidence; for Sanders and Price, civilizations are simply larger-scale, more elaborate versions of chiefdoms. It is probably impossible to define a chiefdom/state dichotomy that would be useful in a prehistoric context, i.e. a qualitative distinction with archaeologically recognizable criteria.

A more useful definition of civilization would allow prehistoric cultures which meet the criteria to be identified archaeologically. This is not a trivial semantic issue but one that involves increased explicitness in hypotheses and conclusions. Distinguishing the essential features of a civilization from the archaeological markers for them should clarify the different kinds of evidence necessary to identify a civilization, to reconstruct its features and to recognize important processes involved in its emergence. Increased clarity and explicitness in these areas will increase our understanding of the development of complex culture in Mesoamerica and elsewhere.

An elaborate and powerful political organization is a prominent and vital characteristic of the various cultures that have been called pristine civilizations. The state is therefore a particularly suitable criterion, if the state is defined so that it is recognizable archaeologically.

Definitions of the state which involve legal constitution and integration through mechanisms of legitimized force (e.g. Service 1962: 173-4) are not useful in a prehistoric context. The state is better defined as an elaborate political organization with specialists who have sufficient authority and coercive power to exercise effective control over a large area; this involves the ability to manage the human and natural resources of an area on a long-term basis—extracting and restricting the use of precious natural resources, mobilizing and organizing the labor of substantial segments of the population, and probably monopolizing the most productive land.

Attempting to specify a minimum size for the area so controlled is not productive; it is as arbitrary as attempting to specify a population threshold for urbanism. Among pristine civilizations the area of effective centralized political control varies enormously. The city-state pattern of Early Dynastic Mesopotamia suggests that political control over a large area need not be centralized to the point that a nation-state can be recognized. Population size is more important than geographical area. In a state, political control encompasses multiple communities and a population substantially larger than would normally experience face-to-face interaction, whether people are densely concentrated in an urban environment or widely dispersed. The cultural systems that accompany the state ensure that the larger area is organized into a single cultural or social system. In the case of a decentralized political system like that in Mesopotamia, the cultural and social mechanisms play a larger role, producing a cultural uniformity that embraces several politically independent units. The same may be true of the Classic Maya. Although states may typically include more than one ethnic group, in dominant/subordinate relationships (e.g. Patterson 1973: 91-2), this is not a necessary or universal feature.

The state so defined can be recognized archaeologically in features which indicate massive mobilization and organization of labor resources. Large-scale continuing construction activity—more broadly, public-works projects—are the best indicators, even if the precise amount of labor involved cannot be calculated. Sanders and Price (1968: 140) are correct in asserting that monumental architecture is a good index of social complexity. Monumental architecture and massive public works often have clear religious significance, and this has produced the impression that many early civilizations were dominated by religion and religious specialists (Willey 1962). Despite the undoubted religious aspects of many public works, their true significance is as indicators of the existence of the state.

Another marker is large-scale procurement of valuable commodities, especially from distant areas, and restriction of access to them to an elite ruling group. This also implies extreme social stratification and the existence of a class-like group, as does control of the most productive land by an elite group. Social stratification is inseparable from political power and the state, as Fried (1967) emphasizes. Many other features often associated with early civilizations are secondary to the state, or are difficult to recognize and use as defining criteria.

The state is the best defining feature for civilizations because it is important, and because it is the feature most likely to be identifiable in an archaeological context, since there are so many possible ways in which it may leave recognizable material traces. This definition does not preserve the distinctions between chiefdoms and civilizations or between ranking and social stratification. When such distinctions are based upon archaeological criteria they are totally arbitrary. It should not be disturbing that societies which some would classify as chiefdoms should be included with those universally recognized as civilizations. All are complex cultures.

Under this definition, the Olmec created the first civilization in Mesoamerica. Construction and public-works projects alone are enough to indicate a state. The massive scale of this activity at the heartland centers of San Lorenzo and La Venta provides vivid documentation of the power, authority, and organizational ability of the Olmec elite group at whose behest, under whose direction, and for whose benefit these projects were undertaken. Olmec leaders had vast human resources at their disposal. Given the non-urban dispersed settlement pattern of the Olmec heartland, the leaders must have exercised effective political control over very large areas. The public-works projects of San Lorenzo and La Venta were not sporadic, spontaneous bursts of activity, and they could not have been effectively organized by transient secular leaders on the basis of personal prestige. Transport of basalt from the Tuxtla mountains for hundreds of multi-ton monuments must have been a regular activity. The construction, enlargement, and resurfacing of the mound-plaza complexes must also have been nearly continuous; it was carried out in accordance with definite overall plans. This implies long-term effective political control and organization by what was doubtless a complex political leadership. It also implies that authority and power and organizational functions were institutionalized so that continuity in planning was maintained over the several or many generations spanned by construction projects. These political functions were incorporated into specialists' roles, although they may also have had religious roles. The public-works activity may even have been cast principally in a religious context, and religion may have provided the source of the power and authority. As Willey (1962) argued, the great Olmec centers were surely sacred establishments, and the art that is concentrated in them served in part to symbolize a religion, which could have been a strong mechanism for unifying and expanding a dispersed social universe. But secular political institutions and specialists were involved as well.

San Lorenzo and La Venta are at least equivalent to Mesopotamian city-states in terms of the authority, power, and managerial skill exhibited by the ruling groups and the size of the labor force under their control. It is more difficult to determine whether either was the capital of a political entity on the scale of a nation-state. Both San Lorenzo and La Venta controlled valuable natural resources at considerable distances. The basalt of the Tuxtla Mountains was imported in enormous quantities at both centers; it was used exclusively for monumental art and architecture—by the elites. Other valuable commodities, particularly exotic raw materials for the manufacture of luxury goods, were procured from great distances through an economic network dominated by the heartland elite group. The flow of these commodities was overwhelmingly into the Gulf-coast area, and they were used by the heartland elite group (and in some cases, perhaps by external local elite groups who were imitating them). In at least some instances this led to the extension of La Venta's political control over the distant sources of these imports, but it is difficult to determine the extent of Olmec political control outside the Gulf-coast area.

Very thorough domination of large areas by militaristic empires may leave remarkably little trace in the archaeological record. In much of the vast area outside the Cuzco basin known to have been part of the Inca empire, identifiable traces of the Inca state are limited to administrative centers. In contemporary settlements under the control of these centers there are few traces of Inca domination, often not even traces of the Cuzco style in ceramics (Murra 1962; Morris and Thompson 1970; Morris 1972). The same is true for parts of the Aztec empire. Although the Aztecs exacted tribute from the Costa Grande area of Guerrero and exerted considerable political influence or military control in the area, the material record contains remarkably little that can be called Aztec (Barlow 1949; E. Brush 1968: 202-3). The series of frontier forts or outposts maintained by the Tarascans to counter Aztec expansion are identifiable only from ethnohistorical information. Their military function is reflected only in their strategic topographic locations; there are no actual fortifications and few identifiably Tarascan elements in the material culture (Gorenstein 1973).

Since the material traces of the Olmec outside the Gulf coast are so strong, the possibility of some militarism in connection with Olmec expansion must remain open, but there is no evidence suggesting militarism as a primary factor. The notion that coercion is the key element in the emergence of civilization and the state has a long history (Carneiro 1970); however, it is not a plausible hypothesis for the rise of Olmec civilization, except to the extent that power and coercion are always features of the state. Luxury goods and other commodities procured exclusively for the elite group are plain indicators of social stratification and also mark Olmec culture as a civilization. Procurement of such goods was evidently the primary function of the enormous heartland-centered economic network.

Since the flow was largely one way, the network itself presumably operated by virtue of political power and state institutions. It eventually stimulated and facilitated state expansion.

Differential access to valuable commodities certainly characterized Olmec civilization. Differential access to resources that sustain life, particularly land, is also fundamental to social stratification (Fried 1967). Differential access to the most productive land may have been a primary mechanism for the concentration of economic and political power, both in Mesoamerica (Flannery et al. 1967: 453-4; Flannery and Coe 1968: 282; Coe 1969: 20) and in other areas where early civilizations appeared (Flannery 1969: 92-4), but it is extraordinarily difficult to document archaeologically.

Intensive agricultural practices, especially irrigation, by exaggerating differential productivity may have an important role in reinforcing social stratification and the concentration of wealth and power. Irrigation has been emphasized again and again in discussions of the emergence of complex societies and state-level political organization in Mesoamerica. The "hydraulic society" approach has been extremely influential in the theoretical literature on the emergence of civilization (e.g. Wittfogel 1957; 1972; Sanders and Price 1968). Despite increasing evidence of the early importance of water-control technique in parts of highland central Mexico, irrigation certainly had no role in the emergence of Olmec civilization in the Gulf-coast lowlands. Even in Mesopotamia the scale and complexity of irrigation systems and their relationship to the growth of state institutions has been exaggerated; large-scale irrigation does not precede civilization and the state there (e.g. R. M. Adams 1962; 1969; Adams and Nissen 1972).

Increasing agricultural productivity and growing population and community size—based in part upon small-scale water-control techniques—may have facilitated the expansion of Olmec influence into central Mexico, but there is no evidence that agriculture in the Gulf-coast area was intensive. Evidence from other coastal lowland zones, particularly Soconusco, suggests a very old tradition of sedentism, in which wild-food resources continued to be of great importance after considerable cultural complexity had been achieved (Coe and Flannery 1964a; 1967). Any subsistence base that permits sedentary life permits, but does not cause, the emergence of complex societies. A striking illustration is the remarkable appearance of features usually associated with civilizations, particularly monumental public constructions, in coastal Peru at the end of the Preceramic period, before agriculture became the primary subsistence strategy (Lanning 1967: 57-79; Patterson 1971b; Moseley 1975). This level of cultural complexity evidently does not even require primary reliance upon food production, much less intensive agriculture or elaborate water control.

Urbanism has been emphasized even more than irrigation in discussions of early civilizations and their origins, to the extent that explaining the emergence of urban society is sometimes thought to account for the rise of civilization (e.g. R. M. Adams 1966; Sanders and Price 1968). No known Olmec center can be classed as urban if population density is taken as the key factor. The appearance of urbanism is largely irrelevant to the questions of the emergence of civilization in Mesoamerica and the nature of Olmec civilization.

There are hints that increasing population and settlement size in the central highlands may have conditioned Olmec expansion into this area. It is also true that centers such as San Lorenzo and La Venta were the focal points of large sustaining areas with substantial populations. They regularly drew in many people for public-works projects, ceremonial occasions, and other events. The economic network would have assured a continual influx of people as well as goods. People were exposed to the monumental art and architecture—visible public expressions of the prestige and authority of the elite ruling group. All of these factors must have reinforced social stratification and the centralization of political power. The regular influx of people also vastly increased opportunities for interaction and exchange of ideas as well as goods. Every indication is that this kind of interaction among people from different areas is crucial in the emergence of complex cultures.

A center with a small permanent population can function as a "magnet" (Mumford 1960) as effectively as a true city. Some Mesopotamian cities arose by actually pulling in the population of their hinterlands permanently (R. M. Adams 1972; Adams and Nissen 1972: 9–33). The same process operated at Teotihuacán (Parsons 1968). Other early civilizations which are often thought of as urban also show aspects of the "ceremonial"-center pattern. Shang cities were networks of settlements focused on political-economic-ceremonial nuclei where the elite ruling group resided, and where political and economic power was concentrated (Chang 1968: 240–1; Wheatley 1971).

Religion is a third factor that is often emphasized in interpretations of early civilizations. The notion that Olmec material outside the Gulf-coast heartland, particularly the prominent representations of the Olmec art style, reflects the spread of a religious cult is persistent (e.g. Willey 1962).

Patterson (1971a) discussed Chavín in precisely these terms, drawing an apt parallel between the spread of the Chavín style in the central Andes and the expansion of the art associated with early Christianity in the Mediterranean. Like the Olmec Blackware horizon, Chavín-related material spreads very rapidly over a wide zone outside the presumed core area around Chavín de Huantar. In contrast with Olmec art, however, the Chavín style coalesced from elements that were already current in various parts of the area over which the style later spread. It is not even possible to pinpoint the area in which this crystallization took place. The Chavín style is not really homogeneous—regional variation is apparent in each of the areas into which it spread. This is precisely what is to be expected of an art style that is the expression of a religious cult, especially one not expanding under the aegis of a powerful state. In each area it will be adopted and expressed differently, with different aspects emphasized and omitted; this is inevitably reflected in associated art as regionalization of the style. The material associated with the Olmec horizons everywhere represents a coherent Olmec style that is not comprised of a series of regionalized substyles. The Olmec expansion cannot be explained primarily in terms of proselytizing missionaries and an expanding religious cult.

Olmec centers and their monumental constructions are generally characterized as ceremonial, and they no doubt did have important ceremonial aspects (Willey 1962). They also reflect related political and economic systems; because of the economic bias of archaeological evidence, they are easier to interpret, or at least to discuss, in these terms. Undoubtedly, some Olmec art was produced and functioned in a religious or ceremonial context; it includes mythical and religious themes. Secular themes and functions related to political and economic systems can also be identified, particularly in the monumental art outside the heartland. These have been emphasized above.

Political, economic, and religious systems do not operate in isolated compartments. The secular functions of Aztec temples, images, and sacred bundles as symbols of the authority and sovereignty of political entities is a case in point. The intimate interrelationships of Aztec religion, world view, human sacrifice, warfare, political expansion, economy, and demography are striking. The economic importance of the temples in early Mesopotamian city-states is conspicuous (Deimel 1931; Falkenstein 1954; Diakonoff 1969). In central Peru during the Late Horizon, the oracle at Pachacamac was the center of an economic network— entirely independent of the Inca empire and its redistributive system—which brought in valuable commodities from as far away as northern Ecuador. There are hints that this may be a very old pattern in the Andes (Patterson 1973: 71-2). There is little doubt that religion was extremely important in early civilizations, permeating many cultural realms, but there is no evidence that they were theocracies. The role of religion in the processes of the emergence of civilization will always be more difficult to determine than the roles of economic and political factors, since the latter are so much more likely to be reflected in archaeological evidence.

Future research focusing on the elaborate Olmec economic network has a tremendous potential for throwing new light on the nature of Olmec civilization and its interaction with the rest of Mesoamerica. This would also be a productive approach to the problem of Olmec origins. It is already apparent that there were economic links between the Gulf coast and other areas of Mesoamerica before the emergence of a recognizable Olmec civilization (Cobean et al. 1971).

Economic interaction of major proportions led to a rapid upsurge in prosperity, population, and community size just at the time that civilization emerged in the coastal lowland zone. Maize agriculture was introduced from the highlands into the coastal lowlands, where the rich wild-food resources of closely spaced microenvironments, and perhaps a lowland tradition of root-crop agriculture, already permitted a certain degree of sedentism (Coe and Flannery 1964a; 1967; Flannery and Coe 1968). Economic interaction must have been accompanied by many kinds of communication and exchange. Economic networks are also important in other early civilizations and in the periods preceding their emergence (e.g.

Renfrew et al. 1966; Dixon et al. 1968; Patterson 1971b; 1973: 97). Exchange is often identified as the cause of increasing sociocultural complexity and political integration (e.g. Steward 1955).

Çatal Hüyük in Turkey (Mellaart 1967) is a suggestive example. Although it does not represent a civilization, its scale and complexity make it appear extremely anomalous for most theories on the origins of civilization. There is no hope of explaining Çatal Hüyük in terms of irrigation systems, but an economic network emphasizing local obsidian resources is a strong probability.

Systematic investigation of the early economic networks of Mesoamerica has a tremendous potential for clarifying crucial aspects of Mesoamerican culture history, and what may turn out to be general processes involved in the emergence of complex cultures.

Appendix 1. Atopula Ceramics

Analysis

The analysis of the ceramic complexes from Atopula is consistent with type-variety analysis as it has been elaborated for the description and classification of pottery from the Maya lowlands (Smith et al. 1960; Willey et al. 1967). This approach has been simplified on general grounds and because of the nature of the ceramic sample from Atopula.

A principal aim of the type-variety system is to encourage sufficient consistency in ceramic analysis and description so that units of data will be comparable from one site to another. While this goal must not be abandoned, slavish adherence to the complexities of the elaborated methodology, with no allowance for analytical flexibility, may produce categories that are needlessly complex or meaningless, or actually misrepresent the data.

Although types should be considered tools for the solution of space-time problems (Sears 1960), they must also function adequately as descriptive devices. If they do not, no independent evaluation of the conclusions reached by the analyst is possible, and others may find it difficult or impossible to use the ceramics in question for comparative purposes or for the solution of new and different problems. The remedies—reexamination of the ceramics themselves or the publication of separate detailed descriptions—are inefficient and expensive. Type-variety analysis, as long as it remains flexible, is the best compromise.

Strict analysis, in which types and varieties are treated as monothetic categories (Hammond 1972: 451-2), can produce misleading descriptions. The difficulties are pronounced when vessels combine two different kinds of decoration, when decoration is limited to certain parts of the surface area, or when variation in firing produces different colors on the same paste or slip.

More serious, this kind of classification departs from "reality" in the sense of approximating the cultural categories of the potters themselves. Types and varieties are often said to provide the best possible approximation of these categories (e.g. Smith et al. 1960); in fact, this is a subjective judgment. Plainly, a system in which sherds from a single vessel are placed in different categories is an imperfect reflection of the native categories. Michael Coe's (1961: 30) example of a jar from Illinois which embodies the features taken to be distinctive of four separate "types" is devastating.

The problem of assigning sherds from the same vessel to different types is extremely serious in the case of ceramic samples with few or no complete vessels, particularly when individual sherds are so small that few complete vessel profiles are represented. The potential inadequacy of rigid type-variety analysis may be illustrated by a hypothetical case: vessels of a particular paste and surface treatment which occur either as undecorated hemispherical bowls or as flat-based bowls with incisions encircling the rim. If sherds representing complete vessel profiles were not recovered, the flat bases would be described as characteristic of the undecorated type, in which they did not occur, and would be absent from the incised type, in which they occurred exclusively.

Treating units of ceramic analysis as polythetic categories (Hammond 1972: 451-2), in which no single attribute is either necessary or sufficient for group membership, has the effect of increased lumping and provides a partial remedy to the problem. Each attribute is characteristic of several types, which overlap one another in their constituent attributes. Subjectively this seems to provide a closer approximation of individual variation within a culturally patterned framework. On the other hand, it would be easy to go too far in this direction, and it is well to remember that it is difficult to split established categories (especially for someone other than the original analyst).

R. E. W. Adams (1971: 7) stresses the importance of flexibility in the application of the type-variety methodology and the desirability of adapting the system to the requirements of particular sites and particular ceramic samples. The methodology must be capable of accommodating the most complex possible situation, but only those distinctions demanded by the complexity of the ceramic sample in question need be made. As Sabloff and Smith (1969: 279) point out, when a ceramic sample is not amenable to categorization at the level of the type, the analysis need not proceed beyond the level of ceramic group or ware (for them, the level at which attributes of paste composition and surface finish are distinctive).

Drawbacks in type-variety analysis may become extremely severe when ceramic samples are small, when there are few whole or reconstructable vessels and few sherds representing full vessel profiles, and when there are few indications of decorative features or variation in vessel form. In these circumstances a purely modal analysis has sometimes been advocated as the best alternative.

Charles Brush (1969: 26-68), faced with a large ceramic sample with little decoration and minimal detectable variation in color, surface treatment, and vessel form, chose to concentrate on attributes, eschewing traditional typological analysis. A modal analysis ideally permits subsequent typological analysis by investigators who are not bound by a prior selection of a few diagnostic attributes (Rouse 1960: 318). This is possible only if the original modal analysis includes adequate tabulation of attributes and their associations. In fact, modal analysis is necessarily selective; modes are *significant* culturally determined attributes (Rouse 1960: 313-4; Sabloff and Smith 1969: 281). Despite extensive illustrations, tables, and verbal descriptions, Brush's selection of modes and presentation of the correlations among them make it difficult to use his pottery for intersite comparisons.

While a pure modal analysis may make the use of data for comparative purposes very difficult, modal and typological analyses are not mutually exclusive but complementary (Sabloff and Smith 1969). The typological approach necessarily involves the recognition of significant attributes (modes), since types are recurring combinations of attributes. In practice, most type-variety analyses make considerable use of modes, although not always explicitly. Determining the temporal boundaries of phases or defining temporal facets of complexes frequently depends as much upon changes in attributes as upon changes in types. Intersite comparison has almost always been approached in terms of shared modes (horizontal markers) (Willey et al. 1967: 305; Sharer and Gifford 1970: 458). Extremely detailed attribute analyses have permitted inferences and interpretations which could not have been based upon a typological approach alone—for example, in reconstructing aspects of prehistoric social organization (e.g. Deetz 1965; 1968; Hill 1966; 1970; Longacre 1970).

A modified type-variety approach is most appropriate for the ceramic sample from Atopula. The sample is rather small and it includes no complete vessels and few sherds that represent complete vessel profiles. In these circumstances the use of attributes of decorative techniques and vessel form as the primary criteria for classification at the level of type (Sabloff and Smith 1969: 278) would lead to ambiguities and distortions for the reasons noted above. Instead, the initial sorting units, and therefore ultimately the types, were defined in terms of the characteristics of the paste, surface treatment, and firing. This procedure has the advantage of permitting the largest possible proportion of the ceramic sample to be classified. Differential weathering is the only major factor that skews the proportional representation of the categories. In a system of analysis which emphasizes modes of vessel form, rim form, and decoration as primary criteria, skewing produced by such factors as differential breakage patterns can be quite serious.

This approach is identical in every respect (except terminologically) with the procedure advocated by Sabloff and Smith (1969: 279) for situations in which weathering and breakage militate against primary reliance on modes of decoration and vessel form in classification: namely, emphasis on the ceramic ware, which they define on the basis of attributes of paste and surface finish. It is equivalent to operating just above the level of the type and has the added advantage of restricting the proliferation of named types.

The Atopula pottery, like many Preclassic ceramic complexes, also exhibits what Coe (1961: 47) has called the "family effect." That is, there is a wide but fairly continuous range of variation in paste and surface characteristics, especially color. This situation was produced, as at La Victoria, by varying firing conditions on a few types of paste clays and slips. Even with the relatively small sample size and the typically small size of individual sherds, it quickly became apparent that paste and slip color varied considerably on individual vessels; many of the original sorting units had to be combined into a relatively small number of final types. Even so, there remains considerable overlap among types, as is to be expected with polythetic categories. The formal type descriptions define this variability and overlap, as well as the typical attribute combinations.

The guiding principle in the classification is not an abstract notion of what class of attributes ought to be primary in distinguishing types (e.g. Sabloff and Smith 1969: 278), but rather an attempt to produce a set of types which minimizes the possibility of sherds from a single vessel being classified in different types. Thus the amount of variability present on individual vessels sets a lower limit to the amount of variability within a type. In practice this is approximated by the range of variation detected on individual sherds. The upper limit remains arbitrary. Emphasis on the variation present on individual vessels need not be restricted to such special situations as at Atopula; the vessel is one prehistoric cultural category that can be recognized with certainty. The possibility that this approach might produce types that embrace different amounts of variation at different sites is not necessarily a drawback—if this were the case, it might prove to be a fact of cultural significance.

The "special" features of the Atopula ceramic sample are not really unusual for Preclassic, especially Early Preclassic, ceramic complexes in Mesoamerica. Pottery frequencies and densities are typically quite low. For example, fewer than 15,000 sherds were recovered from MacNeish's (1954: 553, chart 1) excavations near Panuco; Piña Chán's (1955a: 44; 1958a: 35, 70, tables 1, 2) stratigraphic excavations at Tlatilco, Atoto, and Chalcatzingo; Cerro Chacaltepec (Grove 1968b); several of the Early Preclassic complexes from Tehuacán (MacNeish et al. 1970: 3-6, table 6); Altamira (Green and Lowe 1967: 81, tables 2-6, 9-16); and the Mound 30a excavations at Izapa (Ekholm-Miller 1969: 23). Although it is difficult to determine the precise volume of earth moved in each case, the pottery densities, not just total sherd frequencies, are low. Analyses of Early Preclassic ceramic complexes have been useful and important, despite very small sample sizes. Ekholm-Miller's (1969: 23) classification of Izapa pottery is based on 3500 sherds, and Dixon's (1959: 4, 19) analysis of Cotorra- and Dili-phase pottery from Chiapa de Corzo is based on 2224 sherds. The most striking examples are the Purrón complex, established on the basis of 127 sherds, and the Barra complex, based on very few more (Green and Lowe 1967: 56, 97-104; MacNeish et al. 1970: 21).

The small size of ceramic samples in Early Preclassic components has not been emphasized, presumably because of the importance of the notable exceptions: La Victoria (Coe 1961), Salinas La Blanca (Coe and Flannery 1967), San Lorenzo Tenochtitlán (Coe 1968b, 1970). In view of the much larger size of many Middle Preclassic ceramic samples, even from comparable exposures in the same areas or sites (e.g. MacNeish et al. 1970: table 6), it may be that the low frequencies of ceramics in Early Preclassic components are culturally significant. It is not exclusively a function of small exposures, although this may be a factor in some cases.

Earlier Preclassic ceramic assemblages deserve detailed ceramic analyses despite their small size. Types established on the basis of samples that do not perfectly reflect the full range of variation in the ceramic complexes need not become fossilized in the literature. Type-variety analysis is not intended to create immutable categories; on the contrary, types should remain in flux, being continuously redefined, expanded, or narrowed, as knowledge of the ceramic history of an area is refined (Smith et al. 1960: 336-7).

Most Early Preclassic ceramic complexes have been described in a modified type-variety framework, perhaps because of small sample size and the "family effect." Almost all Early Preclassic ceramic types (and, outside the Maya lowlands, Middle Preclassic types as well) have been defined on the basis of characteristics of paste, firing, and surface treatment. This is the best argument for adopting a similar approach in the analysis of the ceramics from Atopula. Analysis of ceramic complexes from an archaeologically unknown zone like Guerrero must in the first place contribute to the establishment of a chronological framework. A basically taxonomic approach is best suited to solving such chronological problems. Maximum compatibility with the descriptive and taxonomic frameworks that have been applied to contemporary complexes from nearby areas is essential.

Type Descriptions

The descriptions of pottery types which follow include those visual features and physical characteristics that could be readily determined without elaborate equipment. Much of the same data is presented in the accompanying tables and charts.

A full description of each type is given under the phase in which it first appeared (even though this may not be the phase in which it reached its highest frequencies). Types that continue to be manufactured in later phases also have abbreviated entries in the corresponding sections, in which new or changed features are catalogued. Type names consist of a local geographical name from the Atopula area combined with a descriptive term (or terms).

Paste and Surface

The terms used to describe the colors of the pastes and slips are those of the Munsell system (Munsell Color Co., Inc. 1954). The Munsell numerical notation corresponding to each color name appears after it, in parentheses. The determination is given to the nearest color chip, as no greater accuracy was thought to be possible (or desirable). In most cases the colors represented on a single vessel are far from uniform. No attempt has been made to give a value for every shade; the designations given represent the dominant colors and the normal range of variation.

Hardness of the pastes was estimated by means of a mineral scratch-test kit, and the designation is given according to the Mohs scale. Pastes and tempering materials were examined with a hand lens. The tempering material is quite uniform among the major types represented at Atopula. Particles of quartz, mica, and whitish particles of limestone or calcite, and occasionally other shiny black or red mineral particles, are recognizable; this tempering material is designated for convenience "quartziferous sand." The homogeneity of tempering material probably is the result of the use of one, or perhaps two, local clay sources naturally rich in aplastic particles (such as decomposing granite or tufaceous sediment). The Preclassic potters of La Victoria and Salinas La Blanca almost certainly used naturally tempered clays of this sort, as do modern potters on the coast of Guerrero (Coe and Flannery 1967: 21-2; C. Brush 1969: 134). Under these circumstances, trade sherds are easily distinguished from locally manufactured pottery. The size of temper particles is approximated according to the Wentworth scale (Shepard 1965: 118). The porosity of the paste was simply estimated.

Form Terminology

The terms used to describe vessel form are common ones in the literature on Mesoamerican ceramics. Where multiple terms are available for the same shape, those used by David Grove (1968b: 43-8) in his description of ceramics from Morelos have generally been adopted. The close ties between the Preclassic ceramic assemblages of Morelos and northeastern Guerrero make descriptive compatibility highly desirable.

The terms "restricted" and "unrestricted" are applied to vessel mouths rather than to whole vessels. Restricted orifices refer to converging walls at the rim, and unrestricted orifices to vertical or expanding walls at the rim.

The categories of vessel form follow.

TECOMATE. Globular neckless jar with restricted, generally small orifice; body roughly hemispherical, with uniformly convex wall. (Also called seed jar, neckless olla.) Should be distinguished from incurved-rim bowl.

DEEP TECOMATE. Globular neckless jar with restricted, generally small orifice; tall and deep rather than hemispherical; upper vessel wall more strongly convex. Close to Mode 17 and 17A tecomate forms in the Tehuacán Valley (MacNeish et al. 1970: fig. 5).

OLLA. Jar with flaring or vertical neck and unrestricted orifice above globular body; may have sharp break in curvature at or near neck–body junction. (Also called necked jar.)

OPEN BOWL. Unrestricted orifice and outslanting wall, straight or slightly concave; often relatively shallow, with flat base. Grove (1968b: 44-5) includes this shape in his "flaring-wall bowl" category.

FLARING BOWL. Unrestricted orifice and strongly concave or flaring wall; usually relatively shallow, with flat base.

CONVEX BOWL. Simple, uniformly convex wall; orifice unrestricted or very slightly restricted, but not incurved. (Also called simple bowl, simple-silhouette bowl.)

INCURVED-RIM BOWL. Restricted orifice and convex wall; intermediate between tecomate and convex bowl.

BEAKER. Relatively deep vessel with unrestricted orifice and flat base; wall straight, vertical or more commonly very slightly outslanting. (Also called cylindrical bowl, cylindrical jar.)

COMPOSITE-SILHOUETTE BOWL. Upper wall slants sharply inward (or outward) above sharp break in curvature.

BOTTLE. Vessel with narrow neck and mouth (unrestricted) above globular body. (Also called *botellon*.)

MOLCAJETE. Unrestricted bowl with ring base or supports and deep incision on interior base; functioned as a grater bowl.

Auxiliary features. 1. Lug or slab handle: wide flattened projection on exterior of vessel, presumably a handle. 2. Loop handle: roughly semicircular, round in cross-section, attached to exterior of vessel. 3. Strap handle: roughly semicircular, flattish to elliptical in cross-section, attached to exterior of vessel.

Lip forms are described according to the following modes. 1. Rounded. 2. Blunted; slightly to moderately flattened but still rounded. 3. Beveled; straight, with sharp edges. 4. Tapered. 5. Thickened interior; slight swelling to "comma-shaped." 6. Thickened exterior; slight swelling to incipient bolster. 7. Bolstered; rounded projection or flange. 8. Everted; turned sharply outward and thickened, flat to very slightly rounded.

Plastic Decorative Techniques

The major categories used in the description of decoration by plastic surface alteration follow.

INCISION. Narrow (up to 3 mm.) linear designs cut into surface of vessel before firing. Edges smooth or ragged, depending whether incision done while paste was still plastic or had partially dried.

GROOVING. Broad incision; always smooth, regular, and relatively shallow—done while paste was plastic.

EXCISION. Broad bands or zones carved out of surface of vessel before firing but after paste was partially dry. Edges and bases of these zones always ragged and slightly irregular.

MOLCAJETE BASE. Deep incision on interior base of bowl (usually flattened); often in form of multiple parallel straight lines. Base interior generally quite worn, indicating actual use as grater.

PSEUDO-GRATER FONDO. Relatively shallow incision on interior base of bowl (usually flattened); frequently in patterns such as the so-called sunburst motif (Coe 1961: 67), rather than simple parallel lines. These look like ornamental rather than strictly functional designs, but they are sometimes worn, showing actual use as graters.

Comparisons

Comparisons with other ceramic complexes are made in terms of both types and modes (generally modes of decoration). Ceramics from neighboring areas, such as Morelos and the Tehuacán Valley, are compared in terms of paste characteristics as well as features of surface treatment, form, and decoration. Comparisons with more distant areas emphasize the latter features.

Appendix 2. The Preclassic Pottery of Atopula

Pottery Types of the Cacahuananche Phase

Tlapala Red (Fig. 12)

Paste. Relatively porous; hardness near 2.5. Temper coarse, a few very coarse inclusions, composed of the usual quartziferous sand, predominantly quartz crystals and occasional yellow plates of mica. Paste typically oxidized to light red (2.5 YR 6/6-8) near surface, dark reddish gray to dusky red (10 R 3/1-2) core. Walls sometimes oxidized near exterior surface, interiors remain dusky red. In less completely oxidized examples, areas near surface are fired red (10 R 5/6-8; 2.5 YR 5/6-8). In occasional firing variation, a portion of vessel partially oxidized to red or light red near exterior surface, elsewhere reddish gray to dusky red throughout.

Surface. Slip applied to well-smoothed exterior surface, sometimes over lip onto upper interior wall (esp. deep tecomates). Slip typically oxidized, firing to red (10 R 5/6-8; 2.5 YR 5/6-8) or light red (2.5 YR 6/6). Less completely oxidized vessels, or portions of, are darker (10 R 4/6-8, or rarely 10 R 3/6). Slip usually polished, but seldom exhibits high luster; tends to adhere poorly to vessel surface and frequently almost eroded away. Bagre Coarse, the residual unslipped category, presumably includes many eroded examples of Tlapala Red. Weathering may also account for absence of lustrous surface. Unslipped surfaces, exclusively tecomate body interiors, coarse and pitted and grainy from protruding temper particles. Few indications of attempts to smooth these surfaces, but occasionally unslipped upper interior walls were smoothed with a soft, yielding material (hand, fabric?) while paste was plastic.

Form. Wall thickness 8–12 mm., typically 9–10 mm.

TECOMATE. Diameter 15–17 cm. Overall vessel shape roughly hemispherical. Base form unknown, presumably rounded. Lip form: beveled or thickened interior.

DEEP TECOMATE. Diameter 6–10 cm. Overall shape not hemispherical or flattened (pumpkin-shaped) as is typical tecomate: vessel relatively deep. Lower wall may even be nearly vertical, with upper wall more strongly convex (occasionally with break in curvature). Rim occasionally turned upward, forming very low "collar." Base form unknown. Lip form: blunted or thickened interior.

Decoration

GROOVING. 1. Pair of broad shallow slightly curving grooves intersecting to form "V" shape, on upper exterior of one tecomate. Pre-slip grooves quite smooth and regular and made while paste was plastic.

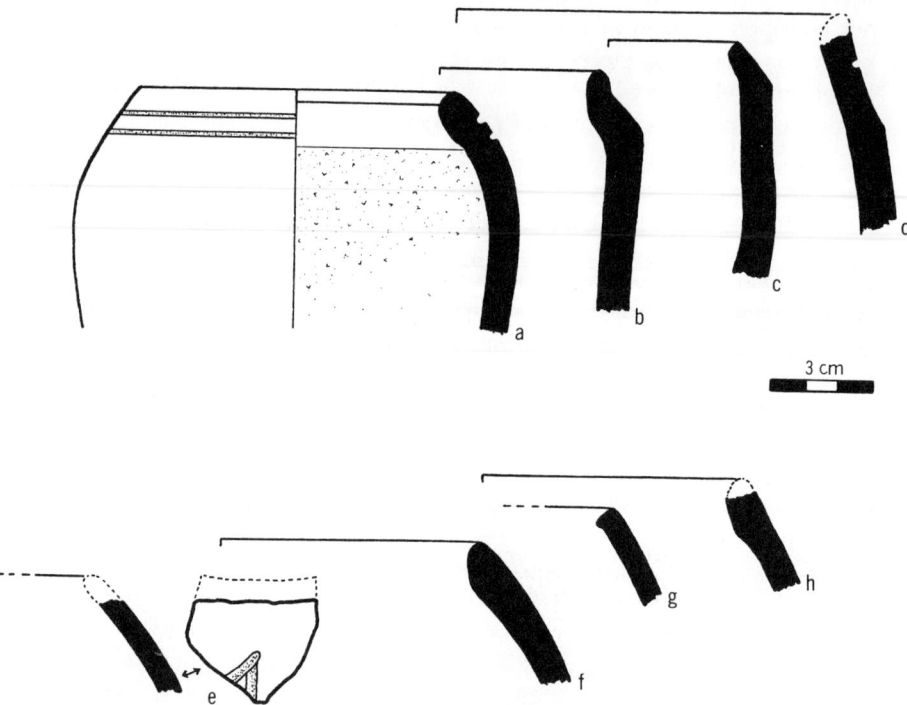

Fig. 12. Tlapala Red pottery, Cacahuananche phase: *a–d*, deep tecomates; *e–h*, tecomates.

INCISION. 1. One or two lines encircling exterior of deep tecomates just below and parallel to rim. Pre-slip incisions shallow and quite smooth and done while paste was plastic. May be firm and regular or somewhat erratic, as though done with a wavering hand.

Comparative material

TEHUACÁN VALLEY. Ajalpan Coarse Red of the Ajalpan phase quite similar in paste, surface treatment, and thickness, although Tlapala Red is slightly darker, less completely oxidized, and has true slip rather than a wash. Tecomate shape occurs in Ajalpan Coarse Red (at least in the Late Ajalpan phase). Most common Tlapala Red form (deep tecomate) similar to ellipsoidal tecomate shape of Ajalpan Coarse, which also has similar paste characteristics but lacks red wash. Ajalpan Coarse diagnostic of the Ajalpan phase, and most popular in Early Ajalpan. One sherd of Ajalpan Coarse Red ellipsoidal tecomate found in a Late Ajalpan level. Ajalpan Coarse Red has no decoration besides red wash, but a few aberrant Late Ajalpan sherds with paste like Ajalpan Coarse have incised lines encircling vessel exteriors and curvilinear grooving or wide-line incision on vessel exteriors (MacNeish et al. 1970: 26–9, 41–2, 51, figs. 10, 20, 26, tables 14, 18).

SOCONUSCO. Mapache Red-rimmed and Ocós Specular Red of Ocós and Cuadros phases at La Victoria and Salinas La Blanca generally similar in surface treatment and form, although slip of Tlapala Red is not specular and not confined to band at rim. Deep tecomate form not precisely duplicated, but Ocós-phase examples of both types are closer than Cuadros-phase Mapache Red-rimmed tecomates. Incised lines encircling upper vessel exteriors occur in both types, but other decoration (punctation, pattern-burnishing) of Cuadros-phase Mapache Red-rimmed tecomates not in Tlapala Red (Coe 1961: 50-1, figs. 14-17; Coe and Flannery 1967: 26, fig. 9, pl. 12). Cotán Grooved Red of Barra and Ocós phases at Altamira includes tecomates with oblique grooving, encircling incision, upturned lips. Ocós Specular Red and Michis Thin Tecomate types of Izapa-Ocós and Altamira-Ocós phases also similar, as is Mapache Red-rimmed of Izapa-Cuadros and Altamira-Cuadros phases, again excepting rows of punctations. Deep tecomate form duplicated in one Early Preclassic Negruzco Coarse vessel (Green and Lowe 1967: 97-100, 104-6, 112, figs. 22, 72, 77, 78, 85; Ekholm-Miller 1969: 27-9, 47-8, figs. 19, 36, 37).

CENTRAL CHIAPAS. The "Unslipped" category of the Cotorra phase at Chiapa de Corzo includes similar tecomate forms with encircling incision and red paint or slip, although usually confined to limited areas such as rim band (Dixon 1959: 16-17, figs. 19, 52). Closely related Cotorra-phase occupations of Santa Marta rock shelter and Padre Piedra characterized by tecomates with encircling incision and grooving and red paint, again generally confined to rim band (Navarrete 1960: 23, 24, fig. 22; MacNeish and Peterson 1962: 32, 33, pl. 6; Green and Lowe 1967: 43, fig. 52). At Santa Cruz, very similar tecomates are classified as Burrero Red, which may pertain to the Burrero period, aligned with the Dili phase, or to an earlier undefined occupation contemporary with the Cotorra phase (Sanders 1961: 17, fig. 16).

CENTRAL HIGHLANDS. In the Valley of Mexico, red-rimmed tecomates occur at Ayotla (Tlapacoya) in Ayotla and Justo subphases of the valley-wide Ixtapaluca phase. Red-slipped tecomates in the Iglesia subphase (initial Zacatenco phase) at Tlatilco; very similar polished red-slipped tecomates, including forms resembling the deep tecomate with incision encircling rim, in Tlatilco graves (Piña Chán 1958a: 35, 36, 48, 85, figs. 8, 16, 41, cuadro 2; MacNeish et al. 1970: 277). Tecomates with red slip or paint, usually confined to rim band, in Tierras Largas and San José phases in the Valley of Oaxaca (esp. at Tierras Largas and San José Mogote) (Flannery 1968: 82; MacNeish et al. 1970: 270).

GULF COAST. A few red-slipped tecomate-like vessels included in the Heavy Plain category of the Ponce phase in northern Veracruz (MacNeish 1954: 571, fig. 17, charts 2, 5). Tecomate form, including examples with red slip or red-painted zone, common in Trapiche I period at El Trapiche and Chalahuite. One form very similar to the deep tecomate of Tlapala Red (García Payón 1966: 95-9, láms. 36, 37; MacNeish et al. 1970: 273). Red-slipped tecomates with encircling incision occur in Chicharras and San Lorenzo phases at San Lorenzo Tenochtitlán, and red-slipped and red-rimmed ones in earlier Ojochi and Bajío phases there and in Squier's "pre-Complex A" material from La Venta (Coe 1970: 21-7; MacNeish et al. 1970: 279).

COASTAL GUERRERO. Tecomates are dominant form in Pox, Uala, and Tom periods at Puerto Marqués and Zanja; are often red-slipped and, esp. in Uala period, often bear one or two encircling incised lines. One tecomate variant is close to deep tecomate shape of Tlapala Red (C. Brush 1969: 57-8, 135, 144, figs. 6, 12, 21, table 8).

Remarks. Tlapala Red is never overwhelmingly common in terms of sherd counts or percentages, but is the most distinctive marker of the Cacahuananche phase. It continues to appear in early levels of the succeeding Atopula phase, but in minute quantities, and disappears entirely before the end of the Atopula phase. By Atopula times it is almost entirely superseded in popularity by Jiménez Red, to which it, or a firing variant, may be ancestral. Jiménez Red occurs in small quantities in Cacahuananche-phase levels as well. Tlapala Red and Jiménez Red are genetically related in that both are relatively thick, have a red-firing slip, and are manufactured from the same local clay and tempering materials (as is all locally manufactured pottery—virtually all the pottery recovered).

In a few cases, distinction between the two types is hard to draw, and assignment of some sherds to one or the other appears arbitrary, presumably reflecting incomplete divergence of the types in late Cacahuananche and early Atopula times. In general, however, the two types are easily distinguishable by surface treatment (Tlapala Red is polished, Jiménez Red is not), and firing (Jiménez Red slip is darker, reflecting a general trend toward less complete oxidation in Atopula-phase pottery). More striking is the total divergence in forms; the deep tecomate form appears only in Tlapala Red of the Cacahuananche phase. In terms of surface treatment (polishing), Tlapala Red seems to be ancestral to Guamuchil Polished Black, which first appears in Cacahuananche-phase levels. In the Atopula phase, as Tlapala Red disappears, Guamuchil Polished Black increases in popularity, and in the technical proficiency of its polish.

Jiménez Red (Fig. 13)

Paste. Relatively porous; hardness near 2.5, a few examples slightly harder (3.0). Temper coarse, occasional very coarse inclusions, is the usual quartziferous sand, predominantly quartz crystals and yellow mica plates, with a few small whitish particles of calcite or limestone. Paste typically incompletely oxidized: red (10 R 5/6-8; 2.5 YR 5/6-8) near surface, dark reddish gray to dusky red (10 R 3/1-2) core. Occasional vessels have limited areas near exterior surface oxidized to red, elsewhere less completely oxidized (dark reddish gray to dusky red) throughout.

Surface. Bowls almost always slipped on both surfaces; occasional convex bowls with unslipped interior may simply be worn grater bowls. Ollas generally have slip applied to exterior surface, often extending over lip to cover upper interior surface of flaring neck. Slip typically oxidized to red (10 R 4/6-8) or occasionally dark red (10 R 3/6). Slipped surfaces relatively well smoothed but rarely polished, and never a high luster. Like Tlapala Red, slip does not adhere well to surface, is

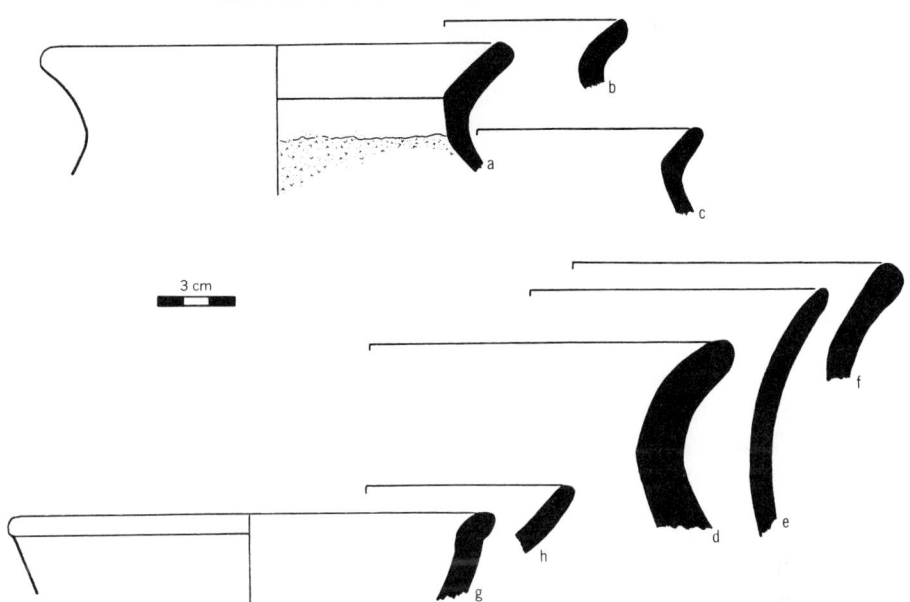

Fig. 13. Jiménez Red pottery, Cacahuananche phase: *a–f*, ollas; *g, h*, convex bowls.

often almost eroded away. Many eroded examples of Jiménez Red have undoubtedly been counted with the residual unslipped category, Bagre Coarse. Unslipped surfaces, almost exclusively body interior of ollas, coarse and pitted, and grainy from protruding temper particles. Usually no evidence of attempts to smooth surfaces, although occasionally unslipped upper interior of ollas were smoothed with a soft yielding material while paste was plastic.

Form. Wall thickness 8–19 mm., typically quite thick, 10–12 mm. Maximum thickness occurs in ollas at point of curvature change, where neck begins to flare.

OLLA. Diameter 14–28 cm. Exterior profile smooth; interior occasionally has very sharp break in curvature where neck flares strongly outward. Base form unknown, presumably rounded. Lip form: rounded, blunted, beveled, or slightly thickened exterior.

CONVEX BOWL. Diameter 16–20 cm. Wall uniformly convex. Base rounded. Lip form: blunted or thickened exterior.

Decoration. Limited to red slip in Cacahuananche phase.

Comparative material

TEHUACÁN VALLEY. Ajalpan Coarse Red of the Ajalpan phase quite similar in paste, surface treatment, and thickness, although Jiménez Red is darker, less completely oxidized, and has true slip rather than a wash. Ollas with flaring necks most common form in both types, and convex bowls a minor form in both—the only two shapes in Jiménez Red and Early Ajalpan-phase Ajalpan Coarse Red. Neither has decoration besides red slip or wash (MacNeish et al. 1970: 41–2, fig. 20, table 18).

SOCONUSCO. Similar surface treatment and wall thickness typical of Pacaya Red of Cuadros and Jocotal phases at Salinas La Blanca; olla most frequent form in this type; convex bowl occurs as minor form (Coe and Flannery 1967: 36–7, fig. 16). Tustlán Red of the Izapa-Ocós phase includes ollas and convex bowls; Tusta Red of the Barra phase at Altamira includes convex bowls (Green and Lowe 1967: 104, fig. 76; Ekholm-Miller 1969: 25–7, fig. 18).

CENTRAL CHIAPAS. Red-and-White Bichrome category of the Cotorra phase at Chiapa de Corzo includes slightly convex bowls with red slip, and one sherd of a red-slipped olla (Dixon 1959: 12–16, figs. 14, 15, 17). The closely related Burrero Red type of Santa Cruz also includes red-slipped convex bowls that may pertain to the Burrero period or to an earlier undefined occupation equivalent to the Cotorra phase (Sanders 1961: 17, fig. 16).

CENTRAL HIGHLANDS. Generally similar forms occur in Brown pottery of La Juana (Early Nexpa) phase in Morelos; true red-slipped pottery does not appear in quantity until the following San Pablo A (Middle Nexpa) phase (Grove 1972: 59, fig. 16). Ollas and convex bowls typical of Piña Chán's (1955a: 11, 17–18, láms. 4, 12) Café Rojizo and (to a lesser extent) Roja Pulida types, and of Cyphers' (1975) Montefalco Bichromes from Chalcatzingo (phase A). Red-slipped ollas and convex bowls occur in Gualupita I (Vaillant and Vaillant 1934: figs. 18, 24). Similar red-slipped convex bowls in the Iglesia subphase (initial Zacatenco phase) at Tlatilco, and found by *huaqueros* in Tlapacoya graves. These and red-slipped ollas in Tlatilco graves (Piña Chán 1958a: 35–6, 85, figs. 8, 45; Weaver 1967: 33, pl. 22). In the Matadamas complex of San José Mogote in the Valley of Oaxaca, forms limited to ollas and convex bowls, which may bear red slip. Coatepec Red-on-Buff is dominant type in the Tierras Largas phase, and includes ollas and esp. convex bowls with at least partial red slip, or red-painted zone. Red (unslipped) ollas and polished red-slipped bowls very common in the San José phase (Flannery 1968: 82; MacNeish et al. 1970: 46–9, 269–70, fig. 23).

GULF COAST. Very similar red-slipped ollas (Heavy Plain) common in Pavón and Ponce phases of northern Veracruz (MacNeish 1954: 567–9, 571, fig. 17, chart 2). Very similar ollas and a few slightly convex bowls with red slip (or red-painted zone) occur in Trapiche I at El Trapiche and Chalahuite (García Payón 1966: 95–9, láms. 4, 41, 42; MacNeish et al. 1970: 273). Red-slipped bowls at San Lorenzo Tenochtitlán from the Ojochi phase on; olla form does not appear until the Chicharras phase (Coe 1970: 21–5; MacNeish et al. 1970: 279).

COASTAL GUERRERO. Similar red-slipped ollas and convex bowls occur in Uala and Tom periods at Puerto Marqués and Zanja (C. Brush 1969: 137–8, 144–5, figs. 6, 13, 14, 22, 23, tables 3A, 3B, 8).

Remarks. Jiménez Red is distinctly a minority type in the Cacahuananche phase, achieving greatest popularity, with considerably greater diversity of forms and varieties of decoration, during the Atopula and Tecolotla phases, although never the most numerous type. Probably a descendant of Tlapala Red (see discussion above, under Tlapala Red).

Pozo Thin Red (Fig. 14)

Paste. Relatively porous; hardness generally near 2.5, a few examples reaching 3.5. Temper coarse to very coarse, with occasional granule-sized inclusions, is the usual quartziferous sand, predominantly quartz crystals and small yellow plates of mica. Paste usually oxidized throughout to red (2.5 YR 5/6); sometimes less completely oxidized to weak red (2.5 YR 5/2), esp. near interior surface. Presumably because of thin vessel walls there are no gray cores.

Surface. Exterior or both surfaces slipped; one bowl has slip on interior only. Slip typically fires to red (10 R 4/6-8, 2.5 YR 4/8), sometimes dark red (10 R 3/6, 2.5 YR 3/6) or dusky red (10 R 3/2, 2.5 YR 3/2) on incompletely oxidized examples. Occasional dark reddish gray (10 R 3/1) firing clouds. Slipped surfaces well smoothed, and slip is polished but seldom has high luster. Unslipped surfaces coarse with grainy texture from protruding temper particles, and generally show little attempt at smoothing. Occasional marks of scraping while paste was leather-hard—pits left by plucked-out temper particles or ridges left by a scraping tool. Single exception is a nondescript body sherd with both surfaces carefully smoothed, and a slip covering interior and part of exterior surface.

Form. Wall thickness 3–7 mm., typically quite thin, 4–5 mm.

TECOMATE. Diameter 8–9 cm. Overall shape hemispherical; wall uniformly convex. Base form unknown, probably rounded. Lip form: rounded or thickened exterior.

OLLA. Diameter 15–17 cm. Small jar with everted to flaring neck. Exterior profile smooth; interior may have sharp break in curvature where neck begins

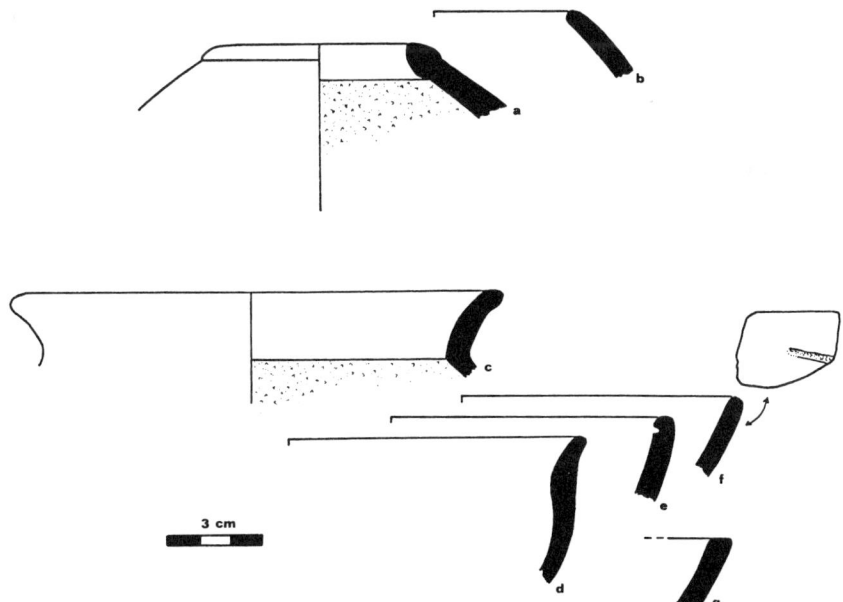

FIG. 14. Pozo Thin Red pottery, Cacahuananche phase: *a, b*, tecomates; *c*, olla; *d–g*, convex bowls.

to flare outward. Base form unknown, presumably rounded. Lip form: rounded or slightly blunted.

CONVEX BOWL. Diameter 18–20 cm. Lower wall uniformly convex; upper wall occasionally curves outward slightly near lip. Base rounded. Lip form: rounded, blunted, beveled, or everted.

Decoration

INCISION. 1. One or two lines encircling interior of convex bowls just below and parallel to rim. Pre-slip incisions shallow, smooth, and regular and done while paste was plastic. 2. Single oblique incision on upper exterior of one convex bowl. Pre-slip incision has slightly rough edges made after paste was partially dry.

Comparative material

TEHUACÁN VALLEY. Ajalpan Fine Red of the Ajalpan phase is quite similar in paste, surface treatment, and thickness, although Pozo Thin Red has nonspecular red slip rather than specular "streaky red wash"; both are polished. Convex bowls common in both types, and small ollas and tecomates occur in both as minor shapes. Ajalpan Fine Red has no decoration other than red wash, but a few examples of Coatepec Buff and Red-on-Buff and a few Late Ajalpan aberrant sherds have incised lines encircling vessel exterior. The only major difference: Ajalpan Fine Red is a minority type in Tehuacán; Pozo Thin Red is a major type at Atopula (MacNeish et al. 1970: 31–3, 51, figs. 12, 26, table 16).

SOCONUSCO. Somewhat similar surface treatment and vessel form typical of Ocós Specular Red, Pacaya Red, and Mapache Red-rimmed (tecomates only) of Ocós and Cuadros phases at La Victoria and Salinas La Blanca. All have encircling incised lines and occasional oblique incision on upper vessel exterior (Coe 1961: 51–2, figs. 17–19; Coe and Flannery 1967: 26, 36, figs. 9, 16). Tustlán Red and Michis Thin Tecomate of Izapa- and Altamira-Ocós phases similar in surface treatment and form; Tustlán Red (convex) bowls have incised lines encircling interior or exterior (Ekholm-Miller 1969: 26–29, figs. 18, 19). Cotán Grooved Red and Tusta Red of the Barra phase at Altamira have similar forms (except ollas) and Tusta Red bowls have incisions encircling interior (Green and Lowe 1967: 97–100, 104–6, figs. 72, 73, 76, 78).

CENTRAL CHIAPAS. The Unslipped category of the Cotorra phase at Chiapa de Corzo includes tecomates with red paint or slip, although usually applied to limited areas. A few slightly convex bowls and one red-slipped olla neck occur in Cotorra-phase Red-and-White Bichrome (Dixon 1959: 12–17, figs. 14, 15, 17, 19, 52). The closely related Cotorra-phase occupations of Santa Marta rock shelter and Padre Piedra also include similar tecomates (Navarrete 1960: 23, 24, fig. 22, table 1; MacNeish and Peterson 1962: 32, 33, pl. 6; Green and Lowe 1967: 43, fig. 52). At Santa Cruz, similar tecomates and red-slipped convex bowls are included in Burrero Red, which may pertain to the Burrero period or an earlier undefined occupation contemporary with the Cotorra phase (Sanders 1961: 17, fig. 16).

CENTRAL HIGHLANDS. Polished red-slipped ollas and convex bowls, occasionally with encircling incised line, occur in Piña Chán's (1955a: 17–18, lám. 12) Roja Pulida type and Montefalco Bichromes (Cyphers 1975) from Chalcatzingo (phase A). Red-slipped ollas and convex bowls also in Gualupita I (Vaillant and Vaillant 1934: figs. 18, 24). Red-rimmed tecomates at Ayotla (Tlapacoya) in Ayotla and Justo subphases (Ixtapaluca phase). Polished red-slipped tecomates and convex bowls with encircling incision in the Iglesia subphase (initial Zacatenco phase) at Tlatilco. Polished red-slipped tecomates, ollas, and convex bowls, occasionally with encircling or oblique incision, in Tlatilco graves, and red-slipped convex bowls were found by *huaqueros* at Tlapacoya (Piña Chán 1958a: 35, 36, 48, 75, 85, figs. 8, 16, 40, 45; Weaver 1967: 33, pl. 22; MacNeish et al. 1970: 277). In the Matadamas complex of the Valley of Oaxaca, forms limited to ollas and convex bowls; latter may have red slip. Coatepec Red-on-Buff, the dominant type in the Tierras Largas phase, includes tecomates, ollas, and esp. convex bowls with at least a partial red slip (or red-painted rim zone). Red (unslipped) ollas, red-rimmed tecomates, and polished red-slipped bowls common in the San José phase (Flannery 1968: 82; MacNeish et al. 1970: 46–9, 269–70, fig. 23).

Remarks. Pozo Thin Red is a very popular type throughout the Preclassic sequence. It steadily increases in popularity during the earlier part of the Cacahuananche phase and maintains its popularity thereafter. Is the most common type in the Cacahuananche phase, with the exception of Bagre Coarse, the residual category.

Guamuchil Polished Black (Fig. 15)

Paste. Relatively porous; hardness 2.5–3.0. Temper coarse, with occasional very coarse inclusions, is the usual quartziferous sand, predominantly quartz crystals, small yellow flecks of mica, and whitish particles of calcite or limestone. Oxidation variable, but never complete; paste typically very dark gray (5 YR 3/1) to gray or reddish gray (5 YR 5/1-2) throughout. Often pink (5 YR 7/4) near one or both surfaces, with dark gray (5 YR 4/1) core.

Surface. Both surfaces slipped, or only exterior in tecomates and bottles. Slip typically fired to black or very dark gray (N 2/0, 3/0); often more completely oxidized to dark reddish gray or brown (5 YR 4/1-3, 3/3), or, rarely, red (2.5 YR 4/6). Sometimes slip is uniformly more oxidized on one surface, producing a dark reddish brown exterior and black interior, or the reverse. Occasional mottled vessels exhibit full color range from dark gray, through dark reddish gray or brown, to red on a single surface. Slipped surfaces carefully smoothed; slip typically polished, with moderate or high gloss, but surfaces are frequently eroded. Unslipped surfaces generally not smoothed or polished; occasional marks of perfunctory smoothing with a yielding tool while paste was plastic, but typically left coarse, pitted, and grainy from protruding temper particles.

Form. Wall thickness 4–9 mm., typically 6–7 mm.

TECOMATE. Diameter 9–12 cm. Base form unknown, presumably rounded. Lip form: slightly blunted or thickened interior.

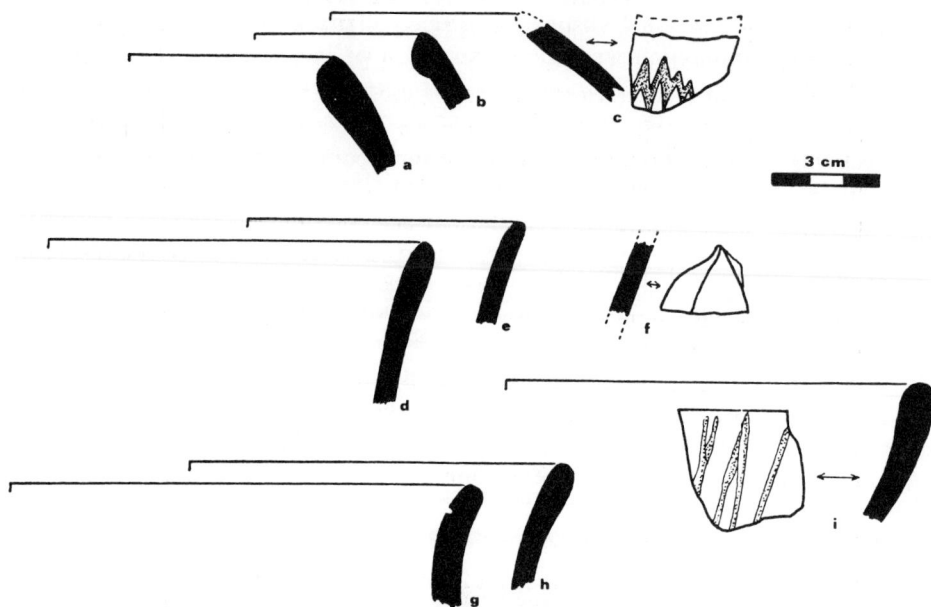

Fig. 15. Guamuchil Polished Black pottery, Cacahuananche phase: *a–c*, tecomates; *d–f*, open bowls; *g, h*, flaring bowls; *i*, convex bowl.

OPEN BOWL. Diameter 16–24 cm. Wall straight and outslanting to very slightly flaring. Base probably flat. Lip form: rounded or tapered.

FLARING BOWL. Diameter 22–32 cm. Wall concave. Form of base unknown, probably flat. Lip form: rounded or slightly blunted.

CONVEX BOWL. Diameter 18–24 cm. Wall uniformly convex. Base rounded. Lip form: slightly blunted or slightly thickened exterior.

Decoration

INCISION. 1. Single line encircling interior of flaring bowl. Pre-slip incision smooth and regular and done while paste was plastic. 2. Two straight intersecting lines on upper exterior of one open bowl. Postslip incision very fine and smooth and done while paste was plastic. 3. Multiple oblique parallel lines on interior surface of convex bowl, perhaps a grater base. Pre-slip incision smooth and done while paste was plastic.

STAMPING. 1. Single band of plain rocker-stamping encircling upper exterior of tecomates.

Comparative material

TEHUACÁN VALLEY. Guamuchil Polished Black forms occur in some Ajalpan-phase types, but polished black pottery occurs there only as aberrant or trade sherds, some exhibiting rocker-stamping. Other Late Ajalpan aberrant sherds have incision on base interior and encircling vessel exterior (MacNeish et al. 1970: 51–2, figs. 26, 27).

SOCONUSCO. Similar surface treatment and vessel forms found in Ocós Black of the Ocós phase at La Victoria, and Morena Black of the Cuadros phase at Salinas La Blanca (but Guamuchil Polished Black exterior is always slipped and often as dark as interior). Encircling incised lines on some forms of both types, and plain rocker-stamping on Ocós Black tecomates. Ocós Black is probably closer; Morena Black has neither tecomates nor convex bowls (Coe 1961: 54–5, figs. 22, 28, 29; Coe and Flannery 1967: 32–3). Morena Black of the Izapa-Cuadros phase has similar surface treatment and forms (but lacks convex bowls), and encircling incised lines on bowl interiors (Ekholm-Miller 1969: 41–2, fig. 31). Petacalapa Black of the Barra phase at Altamira has flaring bowls with interior encircling incision or grooving (Green and Lowe 1967: 100, fig. 74).

CENTRAL CHIAPAS. Similar tecomates and bowls occur in the Cotorra phase at Padre Piedra (Navarrete 1960: 24, figs. 23, 24, table 1). A few tecomates and open or flaring bowls with dark brown-to-black polished slip in the Cotorra-phase occupation of the Santa Marta rock shelter (MacNeish and Peterson 1962: 33–4).

CENTRAL HIGHLANDS. Similar open and convex bowls, without incised decoration, occur in "Black" and "Black-Brown" pottery of the La Juana (Early Nexpa) phase of Morelos (Grove 1972: 61, fig. 14). Piña Chán's (1955a: 10, 12–13, 21–22, láms. 2, 3, 8, 11, 13, 18) Negro Pulido, Café Oscuro, and Café Negruzco types and Cyphers' (1975) Atotonilco Black, Tenango Brown, and Tlatilco Brown types from Chalcatzingo (phase A) include very similar incised polished black and brown bowls. Rocker-stamping occurs in several types. Similar incised black- and brown-slipped bowls in Gualupita I (Vaillant and Vaillant 1934: figs. 20, 21, 23). In the Valley of Mexico, polished black and brown open and flaring bowls and plain rocker-stamping at Ayotla (Tlapacoya) in Ayotla and Justo subphases (Ixtapaluca phase). Similar polished black and black-to-brown tecomates, bowls, and incised grater bases in the Iglesia subphase (initial Zacatenco phase) at Tlatilco. Incised polished black and black-to-brown bowls, grater bases, and tecomates with plain rocker-stamping in Tlatilco graves; also very similar incised polished black-to-brown tecomates and flat-based open and flaring bowls, rocker-stamping, and incised grater bases found in Tlapacoya graves. Incised polished black tecomates and flat-based open bowls also in the Las Bocas cemetery (Porter 1953: pls. 10, 11; Piña Chán 1958a: 36, 41, 51–3, 74, figs. 9, 11, 18, 33–7; 1971: figs. 1, 3, 4; Coe 1965b: ills. 23–6, 33; Weaver 1967: 13–18, figs. 1, 4, pls. 1, 2, 8; MacNeish et al. 1970: 277; Tolstoy and Paradis 1970: 347, fig. 1). In the Valley of Oaxaca, polished black pottery (Ocós Black) and rocker-stamped tecomates in small quantities as trade sherds in the Tierras Largas phase. Polished black (esp. open) bowls common in the San José phase (Flannery 1968: 82; MacNeish et al. 1970: 270).

GULF COAST. Polished (unslipped) black open, flaring, and convex bowls with encircling incision and multiple parallel lines incised on vessel interiors occur in Ponce Black of the Ponce phase of northern Veracruz (MacNeish 1954: 570–1, fig. 17, chart 2). Black tecomates (some with plain rocker-stamping), open and flaring bowls, and a few slightly convex bowls, sometimes slipped, polished, and with encircling incision, in the Trapiche I phase at El Trapiche and Chalahuite (García Payón 1966: 39–45, 109–16, láms. 5–8, 46; 1971: 514; MacNeish et al. 1970: 273). Rocker-stamped tecomates in the Chicharras and San Lorenzo phases at San Lorenzo Tenochtitlán; rocker-stamping itself also in the Bajío phase, and one example in an Ojochi context. Polished black (esp. open) bowls common in the San Lorenzo phase (Coe 1970: 21–7; MacNeish et al. 1970: 279–80). Plain rocker-stamping also at La Venta (Drucker 1952: fig. 28; Coe 1965a: 690, fig. 9; MacNeish et al. 1970: 280).

COASTAL GUERRERO. Polished black- and brown-slipped tecomates and open, flaring, and convex bowls, with incised decoration, occur in the Uala and Tom periods at Puerto Marqués and Zanja. Convex bowls with incised grater bases appear in the Uala period (C. Brush 1969: 135, 139–40, figs. 6, 12, 15, 25, tables 3, 8).

Remarks. Guamuchil Polished Black appears during the Cacahuananche phase; it achieves greatest popularity during the Tecolotla phase. After the Cacahuananche phase, Guamuchil Polished Black is more consistently polished (virtually every example), and is more carefully done, typically achieving a much higher luster than Pozo Thin Red. Also a greater variety of forms and plastic decoration, although some of the same modes appear in low frequencies in the Cacahuananche phase (oblique incision in convex bowl interiors, e.g.). Rocker-stamping is confined to Guamuchil Polished Black of the Cacahuananche phase.

Pedrusco Polished Gray (Fig. 16)

Paste. Relatively porous; hardness 2.5–3.0. Temper coarse to very coarse, occasional granule-sized inclusions, is typical quartziferous sand, predominantly quartz crystals, yellowish plates of mica, occasional small white particles of calcite or limestone. Paste typically incompletely oxidized throughout to dark reddish gray, reddish gray or gray (5 YR 4/2, 5/1–2). Infrequently, more fully oxidized to reddish brown (2.5 YR 5/4) near one or both surfaces.

Surface. Exterior or both surfaces slipped. Slip typically light gray to gray (5 YR 5/1, 6/1); occasionally more fully oxidized to pinkish gray (5 YR 6/2). Slipped surfaces carefully smoothed and slip polished to moderate luster, usually having a distinctly "waxy" feel. Slip generally does not adhere well; is often largely eroded away. Eroded sherds of Pedrusco Polished Gray were probably counted with Bagre Coarse, the residual category. A few examples might be firing variants of Guamuchil Polished Black, although the two are generally easily distinguished. Unslipped surfaces coarse and pitted, with grainy texture from temper particles. Generally no evidence of attempts to smooth unslipped surfaces, but some vessels have marks from scraping with a hard tool (e.g. piece of gourd rind) after paste was partially dry, pits and scratches from dragged temper particles.

Form. Wall thickness 5–10 mm.; typically 6–8 mm.

FLARING BOWL. Diameter 12–28 cm. Wall strongly concave. Base probably flat. Lip form: rounded or beveled.

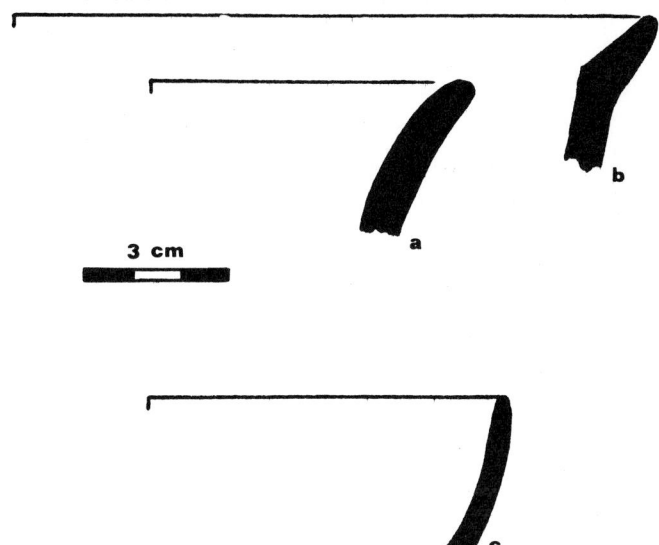

FIG. 16. Pedrusco Polished Gray pottery, Cacahuananche phase: *a, b,* flaring bowls; *c,* convex bowl.

CONVEX BOWL. Diameter 14–17 cm. Wall uniformly convex. Base presumably rounded. Lip form: rounded or slightly tapered.
Decoration. Limited to polished gray slip in Cacahuananche phase.
Comparative material
TEHAUCÁN VALLEY. No very close analogies. A few similarities with Río Salado Gray, but this type is unslipped and very rare in the Ajalpan phase. Same forms occur in a number of Ajalpan-phase types, as well as in Río Salado Gray (MacNeish et al. 1970: 78–83).
SOCONUSCO. Ocós Gray of the Jocotal phase at Salinas La Blanca somewhat similar in surface treatment; flaring bowl one of most common forms. Ocós Black flaring and convex bowls of the Ocós phase at La Victoria include many specimens ranging to gray in slip color (Coe 1961: 54–5, fig. 22; Coe and Flannery 1967: 46–7, fig. 24). Culebra Gray of Izapa-Jocotal and Altamira-Jocotal phases also similar in these respects (Green and Lowe 1967: 118; Ekholm-Miller 1969: 63–5, fig. 56).
CENTRAL CHIAPAS. White Monochrome open and slightly convex bowls of the Cotorra phase at Chiapa de Corzo grade into "pearly gray" in slip color (Dixon 1959: 7–10, figs. 4–6). Gray bowls of Cotorra and Dili phases at Padre Piedra generally similar in form (Navarrete 1960: 25–6, fig. 25, table 1; Green and Lowe 1967: 46, fig. 60). A few gray-slipped sherds from closely related Cotorra-phase occupation of the Santa Marta rock shelter probably represent open or flaring bowls (MacNeish and Peterson 1962: 34).
CENTRAL HIGHLANDS. Polished gray convex bowls in Piña Chán's (1955a: 16, lám. 11) Gris type at Chalcatzingo. In the Valley of Mexico, a few polished gray convex and flaring bowls in Tlatilco and Tlapacoya graves (Piña Chán

1958a: 85, fig. 41; Weaver 1967: 28). In the Valley of Oaxaca, polished gray-slipped bowls with incised decoration in the San José phase; in the Guadalupe phase incised gray, esp. polished waxy gray, pottery shows substantial increase in popularity (Flannery 1968: 82, 94; MacNeish et al. 1970: 270–1).

Remarks. Pedrusco Polished Gray appears in the Cacahuananche phase as a minority type. Several Cacahuananche-phase examples might be firing variants of Guamuchil Polished Black, differing only in lighter color and waxy texture of the slip; this may well reflect the origin of the type. Pedrusco Polished Gray achieves most popularity in the Atopula phase, with much greater diversity of forms, but is never a major type. By the Atopula phase it is distinct from Guamuchil Polished Black in every case. Is less popular at end of the Atopula phase.

Barranca Smoothed Buff (Fig. 17)

Paste. Hardness near 2.5, with occasional softer examples near 2.0. Temper coarse, occasional very coarse inclusions, is the usual quartziferous sand, predominantly quartz crystals, small yellow flecks of mica, and many whitish particles of calcite or limestone. Paste typically oxidized throughout to light reddish brown (5 YR 6/3-4) or pink to reddish yellow (5 YR 7/4-6). Thicker vessels oxidized near surface, gray to very dark gray or reddish gray core (5 YR 3/1, 4/1, 6/1, 5/2); occasionally oxidized near one surface, remaining dark near the other. One sherd has an imperfectly obliterated junction on interior surface, more like the joint of two separate sections than a simple coil joint.

Surface. Exterior or both surfaces carefully smoothed and compacted but not polished or slipped. Compacted surfaces occasionally have very light plastic striations, perhaps rag-polished while paste still wet. In a few cases this produces the effect of a slip of exactly same color as the paste. This float-coat or self-slip seems always simply a result of surface compaction, but more elaborate analysis is required to verify this point. Surfaces typically oxidized: light reddish brown to reddish yellow (5 YR 6/4-6) or pink (5 YR 7/4). Surface-eroded sherds of Barranca Smoothed Buff were probably included in the residual category, Bagre Coarse. Uncompacted surfaces (interior of ollas and tecomates) generally left coarse or slightly smoothed; occasionally have marks of scraping with a hard tool (e.g. edge of piece of gourd rind) while paste was leather-hard; pits and scratches from dragged temper particles.

Form. Wall thickness varies widely, 4–19 mm., maximum at point of curvature change of olla necks or in rims with thickened lips. Typical wall thickness 5–8 mm.

> OLLA. Diameter 20–27 cm. No sharp breaks in profile curvature; smooth transition from convex body to flaring neck. Base form unknown, presumably rounded. Lip form: slightly blunted or everted.
>
> OPEN BOWL. Diameter 16–22 cm. Wall straight and nearly vertical to very slightly outflaring. Base probably flat. Lip form: rounded or tapered.

Auxiliary features. 1. Nubbin foot: solid vessel support with roughly parabolic profile.

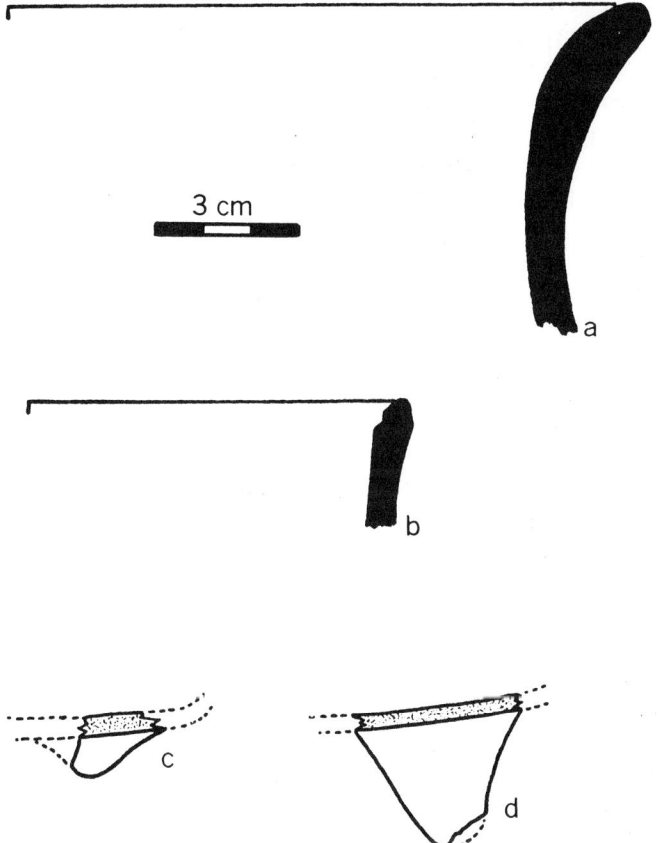

FIG. 17. Barranca Smoothed Buff pottery, Cacahuananche phase: *a*, olla; *b*, open bowl; *c, d*, nubbin feet.

Decoration

INCISION. 1. One line encircling interior of open bowl just below and parallel to rim. Pre-slip incision smooth and regular and done while paste was plastic.

Comparative material. Difficult to find convincing parallels for a plain type with simple forms.

TEHUACÁN VALLEY. Paste, surface treatment, and vessel form similar to Ajalpan Plain and Coatepec Plain, and to a lesser extent to Ajalpan Fine Plain, but latter is thinner and has high polish. None has vessel supports. Closest resemblance is to Coatepec Plain that occurs throughout Ajalpan and Santa María phases, with maximum popularity in Late Ajalpan (MacNeish et al. 1970: 29–35, 44–6, figs. 11, 13, 22, tables 15, 17, 19).

SOCONUSCO. Surface treatment generally similar to Ocós Buff of the Ocós phase at La Victoria, but forms and modes of decoration differ (Coe 1961: 53–4).

CENTRAL HIGHLANDS. Brown pottery of the La Juana (Early Nexpa) phase in Morelos occasionally exhibits same self-slip or float-coat effect; forms generally similar (Grove 1972: 60, fig. 16). Piña Chán's (1955a: 9–10, lám. 1) Café Claro type and Cyphers' (1975) Del Prado Pink from Chalcatzingo (phase A) are somewhat similar in color, surface treatment, and form.

No other resemblances noted to ceramics of distant areas.

Remarks. Barranca Smoothed Buff appears as a minor type in the Cacahuananche phase, and declines gradually in frequency in the later Atopula and Tecolotla phases. Never approaches the popularity of such major types as Guamuchil Polished Black or Pozo Thin Red. The only other nubbin vessel feet occur in Bagre Coarse, also in the Cacahuananche phase.

Bagre Coarse (Fig. 18)

Paste. Quite porous; hardness 2.0–2.5. Temper coarse or very coarse, with granule-sized inclusions, is the usual quartziferous sand, predominantly quartz crystals, small yellow and silverish flecks of mica, and occasional white calcite or limestone particles. Paste typically reddish brown to yellowish red or light reddish brown to reddish yellow (5 YR 5/4-6, 6/4-6) near one surface, less fully oxidized to reddish gray or dark reddish gray (5 YR 4/2, 5/2) near the other. May be a gray to dark gray (5 YR 4/1, 5/1) core; rarely, paste is dark to very dark gray (5 YR 3/1, 4/1) throughout.

Surface. Fired to same color range as paste, typically reddish brown to yellowish red or light reddish brown to reddish yellow (5 YR 5/4-6, 6/4-6). Unslipped and usually coarse and uncompacted; often pitted and grainy. Some vessels show marks of scraping with a hard tool while paste was plastic, such as grooves made by dragged temper particles. Surfaces rarely exhibit light striations from smoothing with a yielding tool, or very shallow grooves produced by pebble- or finger-smoothing while paste was plastic. Many examples have eroded surfaces; this type undoubtedly includes sherds of other types in which distinctive features of surface treatment have weathered away.

Form. Wall thickness quite variable, at least 5–12 mm., typically 7–9 mm.

OLLA. Diameter 26–30 cm. No sharp breaks in profile curvature—smooth transition from convex body to flaring neck. Base form unknown. Lip form: rounded, blunted, or slightly thickened interior.

OPEN BOWL. Diameter 15–18 cm. Wall straight and outslanting. Base probably flat. Lip form: blunted, slightly thickened interior, or thickened exterior.

FLARING BOWL. Diameter 12–18 cm. Wall strongly concave. Base probably flat. Lip form: rounded.

INCURVED-RIM BOWL. Diameter 22–25 cm. Wall uniformly convex. Base presumably rounded. Lip form: rounded.

Auxiliary features. 1. S-shaped foot: solid vessel support with tapering curving profile. 2. Nubbin foot: subconical solid vessel support with hole in one side.

Decoration. None in Cacahuananche phase.

Comparative material. Virtually impossible to find useful comparisons for a residual coarse type.

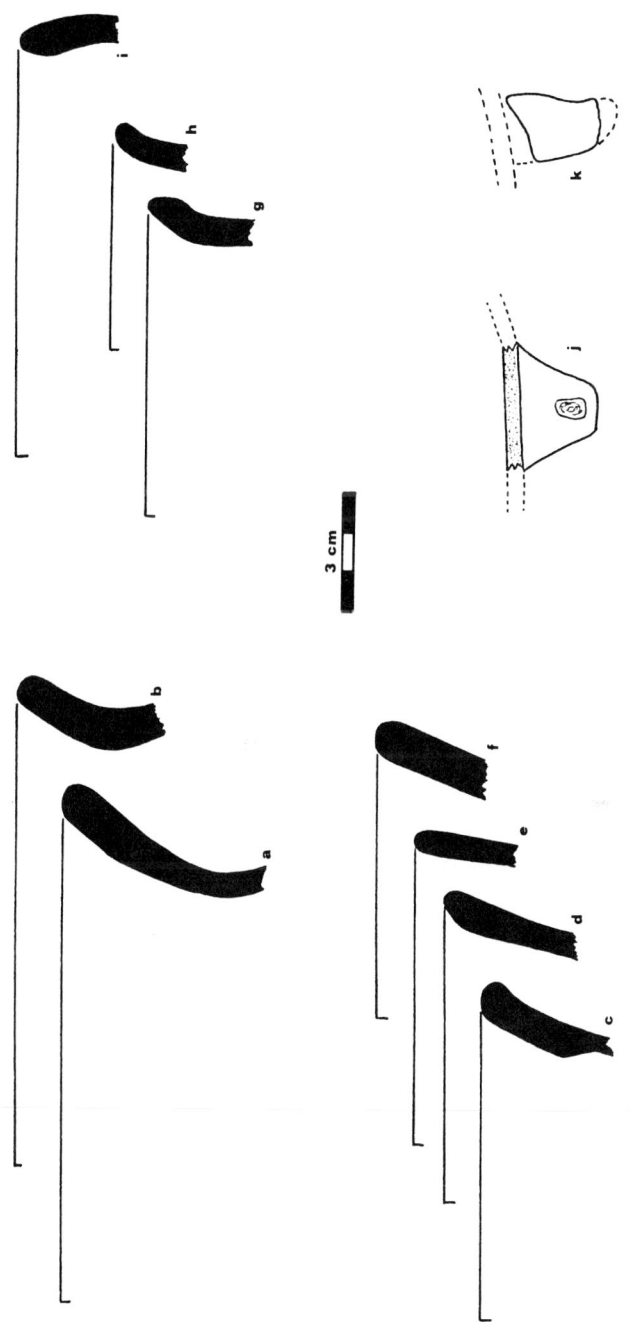

FIG. 18. Bagre Coarse pottery, Cacahuananche phase: *a, b*, ollas; *c–f*, open bowls; *g, h*, flaring bowls; *i*, incurved-rim bowl; *j, k*, nubbin feet.

TEHUACÁN VALLEY. Ajalpan Coarse and Coatepec Buff of the Ajalpan phase more or less similar in paste, surface treatment, and form. Neither type has vessel supports, however (MacNeish et al. 1970: 26-9, 49-51, figs. 10, 25, tables 14, 21).

No close resemblances to more distant areas noted.

Remarks. Bagre Coarse is undoubtedly a residual category. It includes not only vessels originally left unslipped and unsmoothed but also vessels of other types in which slip or other distinctive surface treatment is no longer discernible. Since it cannot have been a native category, it is not meaningful to speak of its popularity. Its only utility is to show a wider range of shapes, lip form, etc. It is well represented in every level, as is expectable for a residual category, and is generally the most frequent type recovered. Its only distinctive features in the Cacahuananche phase are vessel feet.

Rare Pottery Types of the Cacahuananche Phase

Polished Dark Red

Paste. Hardness 3.0-3.5. Temper coarse, with rare very coarse inclusions, predominantly of quartz crystals—not the usual quartziferous sand. Paste typically light reddish brown to pink (5 YR 6/3, 7/3) near exterior surface, reddish brown to light reddish brown (5 YR 5/3, 6/3-4) near interior surface; no dark cores.

Surface. Exterior a uniform red (10 R 4/6-8, 5/6) slip. Slipped surfaces carefully smoothed and occasionally slightly striated from polishing; slip well polished with a slight gloss. Interior unslipped but carefully smoothed and compacted; may even have slight gloss. One sherd has marks of dragged temper particles from scraping with a hard tool while paste was leather-hard.

Form. Wall thickness 3-7 mm., typically quite thin, 4-5 mm. Specific forms unknown.

Decoration. Limited to smoothed surface and polished slip.

Comparative material

TEHUACÁN VALLEY. Surface treatment similar to Coatepec Red-on-Buff, and to a lesser extent to Ajalpan Fine Red, both of the Ajalpan phase, although they have a specular red paint or wash (MacNeish et al. 1970: 31-3, 46-9).

Remarks. The very small sherd sample suggests that this is simply a variant of Pozo Thin Red, yet the differing paste color, hardness, tempering material, and surface treatment argue against it. That it occurs in the Atopula phase as well suggests it is more likely to be an aberrant local type than an import.

Orange

Paste. Hardness usually 2.5; a few softer examples near 2.0. Temper coarse and not the usual quartziferous sand. Oxidation typically thorough to red or light red (2.5 YR 5/6, 6/6-8) throughout. Occasionally, paste incompletely oxidized, gray to pinkish gray (5 YR 6/1-2) near surface or in core of thick vessel walls.

Surface. Exteriors well smoothed and covered with red to yellowish red (2.5

YR 5/8; 5 YR 5/8) slip, slightly polished. Surfaces generally have a slight luster. Interiors unslipped and partially smoothed; frequent scratches of dragged temper particles indicate scraping of leather-hard paste with a hard tool.

Form. Wall thickness 4–8 mm; typically quite thin, ca. 5 mm. Specific forms unknown.

Decoration. Limited to slip.

Comparative material. No close similarities noted. A few very general similarities to Piña Chán's (1955a: 16–17, 19–20) Roja Amarillenta and Naranja Laca types from Chalcatzingo.

Remarks. This is definitely not a variant of one of the more common types. That it occurs again in the Atopula phase may indicate a local aberrant type rather than an import.

Thin Tan (Fig. 19a)

Paste. Hardness 2.5. Temper medium, not the usual quartziferous sand. Paste pinkish gray to pink (5 YR 7/2-4, 7/6) near exterior surface, less completely oxidized, gray to light gray (5 YR 6/1, 7/1) near interior; dark to very dark gray core (N 3/0, 4/0).

Surface. Exterior very well smoothed and has very shallow, somewhat irregular facet-like grooves perpendicular to rim. Traces of reddish yellow (5 YR 7/6) are from firing, not a slip. Interior irregular and unsmoothed.

Form. Wall thickness 3–5 mm.

> BOTTLE. Diameter 0.5–1.0 cm. Apparently this sherd is a fragment of a tiny bottle or flask; shaped almost like a minature tecomate with a neck-like mouth. Base form unknown. Lip form: tapered.

Decoration. Limited to smoothing and grooves.

Comparative material. No close analogies.

> TEHUACÁN VALLEY. Bottle forms rare in the Ajalpan phase. Late Ajalpan imports include small bottles, and one sherd of a cylindrical vessel (resembling Ojochi-phase specimens from San Lorenzo) with very shallow vertical grooves or facets on exterior surface (MacNeish et al. 1970: 51–2, fig. 26).

> CENTRAL HIGHLANDS. Thin buff-to-gray pottery of the Matadamas complex in the Valley of Oaxaca may be similar (MacNeish et al. 1970: 269–70).

Remarks. The sample consists of a single sherd. It is not tempered with the usual quartziferous sand, which suggests an import. However, the tiny size and

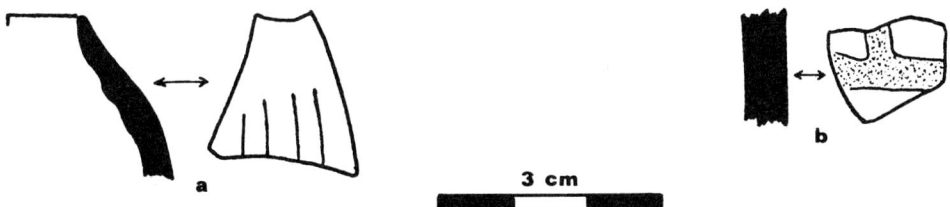

FIG. 19. Rare pottery types, Cacahuananche phase: *a*, Thin Tan; *b*, Red-painted.

irregular surface, thickness, and shape suggest a toy or some other nontypical nonfunctional vessel.

Red-painted (Fig. 19b)

Paste. Hardness 2.5. Temper coarse; includes quartz crystals but predominantly composed of white limestone or calcite particles and unidentified red and shiny black particles. Paste incompletely oxidized, reddish brown to light reddish brown (5 YR 5/3, 6/3).

Surface. Exterior relatively well smoothed; unslipped but has dusky red (10 R 3/4) painted design. Interior surface unslipped and unpainted; no indication of any attempt at smoothing; temper particles produce coarse grainy texture.

Form. Wall thickness ca. 6 mm. Specific forms unknown.

Decoration. Two perpendicular intersecting lines in red paint on exterior.

Comparative material

> TEHUACÁN VALLEY. Coatepec Red-on-Buff of the Ajalpan phase has red stripes on vessel exteriors but is specular paint (MacNeish et al. 1970: 46–9, figs. 23, 24).

Remarks. Since the sample is a single sherd it is tempting to call it an atypically dark example of Pozo Thin Red in which the coloring agent was painted on rather than applied as slip. However, the tempering material is not the usual quartziferous sand, suggesting an import.

Pottery Types of the Atopula Phase

Tlapala Red (Fig. 20)

Paste and surface. Identical with Cacahuananche phase (see above).

Form. Wall thickness 8–12 mm., typically 9–10 mm.

> TECOMATE. Diameter 6–10 cm. Overall shape hemispherical or slightly flat-

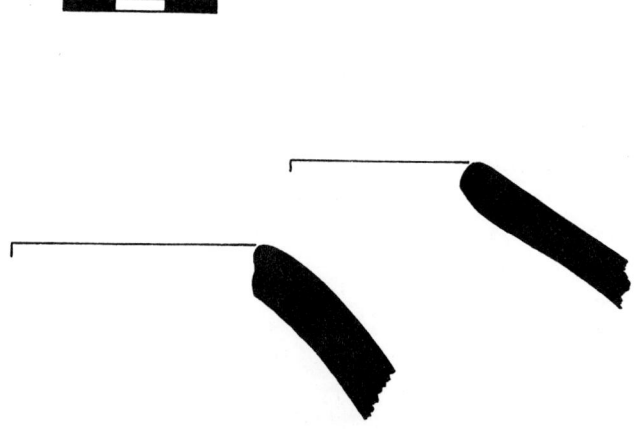

FIG. 20. Tlapala Red tecomates, Atopula phase.

tened, with very small restricted orifice. Base form unknown. Lip form: slightly blunted or beveled.

Decoration. Limited to polished red slip in the Atopula phase.

Comparative material

TEHUACÁN VALLEY. Ajalpan Coarse Red of the Ajalpan phase is quite similar in paste, surface treatment, and vessel thickness, although Tlapala Red is slightly darker and has true slip. Undecorated tecomates occur in Ajalpan Coarse Red, at least in Late Ajalpan. Other common forms of Ajalpan Coarse Red not represented in Tlapala Red (MacNeish et al. 1970: 41-2, fig. 20, table 18).

SOCONUSCO. In surface treatment and vessel form Tlapala Red generally similar to Mapache Red-rimmed and Ocós Specular Red of Ocós and Cuadros phases at La Victoria and Salinas La Blanca, although Tlapala Red slip is not specular and seems not to be confined to rim band. Grooves and punctations that mark Cuadros-phase Mapache Red-rimmed tecomates are absent (Coe 1961: 50-1, figs. 14-17; Coe and Flannery 1967: 26, fig. 9). Cotán Grooved Red of the Barra phase at Altamira, Ocós Specular Red and Michis Thin Tecomate of Izapa- and Altamira-Ocós phases, and Mapache Red-rimmed of Izapa- and Altamira-Cuadros phases all show general similarities in form and surface treatment (Green and Lowe 1967: 97-100, 104-6, 112, figs. 72, 77, 78, 85; Ekholm-Miller 1969: 27-9, 47, 48, figs. 19, 36, 37).

CENTRAL CHIAPAS. The Unslipped category of the Cotorra phase at Chiapa de Corzo includes similar tecomate forms with red slip or paint, although generally applied to limited areas (Dixon 1959: 16-17, figs. 19, 52). Closely related Cotorra-phase occupations of the Santa Marta rock shelter and Padre Piedra also characterized by similar tecomates (Navarrete 1960: 23, 24, fig. 22, table 1; MacNeish and Peterson 1962: 32, 33, pl. 6; Green and Lowe 1967: 43, fig. 52). At Santa Cruz such tecomates classified as Burrero Red, which may pertain to the Burrero period or to an earlier undefined occupation contemporary with the Cotorra phase (Sanders 1961: 17, fig. 16).

CENTRAL HIGHLANDS. In the Valley of Mexico, red-rimmed tecomates occur at Ayotla (Tlapacoya) in the Ayotla and Justo subphases (Ixtapaluca phase), and red-slipped tecomates appear in the Iglesia subphase (initial Zacatenco phase) at Tlatilco. Polished red-slipped tecomates in the Tlatilco graves (Piña Chán 1958a: 35, 36, 48, 85, figs. 8, 16, 41, cuadro 2; MacNeish et al. 1970: 277). Tecomates with red slip or paint, usually confined to rim band, occur in the Valley of Oaxaca in the Tierras Largas and San José phases (Flannery 1968: 82; MacNeish et al. 1970: 270).

GULF COAST. A few red-slipped tecomate-like vessels occur in the Ponce phase of northern Veracruz (MacNeish 1954: 571, fig. 17, charts 2, 5). Tecomates, including specimens with red slip or red-painted zone, common in the Trapiche I phase at El Trapiche and Chalahuite (García Payón 1966: 95-9, láms. 36, 37; MacNeish et al. 1970: 273). Red-slipped tecomates with encircling incision in Chicharras and San Lorenzo phases at San Lorenzo

Tenochtitlán; red-slipped and red-rimmed tecomates also in the earlier Ojochi and Bajío phases there and in Squier's "pre-Complex A" material from La Venta (Coe 1970: 21–7; MacNeish et al. 1970: 279).

COASTAL GUERRERO. Tecomate form is dominant in Pox, Uala, and Tom periods at Puerto Marqués and Zanja; often red-slipped (C. Brush 1969: 57–8, 135, 144, figs. 6, 12, 21, table 8).

Remarks. Tlapala Red declines rapidly in popularity at the end of the Cacahuananche phase; is hardly represented at all in Atopula-phase levels, being replaced by Jiménez Red. The deep tecomate form does not survive the Cacahuananche phase (see discussion above).

Jiménez Red (Figs. 21–24)

Paste and surface. Identical with Cacahuananche phase (see above).

Form. Wall thickness 8–19 mm.; maximum thickness occurs in ollas where neck begins to flare; body walls typically quite thick, 10–12 mm.

OLLA. Diameter 24–30 cm. Exterior profile smooth; interior surface occasionally has very sharp break in curvature where neck flares strongly outward. Base form unknown. Lip form: rounded, slightly blunted, beveled, or thickened exterior.

OPEN BOWL. Diameter 16–29 cm. Wall straight and outslanting to very

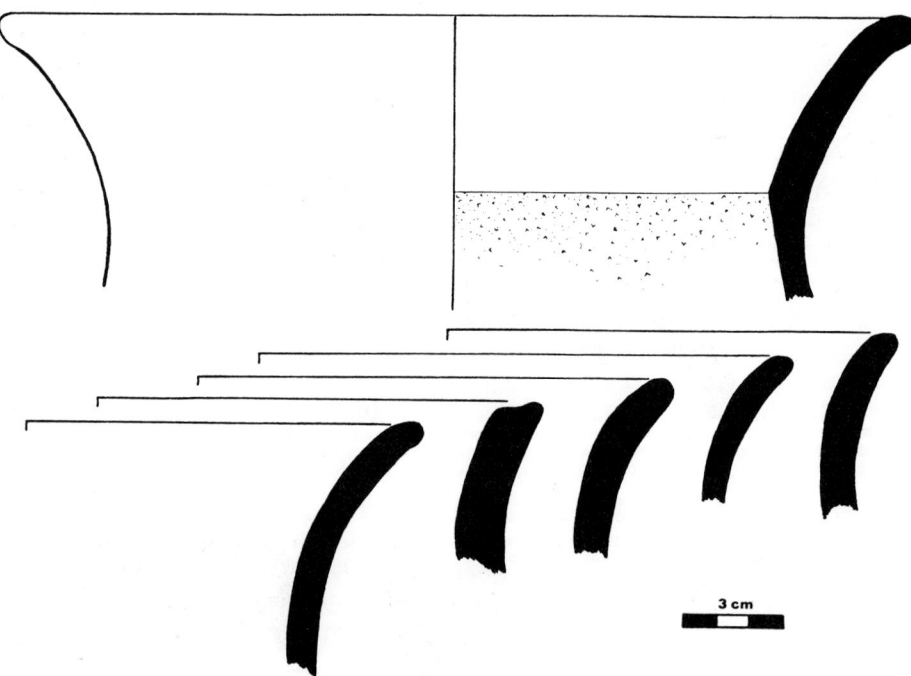

FIG. 21. Jiménez Red ollas, Atopula phase.

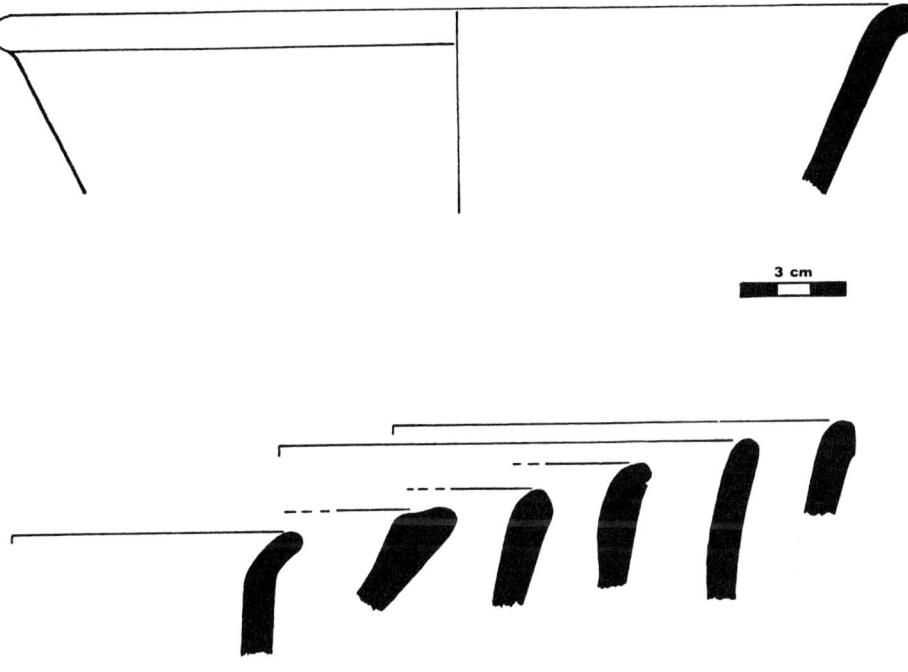

FIG. 22. Jiménez Red open bowls, Atopula phase.

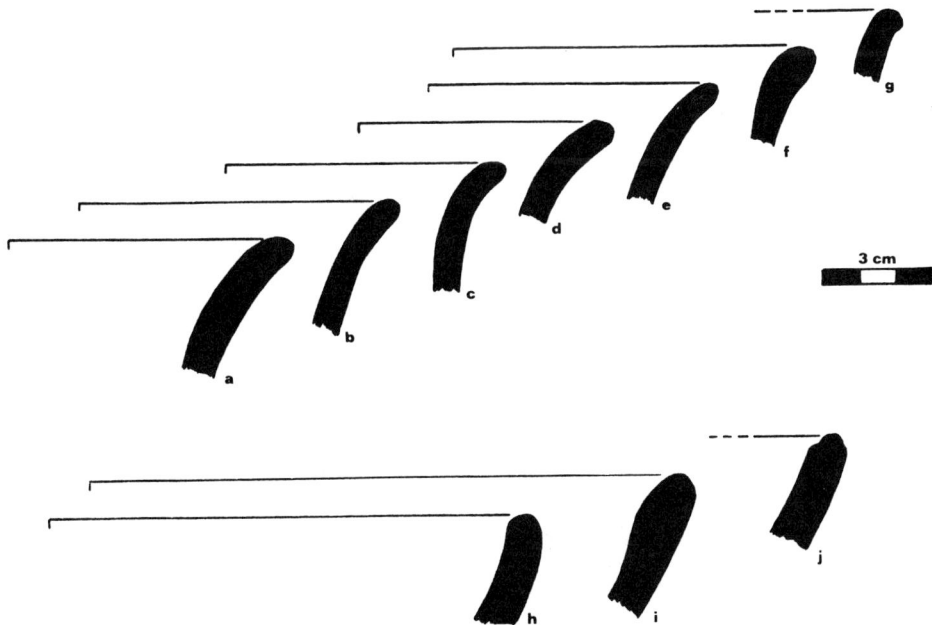

FIG. 23. Jiménez Red pottery, Atopula phase: *a–g*, flaring bowls; *h–j*, convex bowls.

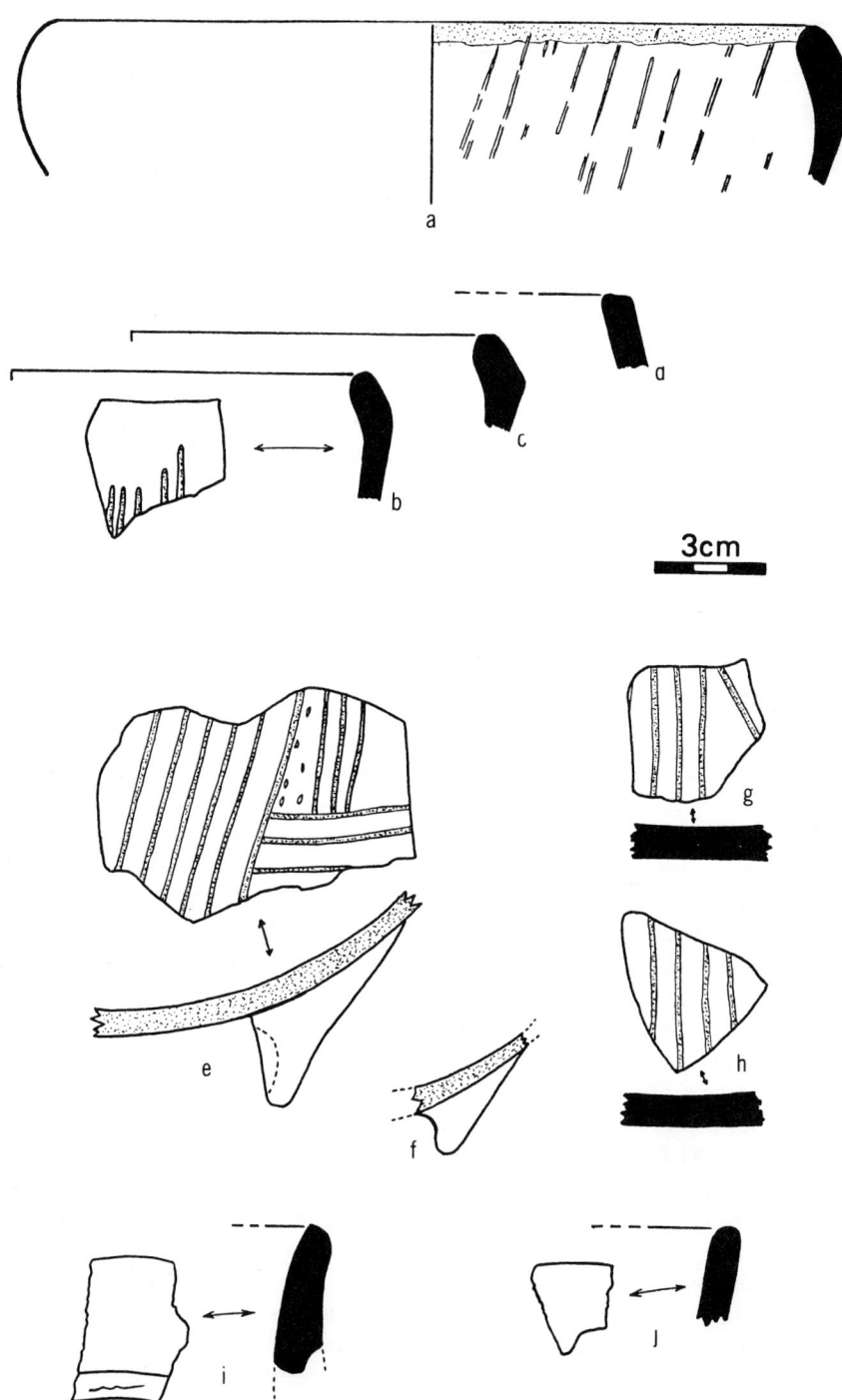

FIG. 24. Jiménez Red pottery, Atopula phase: *a–d*, incurved-rim bowls; *e*, molcajete with ring base; *f*, ring base; *g, h*, molcajete bases; *i, j*, aberrant sherds slipped on both surfaces and two smooth edges.

slightly flaring. Base probably flat. Lip form: rounded, slightly blunted, slightly tapered, very slightly thickened exterior, or bolstered.

FLARING BOWL. Diameter 12–20 cm. Wall strongly concave. Base flat. Lip form: rounded, slightly blunted, or slightly thickened exterior.

CONVEX BOWL. Diameter 26–32 cm. Wall uniformly convex. Base rounded. Lip form: rounded or beveled.

INCURVED-RIM BOWL. Diameter 18–22 cm. Upper wall becomes very strongly convex, restricting mouth. Form of base unknown, presumably rounded. Lip form: rounded, blunted, or beveled.

FOOTED MOLCAJETE. Open or convex-bowl form with molcajete grater base (deep incision, see below) and slab feet.

MISCELLANEOUS. Aberrant sherds slipped on both surfaces and on two smooth edges. Conceivably fragments of strap handles, but edges are diverging in one case, curved and parallel in the other; probably represent rim sherds of vessels with cutout designs below.

Auxiliary features. 1. Slab foot: wide, curved, slightly tapering vessel supports on open or convex bowls with molcajete grater bases.

Decoration

GROOVING. 1. Single broad shallow groove encircling rim of convex bowl along interior edge of lip. One vessel also has a slightly deeper groove along exterior edge of lip.

INCISION. 1. Multiple oblique (nearly vertical) lines on interior surface of incurved-rim bowl. Incision deep and smooth and done while paste was plastic. Interior surface very worn, probably used as grater; no trace of slip remains. 2. Flattened molcajete bases. Designs based on sets of parallel lines, sometimes combined with dotted or jabbed zones; similar to Opposed Areas of Parallel Lines and sunburst motifs (MacNeish 1954: fig. 12; Coe 1961: 67). Incisions broad and deep; traces of slip remain on a few examples even though generally quite worn from use as graters. This type of incision not exclusively decorative.

OTHER. 1. Very slightly raised sharp ridge encircling exterior of one open bowl 1 cm. below lip.

Comparative material

TEHUACÁN VALLEY. Paste, surface treatment, and vessel thickness quite similar to Ajalpan Coarse Red of the Ajalpan phase, although Jiménez Red is darker and has true slip. Ollas with flaring necks most common form in both types. Flaring, open, and incurved-rim bowls, appearing first in Jiménez Red in the Atopula phase, also first appear in Ajalpan Coarse Red in the Late Ajalpan phase. Ajalpan Coarse Red has no decoration but red wash, no appendages, and no molcajetes. A few examples of Coatepec Buff and Red-on-Buff and a few Late Ajalpan aberrant sherds have incised lines or grooves encircling vessel exteriors, and a few have incised interior bases (MacNeish et al. 1970: 41–2, 51, figs. 20, 26, table 18).

SOCONUSCO. Pacaya Red of Cuadros and Jocotal phases at Salinas La Blanca has similar surface treatment and wall thickness; olla is by far most common form in both types (but Pacaya Red ollas have more vertical necks). Open, flaring, and convex bowls occur in both types as minority forms; incurved-rim bowls and other cognate forms in Ocós Specular Red of the Ocós phase at La Victoria. Encircling grooves or incisions on some Pacaya Red vessels and on Ocós Specular Red bowls. Very similar grater bowls in Conchas White-to-Buff in the Conchas phase at La Victoria (Coe 1961: 52, 63, 67–8, figs. 18, 24, 26, 52, 53; Coe and Flannery 1967: 36–7, fig. 16). Tustlán Red of the Izapa-Ocós phase has similar range of forms, including open and flaring bowls with encircling incised lines (Ekholm-Miller 1969: 25–7, 58–62, figs. 18, 41–50, 52, 53). Tocanaque Red-unburnished of the Izapa-Jocotal phase has similar surface treatment; forms include ollas and open and flaring bowls. Xquic Red, of the Izapa- and Altamira-Jocotal phases, is characterized by open, flaring, and convex bowls with encircling incision (Green and Lowe 1967: 116–18, fig. 89).

CENTRAL CHIAPAS. Similar open bowls, a few slightly convex bowls, occasionally incised, and one olla sherd with red slip occur in the Red-and-White Bichrome category of the Cotorra phase at Chiapa de Corzo (Dixon 1959: 12–16, figs. 13–15, 17). Similar bowl forms in the Cotorra phase at Padre Piedra (Navarrete 1960: 23–4, figs. 22, 23, table 1; Green and Lowe 1967: 43, fig. 52). The closely related Burrero Red type of Santa Cruz, which may pertain to the Burrero period or an earlier undefined occupation contemporary with the Cotorra phase, also includes red-slipped open, flaring, and convex bowls (Sanders 1961: 17, fig. 16).

CENTRAL HIGHLANDS. Red-slipped Brown bowls of the San Pablo A (Middle Nexpa) and San Pablo B (Late Nexpa) phases of Morelos similar in form but generally undecorated (Grove 1972: 60–1, fig. 18). Ollas and open, flaring, and convex bowls occur in Piña Chán's (1955a: 11, 17–18, láms. 3, 4, 12) Café Rojizo and Roja Pulida types from Chalcatzingo; the latter has occasional encircling incision. A slab-footed bowl occurs in the Café Negruzco type. Montefalco Bichromes of Chalcatzingo A (Cyphers 1975) include similar red-slipped ollas and convex bowls. Similar red-slipped vessel forms in Gualupita I (Vaillant and Vaillant 1934: figs. 18, 20, 24). In the Valley of Mexico, similar red-slipped bowl forms with encircling incision, some red-slipped ollas, and incised molcajete bases or pseudo-grater fondos at Ayotla (Tlapacoya) in the Bomba subphase, at Tlatilco in the Iglesia subphase, and at El Arbolillo and Zacatenco in the El Arbolillo subphase, all of the initial Zacatenco phase. Also found in the Tlatilco and Tlapacoya graves (Vaillant 1930: 31, 32, pl. I; 1935: 219–23; Porter 1953: pl. 10; Piña Chán 1958a: 35, 36, 85, figs. 8, 9, 34, 38, 45; 1971: fig. 5; Weaver 1967: 33, fig. 4, pl. 22; MacNeish et al. 1970: 277, 278; Tolstoy and Paradis 1970: 345–7, fig. 1). In the Matadamas complex of the Valley of Oaxaca, forms limited to ollas and convex bowls that may bear red slip. Coatepec Red-on-Buff, dominant type of the Tierras Largas phase, includes similar ollas and bowls with at least partial red slip. Red (unslipped) ollas and polished red-slipped open and flaring bowls very common in the

San José phase (Flannery 1968: 82; MacNeish et al. 1970: 46–9, 269, 270, fig. 23).

GULF COAST. Very similar red-slipped ollas common in Pavón and Ponce phases of northern Veracruz. Aguilar Red of Ponce and (esp.) Aguilar phases includes open, flaring, and incurved-rim bowls; very similar incised grater bases; and vessel feet (MacNeish 1954: 567–75, figs. 14, 17, chart 2). Very similar red-slipped (or zoned red-painted) ollas, open and flaring bowls, and a few slightly convex and incurved-rim bowls occur in the Trapiche I phase at El Trapiche and Chalahuite. Molcajetes or pseudo-grater fondos, including footed forms, in Trapiche I and II (García Payón 1966: 95–9, 117–20, láms. 4–6, 36, 37, 41, 42, 47–9; MacNeish et al. 1970: 273). Red-slipped (esp. flaring) bowls, at San Lorenzo Tenochtitlán from the Ojochi phase on; olla does not appear until the Chicharras phase (Coe 1970: 21–5; MacNeish et al. 1970: 279).

PETÉN. Similar red-slipped ollas and open, flaring, and incurved-rim bowls with encircling grooving or incision occur in the Xe-sphere complexes at Altar de Sacrificios and Seibal (Willey et al. 1967: 293; MacNeish et al. 1970: 285; Willey 1970: 324–33, figs. 3–10; R.E.W. Adams 1971: 20, 42, figs. 1–7, chart 1).

COASTAL GUERRERO. Similar red-slipped ollas and open, flaring, convex, and incurved-rim bowls, occasionally with encircling grooving, occur in Uala and Tom periods at Puerto Marqués and Zanja. Red-slipped convex bowls with deeply incised grater bases in the Uala period (C. Brush 1969: 137–46, figs. 6, 13–17, 22–24, tables 3A-3C, 8).

Remarks. Jiménez Red appears in slight quantities in the Cacahuananche phase. It reaches greatest popularity in the Atopula and Tecolotla phases when it essentially replaces Tlapala Red, from which it may be descended. Even in the Atopula phase, with its expanded range of forms and decoration (now including open, flaring, and incurved-rim bowls as well as ollas and convex bowls carried over from the Cacahuananche phase) Jiménez Red does not approach Pozo Thin Red or Guamuchil Polished Black in popularity. True molcajete grater bowls with supports occur only in Jiménez Red in the Atopula and Tecolotla phases, but similar deep molcajete-base incision and more decorative pseudo-grater fondos occur also in Pozo Thin Red, Guamuchil Polished Black, and Bagre Coarse in these phases. Most of the same forms and types of decoration continue into the Tecolotla phase.

Pozo Thin Red (Figs. 25, 26)

Paste and surface. Identical with Cacahuananche phase (see above).
Form. Wall thickness ca. 3–7 mm., typically quite thin, 4–5 mm.

TECOMATE. Diameter 6–16 cm. Overall shape hemispherical, wall uniformly convex. Form of base unknown, presumably rounded. Lip form: rounded, slightly blunted, slightly tapered, thickened interior.

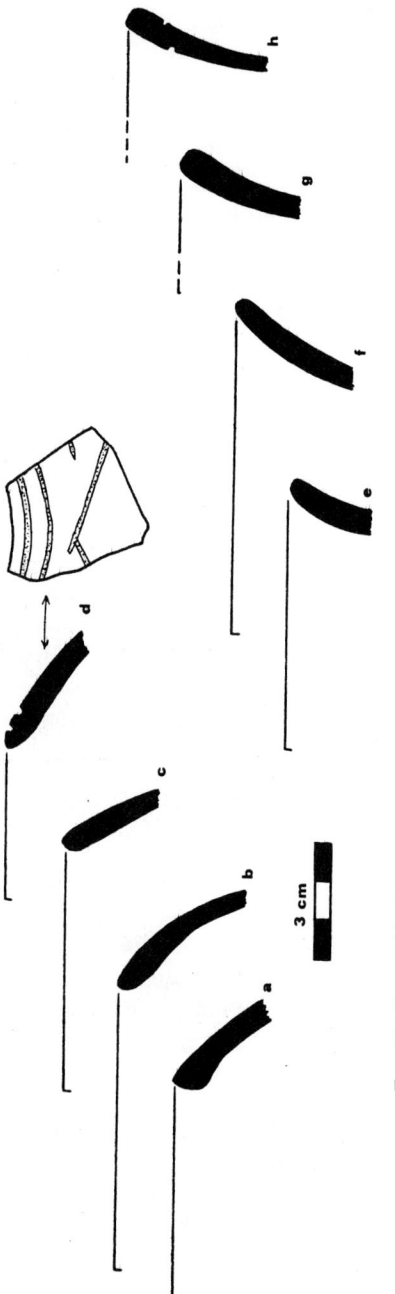

FIG. 25. Pozo Thin Red pottery, Atopula phase: *a–d*, tecomates; *e–h*, flaring bowls.

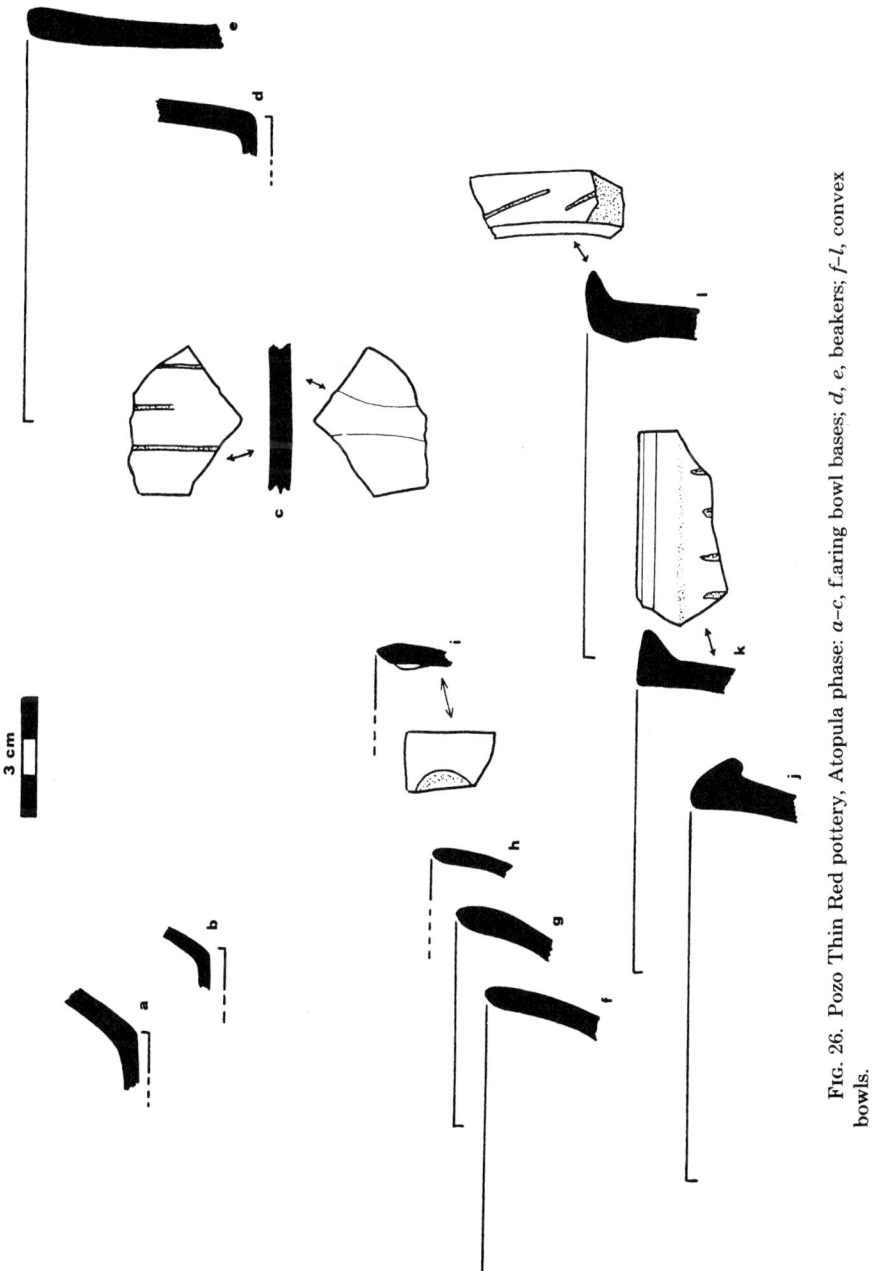

FIG. 26. Pozo Thin Red pottery, Atopula phase: *a–c*, f.aring bowl bases; *d, e*, beakers; *f–l*, convex bowls.

FLARING BOWL. Diameter 14–18 cm. Wall flares strongly outward. Base flat or flattened. Lip form: rounded or slightly blunted.

CONVEX BOWL. Diameter 10–18 cm. Wall uniformly convex. Base rounded. Lip form: rounded, tapered, bolstered, or everted.

BEAKER. Diameter 20–22 cm. Wall straight and nearly vertical to slightly outslanting. Base flat. Lip form: blunted.

Decoration

INCISION. 1. Two lines encircling tecomates just below and parallel to rim. May also be a band of opposed oblique intersecting lines (nearly crosshatching) just below. Pre-slip incision very shallow, smooth, and regular and done while paste was plastic. 2. Single line encircling interior of flaring bowls just below and parallel to rim. Exterior may also have one encircling line. Pre-slip incision irregular, with rough edges and done after paste was partially dry. 3. Single very wide straight line on one unslipped bowl interior. Incision quite smooth and regular and done while paste was plastic. 4. Deep oblique lines across flat everted lip of convex bowl. Pre-slip incision smooth and regular and done while paste was plastic. 5. Multiple parallel straight lines on unslipped (or worn?) flat bowl interiors. In one case exterior base of same bowl has very shallow opposed arcs. Pre-slip incision slightly irregular with rough edges and done after paste was partially dry.

PUNCTATION. 1. Row of deep vertical punctations or jabs encircling exterior of convex bowl just below and parallel to everted lip.

OTHER. 1. Slightly raised area (roughly circular) on interior of one convex bowl just below rim; might not be intentional decoration.

Comparative material

TEHUACÁN VALLEY. Ajalpan Fine Red of the Ajalpan phase quite similar in paste, surface treatment, and vessel forms, although Pozo Thin Red has nonspecular red slip, often covering both surfaces. Both types polished. Major difference: Ajalpan Fine Red is a minor type in Tehuacán; Pozo Thin Red is a major type at Atopula. Ajalpan Fine Red has no decoration other than red wash, but a few examples of Coatepec Buff and Red-on-Buff and a few Late Ajalpan aberrant sherds have incised lines encircling vessel exteriors, and some have incised interior bases. Molcajete bases are similar to bases of pseudo-grater bowls of Canoas White and Río Salado Gray (MacNeish et al. 1970: 31–3, figs. 12, 26, 36, 42, table 16).

SOCONUSCO. In surface treatment and vessel form some similarities to Ocós Specular Red, Pacaya Red, and Mapache Red-rimmed (tecomates only) of Ocós and Cuadros phases at La Victoria and Salinas La Blanca, except that Pozo Thin Red has a nonspecular red slip covering entire exterior. Mapache Red-rimmed tecomates (nonspecular) of the Cuadros phase have very similar encircling grooves and latticework (like Ocós-phase specular examples). Incised lines encircle some forms of all these types. Conchas White-to-Buff convex and grater bowls of the Conchas phase at La Victoria have similar incised bases (Coe 1961: 51–2, 66–8, figs. 16–19, 26; Coe and Flannery 1967: 26, 36, figs. 9, 16). Michis Thin Tecomate vessels of Izapa-Ocós and Altamira-

Ocós phases, and Mapache Red-rimmed tecomates of Izapa- and Altamira-Cuadros phases, have similar form and encircling incision, but slip of former is specular and does not cover entire exterior. Tusta Red of the Barra phase at Altamira, Tustlán Red of the Izapa-Ocós phase, and Xquic Red of Izapa- and Altamira-Cuadros phases all include bowls with encircling incision (Green and Lowe 1967: 104–6, 112, 116–18, figs. 76, 78, 85, 89; Ekholm-Miller 1969: 25–9, 47, 48, 61, 62, figs. 18, 19, 36, 37, 52, 53).

CENTRAL CHIAPAS. The Unslipped category of the Cotorra phase at Chiapa de Corzo includes similar incised tecomates with red slip or paint, although usually applied to a limited area. Similar red-slipped bowls, occasionally with incised decoration, occur in Cotorra Red-and-White Bichrome, and red-slipped beakers appear in this type in the Dili phase. Tecomates, flaring bowls, and convex bowls with polished red slip and encircling incision appear in small quantities in the Dili phase (Dixon 1959: 12–17, 32, 37–8, figs. 13–15, 17, 19, 52). The Cotorra-phase occupation of the Santa Marta rock shelter also includes similar tecomates, and probably red-slipped beakers (MacNeish and Peterson 1962: 32–4, pl. 6). Similar tecomates and bowl forms in the Cotorra-phase ceramics of Padre Piedra (Navarrete 1960: 23–4, figs. 22, 23, table 1; Green and Lowe 1967: 43, fig. 52). At Santa Cruz, similar tecomates and flaring and convex bowls included in Burrero Red, which may pertain to the Burrero period or to an earlier undefined occupation contemporary with the Cotorra phase (Sanders 1961: 17, fig. 16).

CENTRAL HIGHLANDS. Red-slipped Brown ceramics of the San Pablo A (Middle Nexpa) and San Pablo B (Late Nexpa) phases of Morelos include similar flaring and convex bowls. Encircling incision occasionally occurs on incurved-rim bowls or tecomates. Cylindrical vessels first appear in San Pablo B (Grove 1972: 60–1, fig. 18). Piña Chán's (1955a: 17–18, lám. 12) Roja Pulida type and Montefalco Bichromes (Cyphers 1975) from Chalcatzingo (phase A) include similar flaring and convex bowls with occasional encircling incision. Similar red-slipped flaring and convex bowls also in Gualupita I (Vaillant and Vaillant 1934: figs. 18, 24). In the Valley of Mexico, red-rimmed tecomates at Ayotla (Tlapacoya) in the Ayotla and Justo subphases (Ixtapaluca phase). Incised molcajete bases or pseudo-grater fondos appear there in the Bomba subphase, at Tlatilco in the Iglesia subphase and El Arbolillo and Zacatenco in the El Arbolillo subphase—all of the initial Zacatenco phase. Polished red-slipped tecomates, flaring and convex bowls occasionally with encircling incision, and similar incised pseudo-grater fondos in the Tlatilco graves. Red-slipped convex bowls, occasionally with encircling incision, and pseudo-grater fondos were found in the Tlapacoya graves (Vaillant 1930: 31, 32, pl. I; 1935: 219–23; Porter 1953: pl. 10; Piña Chán 1958a: 35, 36, 48, 75, 85, figs. 8, 9, 16, 34, 38, 40, 41; 1971: fig. 5; Weaver 1967: 33, fig. 4, pl. 22; MacNeish et al. 1970: 277, 278; Tolstoy and Paradis 1970: 345–7, fig. 1). In the Valley of Oaxaca, red-slipped convex bowls in the Matadamas complex. Coatepec Red-on-Buff, dominant type of the Tierras Largas phase, includes tecomates and flaring and convex bowls with at least partial red slip or painted zone. Red-rimmed tecomates and polished red-slipped bowls and beakers in the San José phase (Flannery 1968: 82; MacNeish et al. 1970: 46–9, 269, 270, fig. 23).

GULF COAST. A few red-slipped tecomate-like vessels occur in the Ponce phase of northern Veracruz. Aguilar Red of Ponce and Aguilar phases includes very similar flaring bowls and incised bases (MacNeish 1954: 571–5, figs. 14, 17, chart 2). Tecomates, flaring bowls, beakers, and a few slightly convex bowls with red slip (or red-painted zone) and incised molcajete bases or pseudo-grater fondos in the Trapiche I and II phases at El Trapiche and Chalahuite (García Payón 1966: 95–9, 117–20, láms. 5, 6, 36, 37, 39, 47, 48; MacNeish et al. 1970: 273). Red-slipped tecomates with encircling incision and zoned cross-hatching in the Chicharras and San Lorenzo phases at San Lorenzo Tenochtitlán. Red-slipped and red-rimmed tecomates also in the earlier Ojochi and Bajío phases, and in Squier's "pre-Complex A" material from La Venta. Red-slipped (esp. flaring) bowls, at San Lorenzo from the Ojochi phase on (Coe 1970: 21–7; MacNeish et al. 1970: 279).

PETÉN. Similar thin red-slipped tecomates, flaring and convex bowls, and beakers with encircling incision, rows of punctations, and chamfering occur in the Xe-sphere complexes at Altar de Sacrificios and Seibal (Willey et al. 1967: 293; MacNeish et al. 1970: 285; Willey 1970: 324–34, figs. 3–12; R.E.W. Adams 1971: 20, 42, figs. 1–7, chart 1).

COASTAL GUERRERO. Tecomates are dominant during Pox, Uala, and Tom periods at Puerto Marqués and Zanja, often red-slipped and (esp. in Uala period) often have one or two encircling incised lines. Similar red-slipped convex and flaring bowls with encircling incision in the Uala and Tom periods. Incised grater bases appear in Uala period (C. Brush 1969: 57–8, 135, 138–47, figs. 6, 12, 14–17, 21, 23–26, tables 3A-3C, 8).

Remarks. Pozo Thin Red is a major type in all three Preclassic phases. It appears to be an exception to the trend toward less complete oxidation following the Cacahuananche phase, but this may simply reflect the thinness of the vessel walls. The incised decoration is similar to Guamuchil Polished Black in the Atopula phase. It becomes considerably more common on both types in the Tecolotla phase, with a wider range of motifs.

Guamuchil Polished Black (Figs. 27–31)

Paste and surface. Identical with Cacahuananche phase (see above), but polishing is virtually universal and more effective, frequently producing very high gloss.

Form. Wall thickness 4–9 mm., typically 6–7 mm.

TECOMATE. Diameter 14–18 cm. Body hemispherical, uniformly convex. Base form unknown, presumably rounded. Lip form: rounded or thickened interior.

OLLA. Diameter 18–22 cm. Exterior profile smooth; interior sometimes has sharp break in curvature where neck begins to flare strongly. Base form unknown. Lip form: beveled or tapered.

OPEN BOWL. Diameter 14–34+ cm., typically 24–28 cm. Wall straight and

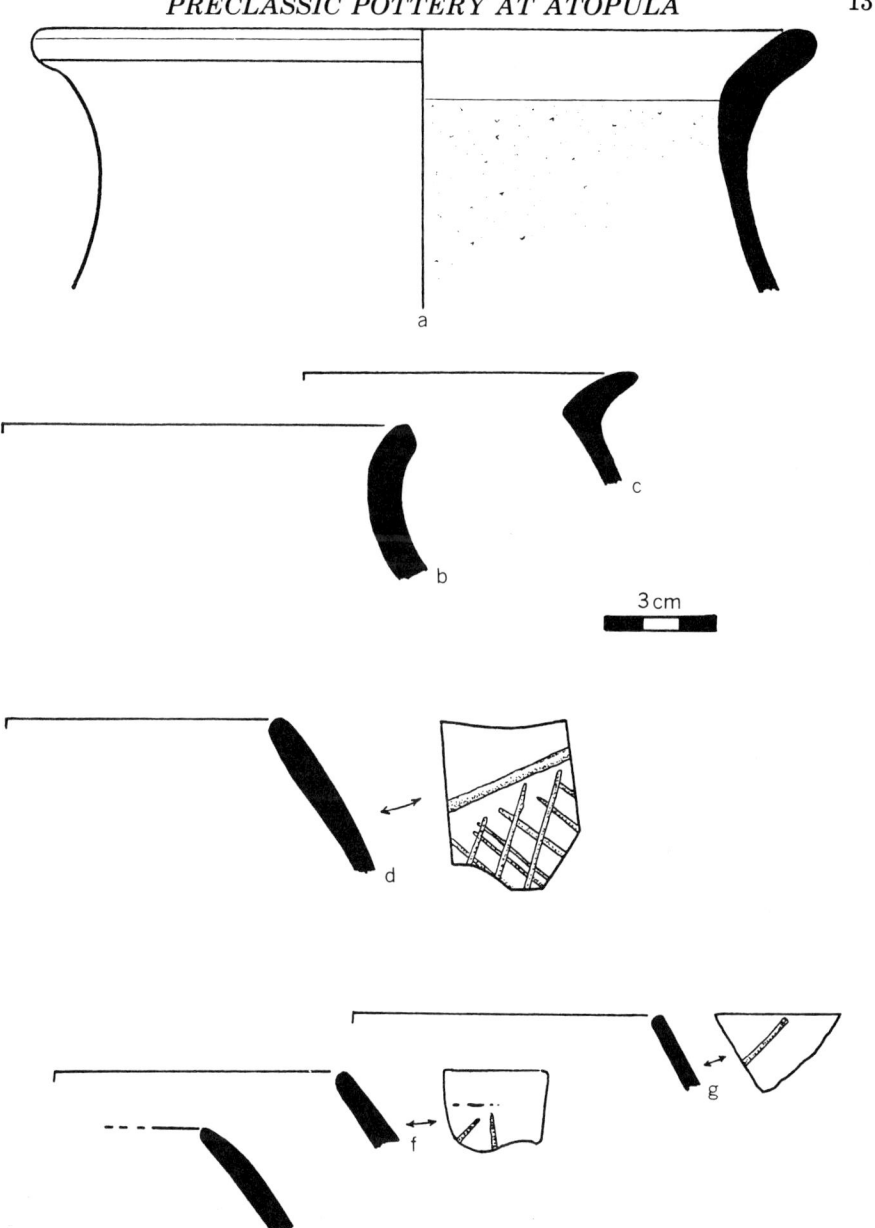

FIG. 27. Guamuchil Polished Black pottery, Atopula phase: *a–c*, ollas; *d–g*, tecomates.

outslanting to very slightly flaring. Base flat; diameter at base 13–14 cm. Lip form: rounded, blunted, beveled, or bolstered.

FLARING BOWL. Diameter 24–32 cm. Wall concave. Base flat. Lip form: rounded or slightly blunted.

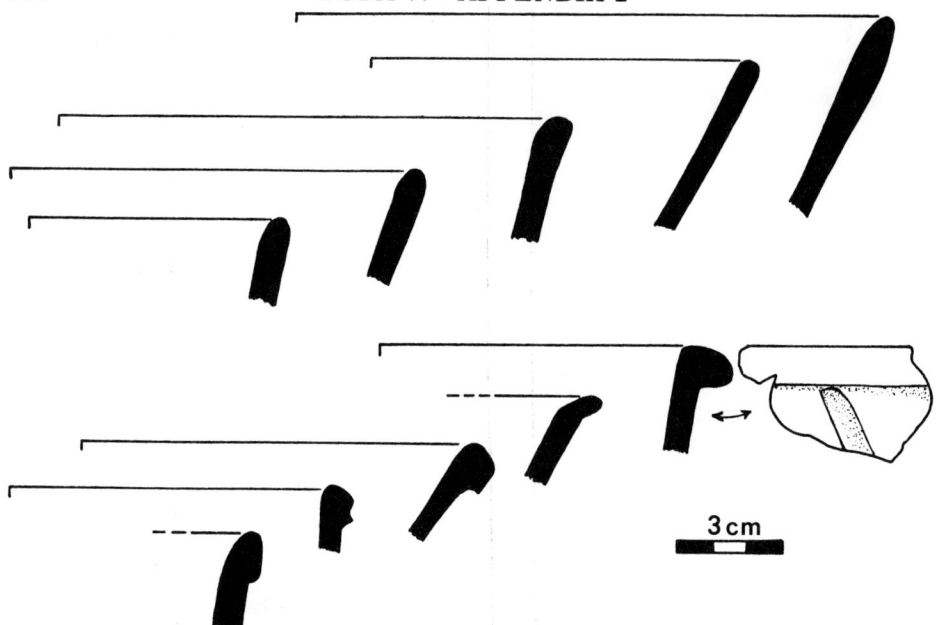

Fig. 28. Guamuchil Polished Black open bowls, Atopula phase.

CONVEX BOWL. Diameter 14–17 cm. Wall uniformly convex. Base rounded. Lip form: rounded, blunted, beveled, or tapered.

INCURVED-RIM BOWL. Diameter 10–22 cm. Base presumably rounded. Lip form: blunted, beveled, or slightly thickened interior.

BEAKER. Diameter 12–18 cm. Wall vertical, producing cylindrical cups or, more commonly, very slightly outsloping, producing typical beaker shape. Base flat; diameter at base 10–16 cm. Lip form: rounded, slightly blunted, or tapered.

BOTTLE. Sherds from cylindrical neck, exterior diameter 2–3 cm. In the only identifiable example the vessel body is convex. Base form unknown.

Decoration

GROOVING. All grooves pre-slip, quite smooth, and made while paste was plastic. 1. Broad, slightly curving, oblique groove on upper exterior of open bowl, with tapering end just below bolster. 2. Parallel vertical grooves on exterior of beakers, with tapering ends just above base. 3. Single very shallow groove encircling exterior of convex bowl just below and parallel to rim.

INCISION. 1. One to three lines encircling vessels parallel to rim, on beakers, convex bowls, incurved-rim bowls, and on body of one bottle. Incisions may be quite regular and perfectly parallel or somewhat erratic; all pre-slip, smooth, and done while paste was plastic. 2. One or more oblique and vertical lines on upper exterior of tecomates, incurved-rim bowls, and convex bowls. Pre-slip incision smooth and regular and done while paste was plastic.

3. Zoned cross-hatching on upper exterior of tecomate, area limited above by oblique line. Incision is deep, smooth, regular, and done while paste was plastic but after slip was applied. 4. Multiple deep oblique lines combined with a series of jabs or punctations on interior surface of incurved-rim bowl. Surface quite worn, presumably from use as grater, but traces of slip remain. Pre-slip incision quite regular and done while paste was plastic.

Comparative material

TEHUACÁN VALLEY. The forms of Guamuchil Polished Black occur in various types of the Ajalpan phase (although bottles and beakers not common). Polished black pottery in that phase only as aberrant or trade sherds. A few examples of Coatepec Buff and Red-on-Buff and a few Late Ajalpan aberrant sherds have incisions or grooves encircling vessel exterior, curvilinear incision on vessel exterior, and incised interior base. One aberrant sherd of a beaker-like vessel (resembling Ojochi-phase specimens from San Lorenzo) has very shallow vertical exterior grooves (MacNeish et al. 1970: 51–2, figs. 24–27).

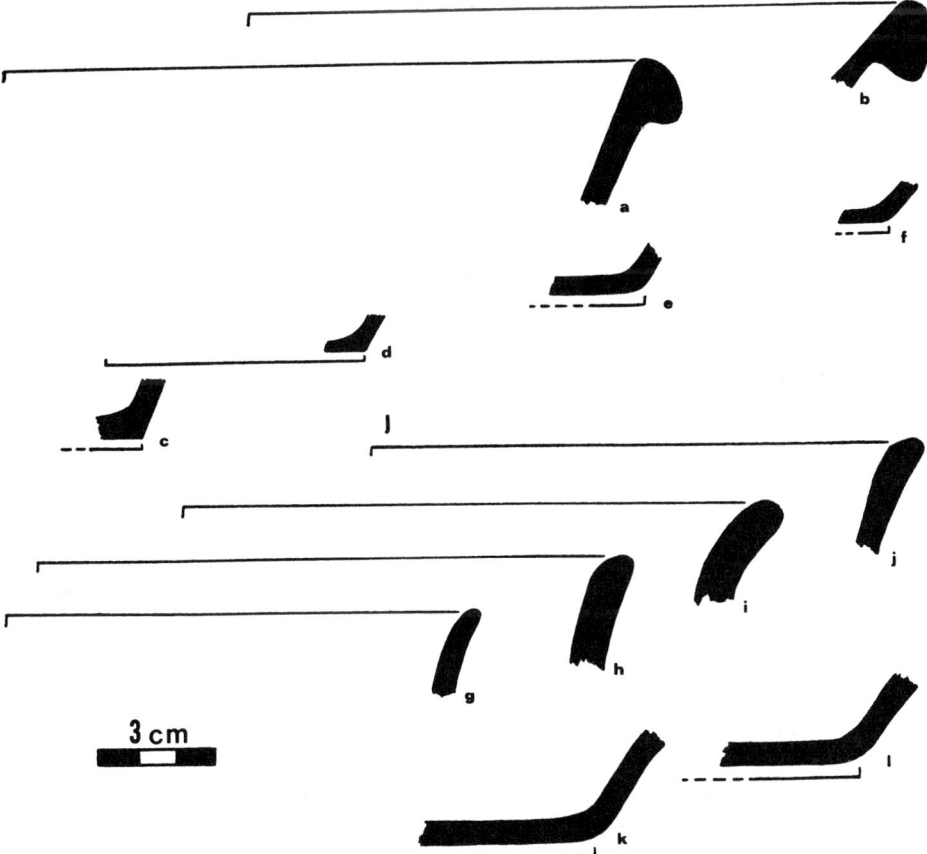

FIG. 29. Guamuchil Polished Black pottery, Atopula phase: *a–f*, open bowls; *g–l*, flaring bowls.

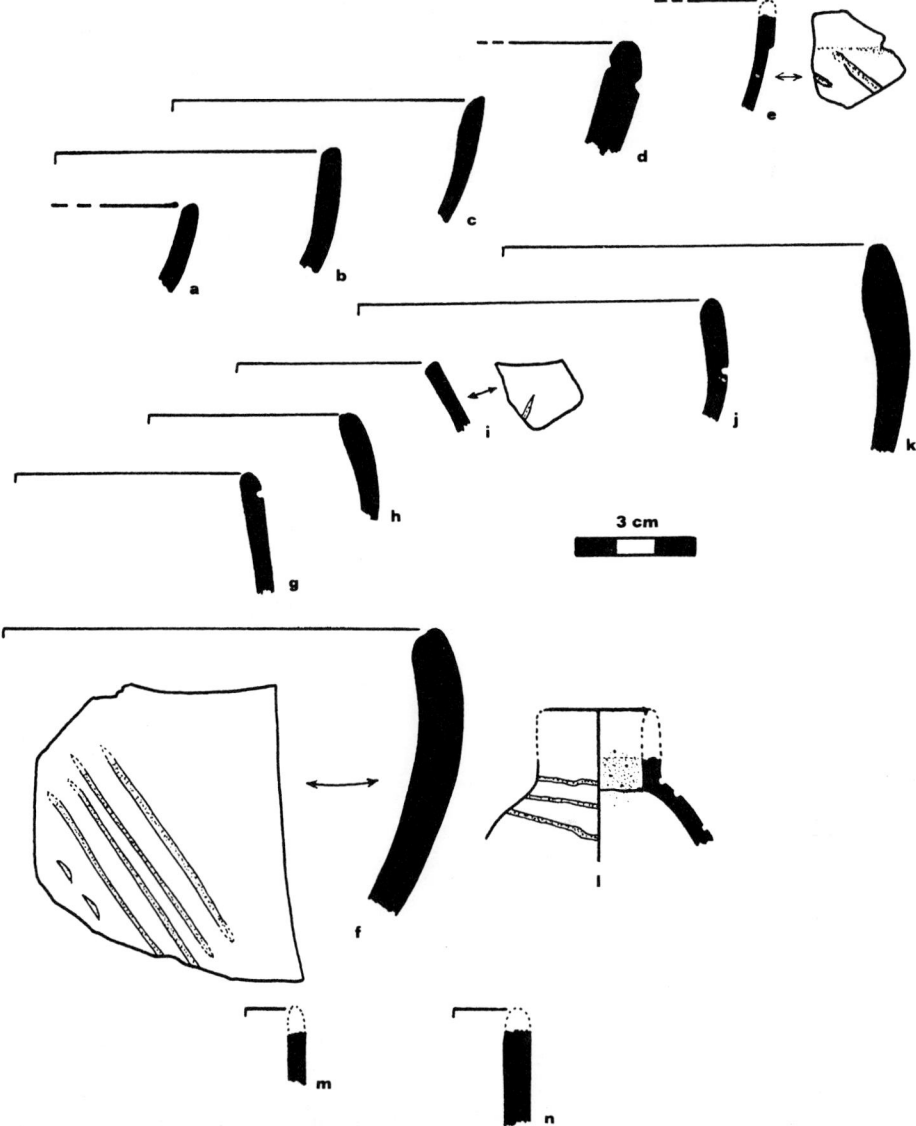

Fig. 30. Guamuchil Polished Black pottery, Atopula phase: *a–e*, convex bowls; *f–k*, incurved-rim bowls; *l–n*, bottles.

SOCONUSCO. Surface treatment and vessel forms (except bottles) similar to those of Morena Black of the Cuadros phase at Salinas La Blanca, which also has encircling grooves and incised designs on bowl exteriors. Crisscrossed lines similar to zoned cross-hatching on Mapache Red-rimmed tecomates of the Cuadros phase. Similar incised interior bases on Conchas White-to-Buff convex and grater bowls of the Conchas phase at La Victoria

(Coe 1961: 66–73, figs. 26, 28, 29; Coe and Flannery 1967: 32–3). Morena Black and Coapa Black of the Izapa-Cuadros phase have similar surface treatment and forms (but no convex bowls or bottles). Encircling incision or grooving on bowls and beakers of these types. Zoned cross-hatched tecomate is identical with one illustrated example of Pijijiapan Zoned from the Izapa-Ocós phase (Ekholm-Miller 1969: 33–5, 41–2, 45–7, figs. 24, 31, 35). One variety of Pampas Black-and-White of the Altamira-Cuadros phase (without white-rimming) includes very similar incised and grooved bowls with thickened and bolstered lips (Green and Lowe 1967: 108, fig. 80).

CENTRAL CHIAPAS. A few open and flaring bowls with polished black slip occur in the Dili phase at Chiapa de Corzo (Dixon 1959: 36–8, fig. 49). Polished dark brown-to-black beakers and a few tecomates, open or flaring bowls, and perhaps ollas in the Cotorra phase at the Santa Marta rock shelter (MacNeish and Peterson 1962: 33–4). Very similar incised black tecomates, bowls, and beakers in the Cotorra-phase ceramics at Padre Piedra (Navarrete 1960: 24, figs. 23, 24, table 1; Green and Lowe 1967: 45, fig. 57). A similar

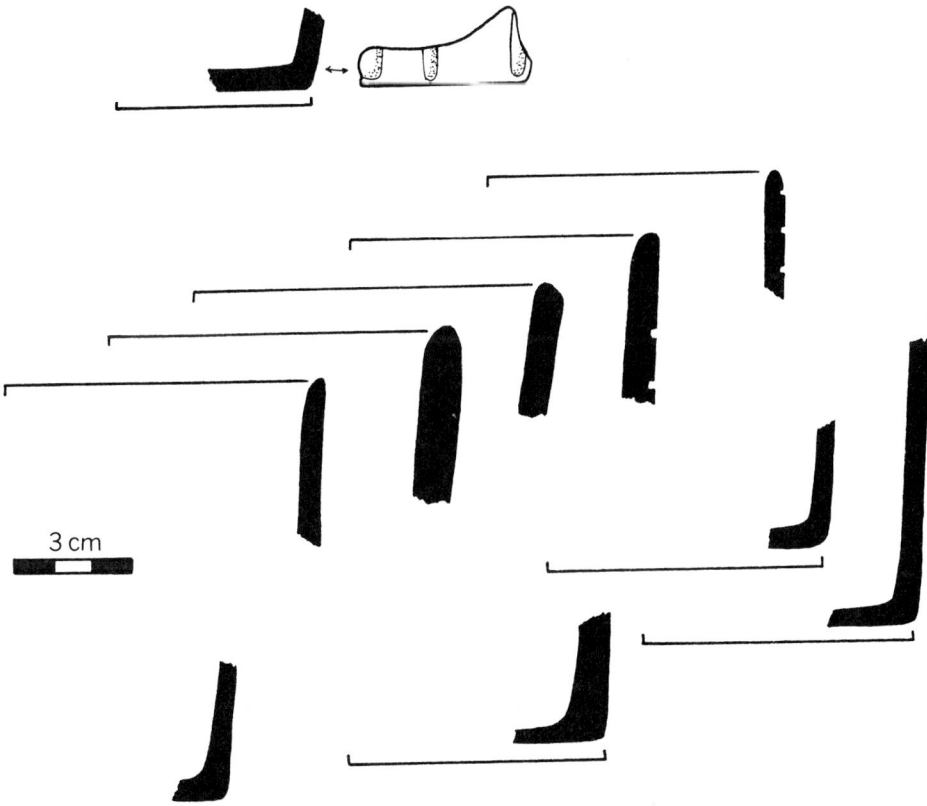

FIG. 31. Guamuchil Polished Black beakers, Atopula phase.

range of forms with incised decoration in the (unslipped and unpolished) black variety of Burrero Gray of the Burrero period (Dili equivalent) at Santa Cruz (Sanders 1961: 19, fig. 18).

CENTRAL HIGHLANDS. A similar range of forms, occasionally with encircling incision, occurs in the Black, Black-Brown and Madera Fine and Coarse types of the San Pablo A (Middle Nexpa) and San Pablo B (Late Nexpa) phases of Morelos. Cylindrical vessels appear only in latter period (Grove 1972: 59–61, figs. 14, 17). Piña Chán's (1955a: 10–13, 21–2, láms. 2, 3, 8, 18) Negro Pulido, Café Oscuro, and Café Negruzco types and Cyphers' (1975) Atotonilco Black, Tenango Brown, and Tlatilco Brown types from Chalcatzingo (phase A) include polished black and brown ollas, open, flaring, and convex bowls, and beakers with closely similar forms and incised and grooved decoration. Similar incised black- and brown-slipped bowls in Gualupita I (Vaillant and Vaillant 1934: figs. 20, 21, 23). In the Valley of Mexico, polished black and brown open and flaring bowls with bolstered rims, beakers, bottles, and zoned cross-hatching occur at Ayotla (Tlapacoya) in the Ayotla and Justo subphases (Ixtapaluca phase). Polished black and black-to-brown tecomates, ollas, beakers, and bowls with encircling incision and incised molcajete bases in the Iglesia subphase (initial Zacatenco phase) at Tlatilco. Very similar highly polished black-to-brown tecomates, open and flaring bowls, beakers, and bottles with incised decoration and molcajete bases or pseudo-grater fondos were recovered from Tlapacoya graves, and (along with polished black-to-brown ollas) these also occur in the Tlatilco graves (Porter 1953: pls. 10, 11; Piña Chán 1958a: 36, 41, 51–3, 74, figs. 9, 11, 18, 33–7; 1971: figs. 1, 3, 4; Coe 1965b: ills. 34, 37; Weaver 1967: 13–18, figs. 1, 2, 4, pls. 1–4, 6–8; MacNeish et al. 1970: 277; Tolstoy and Paradis 1970: 347, fig. 1). In the Valley of Oaxaca, several sherds of polished black trade pottery (Ocós Black) in the Tierras Largas phase. Polished black (esp. open) bowls and beakers common in the San José phase, as is incised decoration (Flannery 1968: 82; MacNeish et al. 1970: 270). Incised polished black tecomates, flat-based open bowls with bolstered rims, and bottles were found in Las Bocas cemetery (Coe 1965b: ills. 23–26, 33, 36).

GULF COAST. Very similar polished black bowls and beakers with encircling incision and multiple parallel lines incised in vessel interiors occur in Ponce Black of the Ponce and Aguilar phases of northern Veracruz (MacNeish 1954: 570–1, 574–5, fig. 17, chart 2). Black tecomates, open and flaring bowls, beakers, and a few convex and incurved-rim bowls and ollas (sometimes slipped, polished, and incised) in the Trapiche I and II phases at El Trapiche and Chalahuite (García Payón 1966: 39–45, láms. 4–11; 1971: 514; MacNeish et al. 1970: 273). Polished black (esp. open) bowls and beakers common in the San Lorenzo phase at San Lorenzo Tenochtitlán. Bottle form esp. typical of the Bajío phase; tecomates occur from the Ojochi phase on, but ollas do not until the Chicharras phase (Coe 1970: 26, 27; MacNeish et al. 1970: 279, 280).

PETÉN. Black-slipped (sometimes polished) tecomates; ollas; open, flaring, convex, and incurved-rim bowls; beakers; and bottles (or spouted vessels) with encircling and oblique incision and grooving and zoned incised crosshatching, occur in Xe-sphere complexes at Altar de Sacrificios and Seibal (Willey et al. 1967: 293; MacNeish et al. 1970: 285; Willey 1970: 341–6, figs. 24–30; R.E.W. Adams 1971: 24, 42, figs. 1, 2, 6, 7, chart 1).

COASTAL GUERRERO. Polished black- and brown-slipped tecomates; open, flaring, and convex bowls; and beakers with similar incised decoration occur in the Uala and Tom periods at Puerto Marqués and Zanja. Convex bowls with incised grater bases appear in Uala (C. Brush 1969: 135, 139–42, 146, figs. 6, 12, 15, 17, 25, tables 3, 8).

Remarks. Guamuchil Polished Black appears in the Cacahuananche phase and continues through the Tecolotla phase when it achieves its maximum popularity. New shapes (ollas, incurved-rim bowls, beakers, and bottles) appear in the Atopula phase. Among major types, the bottle form occurs only in Guamuchil Polished Black in the Atopula phase. The incurved-rim bowl with incised interior is very similar to Jiménez Red incurved-rim bowls and molcajetes of the Atopula phase. Guamuchil Polished Black and Pozo Thin Red together constitute the bulk of Atopula-phase ceramics; they have very similar forms and incised decoration. Guamuchil Polished Black continues as a major type in the Tecolotla phase, with incised decoration becoming even more common.

Arana Black-and-White (Fig. 32)

Paste. Relatively porous; hardness near 2.5, a few examples approaching 3.0. Temper coarse to very coarse, is the usual quartziferous sand, predominantly quartz crystals and small white and yellow flecks of mica. Differential firing typically produces a light rim and dark body (white-rimmed black ware). Two typical situations: (1) dark interior and exterior with white rim, probably produced by oxidizing entire vessel then refiring in a reducing, smudging atmosphere with rim buried; (2) white rim with dark interior and light exterior, probably produced by refiring (inverted) over a vessel containing smudging material, so that exterior and interior rim oxidized but enclosed interior is reduced and smudged; white rim often confined to exterior surface and adjacent paste, presumably produced by refiring with smudging material not contained in a second vessel (or in a vessel of nearly equal diameter). These are equivalent to firing alternatives A and C of Pampas Black-and-White at Salinas La Blanca (Coe and Flannery 1967: 33). Second variety slightly more common. Adjacent to smudged areas, paste is very dark gray to dark reddish gray (N 3/0, 5 YR 3/1, 4/1); core is never more completely oxidized even in white-rim areas. Paste adjacent to surface of white rims oxidized to pink (5 YR 7/3, 7/4). Paste adjacent to oxidized exterior surfaces (variant 2) fired to gray or light reddish brown (5 YR 5/1, 6/1, 6/3, 6/4).

Surface. Typically, exterior and upper interior surfaces are slipped; sometimes both surfaces entirely covered. Slipped surfaces well smoothed and compacted and slip polished to moderate luster. Unslipped interior surfaces relatively well smoothed. Where smudged or reduced, slip is black to dark gray (N 2/0, 3/0; 5 YR 2/1, 3/1, 4/1) or dark reddish brown (5 YR 3/3; 2.5 YR 3/4). Oxidized

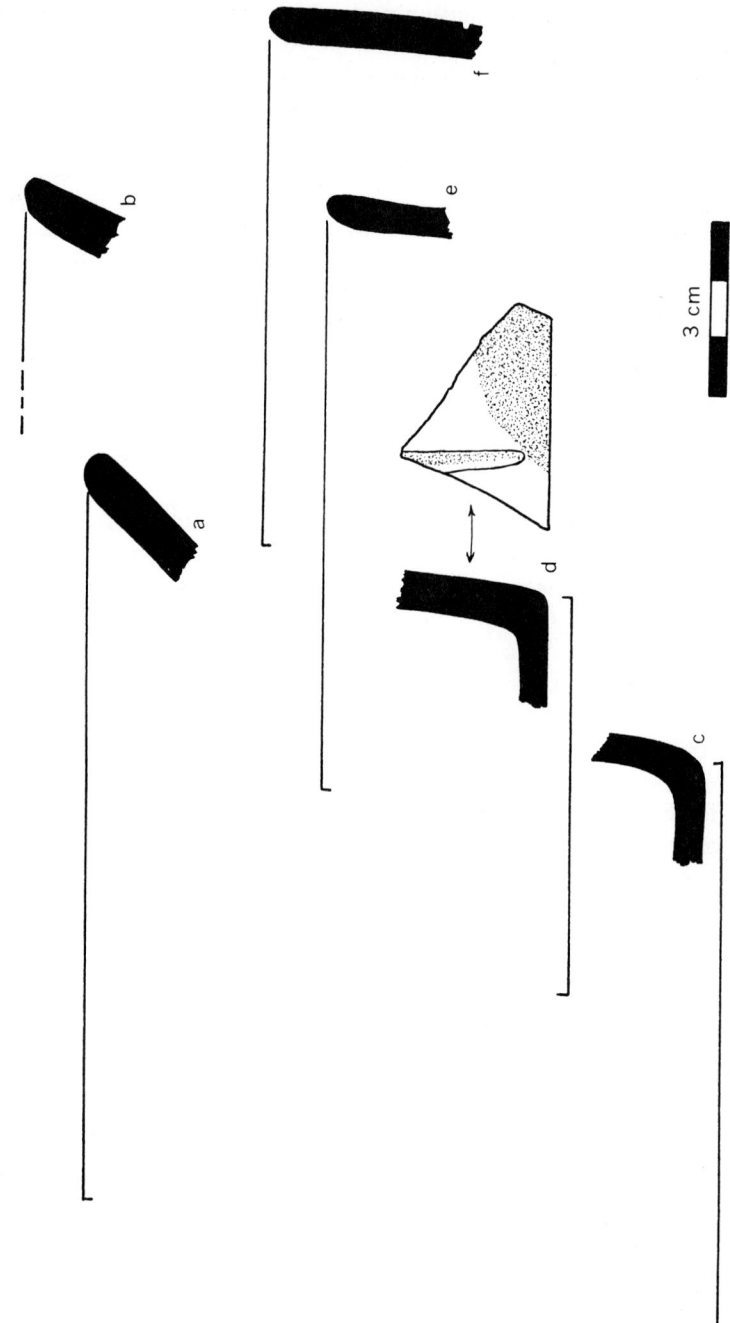

FIG. 32. Arana Black-and-White pottery, Atopula phase: *a, b*, open bowls; *c–f*, beakers.

exteriors have slip fired reddish gray to light reddish brown (5 YR 5/2, 5/3, 5/4). In "white"-rim areas slip is oxidized to pink, pinkish white or, rarely, white (5 YR 7/3-4, 8/1-3; 2.5 YR 8/2).

Form. Wall thickness 5-10 mm., typically 7-8 mm.

OPEN BOWL. Diameter 24-26 cm. Wall straight and outslanting. Base probably flat. Lip form: slightly blunted.

BEAKER. Diameter 16-20 cm. Wall straight and nearly vertical to very slightly flaring. Base flat; diameter at base 10-14 cm. Lip form: rounded or blunted.

Decoration

GROOVING. 1. Vertical grooves on exterior of beaker, with tapering ends just above base. Pre-slip grooves quite smooth and regular and made while paste was plastic.

Comparative material. White-rimmed black wares very widespread in Mesoamerica.

TEHUACÁN VALLEY. Mottled (or differentially fired) white and black bottles occur as trade sherds in the Late Ajalpan phase. Coatepec White-rimmed Black of the Early Santa María phase has same paste, surface treatment, and forms, but lacks vertical grooving. One Late Ajalpan aberrant sherd of a beaker-like vessel (resembling Ojochi-phase specimens from San Lorenzo) has very broad and shallow vertical exterior grooves (MacNeish et al. 1970: 51-2, 108-10, figs. 26, 64, table 35).

SOCONUSCO. Pampas Black-and-White of Cuadros and Jocotal phases of Salinas La Blanca has very similar paste, surface treatment, and forms, but lacks vertical grooving (Coe and Flannery 1967: 33-5, figs, 14, 15). Pampas Black-and-White of Izapa-Cuadros and Izapa-Jocotal phases also similar in these respects, and one bowl has a vertical groove (Ekholm-Miller 1969: 39-41, fig. 30). Pampas Black-and-White of the Altamira-Cuadros phase includes similar open bowls (Green and Lowe 1967: 108, fig. 80).

CENTRAL CHIAPAS. White Monochrome of the Cotorra phase at Chiapa de Corzo includes differentially fired open bowls and beakers (Dixon 1959: 7-9, figs. 2, 4). Revolución Smudged of the Cotorra phase at Padre Piedra includes similar open bowls (Green and Lowe 1967: 43-4, fig. 53).

CENTRAL HIGHLANDS. Differentially fired brown, black, and gray wares occur throughout Early Preclassic sequence in Morelos. Cylindrical vessels first appear in the San Pablo B (Late Nexpa) phase (Grove 1970a: 2; 1972: 35, 61, fig. 15). Chalcatzingo B has differentially fired open bowls and beakers (Cyphers 1975). In the Valley of Mexico, differentially fired black-and-white pottery and open bowl and beaker forms at Ayotla (Tlapacoya) in Ayotla and Justo subphases (Ixtapaluca phase). White-rimmed black open bowls and beakers and vertical grooving in the Iglesia subphase (initial Zacatenco phase) at Tlatilco. Similar white-rimmed black open bowls found by *huaqueros* at Tlapacoya, and differentially fired pottery occurs also in Tlatilco graves (Piña Chán 1958a: 50, 51, figs. 10, 17; 1971: figs. 6, 8; Weaver 1967: 35, 36, pl. 5; MacNeish et al. 1970: 277; Tolstoy and Paradis 1970: 347, fig. 1). In the Valley of Oaxaca, similar differentially fired black-and-white open bowls and beakers in the San José phase (Flannery 1968: 82; MacNeish et al. 1970: 270). White-rimmed black open bowls with grooved or excised decoration were found in the Las Bocas cemetery (Coe 1965b: ill. 27).

GULF COAST. Mottling or simple differential firing, including open bowls and beakers, occurs in Ponce Black of Ponce and Aguilar phases of northern Veracruz (MacNeish 1954: 570-1, 574-5, fig. 17, chart 2). Differentially fired black-and-white open bowls and beakers in Bicolor Natural of the Trapiche I and II phases at El Trapiche and Chalahuite (García Payón 1966: 87-92, láms. 32, 33; 1971: 518; MacNeish et al. 1970: 273). Differentially fired black-and-white pottery, esp. white-rimmed black ware, appears at San Lorenzo Tenochtitlán in the Bajío phase, increases dramatically in popularity during the Chicharras phase, and continues in the San Lorenzo phase when its forms include open bowls and beakers (Coe 1970: 24-7; MacNeish et al. 1970: 279, 280). Differentially fired (esp. white-rimmed black) open bowls also at La Venta (Drucker 1952: 92; Coe 1965a: 692).

PETÉN. White-rimmed black open bowls or beakers occur in the Xe complex at Altar de Sacrificios (R. E. W. Adams 1971: 27, chart 1).

Remarks. Arana Black-and-White is a typical example of the very widespread white-rimmed black wares. It appears only in the Atopula and Tecolotla phases, and always in very small quantities. Except for differential firing, it is quite similar to Guamuchil Polished Black in paste, temper, surface treatment, form, and decoration. Although the range of Arana Black-and-White decoration is more limited, the two types share such unusual features as parallel vertical grooves on beaker exteriors. They might well be considered varieties of a single type.

Pedrusco Polished Gray (Figs. 33, 34)

Paste and surface. Identical with Cacahuananche phase (see above) except that slip is more frequently fired to pinkish gray (5 YR 6/2).

Form. Wall thickness 5-10 mm., typically 6-8 mm.

TECOMATE. Diameter 10-12 cm. Overall form hemispherical, with uniformly convex wall. Base form unknown, presumably rounded. Lip form: rounded or thickened interior.

OLLA. Diameter 16-24 cm. No sharp breaks in curvature, neck grades smoothly into body. Form of base unknown. Lip form: rounded, slightly blunted, or beveled.

OPEN BOWL. Diameter 27-30 cm. Wall straight and outslanting or very slightly outflaring. One vessel so sharply outslanting as to be plate-like. Base slightly rounded. Lip form: blunted or bolstered.

FLARING BOWL. Diameter 14-18 cm. Wall strongly concave. Base probably flat. Lip form: rounded, slightly tapered, slightly thickened exterior, or bolstered.

CONVEX BOWL. Diameter 25-27 cm. Wall uniformly convex. Base rounded. Lip form: blunted.

INCURVED-RIM BOWL. Diameter 12-18 cm. Wall uniformly convex, producing

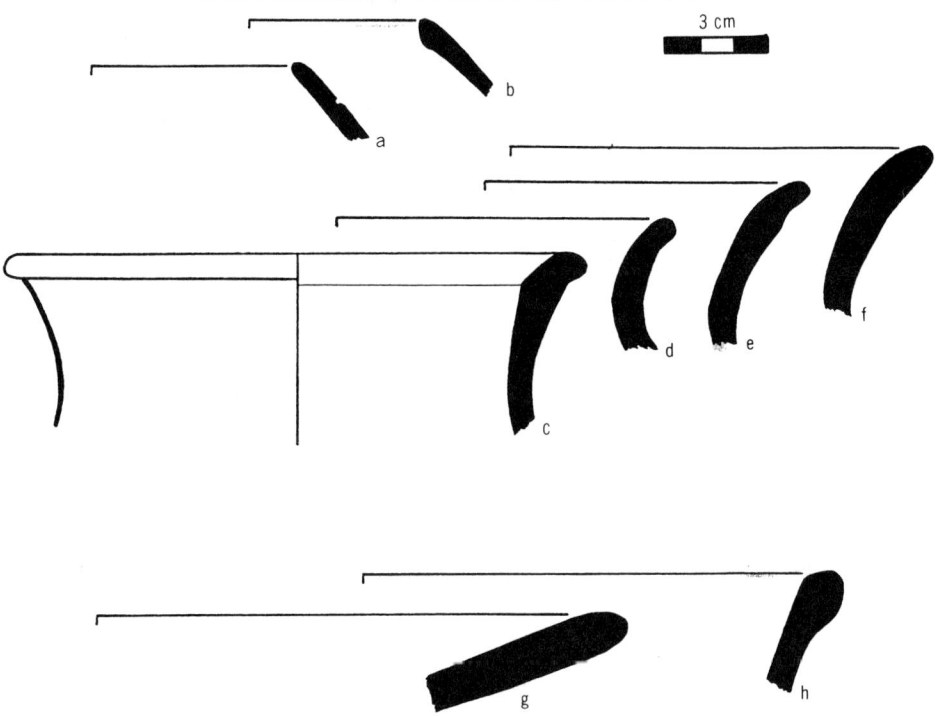

FIG. 33. Pedrusco Polished Gray pottery, Atopula phase: *a, b,* tecomates; *c–f,* ollas; *g, h,* open bowls.

slightly restricted mouth. Base rounded. Lip form: rounded, slightly blunted, or beveled.

Decoration

INCISION. 1. Single line encircling exterior of tecomate just below and parallel to rim. Postslip incision regular and done while paste was plastic.

OTHER. 1. Three flat areas or facets intersect at a point, breaking uniform curvature of upper exterior of one tecomate or incurved-rim bowl; might not be intentional decoration.

Comparative material

TEHUACÁN VALLEY. No close analogies discovered. A few similarities with Río Salado Gray, but this type is unslipped and very rare in the Ajalpan phase. Forms of Pedrusco Polished Gray occur in several Ajalpan-phase types besides Río Salado Gray. Incised lines encircling vessel exteriors in Río Salado Gray, on a few examples of Coatepec Buff and Red-on-Buff of the Ajalpan phase, and on a few Late Ajalpan aberrant sherds (MacNeish et al. 1970: 51, 78–83, figs. 24–26, 42, tables 29, 30).

SOCONUSCO. Ocós Gray of Jocotal and Conchas phases at Salinas La Blanca and La Victoria somewhat similar in surface treatment. Flaring bowls one of most common forms; the other forms of Pedrusco Polished Gray also occur,

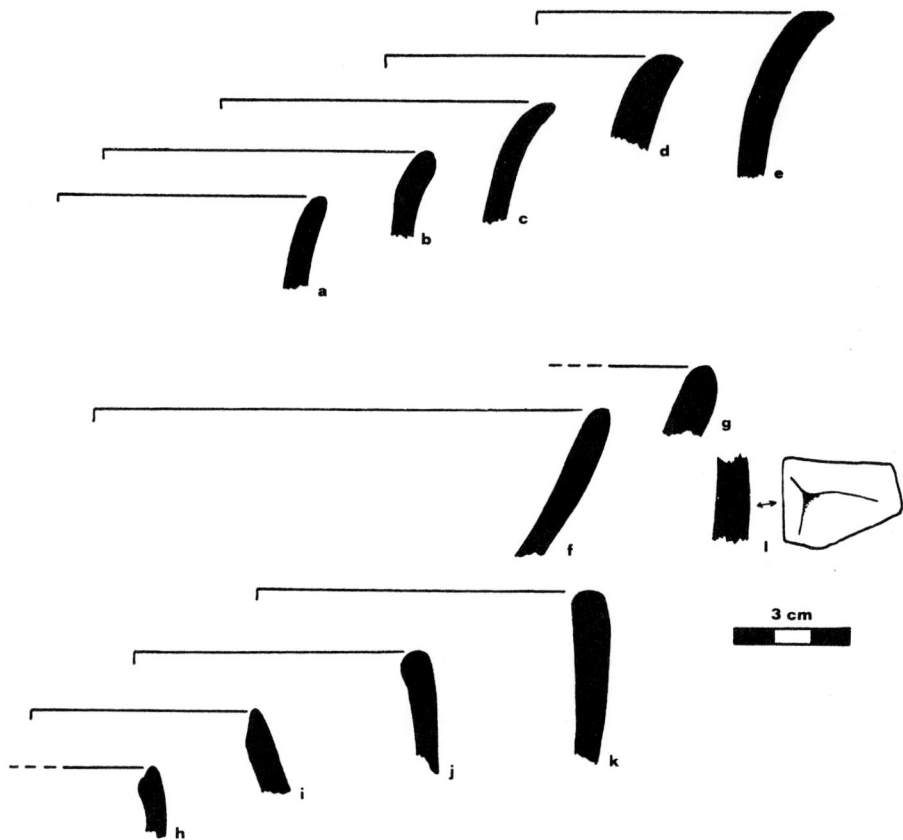

Fig. 34. Pedrusco Polished Gray pottery, Atopula phase: *a–e*, flaring bowls; *f, g*, convex bowls; *h–l*, incurved-rim bowls.

as does encircling incision. Similar forms also in Ocós Black of the Ocós phase at La Victoria, which includes many specimens ranging to gray in slip color (Coe 1961: 54–5, 73, figs. 22, 30; Coe and Flannery 1967: 46–7, fig. 24). Culebra Gray of Izapa-Jocotal and Altamira-Jocotal phases also similar in these respects (Green and Lowe 1967: 118; Ekholm-Miller 1969: 63–5, fig. 56).

CENTRAL CHIAPAS. White Monochrome tecomates, ollas, open bowls, and slightly convex bowls of the Cotorra phase at Chiapa de Corzo grade into "pearly gray" in slip color (Dixon 1959: 7–11, figs. 4–7). A few gray-slipped sherds from closely related Cotorra-phase occupation of the Santa Marta rock shelter probably represent tecomates, ollas, and open or flaring bowls (MacNeish and Peterson 1962: 34). Gray tecomates and bowls of Cotorra and Dili phases at Padre Piedra generally similar in form (Navarrete 1960: 25–6, fig. 25, table 1; Green and Lowe 1967: 46, fig. 60). Similar forms with encircling incision in the unslipped and unpolished Burrero Gray type of the Burrero period at Santa Cruz (Sanders 1961: 19, fig. 18).

CENTRAL HIGHLANDS. Gray pottery of the San Pablo A (Middle Nexpa) phase in Morelos includes generally similar bowls with incised decoration (Grove 1972: 61, fig. 15). Polished gray convex bowls occur in Piña Chán's (1955a: 16, lám. 11) Gris type and Cyphers' (1975) Olmec Grey type from Chalcatzingo (phase B). In the Valley of Mexico a few similar polished gray bowls in the Tlatilco and Tlapacoya graves (Piña Chán 1958a: 85, fig. 41; Weaver 1967: 28). Polished gray-slipped (esp. open and flaring) bowls, with incised decoration in the San José phase of the Valley of Oaxaca. In the Guadalupe phase incised gray (esp. polished waxy gray) pottery substantially increases in popularity (Flannery 1968: 82, 94; MacNeish et al. 1970: 270, 271).

Remarks. Pedrusco Polished Gray achieves its maximum popularity in the Atopula phase, after appearing as a minor type in the Cacahuananche phase. It continues to occur in distinctly reduced quantities in the Tecolotla phase. It is rather similar to Guamuchil Polished Black in form but not in decoration.

Mariposa White (Fig. 35)

Paste. Relatively porous; hardness 2.5–3.5. Temper coarse and is the usual quartziferous sand, predominantly white particles of limestone or calcite, quartz

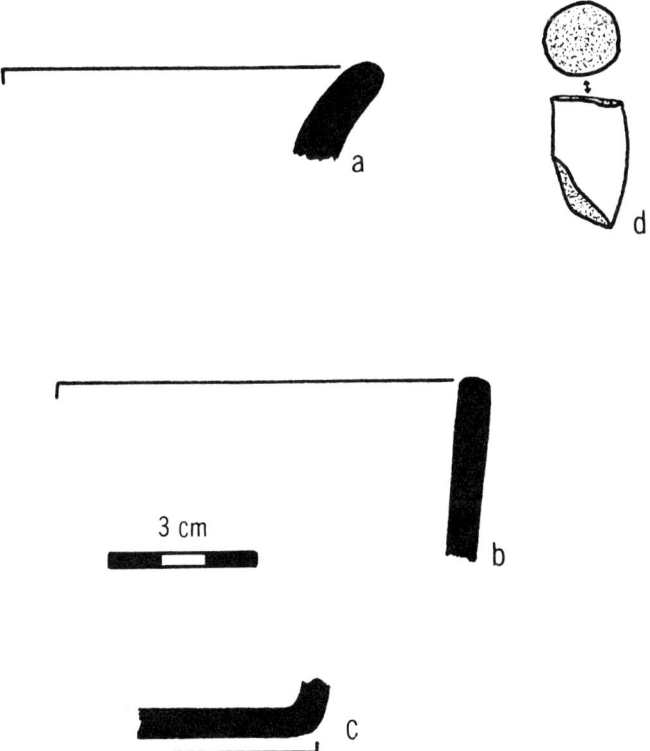

FIG. 35. Mariposa White pottery, Atopula phase: *a*, flaring bowl; *b*, *c*, beakers; *d*, loop handle.

crystals, and yellow plates of mica. Typically, paste oxidized to reddish yellow (5 YR 6/6) throughout; sometimes core or interior surface and adjacent paste less completely oxidized, gray to dark reddish gray (5 YR 4/1-2, 5/1).

Surface. Both surfaces (in one case exterior only) carefully smoothed and compacted, slipped, and polished. Sometimes slip has moderate luster, but is generally matte to chalky, perhaps from weathering. Slip color varies widely: typically pinkish gray to pinkish white (7.5 YR 7/2, 8/2) but may vary from white (10 YR 8/1) to reddish yellow or yellowish red (7.5 YR 6/8; 5 YR 5/6). Sherds in latter range often look streaky.

Form. Wall thickness 5-7 mm., typically quite uniform even at rim and base-wall junction.

FLARING BOWL. Diameter 14-16 cm. Wall concave. Base probably flat. Lip form: rounded or slightly blunted.

BEAKER. Diameter 14-18 cm. Wall straight and slightly outslanting to very slightly flaring. Base flat; diameter at base 12-14 cm. Lip form: slightly blunted.

Auxiliary features. 1. Loop handle: roughly semicircular, round in cross-section, presumably not attached to beaker or flaring bowl but to some form unrepresented in this sample of rim sherds. Conceivably an aberrant sherd of some other type.

Decoration. Limited to white slip in the Atopula phase.

Comparative material

TEHUACÁN VALLEY. In paste, surface treatment, and vessel form Mariposa White virtually identical with Canoas White of the Late Ajalpan and Early Santa María phases. The major difference: incised decoration so typical of Canoas White is not represented on Mariposa White in the Atopula phase, although this may simply reflect the small sample size. Canoas White does not have loop handles, but they do occur in Canoas Heavy Plain and Río Salado Coarse in the Early Santa María phase (MacNeish et al. 1970: 59-68, 75-8, figs. 34-7, tables 23, 24, 27, 28).

SOCONUSCO. Surface treatment and vessel forms quite similar to Conchas White-to-buff of Cuadros and Jocotal phases at Salinas La Blanca and the Conchas phase at La Victoria. Incised decoration not so common on Mariposa White, although encircling incision does occur; loop handles do not occur on Conchas White-to-buff (Coe 1961: 65-9, figs. 25-27; Coe and Flannery 1967: 42-4, fig. 21). Mariposa White similar in same respects to Amatillo White of Izapa- and Altamira-Cuadros phases, to Siltepec White of Izapa- and Altamira-Jocotal phases, to Cuchilla White of the Altamira-Cuadros phase, and to Bobo White of the Izapa-Jocotal phase. One Bobo White olla has a loop handle (Green and Lowe 1967: 110-14, figs. 81, 83, 86; Ekholm-Miller 1969: 48-58, figs. 38, 39, 43-8).

CENTRAL CHIAPAS. Very similar white beakers and flaring bowls occur in Cotorra and Dili phases at Chiapa de Corzo (Dixon 1959: 7-8, 23-8, figs. 4, 23, 24, 28), in the closely related Burrero Cream type of the Burrero period at Santa Cruz (Sanders 1961: 18-19, fig. 17), and in Dili-phase assemblages from Santa Rosa (Brockington 1967: 18), Vergel (Lowe 1959: 29, fig. 35), and Sitio Sevilla (Navarrete 1960: 16-18, 26, figs. 25, 26, table 1). Vergel White-to-buff (Vergel variety) of the Cotorra and Dili phases at Padre Piedra includes similar flaring bowls and lacks incision (Green and Lowe 1967: 44, fig. 55).

CENTRAL HIGHLANDS. "White" ceramics of the San Pablo A (Middle Nexpa) and San Pablo B (Late Nexpa) phases of Morelos generally similar in form and surface treatment; are also rare in these assemblages, and decoration virtually confined to San Pablo B specimens; cylindrical vessels also first appear in later phase (Grove 1972: 61, fig. 15). Similar white flaring bowls and beakers in Piña Chán's (1955a: 11-12, 19, 21, láms. 5-7, 14-17) Blanco Pulido, Blanco Laca, and Amarillenta Laca types and Cyphers' (1975) Amatzinac White type from Chalcatzingo (phases B and C). White-slipped flaring bowls and beakers in Gualupita I (Vaillant and Vaillant 1934: figs. 23, 25). In the Valley of Mexico, white-slipped beakers and flaring bowls at Ayotla (Tlapacoya) in Ayotla and Justo subphases (Ixtapaluca phase), esp. in the Bomba subphase (initial Zacatenco phase); in the Iglesia subphase (initial Zacatenco phase) at Tlatilco; and in Tlatilco and Tlapacoya graves (Piña Chán 1958a: 41, 44, 74, 75, figs. 12, 38; 1971: fig. 5; Coe 1965b: ills. 20, 28; Weaver 1967: 20-7, figs. 4-7, pls. 10, 11, 13, P; MacNeish et al. 1970: 277; Tolstoy and Paradis 1970: 347, fig. 1). In the Valley of Oaxaca, white-slipped bowls and beakers in the San José phase. Incised white pottery, esp. Atoyac Yellow-White, a type closely similar to Canoas White of the Tehuacán Valley, dominates the early Guadalupe phase (Flannery 1968: 82, 90; MacNeish et al. 1970: 270, 271; Drennan 1976).

GULF COAST. Similar flaring bowl forms common in Progreso White of the Pavón, Ponce, and Aguilar phases of northern Veracruz (MacNeish 1954: 566-70, 574, fig. 17, chart 2). White-slipped flaring bowls and beakers appear in small quantities in Trapiche I and II phases at El Trapiche and Chalahuite (García Payón 1966: 63-9, láms. 18-21; 1971; 516, 517; MacNeish et al. 1970: 273). Several types of white pottery occur in the Chicharras and San Lorenzo phases at San Lorenzo Tenochtitlán, but Mariposa White more like the hard incised white wares in the Nacaste phase (Coe 1970: 25-28; MacNeish et al. 1970: 279-80). White-slipped flaring bowls also at La Venta (Drucker 1952: 96, table 6).

PETÉN. White-slipped flaring bowls and beakers (and ollas with handles) occur in the Xe-sphere complexes at Altar de Sacrificios and Seibal (Willey et al. 1967: 293; MacNeish et al. 1970: 285; Willey 1970: 335-41, figs. 16-23; R. E. W. Adams 1971: 25, figs. 1, 2, chart 1).

COASTAL GUERRERO. White-slipped flaring bowls occur in the Tom period (and rarely in the Uala period) at Puerto Marqués (C. Brush 1969: 141, figs. 6, 16, tables 1, 3, 8).

Remarks. Mariposa White is a representative of the very widespread white wares so typical of Terminal Early Preclassic and Early Middle Preclassic ceramic assemblages in Mesoamerica. It appears at Atopula in very small quantities in the later Atopula phase and with slightly greater frequency in the Tecolotla phase. The incised decoration so typical of related types is not represented in the Atopula-phase examples, probably because of the small numbers.

Barranca Smoothed Buff (Figs. 36–38)

Paste and surface. Identical with Cacahuananche phase (see above).

Form. Wall thickness varies widely, 4–19 mm.; maximum at point of curvature change in olla necks or in rim sherds with thickened lips. Typical wall thickness 5–8 mm.

TECOMATE. diameter 10–13 cm. Overall shape hemispherical (to slightly flattened), with uniformly convex wall. Base presumably rounded. Lip form: rounded or tapered.

OLLA. Diameter 22–28 cm. Exterior profile smooth; interior profile may have sharp break in curvature where neck flares outward. Form of base unknown. Lip form: rounded, tapered, thickened exterior, or bolstered.

OPEN BOWL. Diameter 16–23 cm. Wall straight and outslanting to very slightly flaring. Base probably flat. Lip form: rounded, slightly blunted, beveled, or thickened exterior.

FLARING BOWL. Diameter 14–16 cm. Upper wall concave, becoming convex near base, without sharp break in curvature. Base rounded. Lip form: rounded or slightly blunted.

CONVEX BOWL. Diameter 16–18 cm. Wall uniformly convex. Base presumably rounded. Lip form: rounded or slightly blunted.

FIG. 36. Barranca Smoothed Buff ollas, Atopula phase.

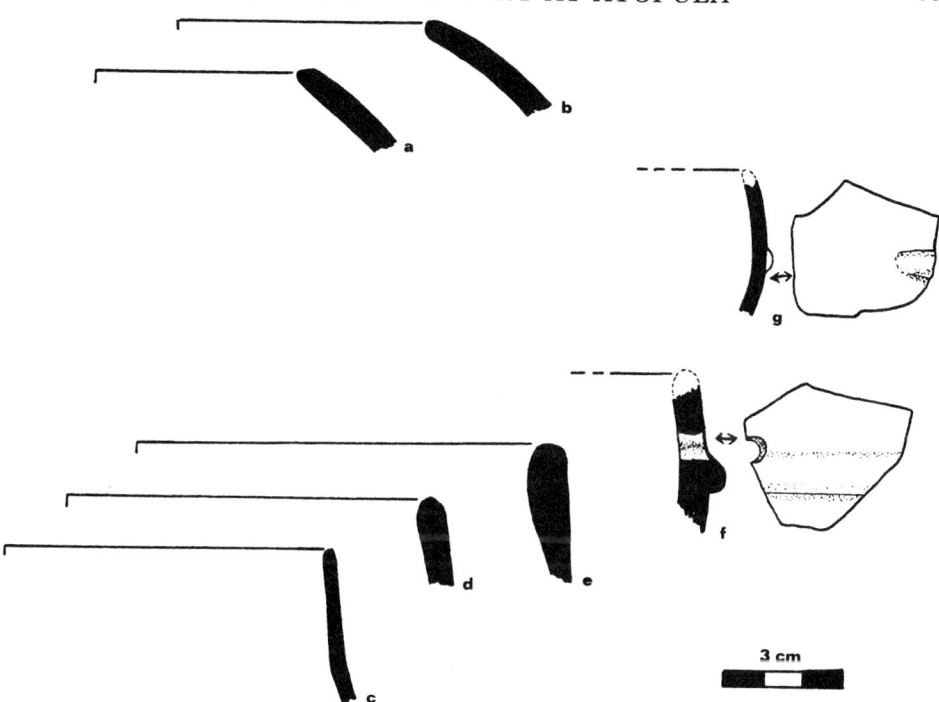

FIG. 37. Barranca Smoothed Buff pottery, Atopula phase: *a, b*, tecomates; *c–g*, incurved-rim bowls.

INCURVED-RIM BOWL. Diameter 16–21 cm. Uniformly convex wall produces slightly restricted mouth. In one vessel, upper wall turned upward so that rim is nearly vertical, forming a "collar," but mouth is still slightly restricted. Base presumably rounded. Lip form: tapered or thickened interior.

Decoration

OTHER. 1. Bolster or flange with roughly semicircular cross-section encircling upper exterior of tecomates or incurved-rim bowls. One sherd has a hole, neatly drilled through wall adjacent to flange after firing, perhaps a repair hole. 2. Raised nubbin or "flange" with roughly semicircular cross-section on upper exterior of one tecomate or incurved-rim bowl; is parallel to rim but extends only 2–3 cm.

Comparative material. Difficult to find convincing analogies for a plain type with simple forms.

TEHUACÁN VALLEY. Paste, surface treatment, and vessel forms similar to Ajalpan Plain and Coatepec Plain, and to a lesser extent to Ajalpan Fine Plain (although latter is thinner and has high polish). None of these types has features analogous to flanges. Coatepec Plain, occurring throughout Ajalpan and Santa María phases, with maximum popularity in Late Ajalpan, is most similar (MacNeish et al. 1970: 29–35, 44–6, figs. 11, 13, 22, tables 15, 17, 19).

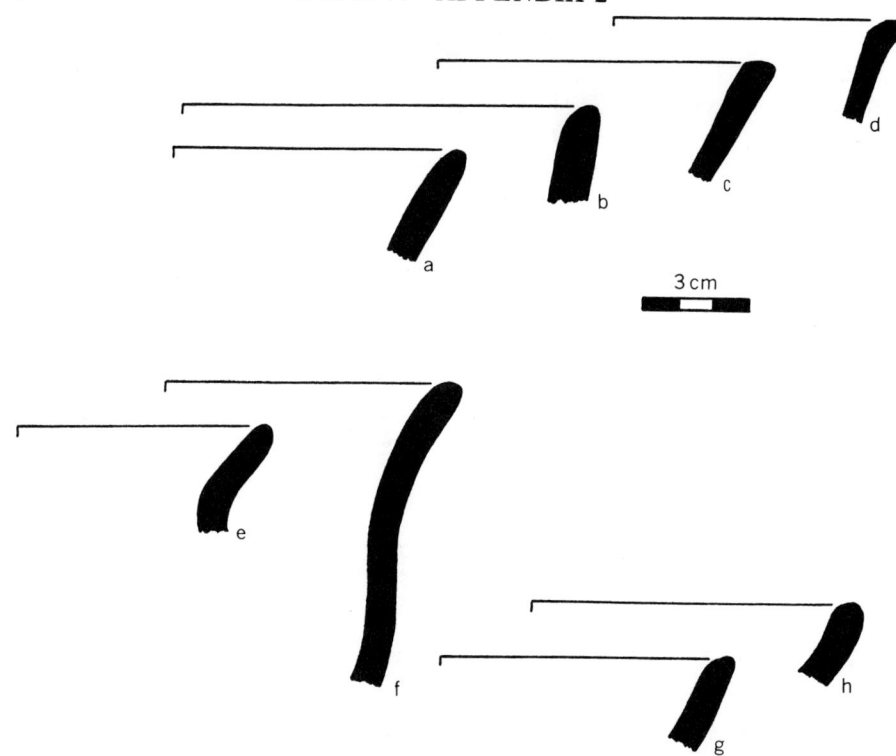

Fig. 38. Barranca Smoothed Buff pottery, Atopula phase: *a–d*, open bowls; *e, f*, flaring bowls; *g, h*, convex bowls.

SOCONUSCO. Surface treatment generally similar to Ocós Buff of the Ocós phase at La Victoria; forms and modes of decoration overlap but are basically different (Coe 1961: 53-4).

CENTRAL HIGHLANDS. "Brown" pottery of the San Pablo A (Middle Nexpa) phase of Morelos occasionally exhibits same self-slip or float-coat effect, and has similar range of forms (Grove 1972: 60, fig. 16). Piña Chán's (1955a: 9-10, lám. 1) Café Claro type and Cyphers' (1975) Del Prado Pink type from Chalcatzingo (phase A) includes ollas and open and flaring bowls with somewhat similar color and surface treatment.

No other resemblances to ceramics of distant areas noted.

Remarks. Barranca Smoothed Buff appears as a minor type in the Cacahuananche phase, and gradually declines in popularity during the later Atopula and Tecolotla phases. At no point does it equal such major types as Guamuchil Polished Black or Pozo Thin Red in popularity. It is characterized by unusual features in every phase: nubbin feet in Cacahuananche, encircling flanges or bolsters in Atopula, and slab handles in Tecolotla.

Bagre Coarse (Fig. 39)

Paste and surface. Identical with Cacahuananche phase (see above).

Form. Thickness of wall quite variable, at least 5–12 mm.; typical wall thickness ca. 7–9 mm.

OPEN BOWL. Diameter 16–22 cm. Wall straight and outslanting to very

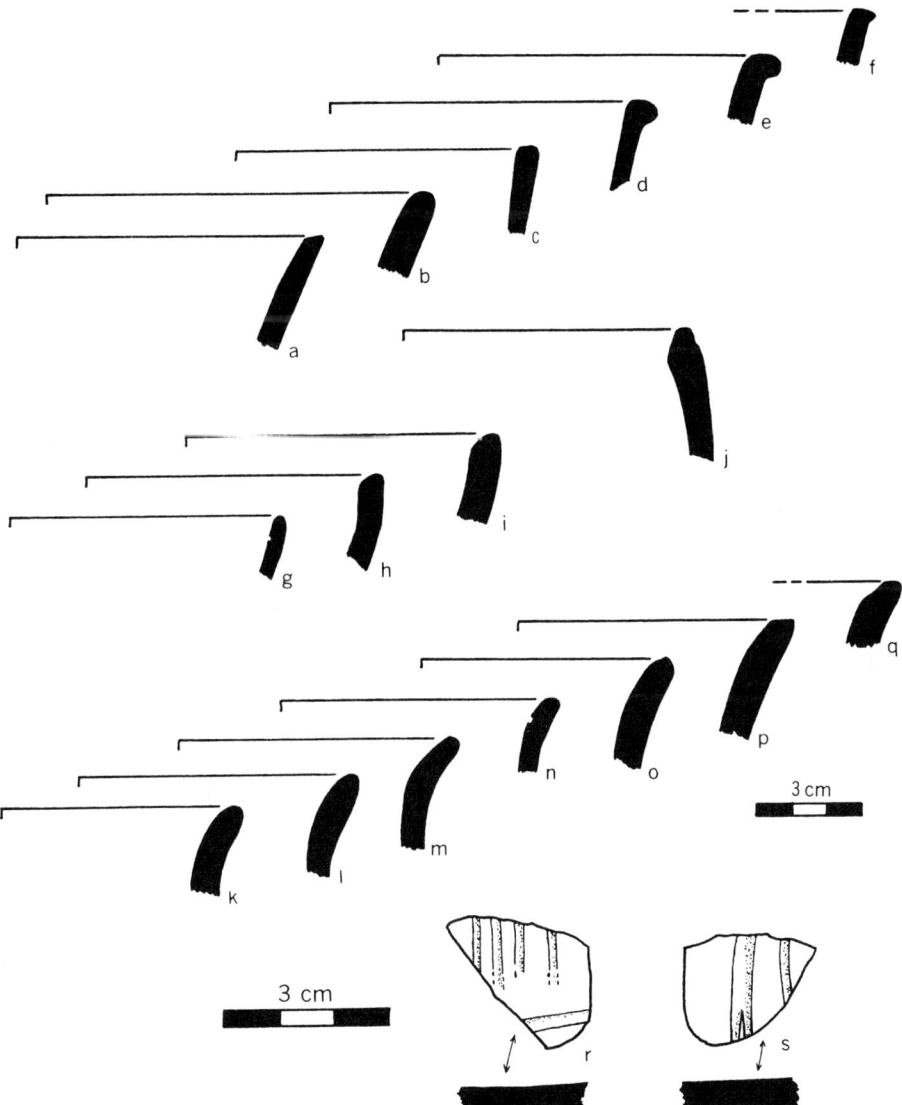

FIG. 39. Bagre Coarse pottery, Atopula phase: *a–f*, open bowls; *g–i*, convex bowls; *j*, incurved-rim bowl; *k–q*, flaring bowls; *r, s*, molcajete bases.

slightly concave. Base presumably flat. Lip form: slightly blunted, beveled, slightly thickened exterior, or bolstered.

FLARING BOWL. Diameter 12–15 cm. Wall strongly concave. Base form unknown, probably flat. Lip form: rounded, slightly blunted, beveled, or tapered.

CONVEX BOWL. Diameter 15–18 cm. Wall uniformly convex. Base probably rounded. Lip form: rounded, slightly blunted, or tapered.

INCURVED-RIM BOWL. Diameter 15–16 cm. Wall uniformly convex, producing slightly restricted mouth. Base presumably rounded. Lip form: slightly blunted or slightly thickened interior.

Decoration

INCISION. 1. Single line encircling upper interior of bowls parallel to rim. Incision smooth and regular and done while paste was plastic. 2. Molcajete base: multiple parallel straight lines on interior of unrestricted bowls. In one, one line bifurcates; in another at least one line is at right angles to the parallel set. Interior surfaces quite worn, presumably used as graters. Incision slightly irregular with rough edges and done after paste was partially dry.

Comparative material. Virtually impossible to find useful comparisons for a residual type.

TEHUACÁN VALLEY. Paste, surface treatment, and vessel forms roughly similar to Ajalpan Coarse and Coatepec Buff. One Coatepec Buff sherd has incised lines or grooves encircling exterior. A few examples of Coatepec Red-on-Buff and some Late Ajalpan aberrant sherds also have encircling incision and incised interior base (MacNeish et al. 1970: 26–9, 49–51, figs. 10, 25, 26, tables 14, 21). No close resemblances at the level of the type noted with ceramics from more distant areas.

Remarks. Bagre Coarse is undoubtedly a residual category. It includes not only vessels originally left uncompacted and unslipped, but also sherds of other types in which slip or other distinctive surface treatment is no longer detectable because of weathering. Since Bagre Coarse cannot correspond to a native category, it is meaningless to speak of its popularity; its only utility is to show a wider range of shapes, modes of lip form, etc. It is well represented in every excavation level, as expectable for a residual type, and is often the most frequent type recovered.

Rare Pottery Types and Trade Sherds of the Atopula Phase

Polished Dark Red

Identical in all features with the Polished Dark Red aberrant type in the Cacahuananche phase (see above).

Orange

Identical in all features with the Orange aberrant type appearing in the Cacahuananche phase (see above).

Red-rimmed (Fig. 40a–d)

Paste. Hardness 2.5. Temper coarse, with occasional very coarse inclusions, is the usual quartziferous sand, predominantly whitish particles of calcite or limestone with occasional quartz crystals. Near surface, paste is typically oxidized:red to light red or reddish yellow (2.5 YR 5/6, 6/6; 5 YR 6/6); core dark gray (5 YR 4/1).

Surface. Rim area has dark red to red (10 R 3/6, 4/8) slip extending 1–2 cm. below lip on interior and exterior. Exterior surface and slipped portions of interior surface carefully smoothed and compacted; slip itself polished and has a slight gloss. Unslipped interior surface occasionally smoothed but not carefully or consistently.

Form. Wall thickness 6–9 mm.

OLLA. Diameter 12–14 cm. Typical shape is small-necked jar with a relatively sharp break in curvature on interior and exterior profile where the nearly vertical neck begins. Vessel body below neck apparently uniformly convex. Form of base unknown. Lip form: rounded or slightly blunted.

Decoration. Limited to red slip or paint.

Comparative material. No very close similarities noted.

TEHUACÁN VALLEY. Coatepec Red-on-Buff short-necked ollas of the Late Ajalpan phase are roughly similar, except that red paint of this type is specular (MacNeish et al. 1970: 46–9, fig. 24).

CENTRAL HIGHLANDS. In Morelos, Piña Chán's (1955a: 15–16, lám. 10) Rojo Sobre Café type from Chalcatzingo includes red-rimmed ollas.

Remarks. This type appears only in the Atopula phase, in minute quantities.

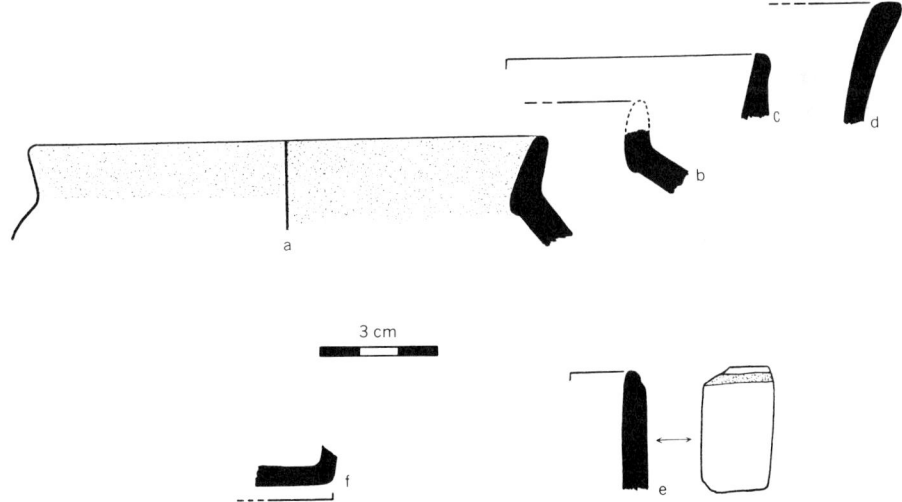

FIG. 40. Rare pottery types and trade sherds, Atopula phase: *a–d*, Red-rimmed ollas; *e*, Red-on-White bottle; *f*, Orange Lacquer flat-based bowl.

Since it is tempered with the usual "quartziferous sand," and the colors of paste and slip are close to Pozo Thin Red, it might be considered a variant of that type. However, given the distinctive vessel form and slip placement, and very uniform slip color, it seems appropriate to treat it as a distinct minority type, although there is nothing to suggest it was an import.

Red-on-White (Fig. 40e)

Paste. Hardness 3.0. Temper coarse, predominantly white particles of limestone or calcite, with frequent quartz crystals, and occasional red particles, not the usual quartziferous sand. Exterior surface and adjacent wall pink (5 YR 7/4; 7.5 YR 7/4); interior less completely oxidized to light brown (7.5 YR 6/4).

Surface. Exterior smoothed and compacted, covered with thin chalky unpolished white (5 YR 8/1) slip, which does not adhere well to surface and is mostly eroded away. Interior not smoothed and has irregular grainy surface from temper particles.

Form. Wall thickness 5–6 mm.

BOTTLE. Diameter 2–3 cm. This sherd represents a tubular bottle neck, not quite cylindrical but very slightly convex, producing a slightly restricted orifice. Form of body and base unknown. Lip form: rounded.

Decoration. Dark red (10 R 3/6) paint applied to exterior of neck over white slip. Occurs as a band in a very shallow groove around neck just below lip; slight traces of red paint lower on neck as well, presumably representing additional linear designs now extremely eroded.

Comparative material

SOCONUSCO. Tilapa Red-on-White of the Cuadros and Jocotal phases at Salinas La Blanca has similar red bands around vessel mouths over white slip, but color is different and Tilapa Red-on-White does not include bottle shapes (Coe and Flannery 1967: 39–40). Tilapa Red-on-White of the Izapa-Cuadros phase is more similar: white slip is matte and the red paint applied in bands delimited by (but not confined to) grooves encircling rim. Here, too, bottle form is absent and paint is a weaker red (Ekholm-Miller 1969: 43–5). One sherd of Tilapa Red-on-White occurs in the Tehuacán Valley as an import (MacNeish et al. 1970: 52).

COASTAL GUERRERO. White-slipped vessels (but not bottles) with red-painted rim bands occur in the Tom period at Puerto Marqués (C. Brush 1969: 138–9, figs. 14, 15).

Remarks. This Red-on-White pottery is represented by a single sherd. The tempering material and unusual paste characteristics (hardness) suggest it may be an import.

Orange Lacquer (Fig. 40f)

One sherd from a late Atopula-phase level represents Piña Chán's (1955a: 19–20) and Cyphers' (1975) Laca type from Chalcatzingo (phase B). Tempering material is not the quartziferous sand typical of locally manufactured Atopula ceramics, but includes shiny black and red particles as well as crystals of quartz and whitish particles of limestone or calcite. Paste is fired pink to light reddish brown (5 YR 7/4, 6/4) at surface, with dark gray core (10 YR 4/1). Vessel first coated with thick pinkish-white (7.5 YR 8/2) slip, and then with a thin streaky orange or reddish-yellow (5 YR 6/8) slip. Surface well smoothed and slip lightly polished. Sherd represents a flat-based vessel, probably an open bowl. No decoration other than slip.

Trade sherds of Morelos Orange Lacquer occur in the Tehuacán Valley in the Early Santa María phase and in the Iglesia subphase (initial Zacatenco phase) at Tlatilco; a few flat-based Orange Lacquer vessels in the Tlatilco graves. Orange Lacquer may also occur as a trade ware at La Venta (Drucker 1952: 97, 98; Piña Chán 1958a: 85, fig. 42; MacNeish et al. 1970: 84, 100, 101, 278, 280).

Pottery Types of the Tecolotla Phase

Jiménez Red (Figs. 41–44)

Paste and surface. Identical with Cacahuananche and Atopula phases (see above).

Form. Wall thickness 8–19 mm.; maximum thickness in ollas at point of curvature change, where neck begins to flare. Typical wall thickness 10–12 mm.

OLLA. Diameter 28–32 cm. Exterior profile smooth; interior profile occasionally has sharp break in curvature where neck flares strongly outward. Form of base unknown. Lip form: rounded, blunted, or beveled.

OPEN BOWL. Diameter 24–34 cm. Wall straight and outslanting to very slightly convex. Base presumably flat. Lip form: rounded, blunted, beveled, thickened interior, bolstered, or everted.

FLARING BOWL. Diameter 16–18 cm. Lower wall concave. Base flat; one specimen has a ring base. Lip form: rounded.

CONVEX BOWL. Diameter 19–24 cm. Wall uniformly convex. Base rounded.

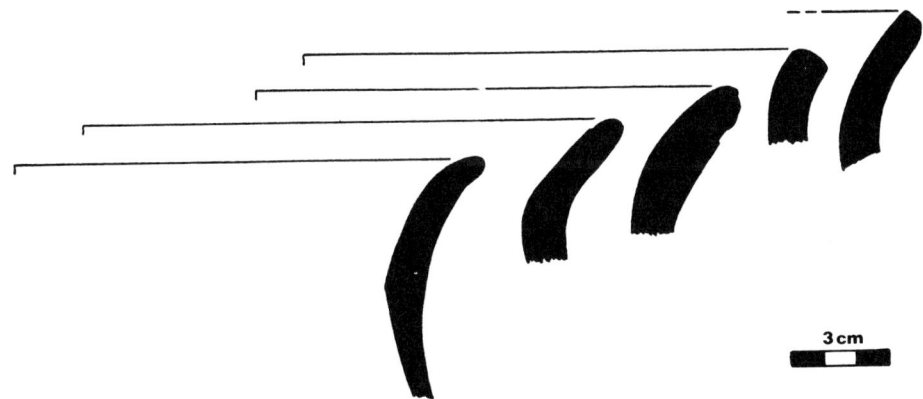

FIG. 41. Jiménez Red ollas, Tecolotla phase.

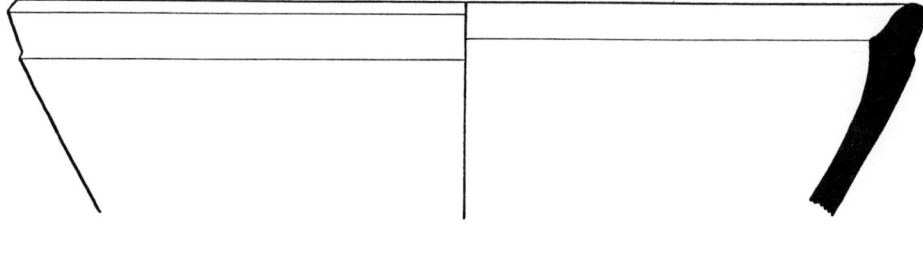

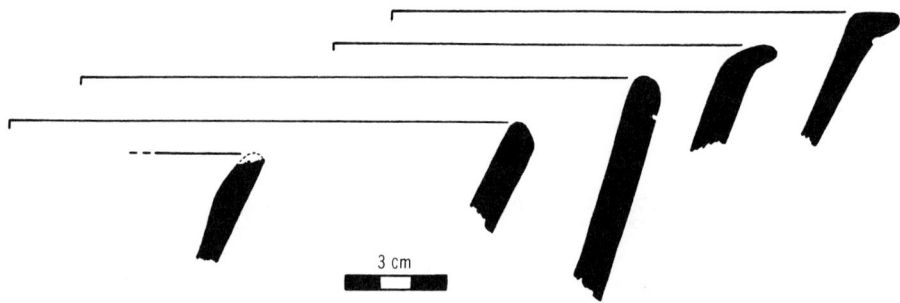

Fig. 42. Jiménez Red open bowls, Tecolotla phase.

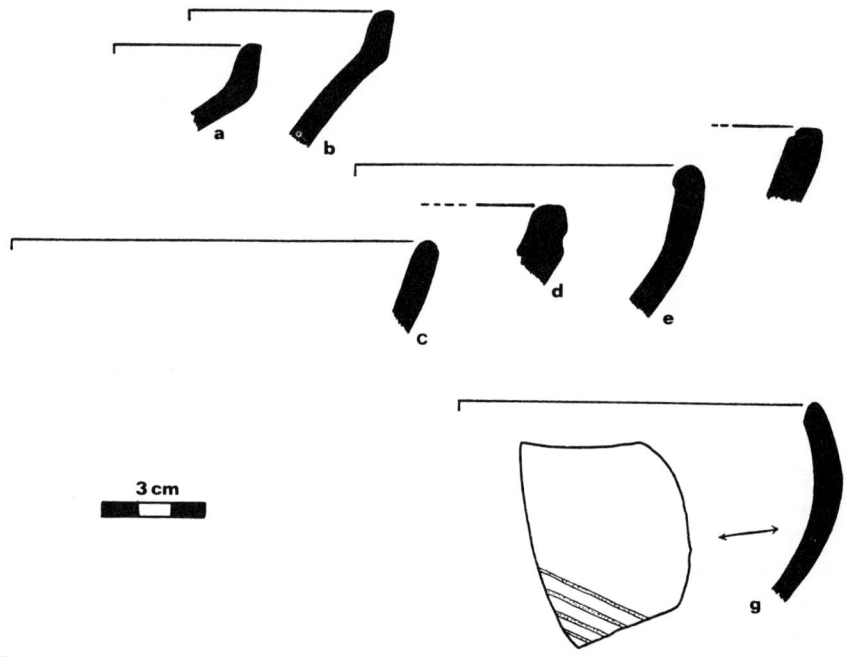

Fig. 43. Jiménez Red pottery, Tecolotla phase: *a, b*, composite-silhouette bowls; *c–f*, convex bowls; *g*, incurved-rim bowl.

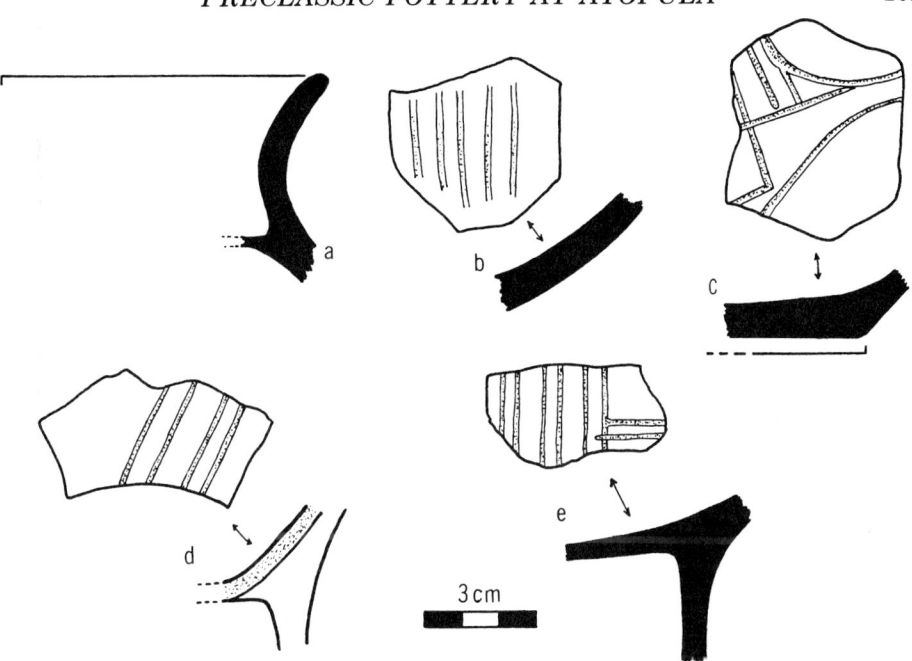

Fig. 44. Jiménez Red pottery, Tecolotla phase: *a*, flaring bowl with ring base; *b*, molcajete base; *c*, pseudo-grater fondo; *d, e*, molcajetes with ring bases.

Lip form: rounded, beveled, or slightly thickened interior.
INCURVED-RIM BOWL. Diameter 20 cm. Wall uniformly convex. Base rounded. Lip form: tapered.
COMPOSITE-SILHOUETTE BOWL. Diameter 8–12 cm. This vessel is a small plate-like bowl with low outslanting walls. Base form unknown. Lip form: blunted.
MOLCAJETE. Diameter 16–18 cm. This vessel is a convex bowl with flattened base. An extension beyond body apparently represents a ring base. Interior base incised with deep parallel lines and is worn from use as a grater. Lip form: rounded.

Auxiliary features. 1. Ring base: on molcajetes and in one case on a flaring bowl.

Decoration
GROOVING. All grooves pre-slip, quite smooth and regular, and made while paste was plastic. 1. One or two shallow grooves encircling exterior of ollas, convex bowls, or open bowls, just below and parallel to rim. 2. Single groove encircling convex bowl at interior edge of lip.
INCISION. All incision pre-slip, quite smooth and regular, and done while paste was plastic. 1. Single line encircling exterior of open bowls just below and parallel to rim; incision very shallow and line sometimes discontinuous. 2. Flat molcajete grater base: designs are deeply incised multiple parallel

straight lines or "Opposed Areas of Parallel Lines" at right angles to one another. Interiors generally quite worn and presumably were graters. 3. Multiple deep oblique parallel lines on interior of incurved-rim bowl, probably used as grater. 4. Pseudo-grater fondo: designs are a combination of pendant arcs and straight lines, the sunburst motif, and occur on flat interior bases of open or flaring bowls. Interiors not very worn, slip basically intact. Vessels probably not used as graters, at least not heavily.

Comparative material

TEHUACÁN VALLEY. Ajalpan Coarse Red of the Early Santa María phase quite similar in paste, surface treatment, and thickness, although Jiménez Red is darker and has true slip. Ollas with flaring necks are most common form in both types, and convex bowls occur in both as minor form. Open and flaring bowls appear in Ajalpan Coarse Red in the Late Ajalpan phase. Composite-silhouette bowls in other Early Santa María types. Ajalpan Coarse Red has no decoration other than red wash, but encircling incisions or grooves and similar incised base interiors (pseudo-grater fondos) occur in several Early Santa María types, notably Canoas White and Río Salado Gray (MacNeish et al. 1970: 41–2, 62, 80, figs. 20, 35, 36, 42, tables 10, 23, 29).

SOCONUSCO. Surface treatment and thickness similar to Pacaya Red of Cuadros and Jocotal phases at Salinas La Blanca. Ollas one of most common forms in both types (but Pacaya Red ollas tend to have more vertical necks); open, flaring, and convex bowls occur in both as minor shapes. Encircling grooves or incisions on some Pacaya Red vessels. Similar incised interior bases in Conchas White-to-buff convex and grater bowls (Coe 1961: 67–8, figs. 26, 52, 53; Coe and Flannery 1967: 36–7, fig. 16). Tocanaque Red-unburnished of the Izapa-Jocotal phase similar in surface treatment; it includes ollas and open and flaring bowls. Xquic Red of Izapa- and Altamira-Jocotal phases characterized by open, flaring, and convex bowls with encircling incised lines (Green and Lowe 1967: 116–18, fig. 89; Ekholm-Miller 1969: 58–62, figs. 49, 50, 52, 53).

CENTRAL CHIAPAS. Similar open bowls and a few slightly convex bowls with a red slip and occasional incised decoration occur in the Red-and-White Bichrome category of the Cotorra and Dili phases at Chiapa de Corzo. One Cotorra-phase sherd represents a red-slipped olla (Dixon 1959: 12–16, 32–3, figs. 13–17, 38–40). The closely related Burrero Red type of Santa Cruz also includes red-slipped open, flaring, and convex bowls; this type may pertain to the Burrero period or to an earlier undefined occupation, contemporary with the Cotorra phase (Sanders 1961: 17, fig. 16). Similar bowl forms in the Cotorra phase at Padre Piedra (Navarrete 1960: 23–4, figs. 22, 23, table 1; Green and Lowe 1967: 43, fig. 52).

CENTRAL HIGHLANDS. Red-slipped Brown pottery of the San Pablo B (Late Nexpa) phase of Morelos includes similar convex and open bowls, but generally undecorated (Grove 1972: 60–1, fig. 18). Similar olla and bowl forms in Piña Chán's (1955a: 11, 17–18, láms. 4, 12) Café Rojizo and Roja Pulida types from Chalcatzingo; the latter has occasional encircling incision. Montefalco Bichromes of Chalcatzingo A (Cyphers 1975) include red-slipped ollas and incised convex bowls. Similar red-slipped ollas and open, flaring, and convex bowls in Gualupita I (Vaillant and Vaillant 1934: figs 18, 24). In the Valley of Mexico, incised molcajete bases or pseudo-grater fondos at Ayotla (Tlapacoya) in the Bomba subphase (initial Zacatenco phase) and, along with similar red-slipped bowls with encircling incision, in the Iglesia subphase at Tlatilco (early Zacatenco phase). Similar ollas and open and flaring bowls, and incised molcajete bases and pseudo-grater fondos, at El Arbolillo and Zacatenco in the El Arbolillo subphase (early Zacatenco phase). Similar red-slipped ollas, bowls, incised molcajete bases, and pseudo-grater fondos in Tlatilco graves. Red-slipped open and convex bowls, occasionally with encircling incision, and similar pseudo-grater fondos found by *huaqueros* at Tlapacoya (Vaillant 1930: 31, 32, pl. I; 1935: 219–23; Porter 1953: pl. 10; Piña Chán 1958a: 35, 36, 85, figs. 8, 9, 34, 38, 45; 1971: fig. 5; Weaver 1967: 33, fig. 4, pl. 22; MacNeish et al. 1970: 277, 278; Tolstoy and Paradis 1970: 345–7, fig. 1). In the Valley of Oaxaca, red (unslipped) ollas and polished red-slipped (esp. open and flaring) bowls very common in the San José phase. Red-washed ollas and open and flaring bowls in the Guadalupe phase (Flannery 1968: 82, 91, 94; MacNeish et al. 1970: 270, 271).

GULF COAST. Very similar red-slipped ollas common in Pavón, Ponce, and Aguilar phases of northern Veracruz. Aguilar Red of Ponce and (esp.) Aguilar phases includes similar open and flaring bowls and molcajete bases (MacNeish 1954: 567–75, figs. 14, 17, chart 2). Very similar incised molcajete bases or pseudo-grater fondos and ollas, open and flaring bowls, composite-silhouette bowls, and a few convex bowls, with red slip (or red-painted zones), in the Trapiche I and II phases at El Trapiche and Chalahuite (García Payón 1966: 95–9, 117–20, láms. 4–6, 36–8, 41, 42, 47–9; MacNeish et al. 1970: 273). Red-slipped (esp. flaring) bowls, at San Lorenzo Tenochtitlán from the Ojochi phase on; olla form does not appear until the Chicharras phase (Coe 1970: 21–5; MacNeish et al. 1970: 279). Open, flaring, convex, and composite-silhouette red-slipped bowls with occasional incision at La Venta, and incised molcajete bases or pseudo-grater fondos and ring bases (Drucker 1952: 96, 97, table 6; Coe 1965a: 690, figs. 8, 9; MacNeish et al. 1970: 280).

PETÉN. Red-slipped unpolished ollas and open and flaring bowls, with encircling grooving or incision, occur in the Xe-sphere complexes at Altar de Sacrificios and Seibal (Willey et al. 1967: 293; MacNeish et al. 1970: 285; Willey 1970: 324–33, figs. 3–10; R. E. W. Adams 1971: 20, 42, figs. 1–7, chart 1).

COASTAL GUERRERO. Similar red-slipped open, flaring, and convex bowls and ollas with occasional encircling incision occur in the Uala and Tom periods at Puerto Marqués and Zanja; deeply incised, red-slipped convex bowl interiors (graters) appear in Uala (C. Brush 1969: 137–47, figs. 6, 13–17, 22–26, tables 3A–3C, 8).

Remarks. Jiménez Red appears in very small quantities in the Cacahuananche phase and achieves its maximum popularity during the Atopula and Tecolotla phases. At no time does it approach Pozo Thin Red or Guamuchil Polished Black in popularity. Molcajetes and incised convex bowl interiors occur also in Jiménez Red and Guamuchil Polished Black in the Atopula phase (and in Bagre Coarse in the Atopula and Tecolotla phases). The pseudo-grater fondo occurs also in Pozo Thin Red (Atopula and Tecolotla phases), and Guamuchil Polished Black (Tecolotla phase).

Pozo Thin Red (Fig. 45)

Paste and surface. Identical with Cacahuananche and Atopula phases (see above).

Form. Wall thickness 3–7 mm., typically quite thin, 4–5 mm.

OPEN BOWL. Diameter 13–26 cm. Wall straight and outslanting to very slightly flaring. Base flat. Lip form: rounded, blunted, beveled, tapered, or thickened exterior.

CONVEX BOWL. Diameter 16–18 cm. Wall uniformly convex. Base rounded. Lip form: rounded, slightly blunted, or thickened interior.

Decoration

GROOVING. 1. Single groove encircling exterior of open bowl just below and parallel to rim. Pre-slip groove quite smooth and regular and made while paste was plastic.

INCISION. All incision pre-slip, quite smooth, and done while paste was plastic. 1. One or two lines encircling exterior of open or convex bowls just below and parallel to rim; in two cases on unslipped exterior of open bowls. Incision quite regular and carefully done or discontinuous and not quite parallel. 2. Pseudo-grater fondo/molcajete base: designs deeply incised, regular, multiple straight or slightly curved parallel lines on flattened interior base of open bowls. Most examples are pseudo-grater fondos, not worn at all, but a few bases quite worn, with few traces of slip; perhaps actually used as graters.

Comparative material

TEHUACÁN VALLEY. In paste, surface treatment, and thickness, Ajalpan Fine Red of Ajalpan and Early Santa María phases quite similar to Pozo Thin Red, but latter has a nonspecular red slip often covering both surfaces; both are polished. Ajalpan Fine Red has no decoration other than red wash, but encircling incisions or grooves and similar incised interiors (pseudo-grater fondos) occur in other Early Santa María types, esp. Canoas White and Río Salado Gray. Major difference: Ajalpan Fine Red is a minor type in Tehuacán, Pozo Thin Red a major type at Atopula (MacNeish et al. 1970: 31-3, 62, 80, figs. 12, 36, 42, tables 16, 23, 29).

SOCONUSCO. Surface treatment and vessel forms of Pozo Thin Red somewhat similar to Pacaya Red of Cuadros and Jocotal phases at Salinas La Blanca. Encircling grooves or incisions appear on some forms of Pacaya Red. Similar incised interior bases on Conchas White-to-buff convex and grater bowls of the Conchas phase at La Victoria (Coe 1961: 67-8, figs. 26, 52, 53; Coe and Flannery 1967: 36-7, fig. 16). Xquic Red of Izapa- and Altamira-Jocotal

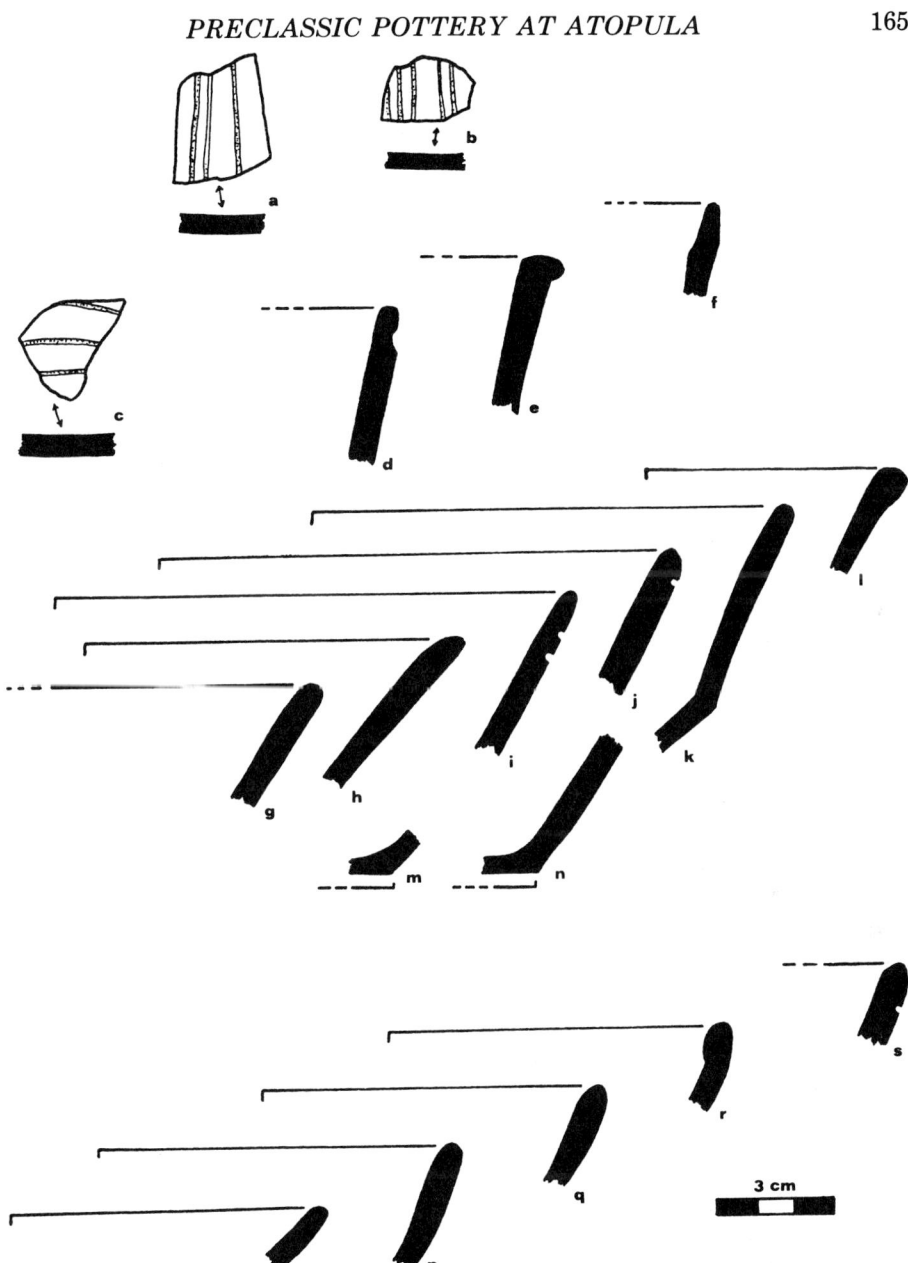

FIG. 45. Pozo Thin Red pottery, Tecolotla phase: *a–c*, pseudo-grater fondos or molcajete bases; *d–n*, open bowls; *o–s*, convex bowls.

phases includes bowls with encircling incision (Green and Lowe 1967: 116-18, fig. 89; Ekholm-Miller 1969: 61-2, figs. 52, 53).

CENTRAL CHIAPAS. Similar red-slipped open and slightly convex bowls with incised decoration occur in Red-and-White bichrome type of Cotorra and

Dili phases at Chiapa de Corzo. In the Dili phase a few such bowls have polished red slip (Dixon 1959: 12–16, 32–3, 37–8, figs. 13–15, 38–40). Closely related Burrero Red type of Santa Cruz also includes similar red-slipped open and convex bowls, which may pertain to the Burrero period or an earlier undefined occupation contemporary with the Cotorra phase (Sanders 1961: 17, fig. 16). Similar bowls also in the Cotorra phase at Padre Piedra (Navarrete 1960: 23–4, figs. 22, 23, table 1; Green and Lowe 1967: 43, fig. 52).

CENTRAL HIGHLANDS. Red-slipped Brown pottery of the San Pablo B (Late Nexpa) phase of Morelos similarly restricted to open and convex bowl forms, although undecorated (Grove 1972: 60–1, fig. 18). Piña Chán's (1955a: 17–18, lám. 12) Rojo Pulida type and Montefalco Bichromes (Cyphers 1975) from Chalcatzingo (phase A) include similar open and convex bowls with polished red slip and occasional encircling incision. Red-slipped open and convex bowls occur in Gualupita I (Vaillant and Vaillant 1934: fig. 24). In the Valley of Mexico, incised molcajete bases or pseudo-grater fondos appear at Ayotla (Tlapacoya) in the Bomba subphase (initial Zacatenco phase) and at Tlatilco in the Iglesia subphase (early Zacatenco phase), along with polished red-slipped bowls with encircling incision. Similar open bowls, incised molcajete bases, and pseudo-grater fondos at El Arbolillo and Zacatenco in the El Arbolillo subphase (early Zacatenco phase). Polished, red-slipped open and convex bowls, occasionally with encircling incision, and incised molcajete bases or pseudo-grater fondos in the Tlatilco and Tlapacoya graves (Vaillant 1930: 31, 32, pl. I; 1935: 219–23; Porter 1953: pl. 10; Piña Chán 1958a: 35, 36, 48, 75, 85, figs. 8, 9, 16, 34, 38, 40, 41; 1971: fig. 5; Weaver 1967: 33, fig. 4, pl. 22; MacNeish et al. 1970: 277, 278; Tolstoy and Paradis 1970: 345–7, fig. 1). In the Valley of Oaxaca, polished red-slipped (esp. open) bowls common in the San José phase. Open and convex bowls continue popular in the Guadalupe phase (Flannery 1968: 82, 94; MacNeish et al. 1970: 270, 271).

GULF COAST. Similar red-slipped open bowls and incised base interiors occur in Aguilar Red of the Ponce and (esp.) Aguilar phases of northern Veracruz (MacNeish 1954: 573, 575, figs. 14, 17, chart 2). Open and a few convex bowls with red slip (or red-painted zone) and molcajete bases or pseudo-grater fondos in the Trapiche I and II phases at El Trapiche and Chalahuite (García Payón 1966: 95–9, 117–20, láms. 4, 5, 36, 47, 48; MacNeish et al. 1970: 273). Red-slipped bowls at San Lorenzo Tenochtitlán from the Ojochi phase on. Red-slipped open and convex bowls, occasionally incised, at La Venta, also incised molcajete bases or pseudo-grater fondos (Drucker 1952: 96, 97, table 6; Coe 1965a: 690, figs. 8, 9; 1970: 21–7; MacNeish et al. 1970: 279, 280).

PETEN. Thin red-slipped open bowls with encircling grooving or incision occur in the Xe-sphere complexes at Altar de Sacrificios and Seibal (Willey et al. 1967: 293; MacNeish et al. 1970: 285; Willey 1970: 324–33, figs. 3–12; R. E. W. Adams 1971: 20, 42, figs. 1–7, chart 1).

COASTAL GUERRERO. Red-slipped open and convex bowls with encircling incision occur in the Uala and Tom periods at Puerto Marqués and Zanja.

Incised grater bases appear in the Uala period (C. Brush 1969: 138–41, 145–7, figs, 6, 14–16, 23–25, tables 3A–3C, 8).

Remarks. Pozo Thin Red is a major type throughout the Preclassic sequence, although fewer forms are represented in the Tecolotla phase. Similar pseudo-grater fondos are characteristic of Pozo Thin Red in both Atopula and Tecolotla phases, and occur also in Guamuchil Polished Black in the Tecolotla phase.

Guamuchil Polished Black (Figs. 46–50)

Paste and surface. Identical with Cacahuananche and Atopula phases (see above).

Form. Wall thickness 4–9 mm., typically 6–7 mm.
OPEN BOWL. Diameter 18–30 cm. Wall straight and outslanting to very slightly flaring. Base flat; diameter 12–14 cm. Lip form: beveled, slightly tapered, thickened exterior, bolstered, or everted.
FLARING BOWL. Diameter 18–22 cm. Lower wall concave; one vessel has wall turned upward, becoming nearly vertical just below rim. Base flattened. Lip form: blunted, tapered, slightly thickened interior.
CONVEX BOWL. Diameter 14–22 cm. Wall uniformly convex. Base rounded. Lip form: blunted.
BEAKER. Diameter 10–14 cm. Wall nearly vertical; straight and slightly

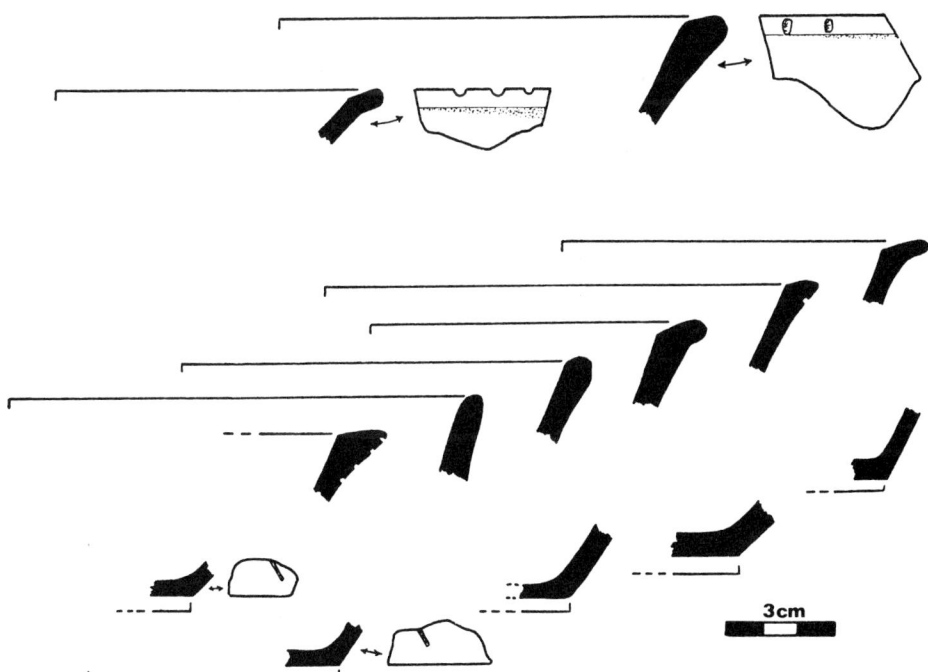

FIG. 46. Guamuchil Polished Black open bowls, Tecolotla phase.

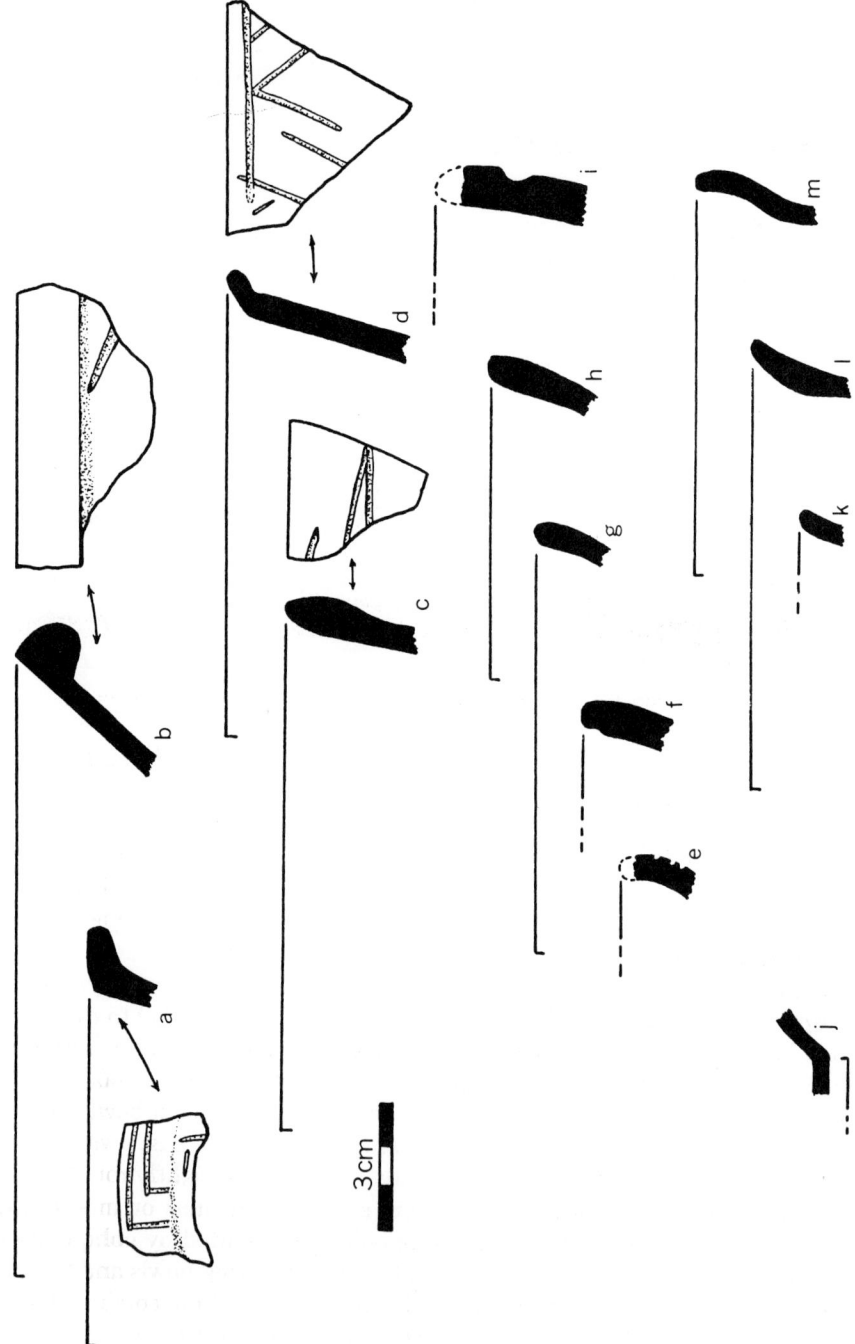

FIG. 47. Guamuchil Polished Black pottery, Tecolotla phase: *a–d*, open bowls; *e–i*, convex bowls; *j–m*, flaring bowls.

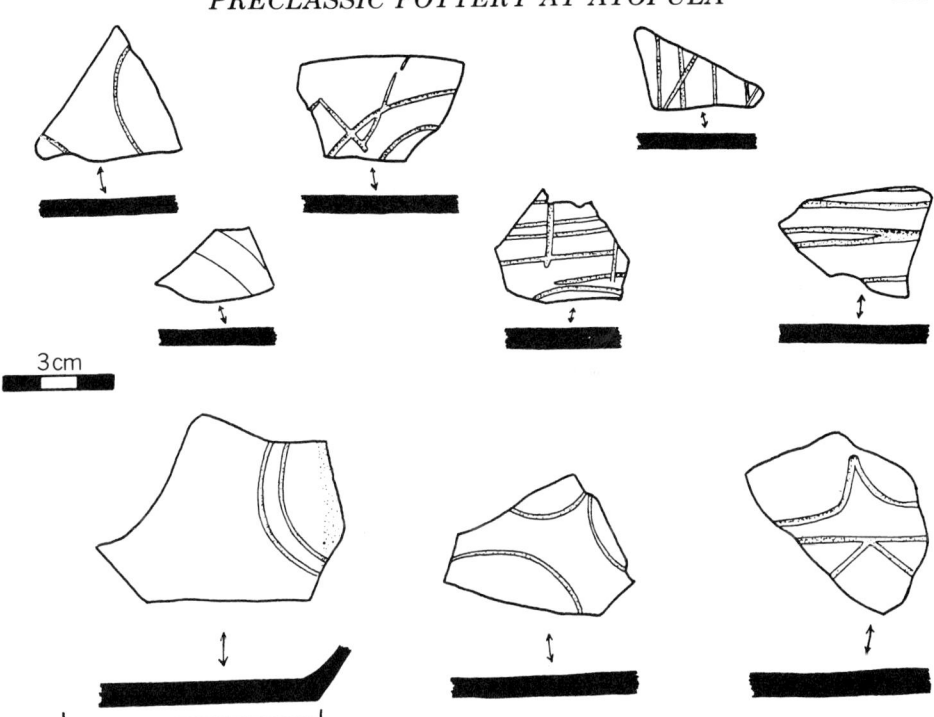

FIG. 48. Guamuchil Polished Black pseudo-grater fondos, Tecolotla phase.

outslanting to very slightly flaring. Base flat; diameter 12–14 cm. Lip form: rounded or tapered.

Decoration

GROOVING. All grooves pre-slip, quite smooth, and made while paste was plastic. 1. Single broad groove encircling bowl exteriors just below and parallel to rim. 2. Single very slightly curved oblique groove on upper exterior of open bowls with tapering end just below bolster.

INCISION. 1. One to four lines encircling exterior or, less frequently, interior of open bowls, convex bowls, or beakers, just below and parallel to rim. Lines may be quite regular and perfectly parallel or somewhat erratic, discontinuous, or turn up at the ends forming a single- or double-line-break motif. A double-line-break encircles top of flat everted lip of one open bowl. Pre-slip incision usually quite smooth and regular and done while paste was plastic; occasionally done after paste was partially dry, and has slightly rough edges. 2. Oblique and/or vertical lines forming e.g. perpendicular or intersecting horizontal and oblique lines, zones of parallel lines limited by oblique lines, and more complex designs on exterior of open and flaring bowls and beakers and occasionally on upper interior of open bowls. Often combined with encircling incision. Incised designs occasionally filled with red pigment. Pre-slip incision quite smooth and regular and done while paste was plastic. 3.

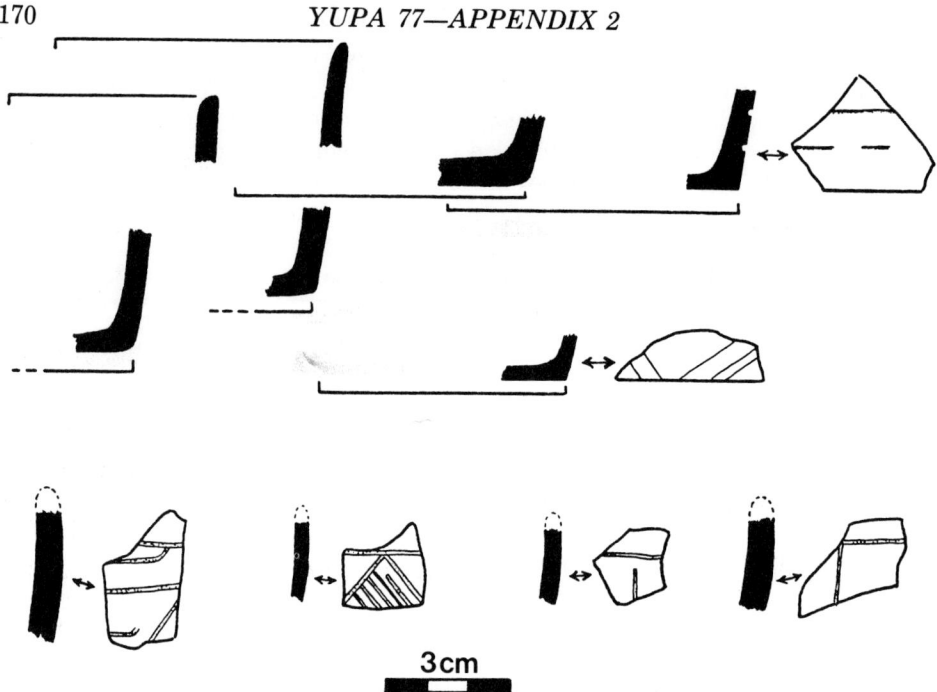

FIG. 49. Guamuchil Polished Black beakers, Tecolotla phase.

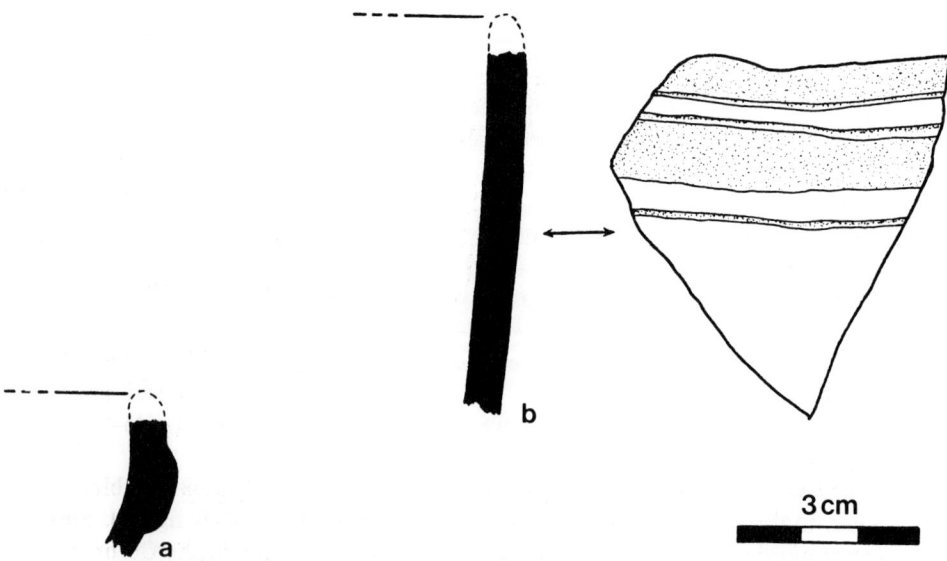

FIG. 50. Guamuchil Polished Black pottery, Tecolotla phase: *a*, convex bowl with flange; *b*, open bowl or beaker with incised lines and excised zones filled with red pigment.

Pseudo-grater fondo: designs are deeply incised multiple parallel lines, pendant arcs, concentric arcs, intersecting sets of parallel straight lines, and complex combinations of arcs and straight lines on flat interior base of open and flaring bowls. Pre-slip incision typically smooth and regular and done while paste was plastic. Occasional rough irregular edges (done after paste partially dry). Interiors rarely worn, apparently not true functional graters.

EXCISION. 1. Roughened or excised bands alternating with two encircling incised lines. Traces of red pigment rubbed into excised areas.

OTHER. 1. Row of evenly spaced notches or punctations encircling exterior of everted lip of open bowl. Notches pre-slip, smooth and regular, and done while paste was plastic. 2. Raised flange or "bolster" encircling upper exterior of vessel parallel to rim, roughly elliptical in cross-section, ca. 1.5 cm. wide.

Comparative material

TEHUACÁN VALLEY. Some resemblances to Quachilco Brown, although Guamuchil Polished Black is typically much darker and has true slip rather than a float-coat produced by polishing. Forms of Guamuchil Polished Black occur in Quachilco Brown and other Early Santa María types. True polished black pottery in the Early Santa María phase only as aberrant or trade sherds (which have incised decoration, sometimes filled with red pigment). Encircling incisions or grooves, multiple-line-breaks, various exterior incised designs, and molcajete and pseudo-grater bases common in Quachilco Brown and other Early Santa María types such as Canoas White and Río Salado Gray (MacNeish et al. 1970: 59–68, 78–85, 114–20, figs. 34–37, 42, 68, 69, tables 23, 24, 29, 30, 37, 38).

SOCONUSCO. Morena Black of Cuadros and Jocotal phases at Salinas La Blanca and the Conchas phase at La Victoria similar in surface treatment and vessel forms. Has similar encircling incision or grooving and incised designs including (in the Conchas phase) red-filled incision, red-filled excision combined with incision, and double-line-break. Similar incised interior base on Conchas White-to-buff grater bowls of the Conchas phase (Coe 1961: 67–73, figs. 26, 28, 29, 52, 53; Coe and Flannery 1967: 32–3). Morena Black and Coapa Black of the Izapa-Cuadros phase and Cambil Black of the Izapa-Jocotal phase have similar surface treatment, forms, and encircling incisions or grooves on bowls and beakers. Coapa Black has excised bands filled with red pigment. A variety of Pampas Black-and-White of the Altamira-Cuadros phase without white-rimming includes very similar bowls with thickened and bolstered lips, decorated with red-filled excision, incision, and grooving (Green and Lowe 1967: 108, fig. 80; Ekholm-Miller 1969: 41, 42, 45–7, 59–61, figs. 31, 35, 51).

CENTRAL CHIAPAS. Several open and flaring bowls with polished black slip occur in the Dili phase at Chiapa de Corzo (Dixon 1959: 36–8, fig. 49). Similar range of forms and similar incised and excised decoration in the Cotorra- and Dili-phase assemblages at Padre Piedra (Navarrete 1960: 24, figs. 23, 24, table 1; Green and Lowe 1967: 45, fig. 57). Beakers and a few open or flaring bowls with polished dark brown-to-black slip appear in the Cotorra-phase assemblage of the Santa Marta rock shelter (MacNeish and Peterson 1962: 33–4). Similar incised vessels included in the black variety of Burrero Gray of the Burrero period at Santa Cruz, but unslipped and unpolished (Sanders 1961: 19, fig. 18). Similar incised open bowls in the Dili-phase assemblage at Villa Flores (Navarrete 1960: 25, figs. 25, 26, table 1).

CENTRAL HIGHLANDS. Very similar range of forms, often with incised decoration, occurs in the Black, Black-brown, and Madera Fine and Coarse types of the San Pablo B (Late Nexpa) phase of Morelos (Grove 1972: 59–61, figs. 14, 17). Piña Chán's (1955a: 10, 12–13, 21–2, láms. 2, 3, 8, 18) Negro Pulido, Café Oscuro, and Café Negruzco types and Cyphers' (1975) Atotonilco Black, Tenango Brown, and Tlatilco Brown types from Chalcatzingo (phases A and B) include polished black and brown vessels with nearly identical forms and incised, excised, and grooved decoration. Very similar incised black- and brown-slipped bowls in Gualupita I (Vaillant and Vaillant 1934: figs. 20, 21, 23). In the Valley of Mexico polished black and brown beakers and open and flaring bowls with bolstered rims at Ayotla (Tlapacoya) in Ayotla and Justo subphases (Ixtapaluca phase) and to a lesser extent in the Bomba subphase (initial Zacatenco phase), along with incised molcajete bases or pseudo-grater fondos and the multiple-line-break motif. Similar polished black-to-brown bowls and beakers with incised and excised decoration, including double-line-break motif and pseudo-grater fondos, in the Iglesia subphase (early Zacatenco phase) at Tlatilco. Polished black bowls and beakers with incised (sometimes red-filled) and grooved decoration, including multiple-line-break motif and pseudo-grater fondos at El Arbolillo and Zacatenco in the El Arbolillo subphase (early Zacatenco phase) and in Tlatilco and Tlapacoya graves. The hachured triangle motif is identical with a motif esp. popular in Tlatilco mortuary vessels (Vaillant 1930: 32, pl. I; 1935: 223–7; Porter 1953: 35, 36, pls. 10, 11; Piña Chán 1958a: 36, 41, 51–3, 74, figs. 9, 11, 18, 33–7; 1971: figs. 1, 3, 4; Coe 1965b: ill. 42; Weaver 1967: 13–18, figs. 1, 2, 4, pls. 1–4, 6–8; MacNeish et al. 1970: 277; Tolstoy and Paradis 1970: 345–7, fig. 1). In the Valley of Oaxaca, polished black (esp. open) bowls and beakers with incised or excised decoration, sometimes filled with red pigment, common in the San José phase. In the Guadalupe phase, polished dark pottery continues popular and double-line-break motif appears (Flannery 1968: 82, 90, 94; MacNeish et al. 1970: 270, 271). Polished black flat-based open bowls with bolstered rims and incised and excised decoration (sometimes filled with red pigment) found in Las Bocas cemetery (Coe 1965b: ills. 25, 26, 33).

GULF COAST. Very similar polished black (unslipped) bowls and beakers with encircling incision and incised base interior occur in Ponce Black of Ponce and Aguilar phases of northern Veracruz (MacNeish 1954: 570–1, 574–5, figs. 13, 17, chart 2). Black open and flaring bowls, beakers, and a few convex bowls, sometimes slipped and polished and with incised or excised decoration, including multiple-line-break motif (occasionally filled with red pigment) and molcajete bases or pseudo-grater fondos, in Trapiche I and II phases at El

Trapiche and Chalahuite (García Payón 1966: 39–45, 75–7, láms. 4–11; 1971: 514; MacNeish et al. 1970: 273). Polished black (esp. open) bowls and beakers common in the San Lorenzo phase at San Lorenzo Tenochtitlán; decoration includes excision filled with red pigment. Multiple-line-break motif appears in the Nacaste phase and in the Palangana phase (Coe 1970: 26–9; MacNeish et al. 1970: 279, 280). Polished black flaring and convex bowls with occasional incision, including multiple-line-break motif and incised pseudo-grater fondos with pendant arcs and sunburst motifs at La Venta (Drucker 1952: 102–4, figs. 33, 34, table 6; Coe 1965a: 690, figs. 8, 9; MacNeish et al. 1970: 280).

PETÉN. Black-slipped (sometimes polished) beakers and open, flaring, and convex bowls with similar encircling grooving and incision (including multiple-line-break motif) and notched everted rims occur in Xe-sphere complexes at Altar de Sacrificios and Seibal (Willey et al. 1967: 293; MacNeish et al. 1970: 285; Willey 1970: 341–6, figs. 24–30; R. E. W. Adams 1971: 24, 42, figs. 1, 2, 6, 7, chart 1).

COASTAL GUERRERO. Polished black and brown beakers and open, flaring, and convex bowls with similar incised decoration occur in the Tom period at Puerto Marqués and Zanja. Incised interior grater bases appear in the Uala period (C. Brush 1969: 137–42, 146, figs. 6, 15, 17, 25, tables 3, 8).

Remarks. Guamuchil Polished Black appears in the Cacahuananche phase and reaches maximum popularity in the Tecolotla phase where it is marked by three distinctive new modes: red pigment in incision or excision, multiple-line-break motif, and concentric-arc motif on pseudo-grater fondos. All are Middle Preclassic marker traits, but the last generally occurs on white wares. Red-filled incision is shared only with Arana Black-and-White; excision is unique to Guamuchil Polished Black. Pseudo-grater fondos occur on Pozo Thin Red in Atopula and Tecolotla phases. Open bowls with oblique groove below bolstered rim also in Guamuchil Polished Black in the Atopula phase, and in Mariposa White in the Tecolotla phase. Open bowls with notched rims appear in Arana Black-and-White and Bagre Coarse in the Tecolotla phase. Raised flanges also in Mariposa White and Pedrusco Polished Gray in the Tecolotla phase. A flaring bowl with "turned-up" rim occurs in Jiménez Red, also in the Tecolotla phase.

Arana Black-and-White (Fig. 51)

Paste and surface. Identical with Atopula phase (see above).

Form. Wall thickness 5–10 mm., typically 7–8 mm.

OPEN BOWL. Diameter 16–32 cm. Wall straight and outslanting. Base flat; diameter at base 12 cm. Lip form: beveled or everted.

BEAKER. Diameter 14–16 cm. Wall straight and nearly vertical to very slightly outslanting. Base flat, diameter 14–15 cm. Lip form: rounded.

Decoration

INCISION. All incision pre-slip, smooth and regular, and done while paste was plastic. 1. Two to four parallel lines encircling interior or exterior of open bowl just below lip. In one, a single incised line encircles top of a flat everted (notched) lip, combined with a line encircling part of upper interior parallel

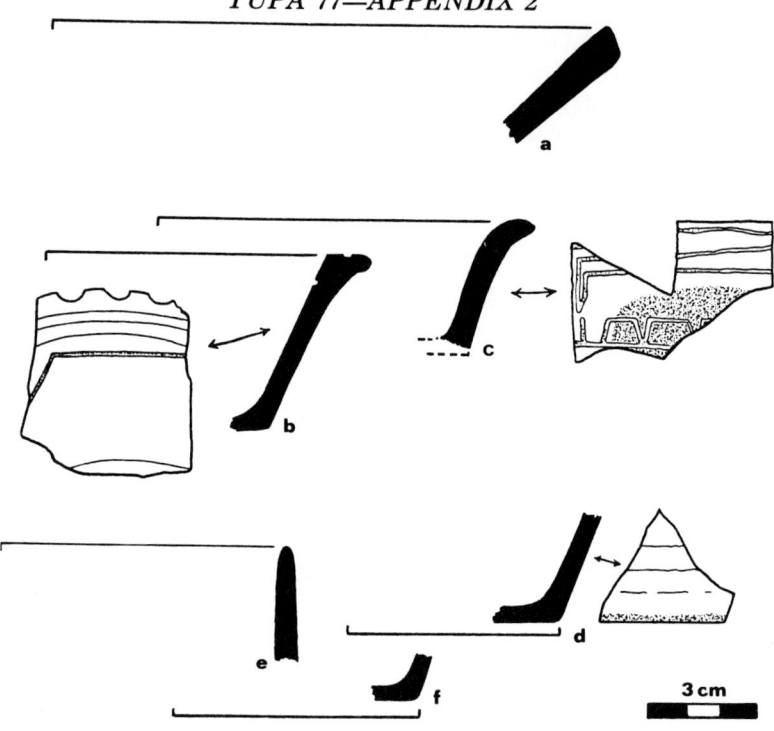

FIG. 51. Arana Black-and-White pottery, Tecolotla phase: *a–d*, open bowls; *e, f*, beakers.

to rim, then turning down sharply at an oblique angle. 2. Triple-line-break on upper interior of one bowl, combined with a complex design including "cleft" motif, just below; design is filled with red pigment.

OTHER. 1. Row of evenly spaced notches encircling exterior edge of everted lip of open bowl. Notches pre-slip, quite smooth and regular, and made while paste was plastic.

Comparative material. White-rimmed black types very widespread in Mesoamerica.

TEHUACÁN VALLEY. Coatepec White-rimmed Black of the Early Santa María phase has same paste, surface treatment, and vessel forms, also generally similar incised decoration, although it is rare and does not include multiple-line-breaks or red-filled incision (MacNeish et al. 1970: 108–10, fig. 64, tables 34, 35).

SOCONUSCO. Pampas Black-and-White of Cuadros and Jocotal phases at Salinas La Blanca has similar paste, surface treatment, and vessel forms but is not incised (Coe and Flannery 1967: 33–5, figs. 14, 15). Pampas Black-and-White of Izapa-Cuadros and Izapa-Jocotal phases also similar to Arana Black-and-White in these respects and is incised as well. Pampas Black-and-White of the Altamira-Cuadros phase includes similar incised open bowls (Green and Lowe 1967: 108, fig. 80; Ekholm-Miller 1969: 39–41, fig. 30).

CENTRAL CHIAPAS. White Monochrome of Cotorra and Dili phases at Chiapa de Corzo includes differentially fired open bowls and beakers with encircling incision, including (esp. in the Dili phase) the double-line-break motif (Dixon 1959: 7–10, 23–8, figs. 2–6, 24–28; Warren 1961: 77). Revolución Smudged of the Cotorra phase at Padre Piedra includes similar incised open bowls (Green and Lowe 1967: 43–4, fig. 53).

CENTRAL HIGHLANDS. Differentially fired brown, black, and gray wares occur throughout the Early Preclassic sequence in Morelos (Grove 1970a: 2; 1972: 35, 61, fig. 15). Chalcatzingo B has differentially fired open bowls and beakers (Cyphers 1975). In the Valley of Mexico, differentially fired black and white pottery and open bowl and beaker forms at Ayotla (Tlapacoya) in Ayotla and Justo subphases (Ixtapaluca phase), and to a lesser extent in the Bomba subphase (initial Zacatenco phase), in which the multiple-line-break motif appears. Mottled or differentially fired black and white open bowls and beakers and the multiple-line-break motif at Tlatilco in the Iglesia subphase (early Zacatenco phase) and at El Arbolillo and Zacatenco in the contemporary El Arbolillo subphase. Similar white-rimmed black open bowls, and black open bowls and beakers with red-filled incision and double-line-break motif were found at Tlapacoya by *huaqueros*. Differentially fired black and white pottery also in Tlatilco graves (Piña Chán 1958a: 50, 51, fig. 17; 1971: figs. 6, 8; Weaver 1967: 13–17, 35, 36, pl. 5; MacNeish et al. 1970: 277, 278; Tolstoy and Paradis 1970: 345–7, fig. 1). In the Valley of Oaxaca, differentially fired black and white open bowls and beakers in the San José phase; double-line-break motif in the Guadalupe phase (Flannery 1968: 82, 90, 94; MacNeish et al. 1970: 270, 271). White-rimmed black bowls with incised or excised decoration, sometimes red-filled, were found in the Las Bocas cemetery (Coe 1965b: ills. 23–25, 27).

GULF COAST. Mottling or simple differential firing characterizes Ponce Black of the Ponce and Aguilar phases of northern Veracruz; it includes open bowl, beaker, and encircling incision (MacNeish 1954: 570–1, 574–5, fig. 17, chart 2). Black-and-white open bowls and beakers with encircling incision and the multiple-line-break motif occur in Trapiche I and II phases at El Trapiche and Chalahuite (García Payón 1966: 87–92, láms. 32, 33; 1971: 518; MacNeish et al. 1970: 273). Differentially fired black and white, esp. white-rimmed black ware, appears at San Lorenzo Tenochtitlán in the Bajío phase, is substantially more popular in the Chicharras phase, and continues into the San Lorenzo phase when it includes open bowls and beakers. The multiple-line-break motif appears in the Nacaste phase and also in the Palangana phase, but differential firing has by then disappeared (Coe 1970: 24–8; MacNeish et al. 1970: 279, 280). Differentially fired, esp. white-rimmed black open bowls, occur at La Venta, also the multiple-line-break motif (Drucker 1952: 92; Coe 1965a: 692).

PETÉN. White-rimmed black open bowls or beakers occur in the Xe complex at Altar de Sacrificios; the multiple-line-break motif there and in the Xe-sphere complex at Seibal (Willey et al. 1967: 293; MacNeish et al. 1970: 285;

Willey 1970: 353; R. E. W. Adams 1971: 27, chart 1).

Remarks. Arana Black-and-White is a typical example of the very widespread white-rimmed black wares. It appears only in the Atopula and Tecolotla phases, and always in very small quantities. Closely related to Guamuchil Polished Black, and might easily be considered a variety of it. In the Tecolotla phase they share such distinctive motifs as notched rims on open bowls and red-filled incision.

Pedrusco Polished Gray (Fig. 52)

Paste and surface. Identical with Cacahuananche and Atopula phases (see above).

Form. Wall thickness 5-10 mm., typically 6-8 mm.

CONVEX BOWL. Diameter 12-14 cm. Wall uniformly convex. Base rounded. Lip form: rounded or tapered.

Decoration

INCISION. 1. Single line encircling exterior of convex bowls just below and parallel to rim. Pre-slip incision smooth and regular and done while paste was plastic.

OTHER. 1. Raised area or flange encircling exterior of convex bowl just below and parallel to rim; roughly elliptical in cross-section and approximately 1 cm. wide.

Comparative material

TEHUACÁN VALLEY. No close analogies noted. A few similarities to Río Salado Gray and Quachilco Gray (which may have similar smooth waxy luster) but these types unslipped. Convex bowls and encircling incision occur in these and other Early Santa María types (MacNeish et al. 1970: 78-83, 120-34, figs. 42, 70-78, tables 29, 30, 39, 40).

SOCONUSCO. Ocós Gray of the Jocotal phase at Salinas La Blanca and the Conchas phase at La Victoria somewhat similar in surface treatment, form, and (in Conchas-phase examples) in encircling incision (Coe 1961: 73, fig. 30; Coe and Flannery 1967: 46-7, fig. 24). Culebra Gray of Izapa-Jocotal and Altamira-Jocotal phases similar to Pedrusco Polished Gray in the same respects (Green and Lowe 1967: 118; Ekholm-Miller 1969: 63-5, fig. 56).

CENTRAL CHIAPAS. Monochrome White convex bowls of the Cotorra phase

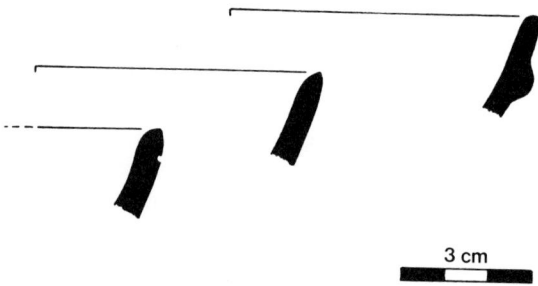

FIG. 52. Pedrusco Polished Gray convex bowls, Tecolotla phase.

at Chiapa de Corzo grade into "pearly gray" in slip color (Dixon 1959: 7-9, fig. 4). Gray convex bowls of Cotorra and Dili phases at Padre Piedra similar in form (Navarrete 1960: 25-6, fig. 25, table 1; Green and Lowe 1967: 46, fig. 60). Similar (but unslipped and unpolished) convex bowls with encircling incision occur in Burrero Gray of the Burrero period at Santa Cruz (Sanders 1961: 19, fig. 18).

CENTRAL HIGHLANDS. In Morelos, polished gray convex bowls with encircling incision and flanged rims occur in Piña Chán's (1955a: 16, lám. 11) Gris type and Cyphers' (1975) Pavon Fine Gray type from Chalcatzingo (phase C). In the Valley of Mexico, a few polished gray convex bowls found in Tlatilco and Tlapacoya graves (Piña Chán 1958a: 85, fig. 11; Weaver 1967: 28). Polished gray-slipped bowls with incised decoration in the San José phase in the Valley of Oaxaca. In the Guadalupe phase, incised gray (esp. polished waxy gray) pottery increases substantially in popularity (Flannery 1968: 82, 94; MacNeish et al. 1970: 270-71).

Remarks. Pedrusco Polished Gray appears in the Cacahuananche phase as a minor type, achieves its greatest popularity in the Atopula phase, and continues in greatly reduced quantities in the Tecolotla phase. Encircling flanges occur also in Guamuchil Polished Black and Mariposa White in the Tecolotla phase.

Mariposa White (Fig. 53)

Paste and surface. Identical with Atopula phase (see above).

Form. Wall thickness 5-7 mm., typically quite uniform, even at rim and base-wall junction.

OPEN BOWL. Diameter 28-32 cm. Wall straight and outslanting. Base presumably flat. Lip form: blunted.

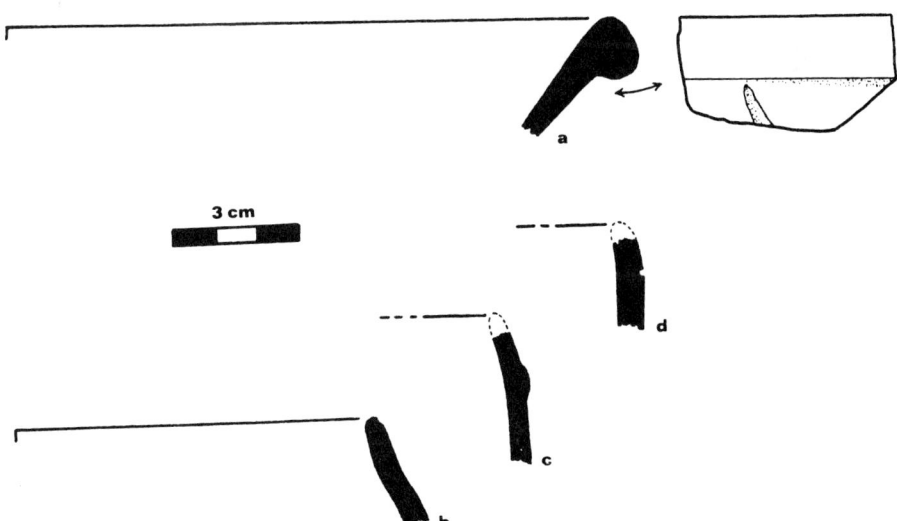

FIG. 53. Mariposa White pottery, Tecolotla phase: *a*, open bowl; *b-d*, incurved-rim bowls.

INCURVED-RIM BOWL. Diameter 16–20 cm. Wall uniformly convex; may turn slightly and smoothly upward just below the lip but still incurving at mouth. Base presumably rounded. Lip form: rounded.

Decoration

GROOVING. 1. Single oblique slightly curved groove on upper exterior of open bowl, with tapering end just below bolster. Pre-slip groove quite smooth and regular and done while paste was plastic.

INCISION. 1. Single line encircling exterior of bowl below and parallel to rim. Pre-slip incision smooth and regular and done while paste was plastic.

OTHER. 1. Raised "flange" encircling upper exterior of one incurved-rim bowl just below and parallel to rim.

Comparative material

TEHUACÁN VALLEY. Paste, surface treatment, and vessel form of Mariposa White virtually identical with Canoas White of the Early Santa María phase. Major difference: incised decoration not heavily represented on Mariposa White, but this may simply reflect small sample size. Canoas White does not have oblique grooving or raised flanges, but one illustrated specimen appears to have a raised area of some kind (MacNeish et al. 1970: 59–68, figs. 34–37, tables 23, 24.

SOCONUSCO. Conchas White-to-buff of the Cuadros and Jocotal phases at Salinas La Blanca and the Conchas phase at La Victoria quite similar in surface treatment and vessel form. Incised or grooved decoration not so common on Mariposa White (Coe 1961: 65–9, figs. 25–27; Coe and Flannery 1967: 42–4, fig. 21). Amatillo White of Izapa- and Altamira-Cuadros phases, Siltepec White of Izapa- and Altamira-Jocotal phases, Cuchilla White of the Altamira-Caudros phase, and Bobo White of the Izapa-Jocotal phase all similar in the same respects. Incurved-rim bowl with wall turned up near rim is identical in form with Bobo White "collared jars" with indistinct collars (Green and Lowe 1967: 110–14, figs. 81, 83, 86; Ekholm-Miller 1969: 48–58, figs. 38, 39, 43–8).

CENTRAL CHIAPAS. Identical open and incurved-rim bowls with encircling incision occur in White Monochrome of Cotorra and Dili phases at Chiapa de Corzo, and the very closely related Burrero Cream type of the Burrero period at Santa Cruz (Dixon 1959: 7–12, 23–8, figs. 5, 25, 27, 30; Sanders 1961: 18–19, fig. 17). Vergel White-to-buff (Vergel variety) of Cotorra and Dili phases at Padre Piedra includes similar bowls without incised decoration (Green and Lowe 1967: 44, fig. 55). Very similar white-slipped incurved-rim bowls in a Dili-phase assemblage from Sitio Sevilla and in the Phase 1 assemblage at Santa Rosa (Navarrete 1960: 16–18, 26, fig. 25, table 1; Brockington 1967: 18, 37, 43, 63).

CENTRAL HIGHLANDS. In Morelos, White ceramics of San Pablo A (Middle Nexpa) and San Pablo B (Late Nexpa) phases generally similar in form and surface treatment. In these too it is a rare type, and incised decoration virtually confined to San Pablo B vessels (Grove 1972: 61, fig. 15). Similar white open and incurved-rim bowls with encircling incision occur in Piña

Chán's (1955a: 11-12, 20-1, láms. 5-7, 15-17) Blanco Pulido and Blanco Laca types and Cyphers' (1975) Amatzinac White type from Chalcatzingo (phases B and C) and in the Gualupita I assemblage (Vaillant and Vaillant 1934: figs. 23, 25). In the Valley of Mexico, incised white-slipped pottery and open bowl form at Ayotla (Tlapacoya) in Ayotla and Justo subphases (Ixtapaluca phase) and (esp.) in the Bomba subphase (initial Zacatenco phase). Incised white open and incurved-rim bowls typical of early Zacatenco subphases at Tlatilco (Iglesia) and El Arbolillo and Zacatenco (El Arbolillo). Very similar white-slipped open and incurved-rim bowls, sometimes with incised or grooved decoration, in the Tlatilco and Tlapacoya graves (Vaillant 1930: 32, 33, pl II; 1935: 227-9, fig. 22; Piña Chán 1958a: 41, 44, 74, 75, figs. 12, 38; 1971: fig. 5; Coe 1965b: ill. 47; Weaver 1967: 20-7, figs. 4-6, pls. 10, 14, 15; MacNeish et al. 1970: 277, 278; Tolstoy and Paradis 1970: 345-7, fig. 1). White-slipped (esp. open) bowls, in the San José phase of the Valley of Oaxaca. Incised white pottery (esp. a type closely related to Canoas White of the Tehuacán Valley) dominates ceramic complexes of the early part of the Guadalupe phase; open bowls and encircling incision particularly common (Flannery 1968: 82, 90; MacNeish et al. 1970: 270, 271).

GULF COAST. Open and incurved-rim bowls and encircling incision occur in Progreso White of Ponce and Aguilar phases of northern Veracruz (MacNeish 1954: 566-70, 574, fig. 17, chart 2). Incised white-slipped open and incurved-rim bowls in small quantities in Trapiche I and II phases at El Trapiche and Chalahuite (García Payón 1966: 63-9, láms. 18-21; 1971: 516, 517; MacNeish et al. 1970: 273). Several types of white pottery in the Chicharras and San Lorenzo phases at San Lorenzo Tenochtitlán, but Mariposa White more similar to the hard incised white wares in the Nacaste phase (Coe 1970: 25-28; MacNeish et al. 1970: 279-80). White-slipped open and incurved-rim bowls, occasionally with encircling incision, also at La Venta (Drucker 1952: 96, table 6).

PETÉN. Similar white-slipped open and incurved-rim bowls with encircling incision occur in the Xe-sphere complexes at Altar de Sacrificios and Seibal (Willey et al. 1967: 293; MacNeish et al. 1970: 285; Willey 1970: 335-41, figs. 16-23; R.E.W. Adams 1971: 25, figs. 1, 2, chart 1).

COASTAL GUERRERO. White-slipped open and incurved-rim bowls with single encircling incised lines occur in the Tom period at Puerto Marqués; raised flanges may occur on incurved-rim bowls (C. Brush 1969: 138-41, figs. 6, 14-16, tables 1, 3, 8).

Remarks. Mariposa White is representative of the very widespread "white" wares so typical of the Terminal Early Preclassic and Early Middle Preclassic. It appears in small quantities at Atopula in the Atopula and Tecolotla phases. The typical incised decoration is not heavily represented in recovered examples, probably because of the small sample size. Mariposa White is similar to Guamuchil Polished Black in form and decoration, including such unusual motifs as flanges and oblique grooving on bolstered-rim open bowls. Guamuchil Polished Black of the Tecolotla phase has a number of incised decorative motifs generally typical of Middle Preclassic white wares. Raised encircling flanges are also shared with Pedrusco Polished Gray in the Tecolotla phase.

Barranca Smoothed Buff (Fig. 54)

Paste and surface. Identical with Cacahuananche and Atopula phases (see above).

Form. Wall thickness varies widely, 4–19 mm.; maximum thickness reached at point of curvature change in olla necks and in rim sherds with thickened lips. Typical wall thickness 5–8 mm.

    OLLA. Diameter 28–34 cm. Profile grades smoothly into flaring neck. Form of base unknown. Lip form: blunted or thickened exterior.

Auxiliary features. 1. Slab handle: projecting handle with roughly elliptical cross-section tapers slightly away from vessel but is not a strap handle; does not reconnect to vessel body.

Decoration. Limited to careful smoothing and compacting of surface in the Tecolotla phase.

Comparative material. Difficult to find useful comparisons for a plain type with simple forms.

    TEHUACÁN VALLEY. Barranca Smoothed Buff similar in paste, surface treatment, and vessel form to Ajalpan Plain, Coatepec Plain, and Ajalpan Fine Plain, but last is thinner and has high polish. Closest resemblances are to Coatepec Plain that occurs throughout Ajalpan and Santa María phases,

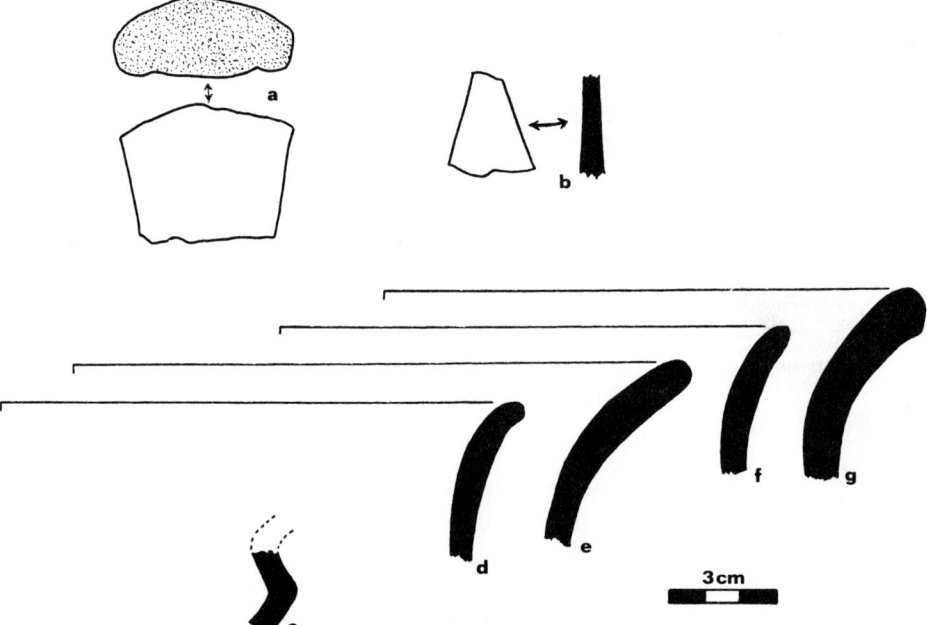

FIG. 54. Barranca Smoothed Buff pottery, Tecolotla phase: *a*, slab handle; *b*, sherd trapezoid; *c–g*, ollas.

with its major popularity in Late Ajalpan. None of these types has appendages, but strap handles occur in Río Salado Coarse in the Early Santa María phase (MacNeish et al. 1970: 29–35, 44–6, 78, figs. 11, 13, 22, tables 15, 17, 19, 28).

SOCONUSCO. Surface treatment of Ocós Buff of the Ocós Phase at La Victoria is generally similar but forms differ. Strap or slab handles occur on Conchas Red Unburnished vessels of the Conchas phase at La Victoria (Coe 1961: 53–4, 63, fig. 24).

CENTRAL HIGHLANDS. Brown ollas of the San Pablo B (Late Nexpa) phase of Morelos occasionally exhibit the same self-slip or float-coat effect (Grove 1972: 60, fig. 16). Piña Chán's (1955a: 9–10, lám. 1) Café Claro type and Cyphers' (1975) Del Prado Pink and Atoyac Unslipped Burnished types from Chalcatzingo (phases A and B) include ollas roughly similar in color and surface treatment.

No other resemblances were noted to ceramics of distant areas.

Remarks. Barranca Smoothed Buff appears as a minor type in the Cacahuananche phase, and declines in popularity in the later Atopula and Tecolotla phases. At no time does it occur in quantities equal to such major types as Guamuchil Polished Black and Pozo Thin Red.

Bagre Coarse (Figs. 55, 56)

Paste and surface. Identical with Cacahuananche and Atopula phases (see above).

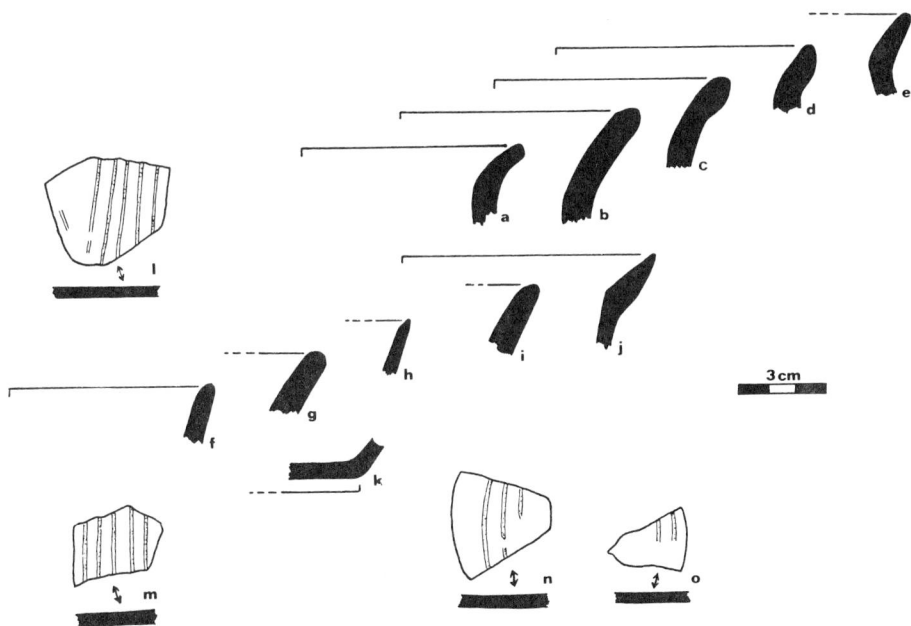

FIG. 55. Bagre Coarse pottery, Tecolotla phase: *a–e*, ollas; *f–k*, open bowls; *l–o*, molcajete bases.

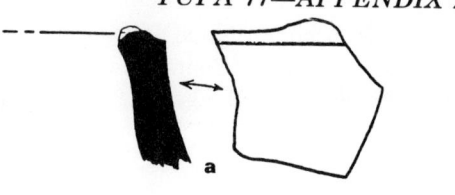

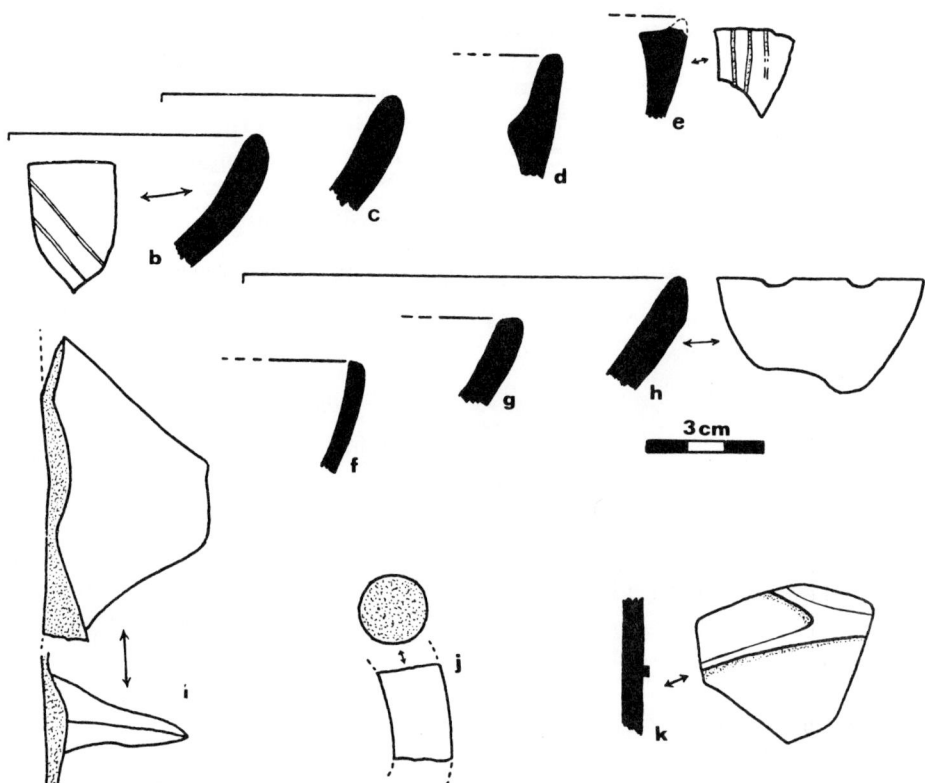

Fig. 56. Bagre Coarse pottery, Tecolotla phase: *a*, incurved-rim bowl; *b–h*, convex bowls; *i*, slab handle; *j*, loop handle; *k*, sherd with raised area on exterior.

Form. Wall thickness quite variable, at least 5–12 mm., typically 7–9 mm.

OLLA. Diameter 15–18 cm. Wall smooth, without sharp breaks in curvature, body grades smoothly into flaring neck. Form of base unknown. Lip form: rounded, slightly blunted, or tapered.

OPEN BOWL. Diameter 14–18 cm. Wall straight and outslanting. Base flat. Lip form: rounded, blunted, or tapered.

CONVEX BOWL. Diameter 12–23 cm. Wall uniformly convex. Base rounded. Lip form: rounded or blunted.

INCURVED-RIM BOWL. Diameter unknown. Lower wall uniformly convex.

Base form unknown, probably rounded. Lip form: blunted or slightly thickened interior.

Auxiliary features. 1. Slab handle: wide flat handle projecting horizontally from vessel (presumably olla) exterior. Roughly elliptical in cross-section, tapering at edges; also tapers slightly away from vessel to a rounded end but is not reattached to vessel body. 2. Loop handle: semicircular, round in cross-section and approximately 1.5 cm. in diameter, projecting from vessel (presumably olla) exterior.

Decoration

GROOVING. 1. Single broad groove encircling exterior of lip of incurved rim bowl. Rim is also eccentric or wavy, with roughly elliptical tabs. Groove smooth and made while paste was plastic.

INCISION. 1. Molcajete base: designs deeply incised multiple concentric arcs or parallel straight lines on flat interior base of open bowls. Incision typically smooth and regular and done while paste was plastic; occasionally done after paste was partially dry and is slightly irregular with rough edges. 2. Multiple parallel oblique lines on interior of convex bowl. Incision smooth and regular and done while paste was plastic. Interior surface worn, presumably from use as grater. 3. Multiple parallel vertical lines on exterior of one convex bowl, perpendicular to rim. Incision shallow and irregular with rough edges, and done after paste was partially dry.

OTHER. 1. Row of broad, evenly spaced notches encircling exterior of lip of convex bowl. Notches smooth and regular and made while paste was plastic. 2. Very slightly raised area on vessel exterior in form of bifurcating line; might not be intentional decoration.

Comparative material. Virtually impossible to find useful comparisons for a residual type.

TEHUACÁN VALLEY. Ajalpan Coarse and Coatepec Buff roughly similar in paste, surface treatment, and vessel form. One Coatepec Buff vessel has incised or grooved lines encircling exterior. Encircling incision and incised flat base interiors (molcajetes or pseudo-grater fondos) occur in a number of other Early Santa María types, notably Canoas White and Río Salado Gray (MacNeish et al. 1970: 26–9, 49–51, 62, 80, figs. 10, 25, 35, 36, 42, tables 14, 21, 23, 29). No close similarities at the type level to ceramics of more distant areas were noted.

Remarks. Bagre Coarse is undoubtedly a residual category, including not only vessels intentionally left unsmoothed and unslipped, but also eroded sherds of vessels that were originally slipped. It occurs in large numbers in every excavation level; it is often the most frequent type, as is expectable for a residual type. Notched rims occur also in Guamuchil Polished Black and Arana Black-and-White in the Tecolotla phase. Similar incised grater bases occur in Guamuchil Polished Black in the Atopula phase, and Jiménez Red and Pozo Thin Red in the Atopula and Tecolotla phases. Designs on some of these bases resemble those of pseudo-grater fondos of Guamuchil Polished Black (Tecolotla phase) and Pozo Thin Red (Atopula and Tecolotla phases). Slab handles are shared only with Barranca Smoothed Buff of the Tecolotla phase.

Appendix 3. The Ceramic Artifacts of Atopula

Figurines of the Cacahuananche Phase
Solid Torso (Fig. 57)

Paste and surface. Hardness near 2.5. Temper coarse to very coarse and is the usual quartziferous sand, predominantly small white particles of limestone or calcite and quartz crystals. Paste oxidized, light red to reddish yellow (2.5 YR 6/6; 5 YR 6/6) throughout and resembles Barranca Smoothed Buff but without the careful smoothing and compaction of surfaces. Surface partially smoothed but has rough irregular texture from temper particles. No trace of slip.

Form. This fragment represents a human torso from upper chest to hip region. Upper portion elliptical in cross-section with no distinction between chest and stomach areas. Lower portion, with plano-convex cross-section, has beginning of a swelling at sides and rear, representing hips and buttocks. Navel indicated by conical punctation and tops of buttocks by a slightly depressed area.

Comparative material. Closest similarities are to the Standing Trackwoman and Venus Body types of the Tehuacán Valley. The Atopula torso is most like the former; breasts on this type quite small and high on the chest; might originally have been present on the missing portion of the Atopula figurine. Navel and swelling of hips and buttocks are more like the Venus Bodies, but slightly less naturalistic and less carefully modeled. Trackwoman bodies occur throughout the Ajalpan phase, Venus Bodies in Late Ajalpan and Santa María (MacNeish et al. 1970: 38, 96, figs. 18, 59).

Similar torso fragments from the San Pablo Pantheon Mound in Morelos date to the San Pablo (Middle-Late Nexpa) phase (Grove 1968b: fig. 31). Some D1 figurine bodies from Gualupita I are similar (Vaillant and Vaillant 1934: fig. 7). No very close resemblances to Valley of Mexico types. A few bodies attached to C1/C2 figurine heads, vaguely similar, occur in the El Arbolillo subphase at El Arbolillo and Zacatenco and the Bomba subphase at Ayotla (Tlapacoya), all of the initial Zacatenco phase. Some D-type figurines, esp. "ball players," from Tlatilco and Tlapacoya graves, have roughly similar torsos (Vaillant 1930: pls. 12, 24; 1935: figs. 15, 16; Porter 1953: pl. 4; Piña Chán 1955b: figs. 4, 9; Coe 1965b: ills. 102, 108, 109, 119; Weaver 1967: pl. C; Tolstoy and Paradis 1970: 345–7, fig. 1).

No very close similarities noted to central Veracruz types, although roughly similar torsos occur in the Ponce phase of northern Veracruz (MacNeish 1954: fig. 24), at El Trapiche and Chalahuite in Trapiche I and II phases (García Payón 1966: láms. 66, 67), and at La Venta (Drucker 1952: pl. 41c).

Roughly similar torsos also at La Victoria in the Conchas phase, and perhaps on a few Ocós-phase specimens; in the Early Preclassic phases at Altamira; in the

CERAMIC ARTIFACTS OF ATOPULA

Dili phase at Chiapa de Corzo; and in Cotorra and Dili phases at Padre Piedra and several related sites (Coe 1961: 92, 97, figs. 39, 58; Lowe and Mason 1965: fig. 9; Green and Lowe 1967: figs. 33, 66; Lee 1969: figs. 16, 17).

Figurines of the Atopula Phase

Solid Helmeted Head (Fig. 58a)

Paste and surface. Hardness near 2.5. Temper medium in size and not the usual quartziferous sand; quartz crystals and tiny white particles of limestone or

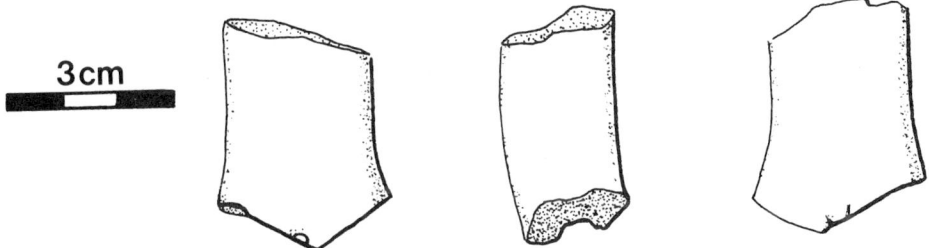

FIG. 57. Ceramic figurine, Cacahuananche phase (solid torso).

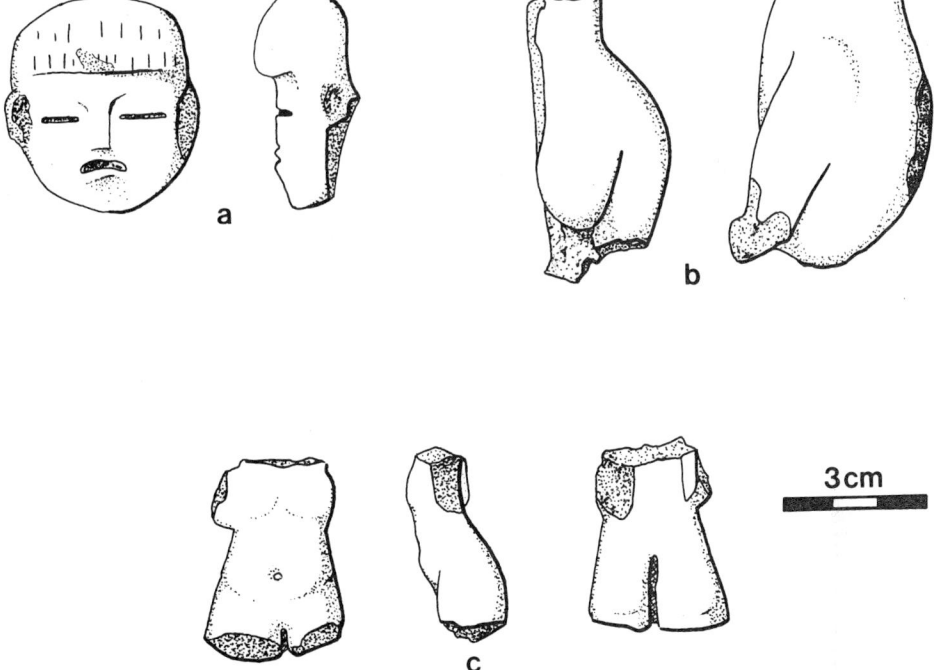

FIG. 58. Ceramic figurines, Atopula phase: *a*, solid Helmeted head; *b*, hollow body fragment; *c*, solid torso.

calcite predominate, with occasional black, red, and brown particles. At surface, paste oxidized to reddish yellow (5 YR 7/6, 6/6) with sharp transition to uniformly gray (5 YR 5/1) core. Except for temper, paste resembles Barranca Smoothed Buff, without the careful surface compaction. Surface smoothed but retains slightly coarse or gritty texture from protruding temper, perhaps from weathering. In such cavities and incisions as eyes, ears, and headdress are traces of white (5 YR 8/1) pigment, esp. in the mouth, indicating additional painted decoration.

Form. Rear of head quite flat, as is the face; only the front of helmet is rounded and slightly projecting. In outline the head (esp. lower facial area) is rounded. Mouth down-turned, formed by crescentic incision. Lips slightly raised and appear even more protruding because of wide flat incision representing chin area, and incision representing base of nose. Nose itself not raised at all but indicated by three incisions. Eyes formed by long straight horizontal incisions, slightly deeper at outer ends. Two more incisions, slanting slightly up and away from top of nose, may represent eyebrows or may define upper limits of eye sockets, indicating closed eyes. Elongated appliqués with two depressions, projecting at each side of face, seem to represent ears, although they extend to base of headdress and might be extensions of it. Helmet-like headdress is rounded at top, sides, and front and projects forward beyond the plane of the face, terminating horizontally across forehead. Four rows of vertical incisions decorate front and top of headdress. Back of head flat to very slightly concave and is featureless. A large portion of rear surface below middle of ears is broken away. No indication that head was ever attached to a body.

Comparative material. Many features of this small ceramic head are strikingly similar to the basalt colossal heads of southern Veracruz and Tabasco. Most striking is the overall effect of a round-faced, puffy-cheeked individual wearing helmet-like headgear. Helmet of typical colossal head is decorated and terminates horizontally, low on forehead. Eyes tend to be horizontal; nose very flat, often indicated more by relief than modeling, and begins just above lips, which project slightly. The heads themselves have nonprojecting features; even in profile face is often nearly a flat plane. Helmets rounded in front, projecting beyond face. Heads and helmets flat in the rear and generally featureless, sometimes even lacking indication of bottom of helmet (Clewlow et al. 1967: esp. figs. 7, 19, pls. 8, 22). Finally, the Atopula ceramic head apparently was never attached to a body.

This head gives strong impression of being a miniature version of a colossal head, if not a copy of a specific head. Ceramic figurine heads from other Mesoamerican sites are similar to this one in particular features but none produces same overall effect.

In the Tehuacán Valley, solid baby-face heads are most similar; they are white-slipped, have similar down-turned mouths and horizontal slit eyes (although appliquéd), and sometimes have similar helmets and red pigment in the mouths. Crescentic Cap heads are white-slipped and have traces of red paint in the mouth (as does one Trapiche Bunned-Helmet head). Helmeted heads have similar headgear but are otherwise dissimilar. All these types occur in the Early Santa María phase (MacNeish et al. 1970: 87–91, figs. 46–7).

Small solid Olmecoid/baby-face heads from San Pablo, Gualupita, and Cerro Chacaltepec (San Pablo and Cerro Chacaltepec I phases) in Morelos show general similarities in facial features (tabular ears, slit eyes, down-turned mouth), but none really resembles the Atopula specimen closely. A few D, K, and solid Olmecoid/baby-face figurines from Cerro Chacaltepec and Gualupita I have roughly similar helmet-like headgear; these small solid figurines occur also at Chalcatzingo (Vaillant and Vaillant 1934: figs. 6–8, 10; Piña Chán 1955a: 50; Grove 1968b: figs. 28–30, 37).

Similar headgear is occasionally found in several Valley of Mexico figurine types, (esp. D1 and D2) that occur in large numbers in the Tlatilco graves; in Ayotla and Justo subphases (Ixtapaluca phase) at Ayotla (Tlapacoya); in the early Zacatenco phase at Zacatenco, El Arbolillo, Tlatilco, and Ayotla (El Arbolillo, Iglesia, and Bomba subphases, respectively); and (perhaps intrusively) in Totolica- and La Pastora-subphase refuse at Tlatilco, Zacatenco, and El Arbolillo (Vaillant 1930: pls. 19, 20; Piña Chán 1958a: 53, fig. 19, tabla 2; 1971: fig. 13; Coe 1965b: ills. 93–112, 128–34; MacNeish et al. 1970: 278; Tolstoy and Paradis 1970: 347).

Olmecoid/baby-face figurines in Gualupita I, in Ayotla and Justo subphases (Ixtapaluca phase) at Ayotla (Tlapacoya), and in the Iglesia-subphase (early Zacatenco phase) refuse at Tlatilco are close in overall effect: occasionally helmeted, have down-turned mouths and puffy facial features, and often have simple slit or grooved horizontal eyes. Some solid and hollow Olmecoid/baby-face figurines from Tlatilco and Tlapacoya graves have same similarities; they are usually white-slipped and may have additional decoration in red pigment. None is entirely similar. The shallow horizontal-slit eye is particularly characteristic of Las Bocas white-slipped solid and hollow Olmecoid/baby-face figurines, which also have down-turned mouths and, often, helmet-like headgear (Vaillant and Vaillant 1934: fig. 14; Porter 1953: 102, pl. 4; Piña Chán 1955b: lám. 42; 1958b: láms. 13, 14, 16; Coe 1965b: ills. 184, 187, 193–9, 201–4; Weaver 1967: pls. E, F, J; MacNeish et al. 1970: 277, 278; Tolstoy and Paradis 1970: 347).

No close similarities with figurines from northern Veracruz, although helmet-like headgear occurs on several Ponce- and Aguilar-phase types, also occasional down-turned mouths and white slip (MacNeish 1954: 588–93, figs. 21–23). Roughly similar helmet-like headgear occurs on several figurine types of Trapiche I and II phases of El Trapiche and Chalahuite. Some small solid white-slipped Olmecoid/baby-face figurines also have puffy features, down-turned mouths, and simple horizontal slit eyes (García Payón 1966: láms. 50, 52, 56). Chicharras and San Lorenzo-phase solid white Olmecoid/baby-face figurines from San Lorenzo Tenochtitlán are similar, esp. in shallow trough eyes (Coe 1968b: 46; 1970: 25–7). Some solid Olmecoid/baby-face figurines from La Venta have similar helmet-like headgear and puffy faces with down-turned mouths, but the eyes generally have punched pupils. None has the same flat profile or produces the effect of a miniature colossal head (Drucker 1952: pls. 26–30, 35, 37, 39–41).

No very close resemblances noted with Conchas-phase figurines from La Victoria, although some have helmet-like headgear, down-turned mouth, white slip, and red pigment in the mouth; eyes almost always large-punched (Coe 1961: 94–7, figs. 54, 55). Figurines from Early Preclassic complexes at Altamira also not particularly similar, although some have helmet-like headgear, puffy features, down-turned mouth, and trough eyes (Green and Lowe 1967: figs. 31, 32, 93, 94).

Some figurine types of the Cotorra and Dili phases of Chiapa de Corzo, Padre Piedra, and allied sites have generally similar helmet-like headgear; mouths are often down-turned, and occasional specimens with horizontal slit eyes and flat triangular noses are quite similar. On a few, a white slip is combined with red pigment (Sorenson 1956: pl. 1; Navarrete 1960: fig. 12; Lowe and Mason 1965: fig. 9; Green and Lowe 1967: 48; Lee 1969: 10–23, figs. 1, 2, 5).

No close resemblances to figurines from highland Guatemala, although some Arévalo- and Las Charcas-phase examples have vaguely similar helmet-like headgear (Kidder 1965: figs. 1, 3–5; MacNeish et al. 1970: 284).

Many small solid Olmecoid/baby-face figurines of the Uala and Tom periods of Puerto Marqués and related sites in coastal Guerrero have similar helmet-like headgear, down-turned mouths, and shallow trough or slit eyes, are often white-slipped, and may be decorated with red pigment as well. In frontal view some produce a similar general effect (E. Brush 1968: 61–70, pls. 2–7, 9, 10, table 4).

Hollow Body (Fig. 58b)

Paste and surface. Hardness near 2.5. Temper coarse and not the usual quartziferous sand; small quartz crystals, white limestone or calcite particles, and occasional shiny black particles predominate. Paste uniformly unoxidized, reddish brown to dark reddish gray (5 YR 4/2, 4/3, 5/3). Surface carefully smoothed and bears traces of a dark reddish brown to dusky red (5 YR 3/2; 2.5 YR 3/2) slip. Paste and slip comparable to Guamuchil Polished Black.

Form. This fragment represents left shoulder, upper arm, and part of back and neck of a large hollow figurine. Left arm bent at elbow, the missing forearm apparently was held in front of body. Arm is solid, but figurine body is hollow.

Comparative material. In Tehuacán, Seated Mother Body figurines, mainly of Late Ajalpan and Early Santa María phases, have arms bent across chest but are smaller and entirely solid. Early Santa María hollow figurines which probably had Olmecoid heads also usually have bent arms but are always white-slipped (MacNeish et al. 1970: 95–6).

Hollow figurines (Olmecoid/baby-face, D and K varieties) occur throughout Early Preclassic sequence in Morelos at Nexpa, La Juana-San Pablo, and Gualupita; no illustrated examples are specifically similar. Bent arms resting across the chest occur in a number of types (Vaillant and Vaillant 1934; Grove 1968b; 1970a; 1970c; 1972).

Large hollow Olmecoid/baby-face figurines, sometimes with one arm bent across the chest, occur in Iglesia-subphase (early Zacatenco phase) refuse at Tlatilco; in Ayotla and Justo subphases (Ixtapaluca phase) at Ayotla (Tlapacoya); in Tlatilco, Tlapacoya, and Las Bocas graves; and in the Guadalupe phase in the Valley of Oaxaca (Porter 1953: 23, 31; Piña Chán 1955b: láms. 41, 43; Coe 1965b:

105, ills. 184-92; Weaver 1967: pls. 24, F; Flannery 1968: 94, fig. 9; MacNeish et al. 1970: 277, 278; Tolstoy and Paradis 1970: 347).

Large hollow figurines of various types, including Olmecoid/baby-face, occur in the Ponce phase of northern Veracruz (MacNeish 1954: 597, fig. 24; MacNeish et al. 1970: 274-5); in the Trapiche II phase (and perhaps in Trapiche I) at El Trapiche and Chalahuite (García Payón 1966: láms. 56, 62, 69; MacNeish et al. 1970: 273); at San Lorenzo Tenochtitlán in the Bajío, Chicharras, and San Lorenzo phases (Coe 1968b: 46; 1970: 24-7); at La Venta (Drucker 1952: pls. 39, 41); in the Conchas phase at La Victoria (Coe 1961: 94, figs. 56, 57); in the Early Preclassic phases at Altamira (Green and Lowe 1967: 24, 124, figs. 30, 94); in the Dili phase at Chiapa de Corzo and in Cotorra and Dili phases at Padre Piedra (Navarrete 1960: fig. 12; Lowe and Mason 1965: fig. 9; Green and Lowe 1967: 48, fig. 66; Lee 1969: 17, figs. 3, 16, 17); and in the Uala and Tom periods at Puerto Marqués, Zanja, and related sites in coastal Guerrero (E. Brush 1968: 58-71, pls. 2-7, 9-11, tables 3, 4). Several Conchas and Dili types have arms bent across the chest.

Solid Torso (Fig. 58c)

Paste and surface. hardness 2.5-3.0. Temper very coarse and not the usual quartziferous sand; shiny black particles, quartz crystals, and large white particles of limestone or calcite predominate. Paste oxidized to light red or reddish yellow (2.5 YR 6/8; 5 YR 6/6). Except for the temper, paste resembles Barranca Smoothed Buff but without compaction of the surface. Surface carefully smoothed with a few protruding temper particles. Polished light gray to white (5 YR 7/1, 8/1) slip now largely eroded away.

Form. This fragment represents a human female torso from shoulders to upper thighs; head, arms, and lower legs missing. Body high-waisted, narrowest above the navel at base of breasts, which are small and rounded. The stomach round and slightly protruding, with large navel. Buttocks also rounded and protruding and separated by a deep vertical incision, which nearly meets a shorter deep incision in the front representing crotch area. An elongated appliqué strip on back of right shoulder apparently represents lower end of a hair braid.

Comparative material. The Solid Polished White "Olmec" figurine bodies from Tehuacán, with their rounded breasts and stomachs, large navels, and high waists, are very similar; one illustrated example is virtually identical. These bodies may go with the Crescentic Cap or Ploughed-eye heads. They occur in the Early Santa María phase. The Venus Body type of the Late Ajalpan and Early Santa María phases, which may go with Helmeted, Baby-face, or Trapiche Bunned-helmet heads, is also quite similar (MacNeish et al. 1970: 96-8, figs. 59, 60).

Very similar torsos occur at Nexpa (Early Nexpa phase) and the San Pablo Pantheon Mound (San Pablo phase) in Morelos. Bodies attached to D2 heads are sometimes quite similar; these occur at Nexpa, La Juana-San Pablo, Cerro Chacaltepec, and Chalcatzingo throughout the Early and Middle Preclassic sequence. Some D1 torsos from Gualupita are also similar (Vaillant and Vaillant 1934: fig. 9; Piña Chán 1955a: 49, 50; Grove 1968b: figs. 28, 31; 1972: 35-7, fig. 11).

D- and C-type figurines of Ixtapaluca and early Zacatenco phases in the Valley of Mexico often have similar torsos. The bodies of D-type (esp. D2) figurines from Tlatilco graves are often very similar; they occasionally have pendant hair braids. Several solid Olmecoid/baby-face figurines from Tlatilco, Tlapacoya, and Las Bocas graves have very similar bodies and hair braids (Vaillant 1930: pls. 10, 19, 24; 1935: figs. 15, 17; Porter 1953: pl. 5E; Piña Chán 1955b: figs. 9, 10, 24, láms. 9, 13; 1958b: láms. 17, 20, 29; 1971: figs. 12, 13, 16; Coe 1965b: ills. 98, 101, 128, 130, 201, 202, 204; Weaver 1967: pls. E, J; MacNeish et al. 1970: 278; Tolstoy and Paradis 1970: 345–7).

Vaguely similar figurine torsos occur in Ponce and Aguilar phases of northern Veracruz (MacNeish 1954: 595–7, fig. 24); in Trapiche I and II phases at El Trapiche and Chalahuite (García Payón 1966: láms. 66, 67); at La Venta (Drucker 1952: pls. 32, 35, 36, 38); in the Conchas phase at La Victoria (Coe 1961: 97–8, figs. 56–58); in the Early Preclassic phases at Altamira (Green and Lowe 1967: figs. 33, 95); in the Dili phase at Chiapa de Corzo (Lowe and Mason 1965: fig. 9; Lee 1969: figs. 16, 17); and in Cotorra and Dili phases at Padre Piedra (Navarrete 1960: fig. 12; Green and Lowe 1967: fig. 66).

Olmecoid/baby-face figurines of the Uala and Tom periods at Puerto Marqués and related sites in coastal Guerrero have roughly similar torsos (E. Brush 1968: 60–71, pls. 8, 12, table 4). Xochipala-style figurines include nude females with similar very naturalistic torsos, often with a deep incision running from the coccyx to the pubic area; they occasionally have braided hair (Gay 1972: 21–30, figs. 9, 10, 12–17).

Figurines of the Tecolotla Phase

Hollow Olmec Head (Fig. 59a)

Paste and surface. Hardness near 2.5. Temper coarse and not the typical quartziferous sand; quartz crystals, whitish particles of limestone or calcite, and gold flecks of mica predominate, with occasional shiny black, red, and brown particles. Near exterior surface paste is oxidized to reddish yellow (5 YR 6/6), grading to pinkish gray (5 YR 7/2) toward center. Except for temper, paste is similar to Barranca Smoothed Buff, but without surface compaction. Carefully smoothed exterior surface has slight traces of light gray (10 YR 6/1) slip. Interior surface coarse and unsmoothed.

Form. This fragment represents mouth and upper lip of a hollow figurine head. Mouth is down-turned, with crescentic upper lip projecting horizontally from plane of face. A broad incision encircles lower edge of upper lip, giving a raised effect to roof of open mouth. A central projection with a vertical incision represents upper incisors.

Comparative material. The mouths of Olmecoid Hollow Lowland-type heads of the Early Santa María phase in the Tehuacán Valley are quite similar (MacNeish et al. 1970: 89, fig. 48).

Hollow figurines occur throughout the Early Preclassic sequence at Nexpa and La Juana-San Pablo; one head fragment from Nexpa (Middle or Late Nexpa

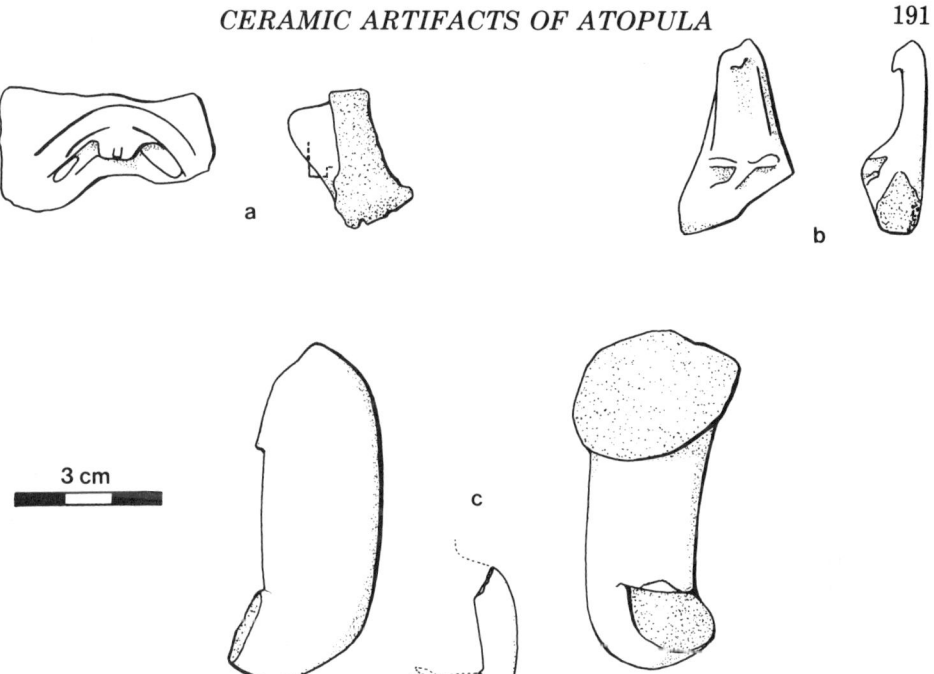

FIG. 59. Ceramic figurines, Tecolotla phase: *a*, hollow Olmec head fragment; *b*, crude solid head; *c*, solid arm fragment.

phase) is quite similar. Large hollow white-slipped Olmecoid/baby-face figurines of the La Juana phase were found in La Juana graves by *huaqueros*. The same types of figurines from Gualupita have similar mouths with projecting crescentic upper lips, often with incisors indicated (Vaillant and Vaillant 1934: figs. 14, 15; Grove 1968b: 128; 1970c: 62; 1972: fig. 13). These figurines also occur in the Ayotla and Justo subphases (Ixtapaluca phase) at Ayotla (Tlapacoya); in the Iglesia subphase (early Zacatenco phase) at Tlatilco; in Tlatilco, Tlapacoya, and Las Bocas graves; in the Guadalupe phase in the Valley of Oaxaca; and in the Uala and Tom periods at Puerto Marqués, Zanja, and related sites in coastal Guerrero (Porter 1953: pl. 5E; Piña Chán 1955b: láms. 41, 43; Coe 1965b: ills. 184-92; Weaver 1967: pl. 24; E. Brush 1968: 58-71, pls. 2-7, 9-11, tables 3, 4; Flannery 1968: 94, fig. 9; MacNeish et al. 1970: 277, 278; Tolstoy and Paradis 1970: 347).

Large hollow figurines of undetermined type occur in the Ponce phase of northern Veracruz (MacNeish 1954: 597, fig. 24; MacNeish et al. 1970: 274-5). Large hollow, white-slipped Olmecoid/baby-face figurines occur in the Trapiche II phase (and perhaps in Trapiche I) at El Trapiche and Chalahuite (García Payón 1966: láms. 56, 57, 62, 69; 1971; MacNeish et al. 1970: 273). They are common in the Bajío, Chicharras, and San Lorenzo phases at San Lorenzo Tenochtitlán (Coe 1968b: 46; 1970: 24-7), and they also occur at La Venta (Drucker 1952: pls. 39, 41).

Vaguely similar large hollow white-slipped figurines appear in the Conchas phase at La Victoria (Coe 1961: 94, fig. 54) and in the Early Preclassic phases at Altamira (Green and Lowe 1967: figs. 30, 94). Large hollow Olmecoid/baby-face figurines with similar protruding crescentic upper lips occur in the Dili phase at Chiapa de Corzo (Lowe and Mason 1965: fig. 9; Lee 1969: 17, fig. 3). Large hollow figurines occur also in Cotorra and Dili phases at Padre Piedra, but the one illustrated specimen is quite dissimilar (Navarrete 1960: fig. 12; Green and Lowe 1967: 48, fig. 66).

Crude Solid Head (Fig. 59b)

Paste and surface. Hardness is 1.5. Temper very coarse and not the usual quartziferous sand; quartz crystals, small whitish particles of limestone or calcite, and tiny red particles predominate. Paste is oxidized reddish yellow (5 YR 7/6, 7/8) to light red (2.5 YR 6/8) throughout. Surface not smoothed and has very coarse texture from protruding temper particles. No trace of slip.

Form. Fragment represents upper part of a very crudely made human head. Eyes indicated by roughly triangular gouges, leaving a raised area between them representing the nose. Lower face broken away. Forehead area slopes sharply back and is continuous with a flat tapering headdress that bends forward slightly at the top.

Comparative material. The headdress gives this head an overall effect very much like that of a surface figurine with a forward-bending headdress, although that head is much larger and more finely made.

No Tehuacán Valley figurine types are particularly similar, nor are those of the Early and Middle Preclassic phases of Morelos and the Valley of Mexico. Aberrant Trapiche II-phase figurines from El Trapiche and Chalahuite have vaguely similar high, forward-curving headdresses, as do a few La Venta figurines (Drucker 1952: pl. 26; García Payón 1966: lám. 63).

Solid Arm (Fig. 59c)

Paste and surface. Hardness near 2.5. Temper coarse and not the usual quartziferous sand; quartz crystals, whitish particles of limestone or calcite, gold flecks of mica, and small shiny black particles predominate. At surface, paste is oxidized to pink or reddish yellow (5 YR 7/4, 6/6), grading to light gray (5 YR 7/1) core. Surface carefully smoothed and compacted. Except for temper, paste and surface treatment comparable to Barranca Smoothed Buff. Very slight traces of what may be a light gray or white (5 YR 7/1, 8/1) slip.

Form. This fragment represents left upper arm of a large human figure; it is broken at shoulder and just below elbow. Arm was bent, with forearm extending across body.

Comparative material. This arm fragment is very similar to the arm attached to an Atopula-phase hollow body fragment, but larger and was probably also attached to a large hollow body.

In the Tehuacán Valley, Early Santa María-phase hollow figurines (probably with Olmecoid heads) usually have bent arms and are about the same size. Seated Mother Body figurines, also primarily Early Santa María phase, have arms resting across the chest but are much smaller (MacNeish et al. 1970: 95–6).

Arms bent across the chest occur on a number of Early Preclassic and Early Middle Preclassic figurine types in coastal Guerrero, the central highlands, the Gulf coast, central Chiapas, and Soconusco—including the white-slipped hollow Olmecoid/baby-face type (e.g. Coe 1965b: ills. 190, 199; García Payón 1966: lám. 69; Weaver 1967: pl. F; see discussion of the Atopula-phase hollow torso fragment).

Surface Figurines

Solid D-Type Head (Fig. 60a)

Paste and surface. Hardness near 2.5. Temper coarse to very coarse and not the usual quartziferous sand; white particles of limestone or calcite predominate, with occasional quartz crystals and shiny black particles. Near surface, paste is oxidized light red to reddish yellow (2.5 YR 6/6; 5 YR 6/6), grading to light reddish brown (5 YR 6/3, 6/4) toward center. Except for temper, paste is comparable to Barranca Smoothed Buff but is somewhat more completely oxidized and lacks the surface compaction. Surface smoothed and regular but is now rough because temper particles have been exposed by weathering. The thick slip, fired from red (10 R 4/6, 4/8) to reddish gray (10 R 6/1) is highly polished.

Form. Head rectangular in overall shape; face is nearly square. Eyes ellipsoidal and slanting, outlined by raised ridges representing lids; eyeball is depressed, most deeply at corners, the pupil represented by a deep punctation in the raised area at center of each eyeball; right eye noticeably higher than the left. Mouth also consists of an ellipsoidal depression, deepest at corners, between raised ridges forming lips. Nose straight, broad at base, and terminates just above upper lip; nostrils represented by two conical punctations. Chin rounded, shallow, and narrow, projecting below the squarish corners of the ears. Ears long and tabular as seen from rear; in front they are not distinguished from the plane of the face. Very deep punctations at lower corners of face presumably represent ear ornaments (or perhaps the auditory meatus). Headdress is a wide rectangular hat slanting back from the face, with a horizontal brim projecting on all sides. Back of head nearly flat except for hat brim and is featureless except to indicate the separation between ears and head. There is a break at what appears to have been top of neck; head originally attached to a body.

Comparative material. This head is very similar in many respects to D- and K-type figurine heads, which are common in Preclassic sites in Morelos and the Valley of Mexico, although it does not fit perfectly into the present classification of subtypes. It is most like D1 heads, which have carefully modeled square faces, slanted eyes depressed at the corners between raised rims (although pupils are often represented, like the mouth, by slits rather than punctations), and small projecting chins. The tendency for one eye to be lower than the other is quite striking. Some features, as well as similar tabular ears, occur also in D2 heads but tend to have pronounced appliqué features, esp. eyebrows. Some features also

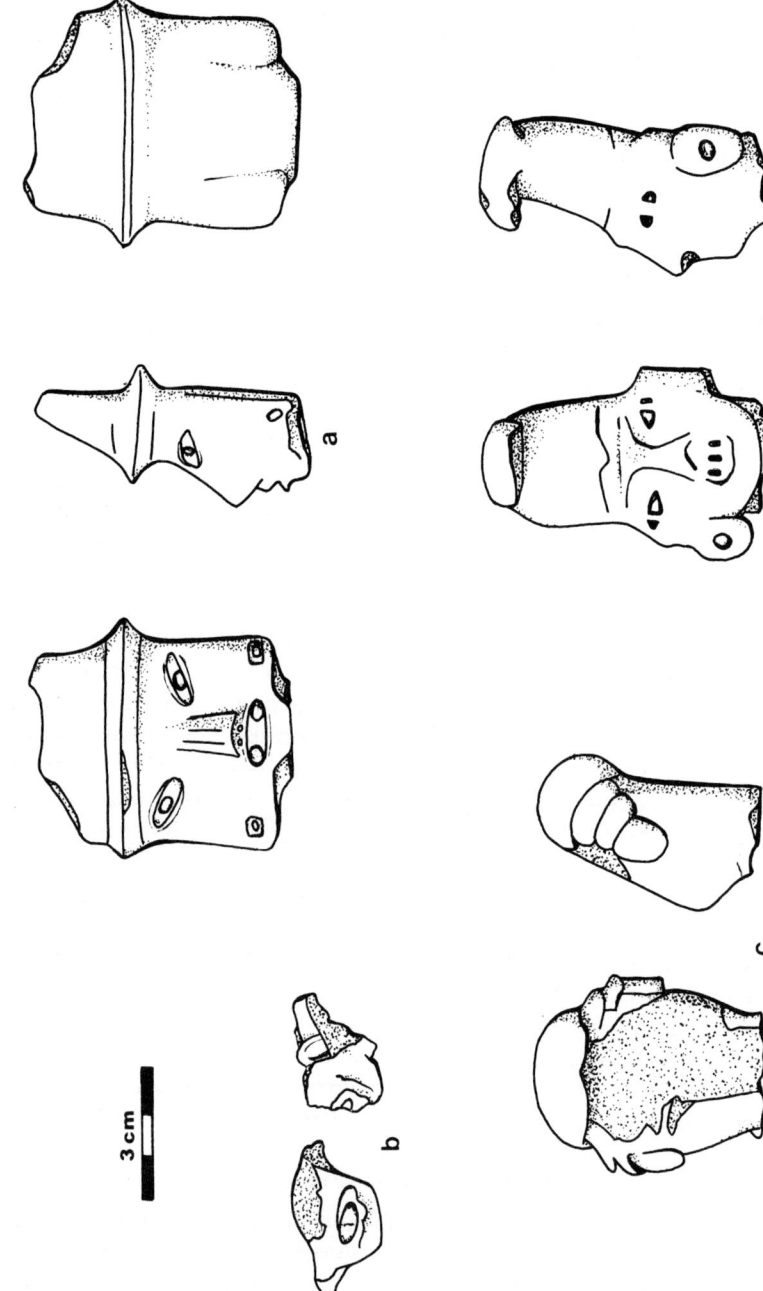

FIG. 60. Ceramic figurines, surface: *a*, solid D-type head; *b*, solid D-type face fragment; *c*, solid Crescent-Cap head; *d*, solid High-Headdress head.

shared with D4 and the Morelos subtypes of K heads (Kma, Kmb, and solid D-K), but these types tend to have ovoid or fan-shaped heads (Piña Chán 1955b: fig. 23; 1971: 170, 171, figs. 13, 16; Coe 1965b: 26, 45, ills. 93–113, 128–34; Noguera 1965: 74, figs. 23, 24; Grove 1968b: 87–91, fig. 3).

Type-D1 heads occur in the Early Santa María phase in the Tehuacán Valley but much more crudely made. Several figurine types of the Late Ajalpan and Early Santa María phases, particularly Crescentic Cap heads, have similar treatment of eyes and mouth (MacNeish et al. 1970: 90–1, figs. 50, 51).

D and K figurines occur in Gualupita I, at Chalcatzingo, and throughout the Early to Early Middle Preclassic sequence at Nexpa, La Juana-San Pablo, and Cerro Chacaltepec. Some D1 and D2 specimens quite similar to this head (Vaillant and Vaillant 1934: figs. 6–8; Piña Chán 1955a: 49, 50; Grove 1968b: esp. fig. 37; 1970c; 1972: esp. figs. 11–13). D1 and D2 figurines occur in the Ixtapaluca phase at Ayotla (Tlapacoya); in the early Zacatenco phase at El Arbolillo and Zacatenco (El Arbolillo subphase), Tlatilco (Iglesia subphase), and Ayotla (Bomba subphase); and (perhaps intrusively) in late La Pastora and Totolica-subphase refuse at Zacatenco, El Arbolillo, and Tlatilco; and in Tlatilco graves. Some of these, esp. the D1's, are quite similar. Figurines like the D types of the Valley of Mexico occur in the San José phase in the Valley of Oaxaca. Projecting-eye figurines of the Guadalupe phase have similar treatment of eyes (Vaillant 1930: pls. 18–20; Porter 1953: 23, 31, pls. 4, 5; Piña Chán 1955b: figs. 9, 10; 1958a: 53, fig. 19, tabla 2; 1958b: láms. 19, 20; Coe 1965b: ills. 93–112, 128–34; Flannery 1968: 82, 94; MacNeish et al. 1970: 270–8; Tolstoy and Paradis 1970: 347).

Several figurine types of Ponce and Aguilar phases of northern Veracruz, esp. the Crescentic and Scalloped-edge Cap, have a similar treatment of eyes and mouth (MacNeish 1954: 589–92, figs. 21, 23). At San Lorenzo Tenochtitlán, figurines with punched eyes do not appear until the Nacaste phase (Coe 1970: 29). A similar treatment of eyes and mouth is found in a number of types from Trapiche I and II phases of El Trapiche and Chalahuite (García Payón 1966); from La Venta (Drucker 1952); from the Dili phase at Chiapa de Corzo (Lowe and Mason 1965: fig. 9; Lee 1969: 10–17, figs. 1, 2); from the Early Preclassic phases at Altamira (Green and Lowe 1967: figs. 32, 94); and from the Conchas phase at La Victoria (Coe 1961: 93, figs. 54, 55).

Some Arévalo- and Las Charcas-phase figurines from highland Guatemala have vaguely similar eyes and mouths (Kidder 1965: figs. 1, 3–5; MacNeish et al. 1970: 284). Many Uala- and Tom-period figurines from Puerto Marqués and related sites in coastal Guerrero have similar eyes (E. Brush 1968: 51, 65, pl. 7).

Solid D-Type Face (Fig. 60b)

Paste and surface. Hardness near 2.5. Temper medium, not the usual quartziferous sand; black and red particles and quartz crystals predominate. Paste unevenly oxidized; in some areas near surface it is pink to light reddish brown (5 YR 7/3, 6/3); other parts of surface and most of core are light gray to gray (5 YR 5/1, 6/1). Surface very carefully smoothed and compacted. Except for temper, paste is comparable to Pedrusco Polished Gray or poorly oxidized examples of Barranca Smoothed Buff. Traces of dark red (10 R 3/6) pigment, apparently a slip, esp. in the corner of the mouth.

Form. This fragment represents lower part of a human head—mouth and chin and adjacent area. Mouth ellipsoidal with deep depressions at corners leaving a raised area in center; lips are appliqué strips. Chin rounded and prominent, clearly differentiated from top of neck. Face above upper lip is missing. A projection at right side of face just above the level of mouth apparently represents base of a long tabular ear.

Comparative material. This fragment similar to the preceding one, except that lips are formed by appliqué strip and face is ovoid or fan-shaped rather than square. It also resembles D and K figurines (types D1, D2, D4, Kma, Kmb, and solid D-K) of highland central Mexico (see discussion above).

Solid Crescent-Cap Head (Fig. 60c)

Paste and surface. Hardness near 2.5. Temper coarse and is the usual quartziferous sand, predominantly small quartz crystals and whitish particles of limestone or calcite. Incompletely oxidized paste is uniformly reddish brown to dark reddish gray (5 YR 4/2, 4/3, 5/3). Surfaces have been partially smoothed but retain slightly gritty texture from protruding temper particles. Paste comparable to Guamuchil Polished Black. No trace of slip, although surfaces are somewhat eroded.

Form. This fragment represents a human head with all facial features broken away. Face was quite prognathous with a strongly projecting lower face. Headgear consists of a crescentic central cap with two overlapping lateral projections and a vertical tabular flap on each side. Back of head is slightly concave and featureless except for the junction between rounded central part of cap and back of head.

Comparative material. Central part of head very similar to caps of Crescentic Cap heads of the Early Santa María phase in the Tehuacán Valley, although these lack the pendant lateral elements (MacNeish et al. 1970: 91, fig. 51).

No illustrated figurines from the Early and Middle Preclassic phases at Nexpa, La Juana-San Pablo, and Cerro Chacaltepec are similar, although central part of headdress is somewhat like headgear of several types (Grove 1968b; 1970c; 1972).

Some Valley of Mexico figurines, mainly D-types and solid Olmecoid/babyface figurines, have headgear roughly similar to the crescentic central part of the headdress. One D2 head (provenience unknown) illustrated by Vaillant (1930: pl. 20) has a similar multitiered cap or helmet with pendant earflaps. Vaguely similar D2 figurines occur in Ixtapaluca and early Zacatenco phases in the Valley of Mexico and in Tlatilco, Tlapacoya, and Las Bocas graves (Porter 1953: pls. 4, 5; Piña Chán 1958a: 53, fig. 19, tabla 2; Coe 1965b: ills. 93, 94, 105, 106, 111, 112, 129–32, 196, 199, 203, 204; Weaver 1967: pls. E, J; Tolstoy and Paradis 1970: 347). Some solid Olmecoid figurines of the San José phase in the Valley of Oaxaca also have roughly similar headgear (Flannery 1968: 82–5, fig. 4; MacNeish et al. 1970: 270).

Headgear resembling crescentic central part of cap is found on figurines of the Ponce and Aguilar phases of northern Veracruz (MacNeish 1954: figs. 21, 23); Trapiche I and II phases at El Trapiche and Chalahuite (García Payón 1966); La Venta (Drucker 1952); the Conchas phase of La Victoria (Coe 1961: figs. 54, 55); the Early Preclassic phases at Altamira (Green and Lowe 1967: figs. 32, 93, 94); the Dili phases at Chiapa de Corzo (Lowe and Mason 1965: fig. 9; Lee 1969: figs. 1-3); the Arévalo and Las Charcas phases of highland Guatemala (Kidder 1965: fig. 1; MacNeish et al. 1970: 284); and the Uala and Tom periods at Puerto Marqués and related sites in coastal Guerrero (E. Brush 1968: 60-70, pls. 2-7, 9-10, table 4).

Solid High-Headdress Head (Fig. 60d)

Paste and surface. Hardness near 2.5. Temper coarse and is the usual quartziferous sand, predominantly small quartz crystals and whitish particles of limestone or calcite. Near surface, paste is oxidized light red to reddish yellow (2.5 YR 6/6; 5 YR 6/6), grading to light reddish brown (5 YR 6/3, 6/4) toward core. Paste comparable to Barranca Smoothed Buff, although more completely oxidized and lacks the careful surface compaction. Surface smoothed but retains a somewhat gritty texture from protruding temper particles. No trace of slip.

Form. This figurine head is tall and relatively narrow. Eyes formed by opposing deep subtriangular punches separated by a central strip continuous with plane of face. No filleting or raised rim. Nose straight, broad at base, and continuous with a slightly projecting brow ridge. Nostrils not indicated. Mouth represented by three deep vertical gashes; no filleting to represent lips. Chin broad, slightly rounded, and very slightly recessed just below mouth, producing effect of a raised mouth area. Ears are long tabular projections at sides of face; left ear broken at base, but the right retains representation of a large discoidal ear plug.

Bottom of headdress marked by light incisions; it continues lines of sides of head and nose, sloping backward slightly and then curving sharply forward and down.

Comparative material. A similar treatment of the eyes, opposing triangular depressions, is common in D and K figurines from highland central Mexico; in some Morelos varieties (Kmb e.g.) eyes also occur without filleted rims. Mouths may have central slits but are always combined with depressions at the corners and raised lips. The overall effect of this head, however, is quite different. No illustrated Early Preclassic specimen from Nexpa and La Juana-San Pablo is similar (Grove 1968b: 88-91, fig. 3; 1970c; 1972). Some K figurines (Kma) from Gualupita I have similar mouths, as do figurines from San Jerónimo, Guerrero (Vaillant and Vaillant 1934: figs. 8, 17). A crude figurine (C5 variant?) from El Arbolillo illustrated by Vaillant (1935: fig. 11) is roughly similar, with high forehead, double-punch eyes, a discoidal earplug, and mouth with three or four vertical slits.

No Tehuacán Valley types are very similar although the Flat, Punched-feature heads of the Early Ajalpan phase have eyes and mouth formed by double punches without fillets. Several Early Santa María types, particularly Crescentic Cap heads, have long tabular ears with discoidal earplugs (MacNeish et al. 1970: 36, 91–4, figs. 15, 51).

Aberrant Trapiche II figurines from El Trapiche and Chalahuite have high forward-curving headdresses somewhat reminiscent of this example, as do a few La Venta figurines (Drucker 1952: pl. 26e; García Payón 1966: lám. 63). A figurine from the Dili phase at Padre Piedra has similar double-punched eyes with no pupil indicated (Sorenson 1956: pl. 1).

Solid Belted Torso (Fig. 61a)

Paste and surface. Hardness near 2.5. Temper coarse and the usual quartziferous sand; quartz crystals and whitish particles of limestone or calcite predominate, with occasional shiny black particles. Paste uniformly oxidized to light red to reddish yellow (2.5 YR 6/8; 5 YR 6/6) throughout. Except for temper, paste is comparable to Barranca Smoothed Buff, although more completely oxidized and lacks the careful surface compaction. Surface smoothed but retains a slightly gritty texture from protruding temper particles. Although surface is eroded, there

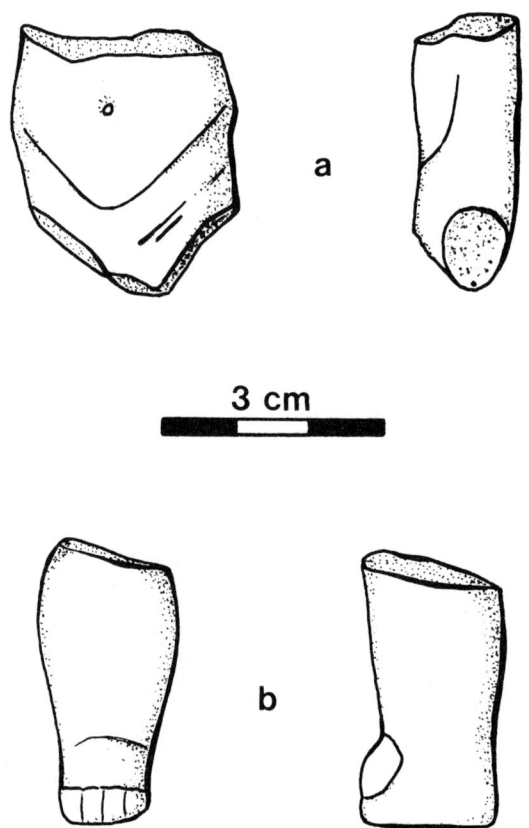

FIG. 61. Ceramic figurines, surface: *a*, solid belted-torso fragment; *b*, solid leg fragment.

are slight traces of what may have been light gray to white (5 YR 7/1, 8/1) slip.

Form. This fragment represents lower torso of a human figure. It is flattened, plano-convex in cross-section, and has a flat featureless back. A raised belt curves down across the lower abdomen in a U-shape. The missing legs were apparently splayed and not fused together at top of thighs: crotch area is continuous from front to back of torso.

Comparative material. No figurine torsos with similar belts found in the Tehuacán Valley. Otherwise, the torso is somewhat like the Standing Gingerbread and Trackwoman bodies of the Ajalpan phase (MacNeish et al. 1970: 37-8, figs. 17, 18).

No illustrated figurines from Early and Middle Preclassic phases at Nexpa, La Juana-San Pablo, and Cerro Chacaltepec have similar belts. In other respects torso not unlike San Pablo-phase fragments from the San Pablo Pantheon mound (Grove 1968b: fig. 31). Roughly similar belts do occur on some D and K figurines from Gualupita I (Vaillant and Vaillant 1934: figs. 7-9) and on some D1 figurines of the Ixtapaluca and early Zacatenco phases in the Valley of Mexico. D-type and esp. "ball-player" figurines in Tlatilco and Tlapacoya graves often have roughly similar belts (Vaillant 1930: pl. 19; Porter 1953: pl. 4; Piña Chán 1955b: figs. 4, 9, lám. 7; Coe 1965b: ills. 97, 100, 108, 109, 111, 119; Weaver 1967: pl. C; MacNeish et al. 1970: 278; Tolstoy and Paradis 1970: 347).

Some solid figurines of the San Lorenzo phase at San Lorenzo Tenochtitlán and from La Venta are belted, but none of the illustrated examples is particularly similar (Drucker 1952: pls. 31, 32, 41; Coe 1970: 27). Roughly similar belts occasionally occur on Dili-phase figurine torsos from Chiapa de Corzo (Lee 1969: fig. 17).

Solid Leg (Fig. 61b)

Paste and surface. Hardness near 2.5. Temper coarse and not the usual quartziferous sand; small quartz crystals and whitish particles of limestone or calcite predominate, with occasional shiny red and black particles. Near surface, paste oxidized light reddish brown to reddish yellow (5 YR 6/4, 6/6), grading to pinkish gray (5 YR 7/2) toward core. Except for temper, paste is comparable to Barranca Smoothed Buff but without the careful surface compaction. Surface partially smoothed but has coarse texture from protruding temper particles. No trace of slip but surface quite eroded.

Form. This fragment represents lower leg and foot of a human figure. Leg elliptical in cross-section, with the long axis from front to back; it swells uniformly from the ankle and begins to contract again just below the break. Foot is quite stubby, with what seems to be an ellipsoidal appliqué across the instep, perhaps part of a sandal. Shallow incisions or scratches represent toes.

Comparative material. This fragment is not very distinctive and not particularly like other reported Mesoamerican types. It is not unlike the squat Booted legs, and legs with sandals with appliqué ornaments of Ajalpan and Early Santa María phases in the Tehuacán Valley (MacNeish et al. 1970: 56, 69, figs. 19, 60, 61).

No specific similarities to Early and Middle Preclassic figurines from Gualupita, Nexpa, La Juana-San Pablo, and Cerro Chacaltepec, although some types have vaguely similar legs (Vaillant and Vaillant 1934; Grove 1968b; 1970c; 1972).

Type C (esp. C1) figurines of the Early Zacatenco phase in the Valley of Mexico (El Arbolillo subphase at El Arbolillo and Zacatenco, Bomba subphase at Ayotla) often have similar pillow-shaped instep appliqués. Roughly similar legs and feet occur on a number of figurines from Tlatilco, Tlapacoya, and Las Bocas graves, esp. C1 and D-types (Vaillant 1930: pls. 10, 24; Porter 1953: pls. 4, 5; Coe 1965b: ills. 91, 92; Weaver 1967: pls. E, J; Tolstoy and Paradis 1970: 345–7).

Very similar figurine legs occur at La Venta (Drucker 1952: pl. 33). Comparable legs and feet occur on Dili-phase figurines from Chiapa de Corzo and Padre Piedra (Lowe and Mason 1965: fig. 9; Green and Lowe 1967: fig. 66; Lee 1969: fig. 17); on figurines from the Early Preclassic phases at Altamira (Green and Lowe 1967: figs. 33, 95); and on Uala- and Tom-period figurines from Puerto Marqués and related sites in coastal Guerrero (E. Brush 1968: 54–7, pl. 1). Several ceramic figurines in the Xochipala style (Gay 1972: figs. 10, 12, 14) have similar instep appliqués.

Miscellaneous Ceramic Artifacts of the Tecolotla Phase

Sherd Trapezoid (Fig. 54b)

This artifact is a perfectly flat trapezoidal sherd. In paste and surface treatment very similar to Barranca Smoothed Buff. It is unslipped, but surface and long straight edges have been very carefully smoothed. This specimen could have been manufactured by grinding a sherd from the flat base of a Barranca Smoothed Buff vessel, although no flat-based forms were represented in this type in Tecolotla-phase levels. Its function is unknown. Comparable artifacts are known only from the Jocotal phase at Salinas La Blanca, in which very similar sherd trapezoids occur. Their function, too, is unknown (Coe and Flannery 1967: 65, pl. 21).

Appendix 4. The Stone Artifacts of Atopula

The inventory of nonceramic artifacts from Atopula is not large; it is limited to stone artifacts. No shell of any kind was recovered, and the only preserved fragments of bone consisted of small unidentifiable splinters of long bone.

Ground Stone of the Cacahuananche Phase

Metates (Fig. 62)

Two large milling stones manufactured from large blocks of reddish sandstone by grinding and pecking: one with both ends broken away was originally ovoid to subrectangular with long edges bowed. Upper grinding surface almost perfectly flat, with slight concavity from side to side. Maximum width of grinding surface 18 cm., preserved length 20 cm. This specimen is 8 cm. thick, roughly tabular in cross-section, with rounded edges; base is flat. The second more nearly complete, with only part of one end missing. Shape again ovoid to subrectangular. Length 28 cm., maximum width 16 cm. This specimen has maximum thickness of 9 cm. and rounded base and edges.

Striations along grinding surfaces of both specimens indicate use as metates, presumably used with loaf-shaped manos like the one recovered from a Tecolotla-phase level.

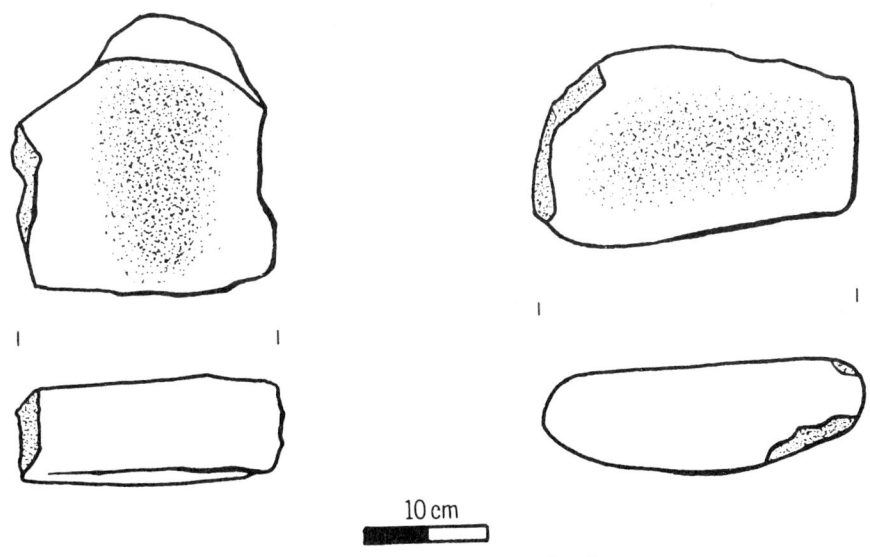

FIG. 62. Metates, Cacahuananche phase.

"Palettes" (Fig. 63)

Two small tabular pieces of gray-brown sandstone or siltstone, roughly trapezoidal in outline with carefully smoothed surfaces and edges; length 6.5–7.5 cm., maximum width 4.5–5.5 cm., thickness 1.0–1.5 cm. One surface of each is slightly convex, opposite face flat with very light striations. Flat faces were grinding surfaces, perhaps for processing mineral pigments, but no detectable pigment traces remain.

Similar small tablets or palettes found at La Victoria in the Ocós or Conchas 1 phase (Coe 1961: 106, fig. 51) and in the Dili phase at Chiapa de Corzo (Lee 1969: 120–3, fig. 82). In the Tehuacán Valley similar tablets, used as pigment grinders, are most popular in the Ajalpan phase (MacNeish et al. 1967: 125, fig. 104, table 19).

Ground Stone of the Atopula Phase

Metates (Fig. 64)

Two fragmentary milling stones manufactured by pecking and grinding; one represents end of an ovoid metate made from gray conglomerate. Edges rounded and base flat; maximum thickness (at edges) 5–6 cm., maximum preserved width 15 cm.

The second specimen, also ovoid, made of reddish-brown basalt, is more complete; preserved length 20 cm., width 18 cm.; maximum thickness (at edges) 10 cm. Edges and base uniformly rounded. In both cases grinding surfaces distinctly trough-like, much more concave than the Cacahuananche-phase metates. Striations paralleling the long dimension demonstrate use as metates.

Stone Bowl (Fig. 65)

Rim sherd of a thin convex bowl of greenish-black volcanic stone (diorite?) manufactured by grinding and polishing; diameter of mouth 17 cm.; base rounded. Vessel wall tapers slightly toward lip, which is sharply beveled. Surface very carefully ground and polished. Similar polished green stone bowls, sometimes with incised or excised designs that may be painted red, have been found in association with Xochipala-style ceramic figurines (Gay 1972: 48–50, fig. 34).

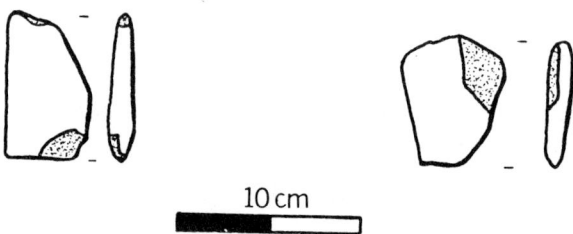

FIG. 63. "Palettes," Cacahuananche phase.

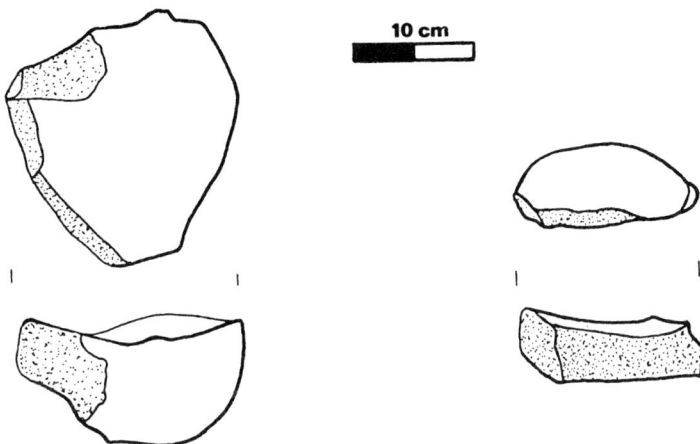

FIG. 64. Metates, Atopula phase.

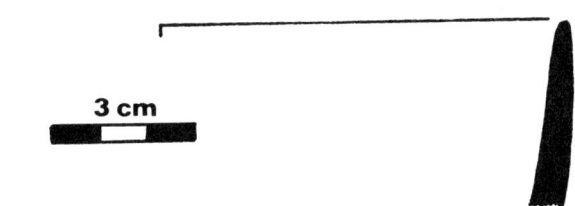

FIG. 65. Stone bowl, Atopula phase.

Ground Stone of the Tecolotla Phase

Metates (Fig. 66a,b)

Two specimens manufactured by pecking and grinding: one, made of gray-brown conglomerate, is only an edge fragment. Shape originally circular or ovoid; base very slightly convex, edges strongly rounded. Maximum thickness (at edges) 13–14 cm.

The second, made of gray-brown sandstone or quartzite, is more complete. Shape roughly rectangular with rounded corners. Maximum preserved length 36 cm., width 17 cm.; maximum thickness (at edges) 16 cm. Base slightly convex and edges strongly rounded. Both specimens deeply concave, with a raised rim encircling entire grinding surface. Upper surfaces of both also striated, indicating grinding function. Striations on the deeper first specimen do not indicate single-direction grinding, and could equally be classified as a mortar; it was used with a pestle rather than a mano.

Pestle (Fig. 66c)

One specimen manufactured from gray basalt by pecking and grinding; nearly square in cross-section with slightly convex faces; tapers gradually toward lower

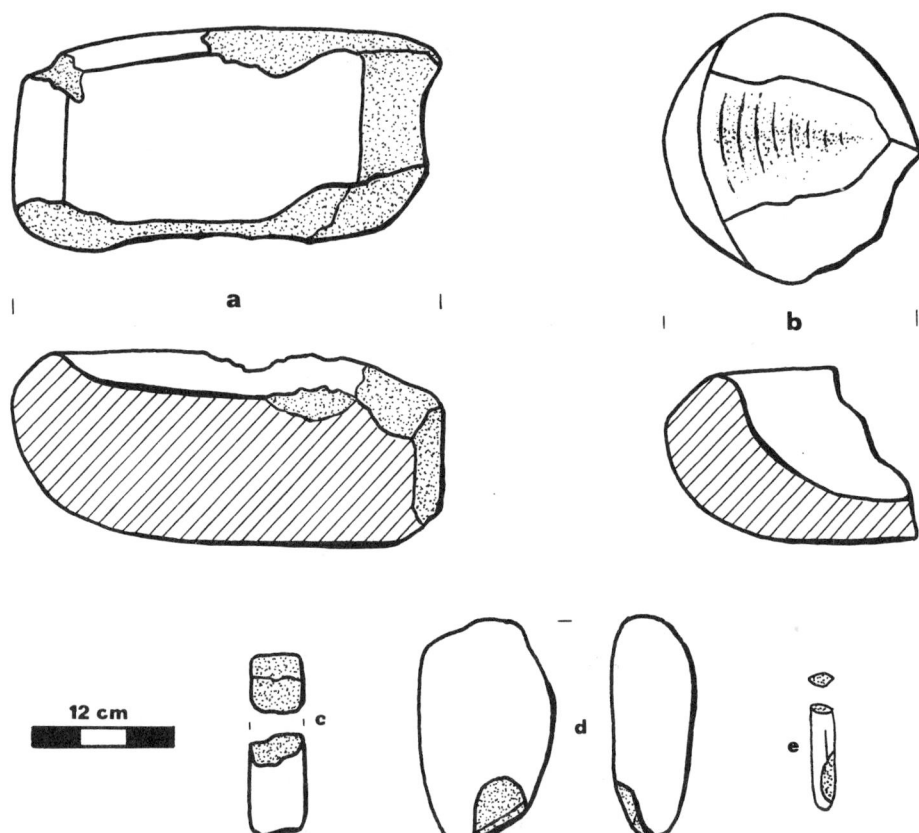

FIG. 66. Ground stone artifacts, Tecolotla phase: *a, b*, metates; *c*, pestle; *d*, mano; *e*, "flaker."

end, which is worn; the other end missing. Each face 5 cm. wide at the break (8 cm. above worn end). Lower end, rather than faces, constituted the grinding surface. This specimen presumably used with a round mortar-like stone rather than a flattened metate.

Stone mortars and (esp.) pestles are relatively rare in Mesoamerica but have been found in Ocós and Conchas phases at La Victoria, the Cotorra phase at Chiapa de Corzo, the Zacatenco phase (at Zacatenco) and the Tlatilco graves in the Valley of Mexico, and in the Miraflores phase at Kaminaljuyú (Vaillant 1930: pl. 45; Dixon 1959: fig. 53f; Coe 1961: 101, 102, figs. 41, 42, 51, 60, 61). A similar long rectangular pestle was found in the Santa María phase in Tehuacán, but this pestle type is most typical of the El Riego phase (MacNeish et al. 1967: 103–5, fig. 84).

Mano (Fig. 66d)

One specimen of gray-brown sandstone manufactured by pecking and grinding; roughly loaf-shaped, ovoid to subrectangular in outline; 18 cm. long, 11 cm. wide,

6–7 cm. thick. The two faces nearly flat and show striations perpendicular to the long dimension, indicating use with a flattish metate in back-and-forth grinding.

"Flaker" (Fig. 66e)

Long narrow spatulate object of gray sandstone or siltstone manufactured by grinding; 7.5 cm. long, 2 cm. wide, 1 cm. thick. Cross-section lenticular. One end broken away, the other rounded and rather battered. This may have been used as a flaker in removing and retouching obsidian blades and flakes.

Discussion

The obvious trend in the grinding-stone complexes is from crudeness to careful shaping and from flattened to concave grinding surfaces. Cacahuananche-phase metates are simple, slab-like, and flat; little effort was invested in shaping them. In the Atopula phase, grinding surfaces are more concave or trough-like, in the Tecolotla phase, they are markedly concave with raised rims and the metates themselves carefully shaped, either rectangular or circular and mortar-like; pestles also appear.

A similar development of grinding-stone complexes may be observed at La Victoria and Salinas La Blanca (Coe 1961: 100–6, tables 7–14; Coe and Flannery 1967: 63–5). Ocós- and Cuadros-phase metates are crude with flat grinding surfaces; in the Conchas and Crucero phases they are more carefully manufactured, with concave trough-like grinding surfaces, and stone mortars become more common. Similarly, in the Valley of Mexico, shallow-basin metates occur in the early Zacatenco phase and in the Tlatilco graves, whereas most of the later Zacatenco-phase metates are deep with an encircling rim. Legged metates are fairly common in the Valley of Mexico, but absent at Atopula (Tolstoy 1971b: 284). In the Tehuacán Valley, oblong basin-shaped metates with deep grinding surfaces and raised rims are most popular in the Santa María phase, and a similar rectangular pestle also occurs in this phase (MacNeish et al. 1967: 120, figs. 96, 99, table 17). "Limited-trough" metates of the Cotorra phase at Chiapa de Corzo are similar to the Atopula- and (esp.) Tecolotla-phase specimens with deep grinding surfaces (Lee 1969: 117, fig. 75).

Cotorra- and Dili-phase manos with oval cross-sections and roughly quadrangular outlines from Chiapa de Corzo (Lee 1969: 114–15, fig. 70) resemble those from Atopula, as do manos of Ocós, Cuadros, and Conchas phases at La Victoria and Salinas La Blanca (Coe 1961: 102–6, figs. 41, 43; Coe and Flannery 1967: 63, pl. 21k), and of the Ajalpan and Santa María phases in the Tehuacán Valley (MacNeish et al. 1967: 108–11, figs. 89–91, table 17).

Chipped Stone of the Cacahuananche Phase

Flakes

Chipped stone from the Cacahuananche-phase levels is almost entirely restricted to unutilized waste flakes and occasional fractured chunks; 75 percent are an off-white or gray agate-like variety of cryptocrystalline quartz which often has pink or red banding; 20 percent are clear gray, gray banded, or opaque black obsidian. The remainder are rare specimens of a black variety of cryptocrystalline quartz and red volcanic stone.

Almost all these flakes are amorphous, with no indication of use or retouch; slight secondary flaking along one edge, which might be from use as scrapers, is seen on a very few.

Blades

Only two blade fragments were recovered from Cacahuananche-phase levels. Both are obsidian and have usage flaking along one or both edges. Probably intrusive from upper levels, since obsidian blades appear in significant numbers only in late levels of the Atopula phase.

Chipped Stone of the Atopula Phase

Flakes

Atopula-phase flaked stone also consists primarily of waste flakes and occasional nodules without secondary modification. A smaller but still substantial proportion (45 percent) is agate-like material, while obsidian now accounts for 35 percent. Clear gray and gray-banded obsidian continue to occur, and cloudy or mottled-gray obsidian appears. The residue consists of a wider variety of materials than in the Cacahuananche phase, including red (jasper-like) and black varieties of cryptocrystalline quartz, gray-brown fine-grained quartzite, and fine-grained green volcanic stone. Slight secondary flaking, perhaps from use, occurs along one edge of some flakes but is still quite rare.

Blades

In upper levels of the Atopula phase obsidian blades (clear gray, gray banded, and cloudy or mottled gray) occur in small quantities, from 1.0 to 1.5 cm. wide; all are fragmentary; the largest has a preserved length of 3 cm. They tend to be triangular or roughly trapezoidal in cross-section and often have considerable usage flaking along one or both edges. There are rare examples of striking platforms, prepared by flaking and grinding, but no other indications of intentional secondary modification. These blades foreshadow prismatic obsidian blades in considerable numbers in the Tecolotla phase.

Chipped Stone of the Tecolotla Phase

Flakes

Unmodified waste flakes and occasional broken chunks still well represented but comprise a smaller proportion of the chipped stone than in the preceding phases. Only 10 percent are of the agate-like material; specimens of red (jasper-like) and black cryptocrystalline quartz and red and green volcanic stone make up 15 percent; 75 percent are clear gray, gray banded, and cloudy or mottled-gray obsidian. Slight secondary flaking along one edge, perhaps from use, occurs rarely. None of the flakes is retouched.

Blades

Prismatic blades of clear gray, gray-banded, and cloudy or mottled-gray obsidian appear in substantial numbers, nearly as numerous as obsidian waste flakes. Uniform in width (8–14 mm.), all are fragmentary, maximum preserved length 4 cm. Almost every specimen shows considerable flaking along one or both edges from use as knife or scraper. Several specimens include remnants of striking platforms prepared by flaking and grinding; several have small almost pointed striking platforms which seem not to have been prepared. Two blade fragments have intentional secondary flaking along one edge, presumably facilitating use as scrapers. One specimen, retouched to produce a pointed end, may have been used as a knife. Two blade fragments have a long narrow flake scar and chisel-like point along one edge produced by accidental "burin blows."

Discussion

The bulk of the chipped stone found at Atopula is obsidian of several colors, indicating the exploitation of several different sources. This in turn implies long-distance economic relationships since there is no source of obsidian near Atopula. None has been located anywhere in the state of Guerrero, although Cobean has suggested an obsidian source in the southeastern highlands of Guerrero (Cobean et al. 1971).

The Preclassic sequence at Atopula shows increased use of obsidian and a replacement of flakes by blades. In the Cacahuananche phase, obsidian comprises 20 percent of the chipped stone, and only two (probably intrusive) blade fragments were recovered. In the Atopula phase, 35 percent of flakes are obsidian; obsidian blades appear in late levels. Obsidian accounts for 75 percent of the Tecolotla-phase chipped stone; blades become nearly as numerous as flakes and are now quite uniform, almost always show usage flaking, and are occasionally retouched. Preclassic sites in the Valley of Mexico indicate a similar early emphasis on a nonobsidian, nonblade tradition of flaked stone. Also, when blades appear there, usage flaking is common but retouch quite rare (Tolstoy 1971b: 273, table 1).

The blade complex at Atopula is restricted to obsidian. Its appearance does not coincide with a change in obsidian sources. Gray-banded and clear gray obsidian occur throughout the Preclassic sequence; at the beginning of the Atopula phase, cloudy or mottled-gray obsidian appears and opaque black obsidian disappears. The appearance of obsidian blades occurs at the end of the phase.

The relatively late appearance of obsidian blades, in Terminal Early Preclassic or initial Middle Preclassic phases, is a phenomenon observed elsewhere in Mesoamerica. At La Victoria and Salinas La Blanca, blades do not appear until the Conchas phase (Coe 1961: 100; Coe and Flannery 1967: 63), and they do not appear in Morelos until the Late Early Preclassic San Pablo B (Late Nexpa) phase (Grove 1972: 40–2). In the Tehuacán Valley, "fine" obsidian blades appear very early, in the Abejas phase (or even in terminal Coxcatlán), but the earliest blades at Atopula seem to fall into the "prepared striking platform" type of Tehuacán, which is popular only in the Purrón and Ajalpan phases. Some

Tecolotla-phase blades appear to match the "pointed striking platform" type, which appears in terminal Ajalpan and becomes popular only in Santa María. This blade type, which appears also in the Chiapa II-IV phases at Chiapa de Corzo, may be a marker for the Middle and Late Preclassic. Blades with retouched edges first appear in the Santa María phase (MacNeish et al. 1967: 17-25, table 1).

At San Lorenzo Tenochtitlán, obsidian blades are absent from Ojochi, Bajío, and Chicharras phases, appearing in significant numbers only in the San Lorenzo phase (Coe 1970; Cobean et al. 1971). The rapid rise in importance of such blades in the San Lorenzo B phase is correlated with an expansion in the number of obsidian sources exploited, seven new varieties appearing at San Lorenzo in that phase.

Without analysis of its chemical composition it is difficult to reach reliable conclusions about the sources of the Atopula obsidian, but information from other sites on Preclassic obsidian exploitation may provide a few clues. At San Lorenzo Tenochtitlán gray-banded or mottled-gray (from the Guadalupe Victoria-Pico de Orizaba area, Teotihuacán, El Chayal, and Ixtepeque Volcano) and black obsidian (from El Paraiso, Queretaro; Teotihuacán; El Chayal; and Ixtepeque Volcano) were imported during Early and Middle Preclassic periods. The importation of dark, translucent, and solid gray obsidian (from Altotongo, Veracruz and Ixtepeque Volcano) begins in the San Lorenzo B phase. The black and gray-banded obsidian used during the Early and Middle Preclassic phases at La Victoria and Salinas La Blanca was surely derived from Guatemalan sources (particularly El Chayal and Ixtepeque Volcano).

Gray-banded obsidian from the Guadalupe Victoria-Pico de Orizaba area is of poor flaking quality because of its irregular texture, and only one prismatic blade of this material was recovered at San Lorenzo. The Atopula gray-banded obsidian has excellent flaking characteristics and was probably derived from a different source. In light of the close ceramic ties with the Valley of Mexico, the Teotihuacán source is most likely. Gray and gray-banded obsidian is predominant in Early and Middle Preclassic components in the Valley of Mexico (Tolstoy 1971b: 271). The solid black obsidian that occurs in small quantities in the Cacahuananche phase might have been derived from the same source (Cobean et al. 1971: 668, table 1).

The translucent gray obsidian at Atopula might have been derived from Altotonga, Veracruz, or from Ixtepeque Volcano; El Ocotito, Guerrero, is another possible source. None of the San Lorenzo artifacts was matched with El Ocotito obsidian, but it is chemically similar to obsidian from Teotihuacán, El Paraiso, and (esp.) Altotonga and El Chayal (Cobean et al. 1971: table 2).

A striking feature of the obsidian complexes at Atopula is the total absence of the famous green obsidian from Pachuca, Hidalgo, during the Preclassic phases. Pachuca obsidian was imported at San Lorenzo Tenochtitlán during the San Lorenzo B and Nacaste phases and at La Venta, probably in Middle Preclassic times (Jack and Heizer 1968: 89; Stross et al. 1968: 61; Cobean et al. 1971: table 1; Jack et al. 1972: table 1). Pachuca obsidian appears at Atopula only in

Postclassic El Clarín-phase levels; it also reappears at San Lorenzo in the Postclassic Villa Alta phase (Cobean et al. 1971: table 1).

Obsidian Hydration Analysis

Twenty-four obsidian flakes from excavated levels at Atopula were submitted to Clement W. Meighan at the University of California at Los Angeles for hydration analysis. Hydration readings were obtained for nineteen of the specimens (Fig. 9, Table 3).

While these data cannot be used uncritically, they are in close accord with the results of the ceramic analysis. The sample size is not enormous but is adequate to provide support for the ceramic dating and to permit detection of a few specimens that are intrusive into the context in which they were excavated.

Re-use of obsidian artifacts does not appear to be a problem at Atopula; the bulk consisted of unretouched flakes and blades rather than carefully finished artifacts that might be used again and again. No retouched specimens were included in the samples submitted for hydration analysis. Only one of the analyzed specimens shows hydration bands that indicate re-use or rebreaking. There is no indication that the obsidian from Atopula was exposed to freak temperature conditions.

The hydration rate is the most serious problem with obsidian hydration dating in Mesoamerica. It has been maintained (Friedman and Evans 1968) that empirical evidence supports a nonlinear rate, but Meighan and others (Meighan et al. 1968a; 1968b; Meighan 1970) have demonstrated from archaeological evidence

TABLE 3. ATOPULA OBSIDIAN HYDRATION READINGS

Phase	Color	Hydration Band Thickness (microns)	Hydration Rate (years/ micron)	Age (years)	Median Calendar Date
El Clarín	Green	2.3	260	598 ± 52	A.D. 1350
El Clarín	Green	2.5	260	650 ± 52	A.D. 1300
El Clarín	Translucent gray	2.5	260	650 ± 52	A.D. 1300
El Clarín	Translucent gray	2.7	260	702 ± 52	A.D. 1250
Tecolotla	Mottled gray	5.5	425	2338 ± 165	390 B.C.
Tecolotla	Translucent gray	9.3/ 11.1	260	2418 ± 140/ 2886 ± 167	470 B.C./ 936 B.C.
Tecolotla	Translucent gray	6.2	425	2635 ± 186	690 B.C.
Tecolotla	Gray banded	6.5	425	2763 ± 195	810 B.C.
Tecolotla	Gray-black opaque	4.6	697	3206 ± 207	1260 B.C.
Tecolotla	Gray banded	7.7	425	3273 ± 231	1320 B.C.
Atopula	Gray banded	3.1	260	806 ± 52	A.D. 1140
Atopula	Translucent gray	9.5	260	2470 ± 143	520 B.C.
Atopula	Mottled gray	7.4	425	3145 ± 222	1200 B.C.
Atopula	Gray opaque	4.7	697	3276 ± 212	1330 B.C.
Atopula	Translucent gray	12.9	260	3354 ± 194	1400 B.C.
Cacahuananche	Gray banded	7.7	425	3273 ± 231	1320 B.C.
Cacahuananche	Gray-black opaque	4.9	697	3415 ± 221	1470 B.C.
Cacahuananche	Gray-black opaque	5.0	697	3485 ± 225	1540 B.C.
Cacahuananche	Mottled gray	8.6	425	3655 ± 258	1710 B.C.

that a linear rate of 260 years/micron is indicated for western Mexico. This rate. is based upon a correlation of obsidian hydration readings with a long series of radiocarbon dates. More recently, Meighan (personal communication) has found that the hydration rate varies with the chemical composition of the obsidian, and that there is at least a second rate (697 years/micron) for western Mexico. He has found that virtually all Postclassic obsidian hydrates at the "short" rate, while most of the earlier obsidian, which is chemically different, hydrates at the "long" rate. A recent application of the rate of 697 years/micron to obsidian from Preclassic sites in the Valley of Mexico produced acceptable ages.

Table 3 shows that the Atopula specimens fall into three groups: the largest consists of specimens for which the rate of 260 years/micron yields dates in the expected chronological range; this group includes all of the El Clarín (Postclassic) specimens. A second smaller group includes those specimens for which the "long" rate of 697 years/micron produces appropriate ages. In this group the dates seem slightly too old, which might suggest that the rate should be slightly shorter for Guerrero. The third group consists of residual specimens for which neither of the two western Mexican rates produces acceptable ages. These presumably represent at least one other hydration rate; in fact, a rate of 425 years/micron produces very acceptable readings for the hydration bands of this group and also for residual specimens from the site of Tetipan (App. 7; Table 4).

There is a very close correspondence between the rate that produces an appropriate age and the color of the obsidian specimens. Green and translucent obsidian correlates with the "short" west Mexican rate, gray-to-black obsidian with the "long" rate, and mottled-gray and gray-banded obsidian with the postulated third rate of 425 years/micron. These color differences probably reflect differences in chemical composition that produce the different hydration rates.

Despite the fact that Atopula is outside the area for which the rates were originally determined and has a slightly different climate, there is a very close fit of the hydration readings with the ages expected on the basis of ceramic comparisons. The specimens within each phase are also remarkably consistent, if the number of error-producing factors that can affect obsidian hydration dating are considered. The only real inconsistencies are a specimen of El Clarín age found

TABLE 4. TETIPAN OBSIDIAN HYDRATION READINGS

Color	Hydration Band Thickness (microns)	Hydration Rate (years/micron)	Age (years)	Median Calendar Date
Mottled gray	5.0	425	2125 ± 150	180 B.C.
Gray banded	5.3	425	2253 ± 159	300 B.C.
Mottled gray	5.4	425	2295 ± 162	350 B.C.
Gray banded	5.5	425	2338 ± 165	390 B.C.
Gray banded	5.7	425	2423 ± 171	470 B.C.
Gray banded	5.8	425	2465 ± 174	520 B.C.
Translucent gray	11.1	260	2886 ± 167	940 B.C.
Gray-black opaque	4.4	697	3067 ± 198	1120 B.C.

in an Atopula-phase level (which probably fell in from an exposed face during excavation) and a few Atopula- and Tecolotla-phase specimens with very old readings (suggesting carry-up from Cacahuananche-phase levels).

It is unfortunate that no radiocarbon determinations are available to serve as a check on the hydration readings, since the specimens from Atopula include some of the thickest hydration bands known from western Mexico. Hydration bands on western Mexican archaeological obsidians rarely exceed 8.5 to 9.0 microns (C. W. Meighan, personal communication), whereas Atopula has produced specimens with bands as thick as 12.9 microns.

Appendix 5. The El Clarín Phase

The El Clarín-phase occupation of Atopula is represented by the uppermost 35–40 cm. of sandy gray-to-brown deposit (Figs. 3–4). The transition to the underlying orange-brown sandy clay representing the Tecolotla phase is relatively sharp in comparison to the transitions between the deposits of the Preclassic phases. This may be the result of the long period of abandonment between the Tecolotla and El Clarín phases, in contrast to the continuous occupation from Cacahuananche through Tecolotla.

The deposits of the El Clarín phase are highly disturbed, and Tecolotla-phase material is mixed with the later artifacts. The pottery (Table 5) in these deposits is generally very poorly preserved, badly eroded and broken into tiny sherds. The types are defined on the basis of characteristics of paste, firing, and surface treatment. The poor condition of the El Clarín pottery and the small sample size have added to the usual problems of defining types. No attempt has been made to go beyond broad descriptive categories. The types defined below will be subject to considerable revision and redefinition with future research into the late prehistoric occupations of this area. The chronological alignment of the El Clarín phase cannot be specified with precision. Such features as serpent-head vessel supports and the high frequency of loop and strap handles in the ceramics, and the hydration reading on El Clarín-phase obsidian (Table 3, Fig. 9), combine to indicate a Postclassic placement.

Ceramics

Huisache Red (Fig. 67)

Paste. Very porous; hardness near 2.5. Temper very coarse and is the usual quartziferous sand. Near surfaces, paste typically oxidized light red to reddish brown (2.5 YR 6/4-8, 5/4); cores often dark gray to reddish gray (5 YR 4/1, 5/1-2).

TABLE 5. POSTCLASSIC (EL CLARÍN PHASE) POTTERY

Type	Sherd Count
Huisache Red	140
Ratón Black-Brown	297
Pulga Orange	180
Venado Orange-Brown	32
Carrancho Coarse	2497
Fine Buff	3
Red-on-White	1
Xilocintla Glaze	16
Total	3166

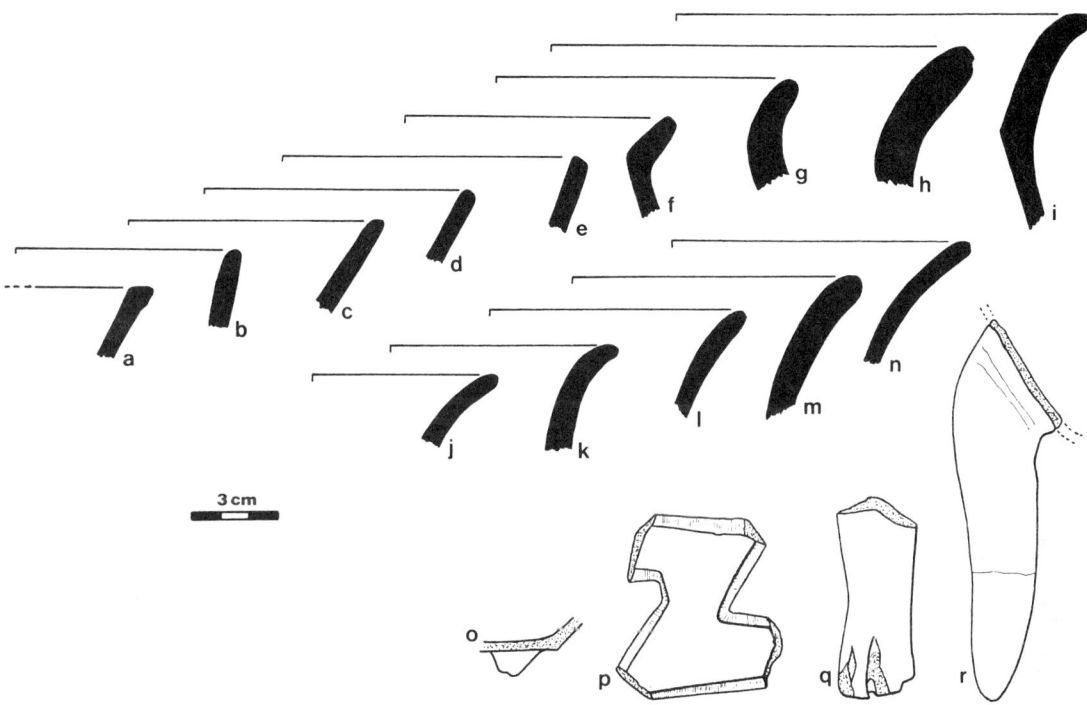

FIG. 67. Huisache Red pottery, El Clarín phase: *a–e*, open bowls; *f–i*, ollas; *j–n*, flaring bowls; *o, r*, conical feet; *p*, z-shaped object; *q*, snake foot.

Surface. Exterior or both surfaces smoothed and slipped. Slip typically oxidized red to dark red (10 R 4/6; 5 YR 5/6, 3/6), not polished. Unslipped surfaces coarse and grainy from protruding temper particles.

Form. Wall thickness 6–16 mm.; typically 8–9 mm.

OLLA. Diameter 18–28 cm. Interior profile occasionally breaks in curvature where neck flares strongly outward; surface unslipped and unsmoothed below this point. Form of base unknown. Lip form: rounded, blunted, beveled, or tapered.

OPEN BOWL. Diameter 14–20 cm. Wall straight and outslanting to very slightly flaring. Base form unknown, probably flat. Lip form: rounded, blunted, beveled, tapered, or slightly thickened exterior.

FLARING BOWL. Diameter 12–20 cm. Wall uniformly concave. Base form unknown, probably flat. Lip form: rounded, blunted, or beveled.

Auxiliary features. 1. Strap handle: scar of attachment of broad flattened lug or handle, roughly plano-convex in cross-section on exterior of one sherd. 2. Conical foot: solid vessel support, circular in cross-section; relatively short and thick or long and tapering with a sharp bend near point of attachment to vessel body. 3. Snake foot: tall solid vessel support terminating in a modeled serpent head. 4. Z-shaped object: this sherd may be from a vessel with cutout decoration.

Decoration

GROOVING. 1. Shallow groove encircling exterior lip of olla. Groove relatively smooth and regular and done while paste was plastic.

Ratón Black-Brown (Figs. 68–69)

Paste. Relatively porous; hardness near 2.5. Temper coarse with occasional very coarse inclusions; is the usual quartziferous sand. Paste typically partially oxidized, with dark gray to dark reddish gray (5 YR 4/1-2) interior and dark brown to dark reddish brown (7.5 YR 4/2; 5 YR 5/3-4) surface.

Surface. One or both surfaces highly compacted and quite smooth, occasionally with slight luster; unslipped. Uncompacted surfaces show marks of perfunctory smoothing with a hard tool while paste was somewhat plastic (dragged temper particles); uncompacted surfaces typically coarse and grainy from protruding temper particles. Surface fired to same color range as paste.

Form. Wall thickness 5–12 mm.; typically 7–9 mm.

OLLA. Diameter 18–34 cm. Interior profile may break in curvature where neck curves strongly outward. Form of base unknown. Lip form: rounded, slightly blunted, tapered, or thickened exterior.

OPEN BOWL. Diameter 14–26 cm. Wall straight and outslanting to very slightly convex. Base form unknown. Lip form: rounded, beveled, tapered, or thickened exterior.

FLARING BOWL. Diameter 14–22 cm. Wall uniformly concave. Form of base unknown. Lip form: rounded, beveled, or thickened exterior.

CONVEX BOWL. Diameter 10–18 cm. Wall uniformly convex. Base presumably rounded. Lip form: rounded, blunted, beveled, or thickened interior.

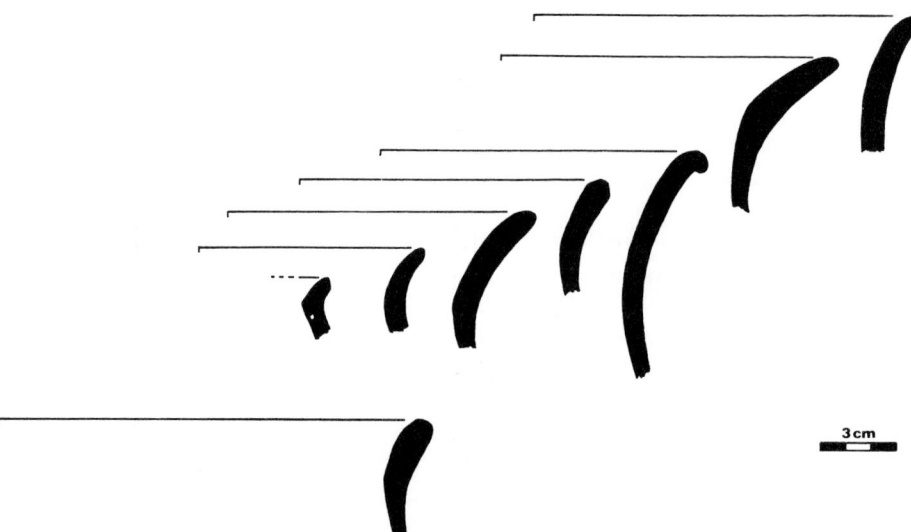

FIG. 68. Ratón Black-Brown ollas, El Clarín phase.

THE EL CLARÍN PHASE

FIG. 69. Ratón Black-Brown pottery, El Clarín phase: *a–f*, convex bowls; *g–j*, open bowls; *k–n*, flaring bowls.

Decoration

INCISION. 1. Single line encircling bowl exterior. Incision very narrow and shallow; slightly irregular and done after paste was partially dry.

Pulga Orange (Figs. 70, 71)

Paste. Relatively porous; hardness ca. 2.0–2.5. Temper coarse with very coarse inclusions; is the usual quartziferous sand. Paste typically reddish yellow (5 YR 6/6, 7/6-8); cores often less completely oxidized, light reddish brown or reddish gray (5 YR 6/3-4, 5/2), as are occasional areas near surface.

Surface. One or both surfaces smoothed and compacted, occasionally with striations from smoothing with a yielding object while paste was plastic; unslipped. Occasional marks of dragged temper grains from smoothing leather-hard paste with a hard tool. Unsmoothed surfaces have grainy texture from protruding temper particles. Surfaces fired to same color range as paste.

Form. Wall thickness 4–10 mm.; typically 7–8 mm.

OLLA. Diameter 20–28 cm. Form of base unknown. Lip form: rounded, beveled, or thickened exterior.

FLARING BOWL. Diameter ca. 13–22 cm. Wall uniformly concave. Form of base unknown. Lip form: rounded or tapered.

CONVEX BOWL. Diameter 12–18 cm. Wall uniformly convex. Base presumably rounded. Lip form: rounded, blunted, beveled, or tapered.

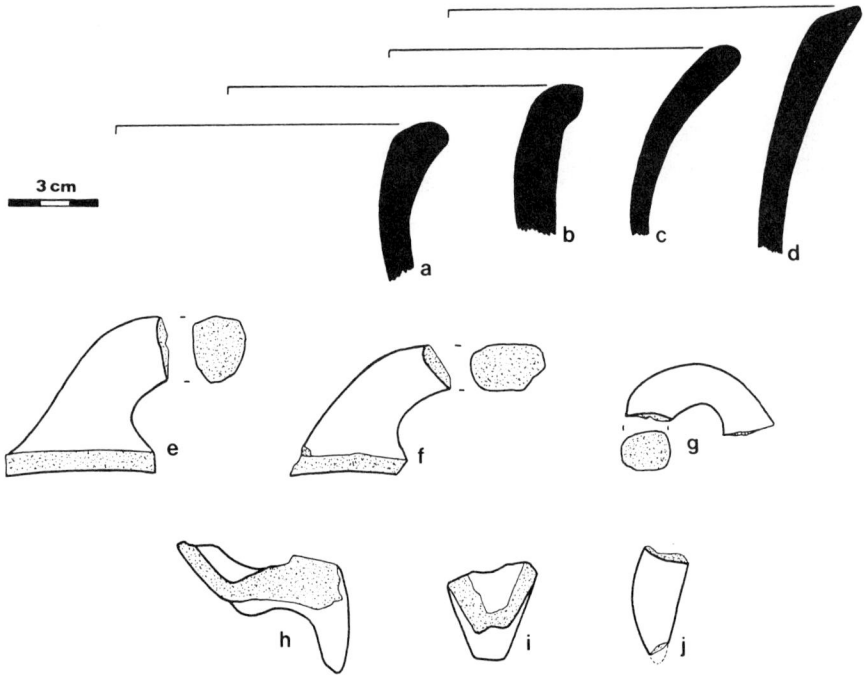

FIG. 70. Pulga Orange pottery, El Clarín phase: *a–d*, ollas; *e–g*, loop handles; *h–j*, nubbin feet.

THE EL CLARÍN PHASE 215

FIG. 69. Ratón Black-Brown pottery, El Clarín phase: *a–f*, convex bowls; *g–j*, open bowls; *k–n*, flaring bowls.

Decoration

INCISION. 1. Single line encircling bowl exterior. Incision very narrow and shallow; slightly irregular and done after paste was partially dry.

Pulga Orange (Figs. 70, 71)

Paste. Relatively porous; hardness ca. 2.0–2.5. Temper coarse with very coarse inclusions; is the usual quartziferous sand. Paste typically reddish yellow (5 YR 6/6, 7/6-8); cores often less completely oxidized, light reddish brown or reddish gray (5 YR 6/3-4, 5/2), as are occasional areas near surface.

Surface. One or both surfaces smoothed and compacted, occasionally with striations from smoothing with a yielding object while paste was plastic; unslipped. Occasional marks of dragged temper grains from smoothing leather-hard paste with a hard tool. Unsmoothed surfaces have grainy texture from protruding temper particles. Surfaces fired to same color range as paste.

Form. Wall thickness 4–10 mm.; typically 7–8 mm.

OLLA. Diameter 20–28 cm. Form of base unknown. Lip form: rounded, beveled, or thickened exterior.

FLARING BOWL. Diameter ca. 13–22 cm. Wall uniformly concave. Form of base unknown. Lip form: rounded or tapered.

CONVEX BOWL. Diameter 12–18 cm. Wall uniformly convex. Base presumably rounded. Lip form: rounded, blunted, beveled, or tapered.

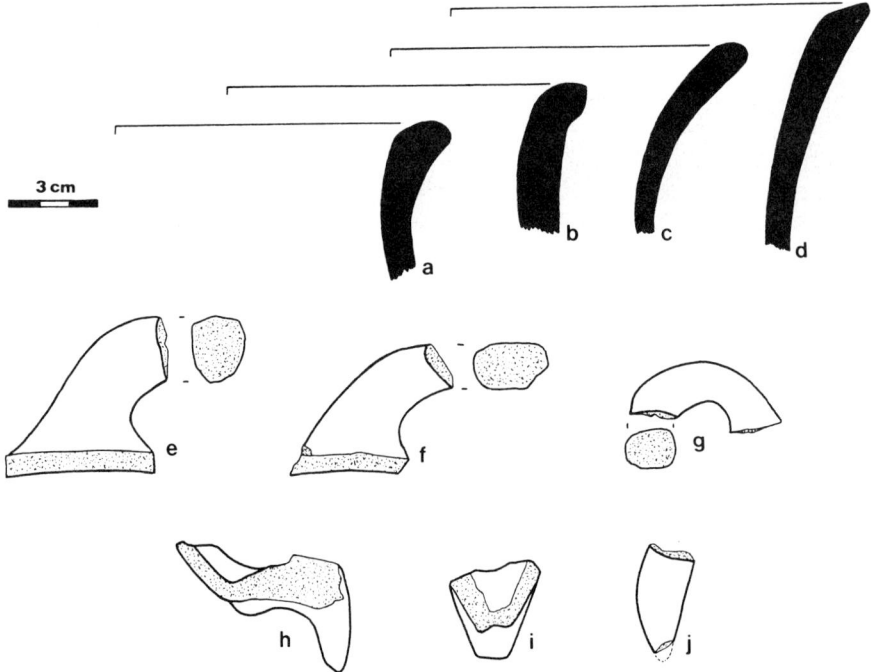

FIG. 70. Pulga Orange pottery, El Clarín phase: *a–d*, ollas; *e–g*, loop handles; *h–j*, nubbin feet.

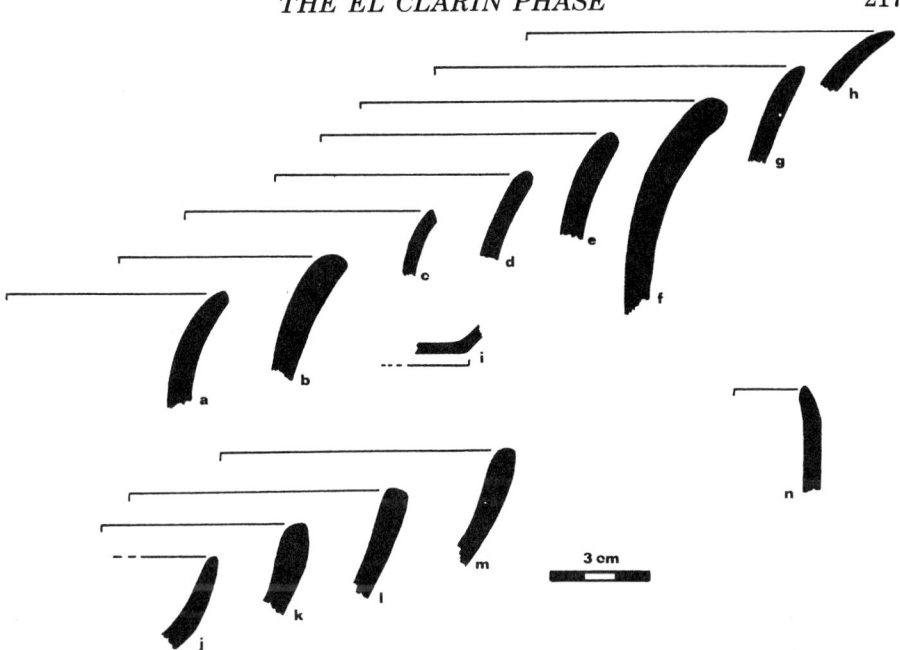

Fig. 71. Pulga Orange pottery, El Clarín phase: *a–i*, flaring bowls; *j–m*, convex bowls; *n*, bottle.

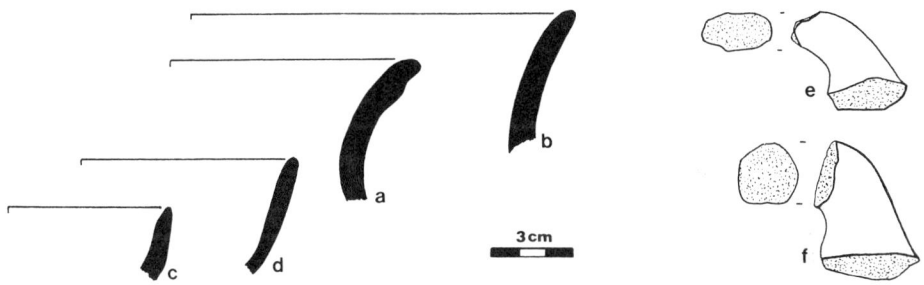

Fig. 72. Venado Orange-Brown pottery, El Clarín phase: *a, b*, ollas; *c, d*, convex bowls; *e, f*, loop handles.

BOTTLE. Fragments of a vertical tubular bottle neck. Diameter 4 cm. Form of vessel body unknown. Lip form: tapered.

Auxiliary features. 1. Loop handle: semicircular, elliptical to plano-convex in cross-section, 1.5–2.5 cm. diameter, projecting from vessel (presumably olla) exterior. 2. Nubbin foot: solid vessel support, roughly parabolic in cross-section.

Decoration. None represented in sample.

Venado Orange-Brown (Fig. 72)

Paste. Relatively porous; hardness ca. 2.5–3.0. Temper coarse and is the usual quartziferous sand. Paste typically reddish brown to light reddish brown to pink

(5 YR 5/3-4, 6/4, 7/3-4). Cores often less completely oxidized to pinkish gray or gray (5 YR 5/1, 6/1-2).

Surface. Exterior or both surfaces smoothed and slip typically oxidized to reddish brown, yellowish red, or reddish yellow (5 YR 5/4-8, 6/6). Slip slightly burnished, with a slight luster in some cases. Unslipped surfaces coarse and grainy from protruding temper particles.

Form. Wall thickness 5-10 mm.; typically 7 mm.

OLLA. Diameter 18-28 cm. Interior profile may have sharp break in curvature where neck flares strongly outward. Form of base unknown. Lip form: rounded or thickened exterior.

CONVEX BOWL. Diameter 12-16 cm. Wall uniformly convex. Base presumably rounded. Lip form: rounded or tapered.

Auxiliary features. 1. Loop handle: semicircular, elliptical to plano-convex in cross-section, 1.5-2.5 cm. diameter, projecting from vessel (presumably olla) exterior.

Decoration. None represented in sample.

Carrancho Coarse (Figs. 73, 74)

Paste. Very porous; hardness 2.0-3.0. Temper coarse to very coarse with occasional granule-sized inclusions and is the usual quartziferous sand. Completeness of oxidation quite variable, and paste ranges from gray and dark gray (5 YR 4/1, 3/1) through reddish brown and light reddish brown (5 YR 5/3-4, 6/3-4) to pink and pinkish gray (5 YR 7/2-3). Cores typically dark gray to dusky red (5 YR 4/1; 2.5 YR 3/2).

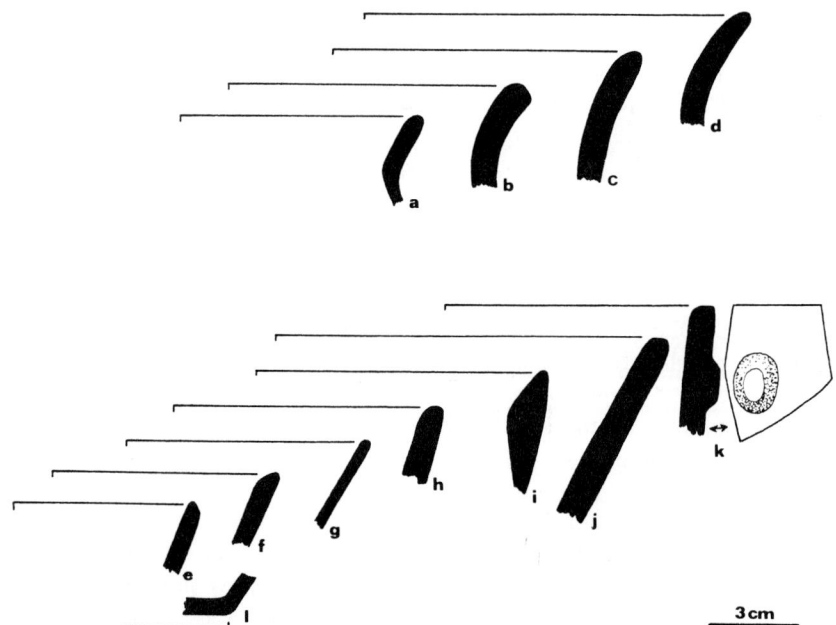

FIG. 73. Carrancho Coarse pottery, El Clarín phase: *a-d*, ollas; *e-l*, open bowls.

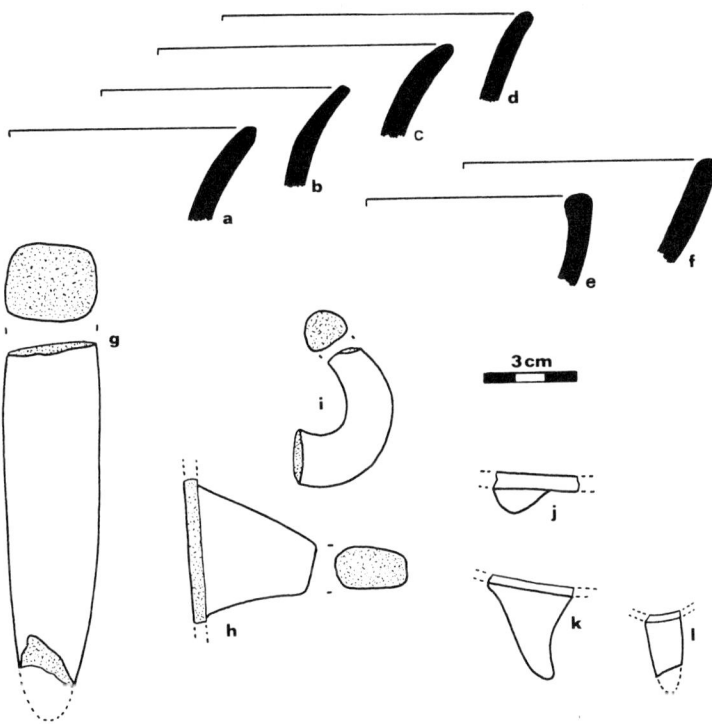

Fig. 74. Carrancho Coarse pottery, El Clarín phase: *a–d*, flaring bowls; *e, f*, convex bowls; *g*, cylindrical foot; *h, i*, loop handles; *j–l*, nubbin feet.

Surface. Fired to same color range as paste; typically coarse, not smoothed or compacted, and unslipped; often pitted and grainy from protruding temper particles. Some vessels indicate minimal attempts at smoothing—marks of scraping with a hard tool while paste was plastic, e.g. grooves made by dragged temper particles.

Form. Wall thickness quite variable, at least 5–13 mm.; typically ca. 7–9 mm.

OLLA. Diameter 16–25 cm. Form of base unknown. Lip form: rounded or blunted.

OPEN BOWL. Diameter 12–25 cm. Wall straight and outslanting. Base flat. Lip form: rounded, blunted, tapered, or thickened interior.

FLARING BOWL. Diameter 16–20 cm. Wall uniformly concave. Base presumably flat. Lip form: rounded or blunted.

CONVEX BOWL. Diameter 14–16 cm. Wall uniformly convex. Base rounded. Lip form: rounded or blunted.

Auxiliary features. 1. Loop handle: semicircular, elliptical to plano-convex in cross-section, 1.0–2.5 cm. diameter, projecting from vessel (presumably olla) exterior. 2. Nubbin foot: short solid vessel support, roughly parabolic in cross-section, ca. 1 cm. diameter. 3. Cylindrical foot: long solid vessel support, roughly circular in cross-section, ca. 3 cm. diameter.

Decoration

APPLIQUÉ. 1. Raised, roughly circular appliqué, ca. 1.5 cm. diameter, on upper exterior of open bowl.

Remarks. Carrancho Coarse is a residual category and includes not only sherds representing vessels originally left unslipped and unsmoothed, but also sherds of other types in which slip or other distinctive surface treatment is no longer discernible. Paste and surface colors consequently cover a wide range.

Fine Buff (Fig. 75a–c)

Paste. Relatively porous; hardness near 2.5. Temper coarse and is the usual quartziferous sand. Near surface, paste typically light reddish brown to pink (5 YR 6/3, 7/3-4); interior remains unoxidized, gray to pinkish gray (5 YR 5/1, 6/1, 7/2).

Surface. Typically oxidized to pink (5 YR 7/3-4). Both surfaces carefully smoothed and compacted but without luster; unslipped. Striations from smoothing while plastic fairly common.

Form. Wall thickness unknown; forms in sample limited to vessel supports.

Auxiliary features. 1. Hollow foot: cylindrical to parabolic vessel support, ca. 2.5 cm. diameter, with rounded base and large opening into hollow interior. 2. Conical foot: solid asymmetrical slender vessel support. One specimen could be a stylized figurine leg.

Decoration. None represented in sample.

Red-on-White (Fig. 75d)

Paste. Relatively porous; hardness near 2.5. Temper coarse and is the usual quartziferous sand. Paste oxidized to pink (5 YR 7/3-4) throughout.

Surface. Exterior smoothed and coated with pinkish white (5 YR 8/2; 7.5 YR 8/2) slip. Slip unpolished and has powdery texture. Unslipped surface coarse and grainy from protruding temper particles.

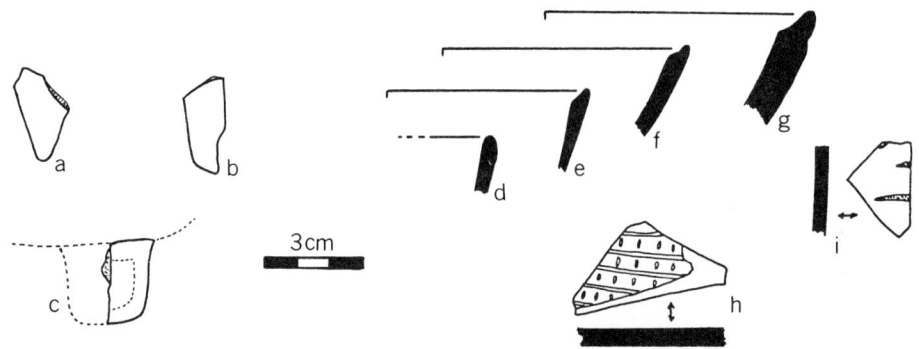

FIG. 75. Minor pottery types, El Clarín phase: *a–c*, Fine Buff solid conical and hollow cylindrical feet; *d*, Red-on-White open bowl; *e–i*, Xilocintla Glaze convex bowls, molcajete base, and painted sherd.

Form. Wall thickness 5–6 mm.

> OPEN BOWL. Diameter ca. 12–14 cm. Wall straight and outslanting. Form of base unknown. Lip form: rounded.

Decoration. Line painted in dark red (2.5 YR 3/6) over white slip.

Xilocintla Glaze (Fig. 75e–i)

Paste. Relatively porous; hardness ca. 2.5–3.0. Temper medium with occasional coarse inclusions; not the usual quartziferous sand. Paste typically oxidized light reddish brown to reddish yellow (2.5 YR 6/4; 5 YR 6/6) near surface, with reddish gray to dark reddish gray (5 YR 5/2, 4/2) core.

Surface. Typically fired light reddish brown to reddish yellow (2.5 YR 6/4; 5 YR 6/6). Both surfaces smoothed; one or both have light olive brown to light yellowish brown to olive yellow (2.5 Y 5/4-6, 6/4-8) glaze. Unslipped surface coarse and grainy from protruding temper particles.

Form. Wall thickness 5–10 mm.; typically 8–9 mm.

> CONVEX BOWL. Diameter 12–16 cm. Wall uniformly convex. Base presumably rounded. Lip form: beveled or tapered.
>
> MOLCAJETE. Bowl with deep linear incisions alternating with rows of deep punctations on interior of flattened base. Incisions and punctations are pre-slip. Base heavily worn from use as grater.

Decoration. Dark brown (7.5 YR 3/2, 4/2-4) linear geometric painted designs appear rarely on exterior surface under the glaze.

Remarks. Xilocintla Glaze is a postconquest type that occurs in very small quantities on the surface and in the uppermost, mixed level of the El Clarín phase deposit.

Stamps (Fig. 76)

Four fragments of flat ceramic stamps: two small thick fragments have paste identical with Pulga Orange and bear linear geometric designs. Two have paste identical with Ratón Black-Brown; both are thin and may be fragments of the same stamp. One bears only parallel lines; the design on the other apparently represents a bird.

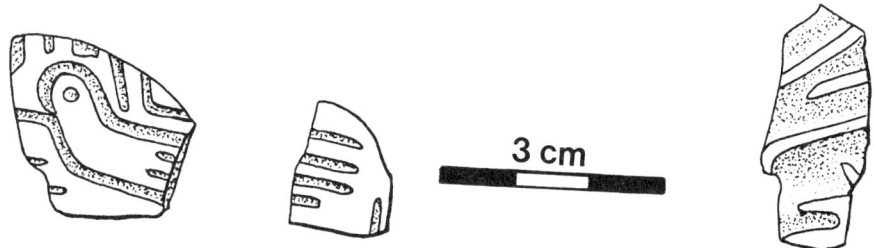

FIG. 76. Ceramic stamps, El Clarín phase.

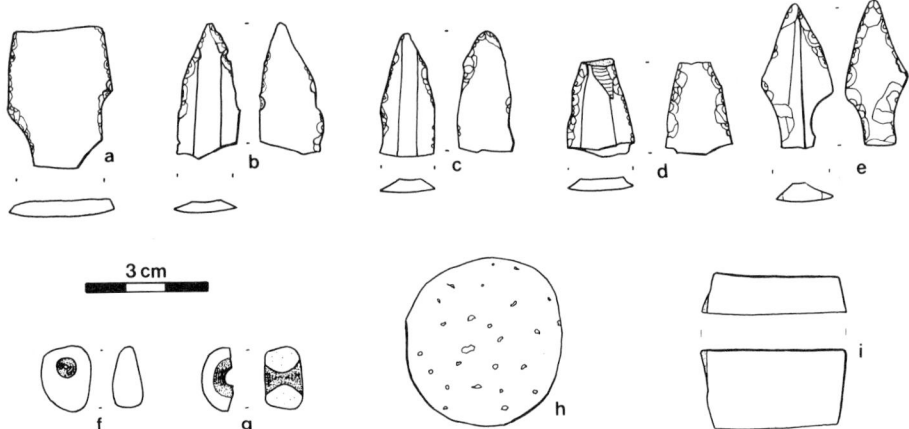

Fig. 77. Stone artifacts, El Clarín phase: *a*, quartz point or knife fragment; *b–e*, obsidian points; *f, g*, green stone beads; *h*, stone sphere; *i*, limestone "polisher."

Stone

Projectile Points (Fig. 77a–e)

One basal point (or knife) fragment of white cryptocrystalline quartz has a wide straight stem and rounded base. Three tip fragments of translucent green and opaque black obsidian are made on prismatic blades. One complete specimen of opaque black obsidian is also made on a prismatic blade; it has a long stem with concave sides and a flat base.

Flakes and Blades

Flakes and prismatic blade fragments are primarily of translucent green and opaque black obsidian; a few are made of cryptocrystalline quartz (mainly a white to pink variety). Several specimens show slight usage flaking, but majority are unretouched and suggest no utilization.

Beads (Fig. 77f, g)

Two bead fragments of green stone with white streaks (jadeite?): one is discoidal with a crude biconical central perforation; the other is amorphous with a carefully drilled off-center biconical perforation.

Ball (Fig. 77h)

A roughly spherical object of gray-white conglomerate; diameter 3.0–3.5 cm.

"Polisher" (Fig. 77i)

Tabular fragment of limestone. Preserved length, 32 mm., width, 18 mm., thickness, 10 mm. This object carefully shaped and smoothed; may have functioned as a polisher.

Appendix 6. Cerro Ototal

Two caves with traces of pre-Hispanic utilization were located at the summit of Cerro Ototal, a high hill some 5 km. east of Huitzuco.

The largest and deepest (H-16) involves a difficult descent of ca. 30 m. to a series of narrow but fairly extensive passageways largely blocked by rock falls. We recovered fragmentary human skeletal remains representing at least three individuals, along with ceramics and green stone beads presumably placed in the cave as burial offerings. The skeletons were completely disarticulated—repeatedly disturbed by modern intruders who also removed most of the intact mortuary offerings. Several stone beads were found with one cluster of bones (Fig. 78). The ceramics (Fig. 79)—particularly the incised white-slipped pottery, identical with Mariposa White of the Tecolotla phase at Atopula and the White ware of Tetipan (App. 7; Figs. 53, 81)—indicate that the cave was utilized primarily during the initial Middle Preclassic period, or perhaps during the Terminal Early Preclassic. Several modern sherds represent minor recent activities.

The second cave (H-17), about 0.5 km. away, is much smaller and shallower, with a drop of about 4 m. to a small open area. Prehistoric remains here consist exclusively of pottery; there are no traces of burials. The ceramics (Fig. 80) represent Atopula pottery types: Pozo Thin Red, Jiménez Red, and Pedrusco Polished Gray. Again, the cave was utilized primarily during the Preclassic period, probably during the Atopula or Tecolotla phase.

Neither cave could have been used as a habitation area, and neither has paintings or other indications of a ceremonial or shrine function. The use of the larger cave for burial may have been a secondary function since the smaller cave definitely was not so used. The Huitzuco area is rich in mineral resources,

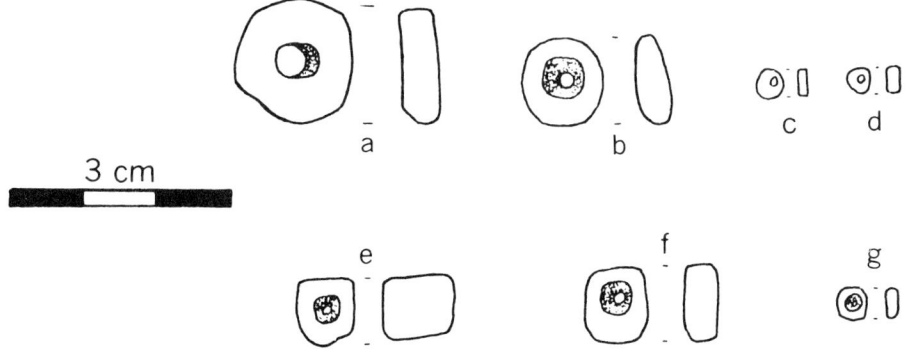

FIG. 78. Stone beads, Cerro Ototal (H-16): *a–d*, white limestone; *e*, fine-grained green stone; *f, g*, green serpentine.

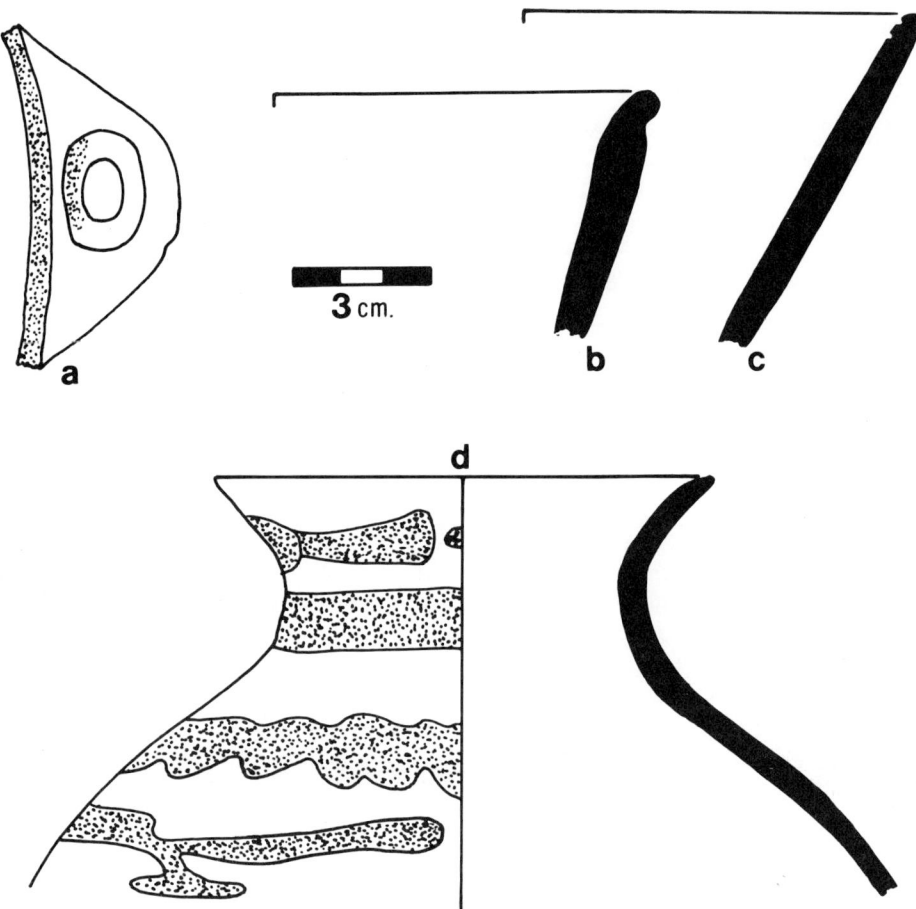

Fig. 79. Pottery, Cerro Ototal (H-16): *a*, black loop handle; *b, c*, Mariposa White open bowls; *d*, Red-painted Buff olla.

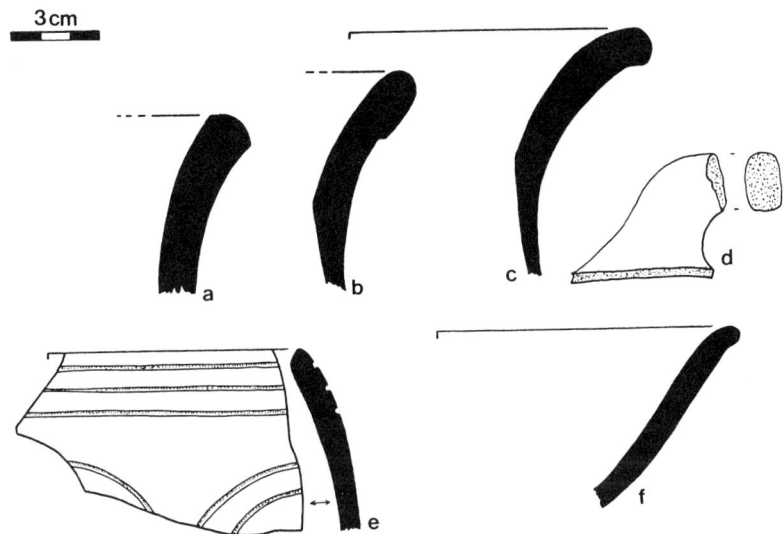

FIG. 80. Pottery, Cerro Ototal (H-17): *a–c*, Jiménez Red ollas; *d*, Jiménez Red loop handle; *e*, Pozo Thin Red tecomate; *f*, Pedrusco Polished Gray convex bowl.

particularly mercury ores. It is a strong possibility that these caves were prehistoric mines; if so, cinnabar was probably the principal mineral sought. Local residents, formerly employed in the mercury-extraction operation at Huitzuco, are firmly convinced that these caves were indeed prehistoric mines. Their prospecting in the caves is responsible for the extreme disturbance of the pre-Hispanic material.

Appendix 7. Tetipan

Tetipan is some 15 km. southwest of Atopula, on the outskirts of the village of Ahuelicán. Like Atopula, it is on a small tributary of the Río Tepecoacuilco (Fig. 1). For some years collectors have obtained Olmec-style pieces of very fine blue-gray jade from local *huaqueros* who systematically loot the large cemetery. There is presumably also a residential zone at Tetipan, but information from the *huaqueros* indicates that pottery which litters the surface represents discarded material from the graves.

By far the most common pottery type in the surface collection is a thin incised white ware homologous to Canoas White of Tehuacán and to the related types typical of Early Middle Preclassic assemblages throughout central Mexico. The abundance of Olmec-style jade mortuary offerings also suggests an Early Middle Preclassic placement for the principal occupation of Tetipan. This is consistent with the obsidian hydration readings (Table 4, Fig. 9).

Red-painted Buff pottery, which is also present in substantial quantities, is identical with the principal type in the Xocohuite surface collection (App. 8); it may indicate that the occupation continues into the Late Middle Preclassic or Late Preclassic period.

Ceramics

White (Fig. 81)

Paste. Relatively porous; hardness near 3.0. Temper coarse with occasional very coarse inclusions; predominantly composed of quartz crystals and occasional gold plates of mica. Paste typically partially oxidized throughout, pink or pinkish gray to light reddish brown or reddish yellow (5 YR 6/2-6, 7/2-4, 8/3).

Surface. Both surfaces well smoothed and compacted, and have a white slip typically polished with moderate to high luster. Rarely, one surface is smoothed and compacted but left unslipped. Slip typically fired to white or very pale brown (10 YR 8/2-3) but is also frequently pinkish gray to pinkish white, pale yellow, or even light yellowish brown (7.5 YR 7/2, 8/2; 2.5 Y 8/4, 6/4).

Form. Wall thickness 4–8 mm.; typically 5–6 mm.

OLLA. Diameter 15–16 cm. Interior profile may have sharp break in curvature where neck flares strongly outward; surface unslipped and unsmoothed below this point. Base form unknown. Lip form: beveled.

OPEN BOWL. Diameter 12–20 cm. Wall straight and outslanting to very slightly convex. Base flat. Lip form: rounded, tapered, or bolstered.

FLARING BOWL. Diameter 12–27 cm. Wall uniformly concave. Base presumably flat. Lip form: rounded, tapered, or thickened interior.

CONVEX BOWL. Diameter 14–16 cm. Wall uniformly convex. Base rounded. Lip form: rounded or tapered.

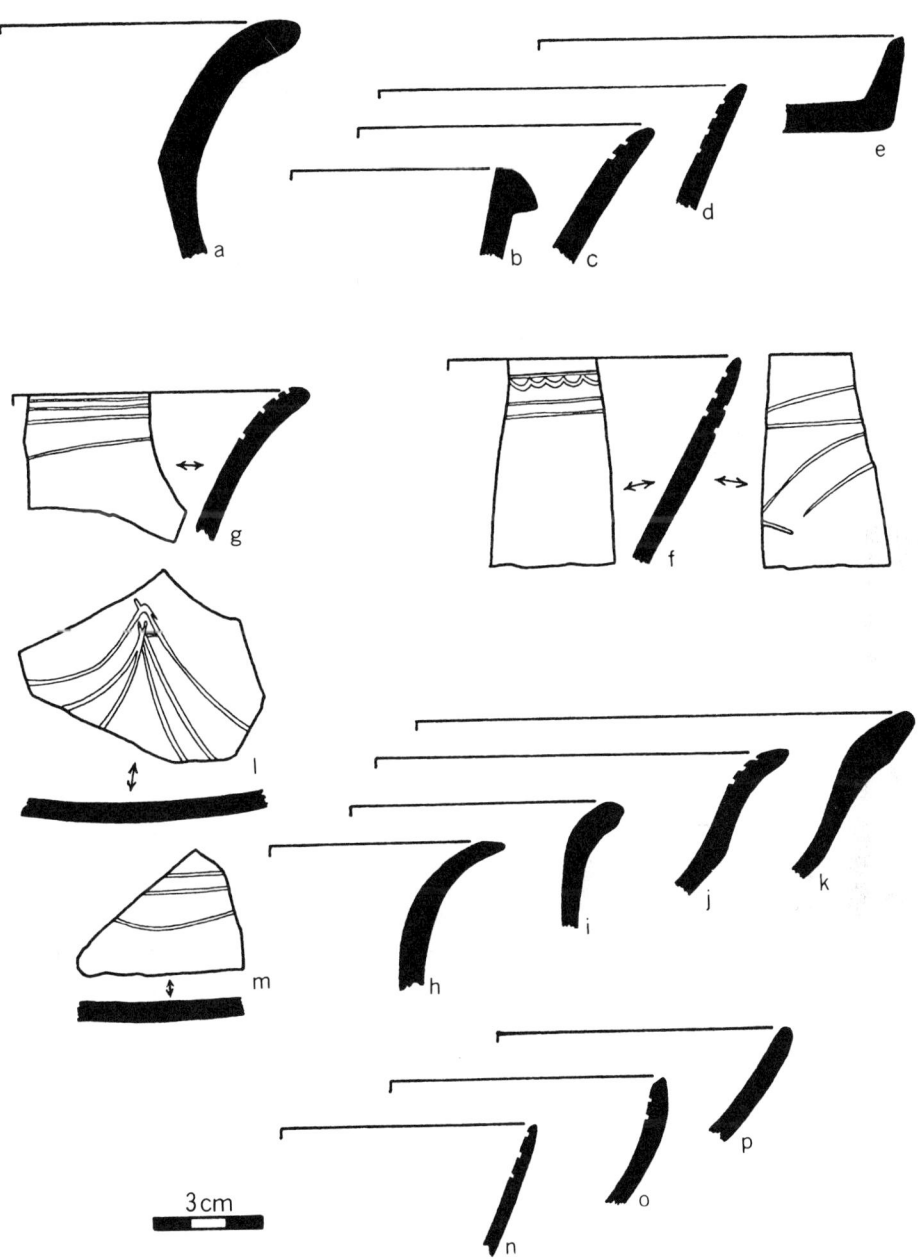

FIG. 81. White pottery, Tetipan: *a*, olla; *b–f*, open bowls; *g–k*, flaring bowls; *l, m*, pseudo-grater fondos; *n–p*, convex bowls.

Decoration

INCISION. All incision is postslip, cutting through slip to expose paste; 1.0–1.5 mm. wide, slightly irregular, with rough edges, and done after paste was partially dry. 1. Two to four incised lines encircling upper interior of open, flaring, or convex bowls just below and parallel to lip. 2. Three incised lines encircling upper interior of open bowl. A series of small arcs is pendant from uppermost line; exterior has two parallel encircling incised lines, and oblique arcs below. 3. Pseudo-grater fondo. Designs are groups of concentric arcs, the "sunburst" motif, occurring on interiors of flattened bases of open or flaring bowls. Interior surfaces not worn from use as grater bowls.

Remarks. This type is identical with the incised white wares typical of Terminal Early Preclassic and particularly Early Middle Preclassic assemblages throughout central Mexico, e.g. Canoas White of the Early Santa María phase in Tehuacán.

Red-painted Buff (Figs. 82, 83)

Paste. Relatively porous; hardness near 2.5. Temper medium to coarse; includes occasional quartz crystals. Paste typically partially oxidized, light reddish brown to pink (5 YR 6/3-4, 7/3-4; 7.5 YR 7/4) throughout.

Surface. Both surfaces typically quite carefully smoothed and compacted but without luster. Marks of smoothing with a yielding object while paste was plastic are relatively common. Occasionally, unslipped surfaces are unsmoothed, pitted and irregular. Surface fired to the same color range as paste. Red paint typically applied to unslipped surface as decoration, but sometimes covers large areas like a partial slip or wash.

Form. Wall thickness 4–10 mm.; typically 5–7 mm.

OLLA. Single fragment of olla neck. Diameter unknown. Form of base and lip unknown.

CONVEX BOWL. Diameter 15–20 cm. Typically deep, with uniformly convex wall. Base presumably rounded. Lip form: rounded or beveled.

COMPOSITE-SILHOUETTE BOWL. Diameter 16–18 cm. Upper wall straight to slightly convex; lower wall, below sharp break in curvature, slightly convex to slightly concave. Base rounded. Lip form: rounded.

Decoration

APPLIQUÉ. 1. Raised ridge or arc on exterior of one vessel just below rim, combined with red painted decoration.

PAINTING. Weak red to red (10 R 4/4-6, 5/4-6) paint, typically applied in wide bands or zones. Thickness and covering ability of paint quite variable, so that single bands or zones may vary in color. Some designs have a "negative" quality, unslipped areas surrounded by red background color, but visible brush marks indicate that red areas were painted in, not produced by resist technique. Design elements include (1) bands along rims on interior or exterior; (2) tapering bands or stripes; (3) irregular polygons outlined by red background.

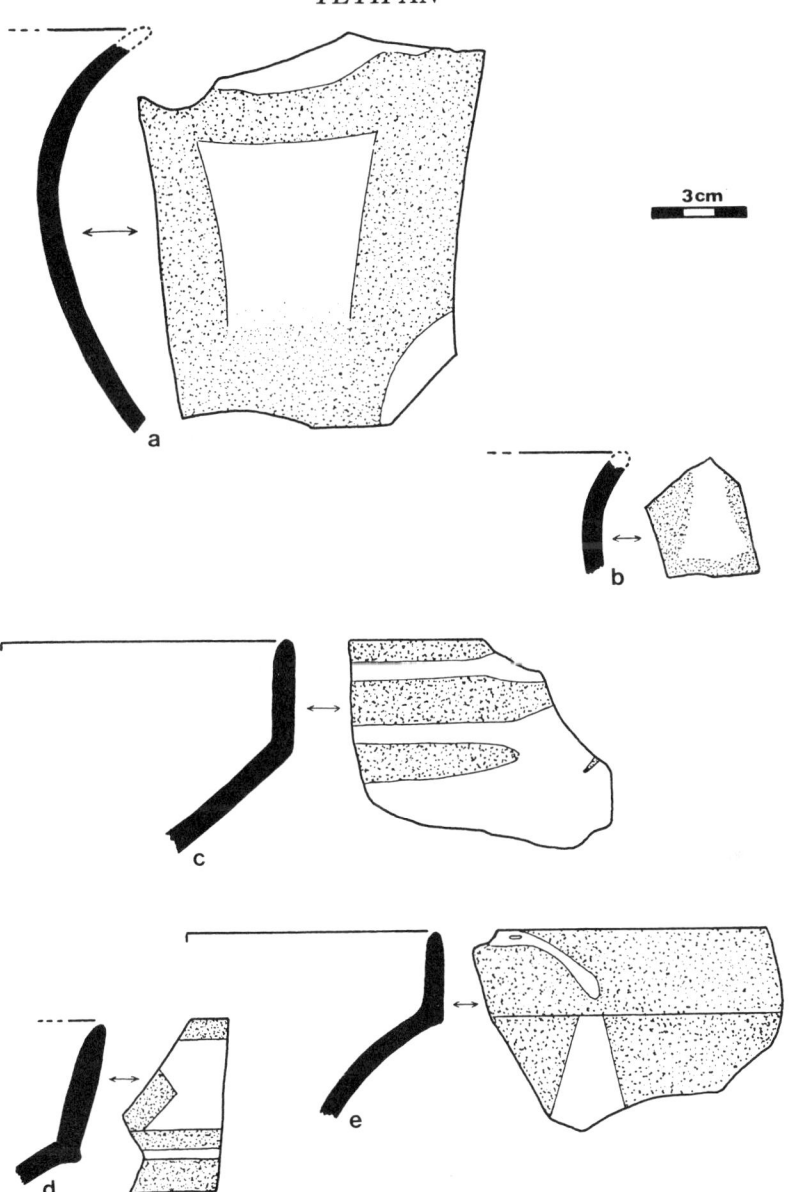

FIG. 82. Red-painted Buff pottery, Tetipan: *a*, olla; *b–e*, composite-silhouette bowls.

Remarks. An identical Red-painted Buff ware is the primary type in the surface collection from Xocohuite (App. 8; Figs. 89, 90). Forms and decoration resemble those of red-on-buff pottery of the Cerro Chacaltepec II phase of Morelos, dated to ca. 400–100 B.C. (Grove 1968b: 57–9, figs. 49, 50; 1970a: 8–9). This may indicate a Late Middle Preclassic or Late Preclassic occupation.

YUPA 77—APPENDIX 7
Excised Brown-Black (Fig. 84)

Paste. Relatively porous; hardness near 3.0. Temper coarse, includes occasional gold flakes of mica. Paste typically reddish gray to dark reddish gray (10 R 5/1, 4/1) throughout, occasionally oxidized to reddish brown (5 YR 5/3) near surface.

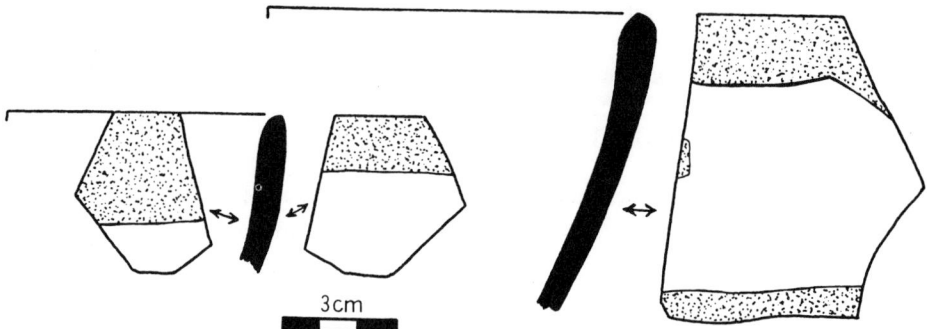

FIG. 83. Red-painted Buff convex bowls, Tetipan.

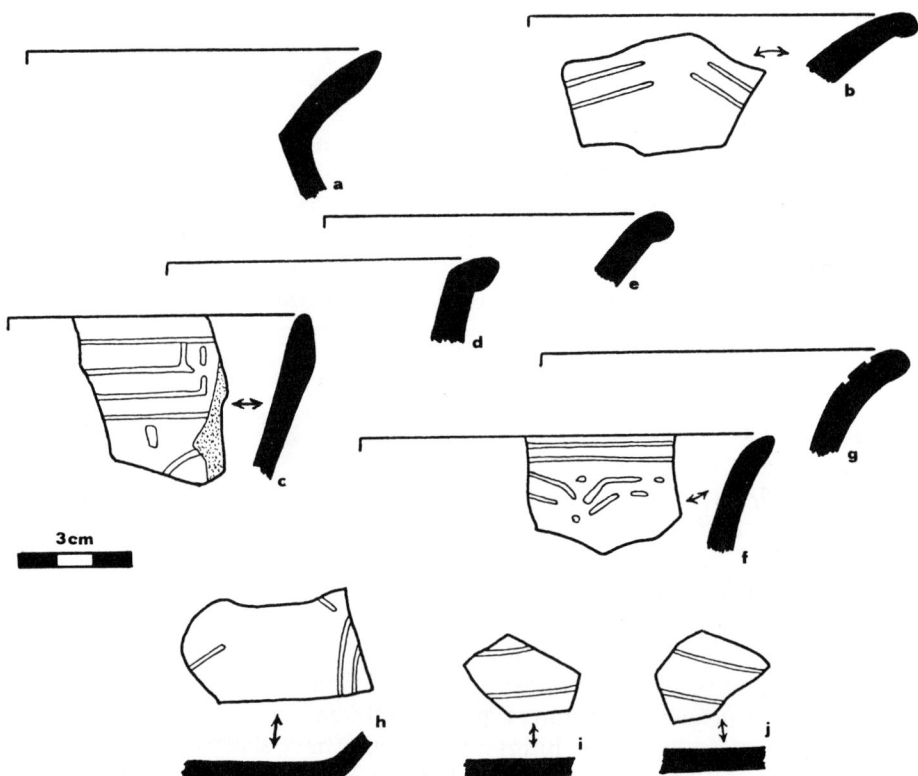

FIG. 84. Excised Brown-Black pottery, Tetipan: *a*, olla; *b–e*, open bowls; *f, g*, flaring bowls; *h–j*, pseudo-grater fondos.

Surface. Both surfaces carefully smoothed and compacted; one or both have a black or very dark gray to dark reddish brown or reddish brown (5 YR 2/1, 3/1, 3/4, 4/3-4) slip, very well polished, with high luster.

Form. Wall thickness 6–9 mm.; typically ca. 7 mm.

OLLA. Diameter 16–20 cm. Interior profile may break in curvature where neck flares sharply outward. Base form unknown. Lip form: rounded.

OPEN BOWL. Diameter 16–20 cm. Wall straight and outslanting to very slightly convex. Base flat. Lip form: slightly thickened exterior or everted.

FLARING BOWL. Diameter 18–22 cm. Wall uniformly concave. Base presumably flat. Lip form: rounded.

Decoration

INCISION. All incision narrow and slightly irregular, with ragged edges, done after paste was partially dry; it is postslip, cutting through the slip to expose paste. 1. Double line encircling upper interior of open or flaring bowl just below and parallel to lip. 2. Pseudo-grater fondo: concentric arcs on interior of flattened base of open or flaring bowl.

EXCISION. Postslip excision typically relatively wide (ca. 2 mm.), with ragged uneven edges and no trace of slip at bottom, done while paste was partially dry. Bottoms of excisions occasionally smoother and more regular, as though paste of vessel-wall interior was still somewhat plastic. Designs limited to (1) two to four lines encircling upper interior of open and flaring bowls, just below and parallel to lip; also multiple-line-break. (2) Complex designs; glyph-like motifs, including arcs and punctations, combined with encircling lines on upper interiors of open and flaring bowls.

OTHER. 1. "Tabbed" or eccentric rim on open bowl.

Remarks. The paste and surface treatment are very similar to those of Guamuchil Polished Black of the Tecolotla phase at Atopula, but the decoration is distinctive. This type is very similar to the Excised Brown-Black pottery in the Xocohuite surface collection (App. 8; Fig. 93).

Red-Black (Figs. 85, 86)

Paste. Relatively porous; hardness 2.5 to 3.0. Temper coarse to very coarse, includes occasional quartz crystals. Paste typically light reddish brown to pink (5 YR 6/3-4, 7/3-4), although cores may remain less completely oxidized, reddish gray to gray or dark gray (5 YR 5/1-2, 4/1).

Surface. Both surfaces typically well smoothed and compacted. Exterior has slip extending over lip onto upper part of interior. Slip typically fired weak red or red (10 R 4/4-6, 5/6), but some vessels have contrasting slip of dark reddish gray to black (10 R 3/1, 2/1). Color change is abrupt, typically forming a black band at rim; it must represent intentional differential firing.

Form. Wall thickness 6–11 mm.; typically 7–8 mm.

OLLA. Diameter 16–28 cm. Interior profile may have sharp break in curvature where neck flares strongly outward, below which surface is unslipped and unsmoothed. Base form unknown. Lip form: rounded, slightly blunted, beveled, tapered, or slightly thickened exterior.

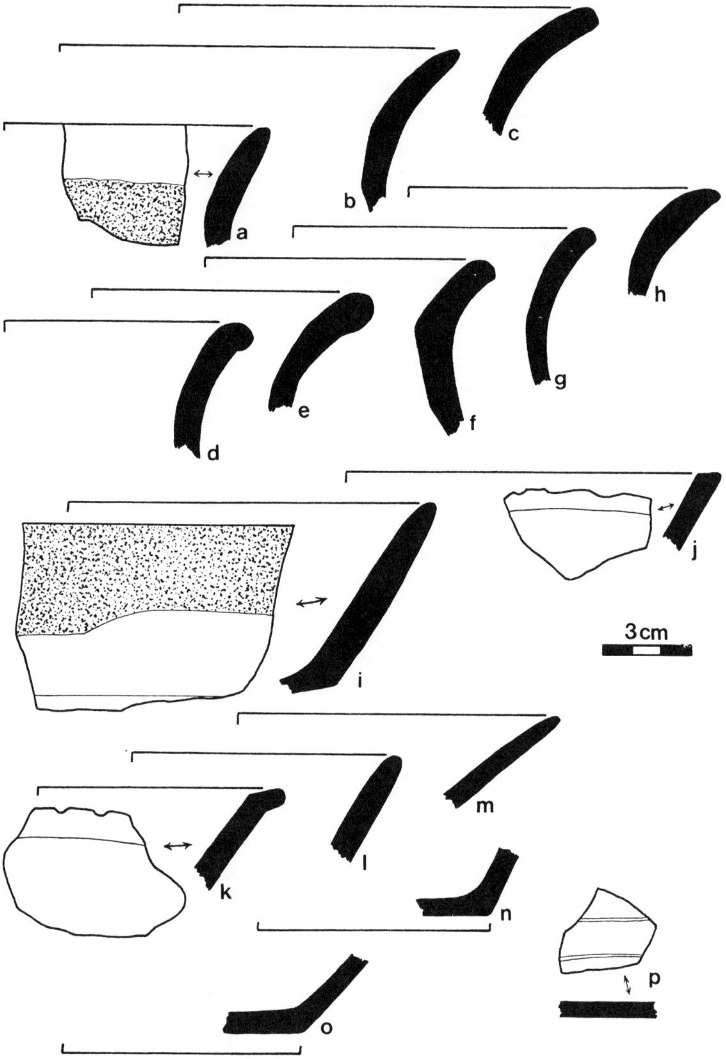

FIG. 85. Red-Black pottery, Tetipan: *a–h*, ollas; *i–o*, open bowls; *p*, pseudo-grater fondo.

OPEN BOWL. Diameter 17–25 cm. Wall straight and outslanting to very slightly convex or concave. Base flat. Lip form: beveled, tapered, or everted.
CONVEX BOWL. Diameter 18–27 cm. Vessel relatively deep with uniformly convex wall. Base presumably rounded. Lip form: rounded, blunted, tapered, or slightly thickened exterior.
BOTTLE. One sherd represents a tubular bottle neck; diameter ca. 3 cm. Form of body unknown. Lip form: rounded.

Decoration

INCISION. All incision pre-slip; slightly irregular but smooth and done while paste was plastic. 1. Single shallow incised line encircling exterior of convex bowls just below and parallel to lip. 2. One or two shallow incised lines on convex-bowl exteriors, along top of encircling flanges; may be short and oblique or partially encircle vessel. 3. Cross-hatching: two pairs of shallow incised lines on a convex bowl exterior, oblique to rim, intersecting near lip. 4. Pseudo-grater fondo: two deep incised concentric arcs on interior of flat base of an open bowl. Base slightly worn, possibly from use as grater.

OTHER. 1. Ridge or flange encircling exterior of convex bowls, 2.5–3.5 cm. below rim, sometimes emphasized by irregular groove below flange. Sometimes an oblique or partially encircling irregular incision along top of flange.

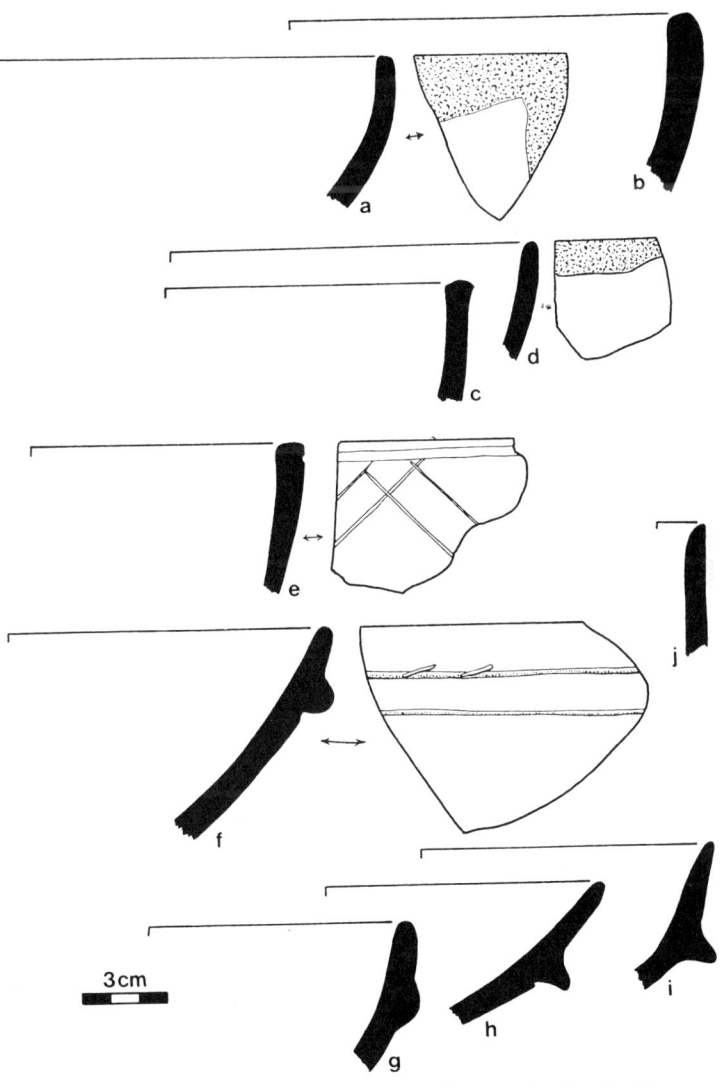

FIG. 86. Red-Black pottery, Tetipan: *a–i*, convex bowls; *j*, bottle.

2. Notched rim: slightly irregular notches, regularly spaced around exterior edge of lip of an open bowl.

Polished Orange (Fig. 87)

Paste. Relatively porous; hardness near 2.5. Temper coarse, predominantly quartz crystals and white particles of limestone or calcite. Paste typically partially oxidized, pinkish gray to light reddish brown to pink (5 YR 6/2-4, 7/2-4) throughout.

Surface. Both surfaces carefully smoothed and compacted and covered with slip fired reddish yellow to yellowish red or red, or even brown to dark brown (5 YR 5/6-8, 6/6-8; 2.5 YR 5/8; 7.5 YR 4/4, 3/2). Slip very well polished, with high luster. Flaring bowls sometimes slipped only on interior.

Form. Wall thickness 3–10 mm.; typically 6–8 mm.

FLARING BOWL. Diameter 18–28 cm. Wall uniformly concave. Base flat. Lip form: rounded, blunted, beveled, tapered, or slightly thickened exterior.

CONVEX BOWL. Diameter 14–18 cm. Wall uniformly convex. Base rounded. Lip form: rounded or tapered.

Decoration

INCISION. All incision postslip, cutting through slip to expose paste; shallow and slightly irregular with ragged edges, done after paste was partially dry.
1. One to four incised lines encircling upper interior or exterior of convex bowls, or upper interior of flaring bowls, just below and parallel to lip.

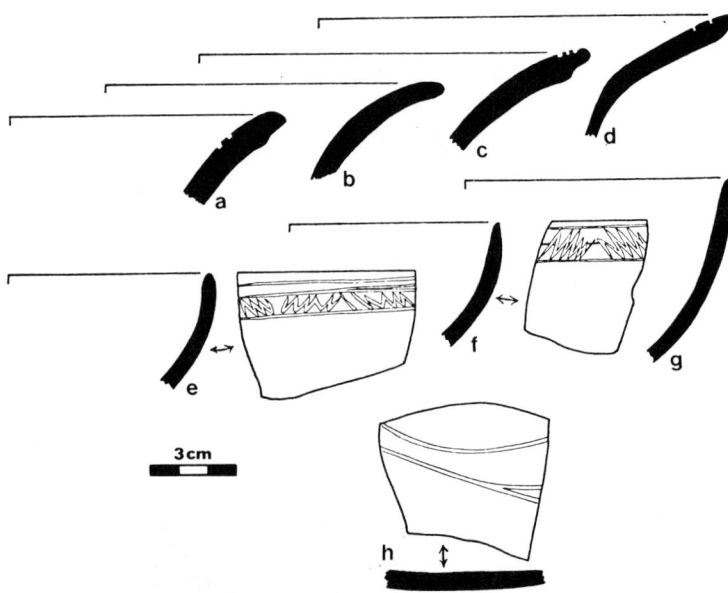

FIG. 87. Polished Orange pottery, Tetipan: *a–d*, flaring bowls; *e–g*, convex bowls; *h*, pseudo-grater fondo.

2. Pseudo-rocker-stamping on upper exterior of convex bowls between encircling lines. Zigzag pattern imitates form of rocker-stamping. 3. Pseudo-grater fondo: concentric arc patterns on interior of flattened base of flaring bowls. No indication of use as graters.

Remarks. This type is identical with Polished Orange pottery in the surface collection from Xocohuite (App. 8; Fig. 91).

Red/White (Fig. 88a)

Paste. Relatively porous; hardness near 2.5. Temper coarse. Paste light reddish brown (5 YR 6/3-4) near surface, with less completely oxidized, pinkish gray to reddish gray (5 YR 5/2, 6/2) core.

Surface. Both surfaces smoothed. Interior has highly polished red (2.5 YR 5/6) slip; exterior has thin, powdery white to pinkish white (5 YR 8/1-2) slip without luster.

Form. Wall thickness 4–5 mm.
 CONVEX BOWL. Diameter unknown. Wall uniformly convex. Base rounded. Lip form: tapered.

Decoration. Other than slips, none represented on the single recovered sherd.

White on-Red (Fig. 88b)

Paste. Relatively porous; hardness near 3.0. Temper coarse, predominantly quartz crystals. Paste light reddish brown to pink (5 YR 6/4, 7/4) near exterior surface, unoxidized, gray (5 YR 6/1) near interior surface.

Surface. Interior unslipped and poorly smoothed, with pitted and grainy texture. Exterior carefully smoothed and compacted and has a reddish yellow (5 YR 7/6) polished slip with slight luster.

Form. Wall thickness 5 mm. Specific form unknown.

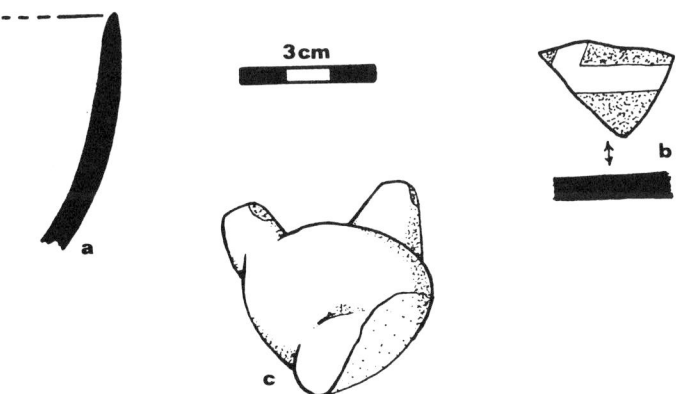

FIG. 88. Minor pottery types and figurine fragment, Tetipan: *a*, Red/White convex bowl; *b*, White-on-Red sherd; *c*, possible animal figurine head.

Decoration. Limited to wide line of thin white (5 YR 8/1) paint on the single recovered sherd.

Coarse Ware

A few sherds represent unslipped ollas; no distinctive features of surface treatment, form, or decoration.

Figurine (Fig. 88c)

Possible animal head; unslipped; the paste is like that of Red-painted Buff.

Appendix 8. Xocohuite

Xocohuite is south of the Río Balsas, some 30 km. south-southwest of Tetipan, on a hill overlooking the western fringes of the village of Xochipala (Fig. 1). Local informants report that *huaqueros* have recovered ceramic figurines and jade from the site, which shows evidence of considerable illicit excavation. It is not clear whether the material recovered from Xocohuite represents the Xochipala style (see above). The site is not one of those mentioned by Gay (1972) as sources of Xochipala-style material.

The surface ceramic collection is dominated by pottery identical with the Red-painted Buff ware from Tetipan (App. 7), except that incised decoration is nearly as common as red painting. In both cases this pottery may indicate a Late Middle Preclassic or Late Preclassic occupation. Polished Orange, Excised Brown-Black, and White pottery also occur at both sites.

Ceramics

Red-painted Buff (Figs. 89, 90)

Paste and surface. Identical with Tetipan type (see App. 7).

Form. Wall thickness 4–10 mm.; typically 5–7 mm.

OPEN BOWL. Diameter 18–20 cm. Wall straight and outslanting to very slightly convex. Form of base unknown. Lip form: rounded, tapered, or slightly thickened interior.

CONVEX BOWL. Diameter 16–24 cm. Wall uniformly convex. Base rounded. Lip form: rounded, slightly blunted, tapered, or slightly thickened interior.

COMPOSITE-SILHOUETTE BOWL. Diameter 16–20 cm. Upper wall straight and outslanting to concave and outflaring; below sharp break in curvature, lower wall convex. Base rounded. Lip form: rounded or beveled.

Auxiliary features. 1. Strap handle: semicircular, ovoid in cross-section, ca. 2 cm. wide, attached to vessel (presumably olla) exterior.

Miscellaneous. 1. Curved cylindrical object, 1.5–2.0 cm. in diameter, with transverse raised bands or flanges almost completely encircling it. Decorated with punctation, longitudinal incised lines, and red painting. Probably a loop handle but could be a figurine arm fragment.

Decoration

PAINTING. Weak red to red (10 R 4/4-6, 5/4-6) painted decoration, typically in bands or zones, with negative designs (but not resist technique). Thickness and coverage of paint variable. Design elements at Xocohuite include (1) bands along rim on interior and/or exterior; (2) regular and irregular bands or stripes; (3) irregular rectilinear and curvilinear zones or spots; (4) polygons outlined by red background.

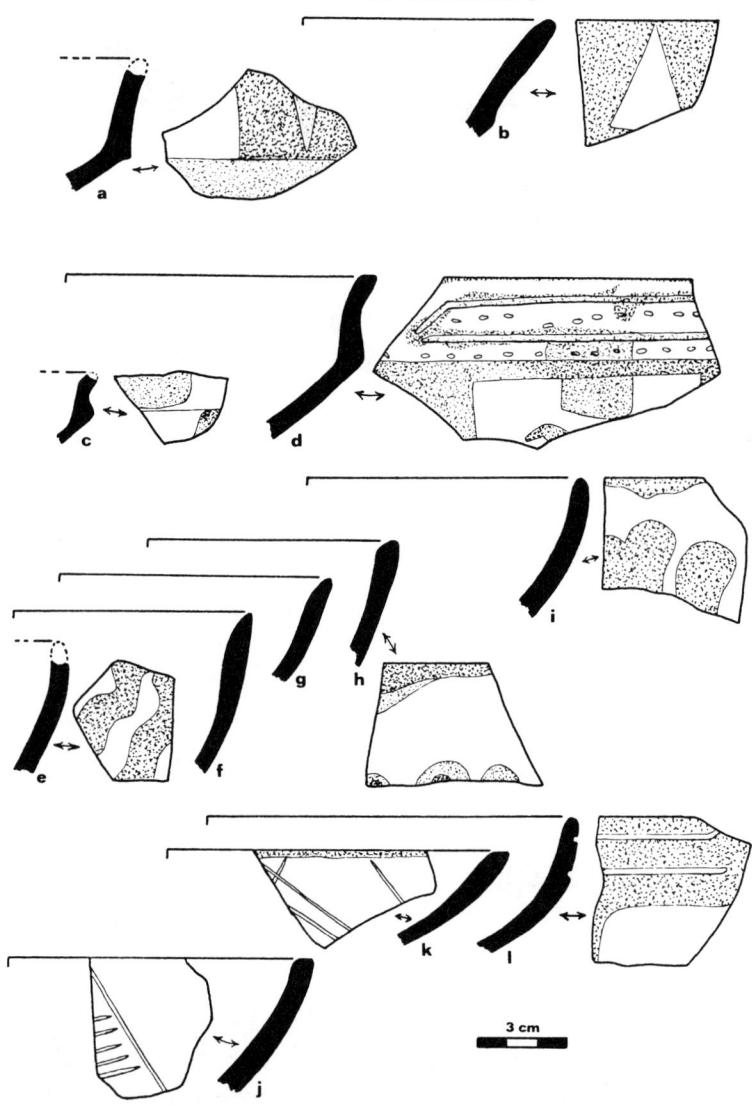

FIG. 89. Red-painted Buff pottery, Xocohuite: *a–d*, composite-silhouette bowls; *e–l*, convex bowls.

INCISION. On unslipped zones; irregular but smooth and done while paste was plastic. 1. Zone of parallel straight lines limited by another line, all oblique to plane of lip, occurring on convex and open-bowl interiors. 2. Two lines encircling upper exterior of convex and composite-silhouette bowls just below and parallel to lip. Motif similar to double-line-break in that upper line may have up-turned (or down-turned) end.

PUNCTATION. 1. Parallel rows of punctations just below and parallel to rim of composite-silhouette bowl exteriors. Pre-slip punctations smooth and done while paste was plastic.

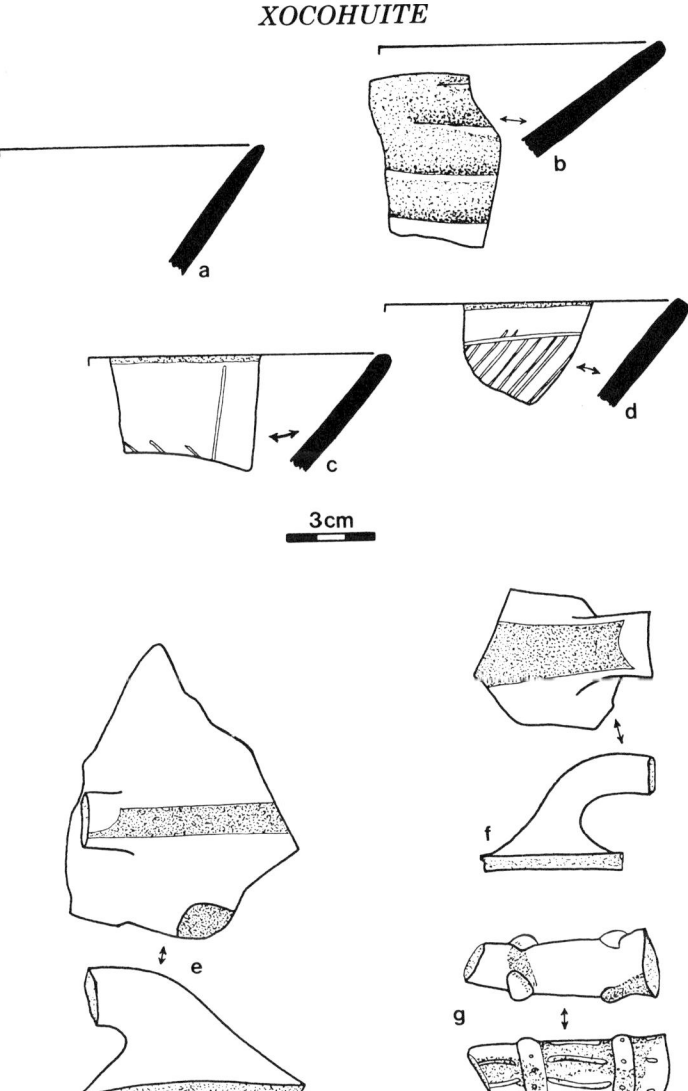

FIG. 90. Red-painted Buff pottery, Xocohuite: *a–d*, open bowls; *e, f*, strap handles; *g*, cylindrical "handle."

Remarks. Except for its incised decoration, this type is identical with Red-painted Buff pottery of Tetipan (App. 7; Figs. 82, 83). Forms and decoration resemble red-on-buff pottery of the Cerro Chacaltepec II phase of Morelos, which is dated to ca. 400–100 B.C. (Grove 1968b: 57–9, figs. 49, 50; 1970a: 8–9) and may suggest Late Middle Preclassic or Late Preclassic occupation.

Polished Orange (Fig. 91)

Paste and surface. Identical with Tetipan type (see App. 7).
Form. Wall thickness 5–9 mm.; typically 6–7 mm.

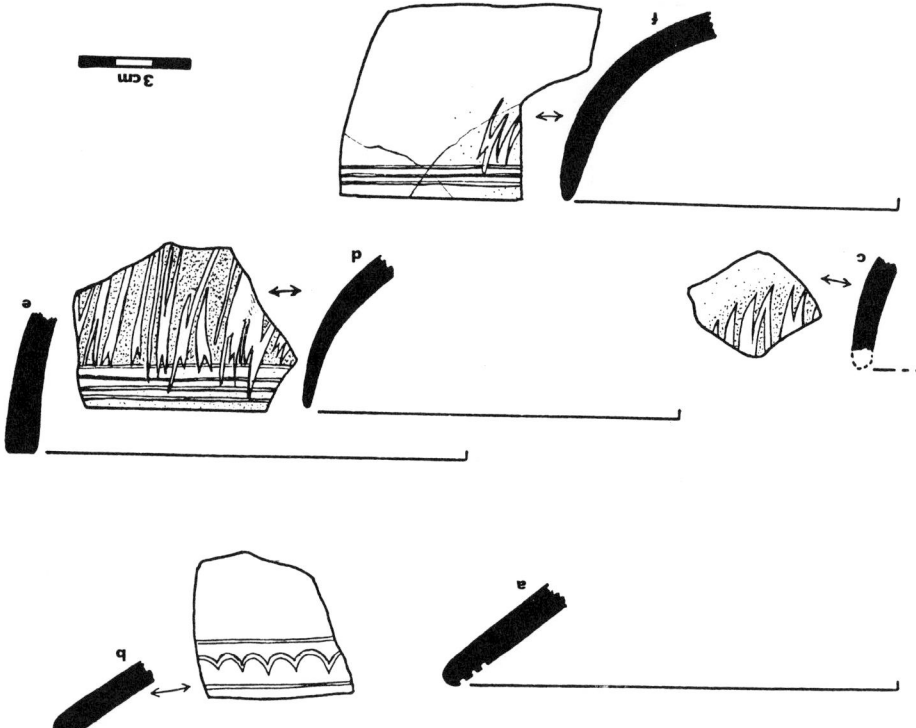

Fig. 91. Polished Orange pottery, Xocohuite: *a, b,* open bowls; *c–f,* convex bowls.

OPEN BOWL. Diameter 24–26 cm. Wall straight and outslanting. Base form unknown. Lip form: rounded.

CONVEX BOWL. Diameter 18–24 cm. Wall uniformly convex. Base rounded. Lip form: beveled or tapered.

Decoration

INCISION. All incision shallow and slightly irregular, done after paste was partially dry; postslip, cutting through slip to expose paste. 1. Two to four incised lines encircling upper interior of open bowls, or upper exterior of convex bowls, just below and parallel to lip. 2. Pseudo-rocker-stamping. Zigzag patterns imitating rocker-stamping extend across encircling lines on upper exterior of convex bowls; one open bowl interior has very similar pendant semicircles between encircling lines.

Remarks. This type is identical in every respect with the Polished Orange pottery in the surface collection from Tetipan (App. 7; Fig. 87) except that open bowls replace flaring bowls.

White (Fig. 92)

Paste and surface. Identical with Tetipan type (see App. 7).

Form. Wall thickness 4–8 mm.; typically ca. 6 mm.

FLARING BOWL. Diameter ca. 22 cm. Wall concave. Base probably flat. Lip form: tapered.

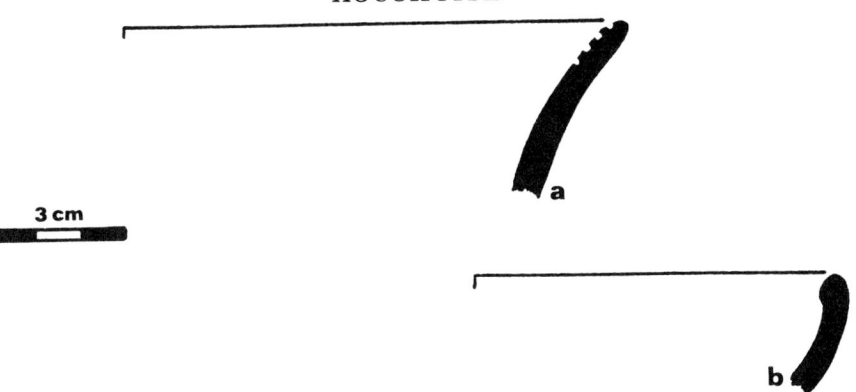

FIG. 92. White pottery, Xocohuite: *a*, flaring bowl; *b*, convex bowl.

CONVEX BOWL. Diameter ca. 16 cm. Wall uniformly convex. Base presumably rounded. Lip form: slightly thickened interior.

Decoration
INCISION. 1. Four parallel lines encircling upper interior of flaring bowl just below and parallel to lip. Incision postslip, cutting through slip to expose paste, but is smooth and regular and done while paste was plastic.

Remarks. This type is very similar to the incised White pottery in the surface collection from Tetipan (App. 7; Fig. 81).

Excised Brown-Black (Fig. 93)

Paste and surface. Identical with Tetipan type (see App. 7).
Form. Wall thickness 6–9 mm.; typically ca. 7 mm.
   OLLA. Diameter 13–14 cm. Form of base unknown. Lip form: tapered.
   OPEN BOWL. Diameter 14–18 cm. Wall straight and outslanting to very slightly convex or concave. Base flat. Lip form: rounded or tapered.
   CONVEX BOWL. Diameter 16–20 cm. Wall uniformly convex. Base rounded. Lip form: beveled or tapered.
   INCURVED-RIM BOWL. Diameter 13–27 cm. Wall convex; near the lip almost straight and inslanting. Base presumably rounded. Lip form: rounded or thickened exterior.

Decoration
INCISION. All incision pre-slip; slightly irregular but smooth, and done while paste was plastic. 1. Three lines encircling exterior of open bowl just below and parallel to lip. 2. Pseudo-grater fondo: multiple parallel straight lines on interior of flat base of open bowls. Bases somewhat worn, perhaps from use as grater bowls. 3. Grater base (?). Widely spaced "cross-hatching" or multiple zones of parallel lines on interior of convex bowls, beginning just below lip. These bowls not worn from use as graters.
EXCISION. 1. Complex design on upper exterior of open bowl composed of zone of parallel excised lines intersecting and limited by other excised lines, all oblique to plane of lip; excised arc below this zone. Excision relatively

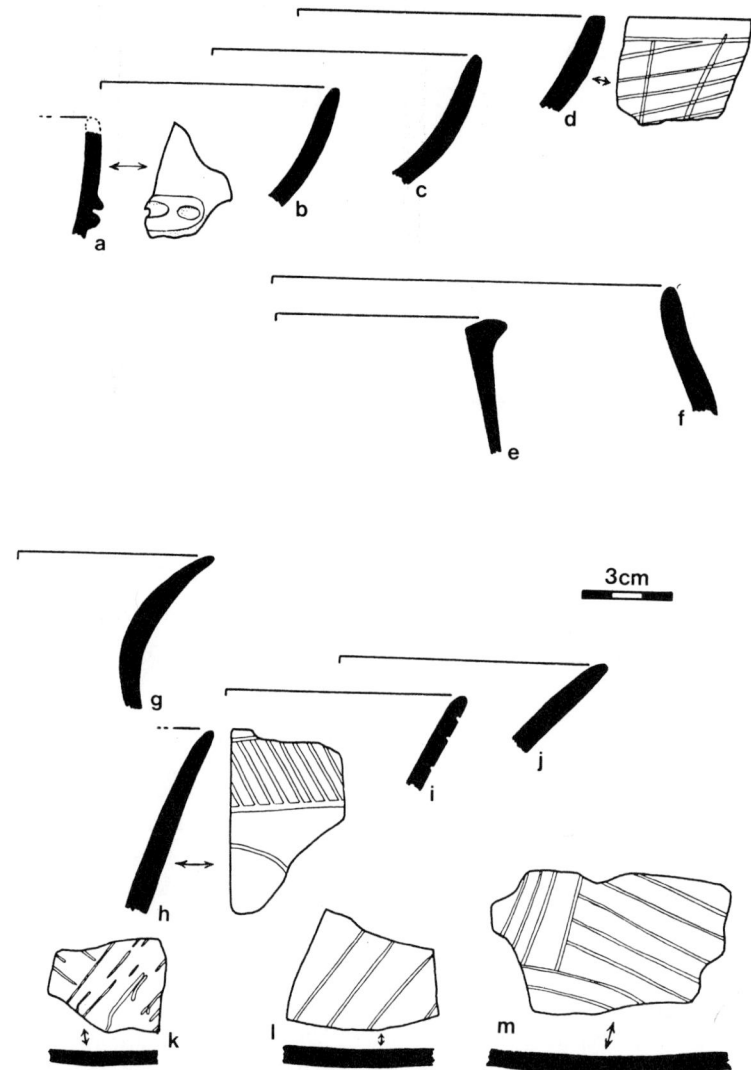

Fig. 93. Excised Brown-Black pottery, Xocohuite: *a–d*, convex bowls; *e, f*, incurved-rim bowls; *g*, olla; *h–j*, open bowls; *k–m*, pseudo-grater fondos.

wide (ca. 2 mm.), with ragged, uneven edges and done after paste was partially dry. It is postslip, cutting through slip to expose paste.

APPLIQUÉ. 1. Oval appliqué with punctations on upper exterior of convex bowl.

Remarks. This type is very similar to the Excised Brown-Black pottery in the Tetipan surface collection (App. 7; Fig. 84).

Coarse Ware

A few sherds representing unslipped convex bowls and ollas have no distinctive features of surface treatment, form, or decoration.

References

ADAMS, RICHARD E. W.
    1970   Suggested Classic Period Occupational Specialization in the Southern Maya Lowlands. In *Monographs and Papers in Maya Archaeology,* Peabody Museum of Archaeology and Ethnology, Papers, vol. 61, pp. 487-502, Cambridge.
    1971   *The Ceramics of Altar de Sacrificios.* Peabody Museum of Archaeology and Ethnology, Papers, vol. 63, Cambridge.

ADAMS, ROBERT McC.
    1962   Agriculture and Urban Life in Early Southwestern Iran. *Science 136*:109-22.
    1966   *The Evolution of Urban Society: Early Mesopotamia and Prehispanic Mexico.* Aldine, Chicago.
    1969   The Study of Ancient Mesopotamian Settlement Patterns and the Problem of Urban Origins. *Sumer 25*:111-24.
    1972   Patterns of Urbanization in Early Southern Mesopotamia. In *Man, Settlement and Urbanism,* ed. by Peter J. Ucko, Ruth Tringham, and G. W. Dimbleby, pp. 735-49. Duckworth, London.

ADAMS, ROBERT McC., AND HANS J. NISSEN
    1972   *The Uruk Countryside: The Natural Setting of Urban Societies.* University of Chicago Press, Chicago.

BALSER, CARLOS
    1964   Some Costa Rican Jade Motifs. In *Essays in Precolumbian Art and Archaeology,* ed. by S. K. Lothrop, pp. 210-17. Harvard University Press, Cambridge.

BARBA DE PIÑA CHÁN, BEATRIZ
    1956   Tlapacoya: Un Sitio Preclásico de Transición. *Acta Antropológica,* época 2, vol. 1, no. 1. Escuela Nacional de Antropología e Historia, Sociedad de Alumnos, Mexico.

BARLOW, R. H.
    1949   *The Extent of the Empire of the Culhua Mexica.* Ibero-Americana, vol. 28, Berkeley.

BAUDEZ, CLAUDE F.
    1966   Niveaux céramiques au Honduras: Une Reconsidération de l'evolution culturelle. *Journal de la Société des Américanistes 55*:299-341.
    1970   *Central America,* trans. by James Hogarth. Barrie & Jenkins, London.

BAUDEZ, CLAUDE F., AND PIERRE BECQUELIN
    1973   *Archéologie de los Naranjos, Honduras.* Mission Archéologique et Ethnologique Française au Mexique, and Centre National de la Recherche Scientifique, Mexico.

BECKER, MARSHALL JOSEPH
    1973   Archaeological Evidence for Occupational Specialization among the Classic Period Maya at Tikal, Guatemala. *American Antiquity 38*:396-406.

BENNETT, WENDELL C.
    1948   The Peruvian Co-Tradition. In *A Reappraisal of Peruvian Archaeology,* ed. by Wendell C. Bennett. Society for American Archaeology, Memoirs, vol. 4, pp. 1-7. Menasha.

REFERENCES

BERGMANN, JOHN F.
   1969 The Distribution of the Cacao Cultivation in Precolumbian America. *Annals of the Association of American Geographers* 59:85–96.

BERNAL, IGNACIO
   1969 *The Olmec World,* trans. by Doris Heyden and Fernando Horcasitas. University of California Press, Berkeley.
   1971 The Olmec Region: Oaxaca. In *Observations on the Emergence of Civilization in Mesoamerica.* University of California Archaeological Research Facility, Contributions, no. 11, pp. 29–50. Berkeley.

BEYER, HERMANN
   1927 Bibliografía: Tribes and Temples. *El México Antiguo* 2:305–13.

BLOM, FRANS, AND OLIVER LA FARGE
   1926 *Tribes and Temples: A Record of the Expedition to Middle America Conducted by the Tulane University of Louisiana in 1925,* 2 vols. Middle American Research Institute, Publication 1, New Orleans.

BOGGS, STANLEY H.
   1950 *"Olmec" Pictographs in the Las Victorias Group, Chalchuapa Archaeological Zone, El Salvador.* Notes on Middle American Archaeology and Ethnology, no. 99. Carnegie Institution of Washington, Division of Historical Research, Cambridge.

BROCKINGTON, DONALD L.
   1967 *The Ceramic History of Santa Rosa, Chiapas, Mexico.* New World Archaeological Foundation, Papers, vol. 23, Provo.

BRUSH, CHARLES F.
   1965 Pox Pottery: Earliest Identified Mexican Ceramic. *Science* 149:194–5.
   1969 "A Contribution to the Archaeology of Coastal Guerrero, Mexico." Ph.D. dissertation, Dept. of Anthropology, Columbia University, New York.

BRUSH, ELLEN S.
   1968 "The Archaeological Significance of Ceramic Figurines from Guerrero, Mexico." Ph.D. dissertation, Dept. of Anthropology, Columbia University, New York.

CARNEIRO, ROBERT L.
   1970 A Theory of the Origin of the State. *Science* 169:733–8.

CASO, ALFONSO
   1938 *Exploraciones en Oaxaca: Quinta y Sexta Temporadas.* Instituto Panamericano de Geografía e Historia, Publicación 34, Mexico.
   1942 Definición y Extensión del Complejo "Olmeca." In *Mayas y Olmecas,* pp. 43–6. Segunda Mesa Redonda, Sociedad Mexicana de Antropología, Mexico.
   1965 ¿Existió un Imperio Olmeca? *Memorias del Colegio Nacional,* vol. 5, no. 3, pp. 11–60, Mexico.

CHANG, KWANG-CHIH
   1968 *The Archaeology of Ancient China,* rev. ed. Yale University Press, New Haven.

CHAPMAN, A. M.
   1957 Port of Trade Enclaves in Aztec and Maya Civilizations. In *Trade and Market in the Early Empires,* ed. by K. Polanyi, C. M. Arensberg, and H. W. Pearson, pp. 114–53. Free Press, Glencoe.

CLEWLOW, C. WILLIAM, JR.
   1974 *A Stylistic and Chronological Study of Olmec Monumental Sculpture.* University of California Archaeological Research Facility, Contributions, no. 19, Berkeley.

CLEWLOW, C. WILLIAM, JR., RICHARD A. COWAN, JAMES F. O'CONNELL, AND CARLOS BENEMANN
    1967   *Colossal Heads of the Olmec Culture.* University of California Archaeological Research Facility, Contributions, no. 4, Berkeley.

COBEAN, ROBERT H., MICHAEL D. COE, E. A. PERRY, JR., K. K. TUREKIAN, AND D. P. KHARKAR
    1971   Obsidian Trade at San Lorenzo Tenochtitlán, Mexico. *Science 174*:666–71.

COE, MICHAEL D.
    1961   *La Victoria: An Early Site on the Pacific Coast of Guatemala.* Peabody Museum of Archaeology and Ethnology, Papers, vol. 53, Cambridge.
    1965a Archaeological Synthesis of Southern Veracruz and Tabasco. *Handbook of Middle American Indians* 3:679–715.
    1965b *The Jaguar's Children: Pre-Classic Central Mexico.* Museum of Primitive Art, New York.
    1965c The Olmec Style and Its Distributions. *Handbook of Middle American Indians* 3:739–75.
    1968a *America's First Civilization.* American Heritage, New York.
    1968b San Lorenzo and the Olmec Civilization. In *Dumbarton Oaks Conference on the Olmec,* ed. by Elizabeth P. Benson, pp. 41–78. Dumbarton Oaks Research Library and Collection, Washington.
    1969   Photogrammetry and the Ecology of Olmec Civilization. Paper read at Working Conference on Aerial Photography and Anthropology, 10–12 May 1969, at Harvard University, Cambridge.
    1970   The Archaeological Sequence at San Lorenzo Tenochtitlán, Veracruz, Mexico. In *Magnetometer Survey of the La Venta Pyramid and Other Papers on Mexican Archaeology.* University of California Archaeological Research Facility, Contributions, no. 8, pp. 21–34, Berkeley.
    1973   *The Maya Scribe and His World.* Grolier Club, New York.

COE, MICHAEL D., AND KENT V. FLANNERY
    1964a Microenvironments and Mesoamerican Prehistory. *Science 143*:650–4.
    1964b The Pre-columbian Obsidian Industry of El Chayal, Guatemala. *American Antiquity 30*:43–9.
    1967   *Early Cultures and Human Ecology in South Coastal Guatemala.* Smithsonian Contributions to Anthropology, vol. 3, Washington.

COHEN, ABNER
    1969   *Custom and Politics in Urban Africa.* University of California Press, Berkeley.

COOK DE LEONARD, CARMEN
    1967   Sculptures and Rock Carvings at Chalcatzingo, Morelos. In *Studies in Olmec Archaeology.* University of California Archaeological Research Facility, Contributions, no. 3, pp. 57–84, Berkeley.

CORDAN, WOLFGANG
    1963   *Secret of the Forest: On the Track of Maya Temples,* trans. by Basil Creighton. Gollancz, London.

COVARRUBIAS, MIGUEL
    1942   Origen y Desarrollo del Estilo Artístico Olmeca. In *Mayas y Olmecas,* pp. 46–9. Segunda Mesa Redonda, Sociedad Mexicana de Antropología, Mexico.
    1943   Tlatilco: Archaic Mexican Art and Culture. *Dyn, The Review of Modern Art,* nos. 4–5, pp. 40–6, Coyoacan.
    1948   Tipología de la Industria de Piedra Tallada y Pulida de la Cuenca del Río

Mexcala. In *El Occidente de México,* pp. 86–90. Cuarta Mesa Redonda, Sociedad Mexicana de Antropología, Mexico.
1957   *Indian Art of Mexico and Central America.* Knopf, New York.

CURTIS, GARNISS H.
1959   The Petrology of Artifacts and Architectural Stone at La Venta. In *Excavations at La Venta, Tabasco, 1955,* by Philip Drucker, Robert F. Heizer, and Robert J. Squier. Smithsonian Institution, Bureau of American Ethnology, Bulletin, no. 170, pp. 284–9, Washington.

CYPHERS, ANN MARIE
1975   "The Preclassic Ceramic Chronology at Chalcatzingo, Morelos, Mexico: Implications for Internal Growth and External Contacts." M.A. thesis, Dept. of Anthropology, University of Wisconsin, Milwaukee.

DEETZ, JAMES D. F.
1965   *The Dynamics of Stylistic Change in Arikara Ceramics.* Illinois Studies in Anthropology, no. 4, Urbana.
1968   The Inference of Residence and Descent Rules from Archaeological Data. In *New Perspectives in Archaeology,* ed. by Sally R. Binford and Lewis R. Binford, pp. 41–8. Aldine, Chicago.

DEIMEL, ANTON
1931   *Šumerische Tempelwirtschaft zür Zeit Urukaginas und seiner Vorgänger: Abschluss der Einzelstudien und Zusammenfassung der Hauptresultate.* Analecta Orientalia, no. 2. Pontificio Istituto Biblico, Rome.

DIAKONOFF, I. M.
1969   The Rise of the Despotic State in Ancient Mesopotamia. In *Ancient Mesopotamia: Socio-economic History,* ed. by I. M. Diakonoff, pp. 173–203. U. S. S. R. Academy of Sciences, Moscow.

DIXON, J. E., J. R. CANN, AND COLIN RENFREW
1968   Obsidian and the Origins of Trade. *Scientific American* 218(3):38–46.

DIXON, KEITH A.
1959   *Ceramics from Two Preclassic Periods at Chiapa de Corzo, Chiapas, Mexico.* New World Archaeological Foundation, Papers, vol. 5, Orinda.

DRENNAN, ROBERT D.
1976   *Fábrica San José and Middle Formative Society in the Valley of Oaxaca.* University of Michigan, Museum of Anthropology, Memoirs, vol. 8, Ann Arbor.

DRUCKER, PHILIP
1952   *La Venta, Tabasco: A Study of Olmec Ceramics and Art.* Smithsonian Institution, Bureau of American Ethnology, Bulletin, no. 153, Washington.

DRUCKER, PHILIP, ROBERT F. HEIZER, AND ROBERT J. SQUIER
1959   *Excavations at La Venta, Tabasco, 1955.* Smithsonian Institution, Bureau of American Ethnology, Bulletin, no. 170, Washington.

EASBY, ELIZABETH K.
1968   *Pre-Columbian Jade from Costa Rica.* Emmerich, New York.

EASBY, ELIZABETH K., AND JOHN F. SCOTT
1970   *Before Cortés: Sculpture of Middle America.* Metropolitan Museum of Art, New York.

EDMONSON, MUNRO S.
1965   *Quiche-English Dictionary.* Tulane University, Middle American Research Institute, Publication 30, New Orleans.
1971   *The Book of Counsel: The Popol Vuh of the Quiche Maya of Guatemala.*

REFERENCES

Tulane University, Middle American Research Institute, Publication 35, New Orleans.

EKHOLM-MILLER, SUSANNA
- 1969 *Mound 30A and the Early Preclassic Ceramic Sequence of Izapa, Chiapas, Mexico.* New World Archaeological Foundation, Papers, vol. 25, Provo.
- 1973 *The Olmec Rock Carving at Xoc, Chiapas, Mexico.* New World Archaeological Foundation, Papers, vol. 32, Provo.

FALKENSTEIN, ADAM
- 1954 La Cité-temple Sumérienne. *Cahiers d'Histoire Mondiale* 1:784–814.

FERDON, EDWIN N., JR.
- 1953 *Tonala, Mexico: An Archaeological Survey.* School of American Research, Monographs, vol. 16, Santa Fe.

FLANNERY, KENT V.
- 1968 The Olmec and the Valley of Oaxaca: A Model for Interregional Interaction in Formative Times. In *Dumbarton Oaks Conference on the Olmec,* ed. by Elizabeth P. Benson, pp. 79–117. Dumbarton Oaks Research Library and Collection, Washington.
- 1969 Origins and Ecological Effects of Early Domestication in Iran and the Near East. In *The Domestication and Exploitation of Plants and Animals,* ed. by Peter J. Ucko and G. W. Dimbleby, pp. 73–100. Aldine, Chicago.
- 1976 *The Early Mesoamerican Village.* Academic Press, New York.

FLANNERY, KENT V., AND MICHAEL D. COE
- 1968 Social and Economic Systems in Formative Mesoamerica. In *New Perspectives in Archaeology,* ed. by Sally R. Binford and Lewis R. Binford, pp. 267–83. Aldine, Chicago.

FLANNERY, KENT V., AND JAMES SCHOENWETTER
- 1970 Climate and Man in Formative Oaxaca. *Archaeology* 23:144–52.

FLANNERY, KENT V., A. V. T. KIRKBY, M. J. KIRKBY, AND A. W. WILLIAMS, JR.
- 1967 Farming Systems and Political Growth in Ancient Oaxaca, Mexico. *Science* 158:445–54.

FRIED, MORTON H.
- 1960 On the Evolution of Social Stratification and the State. In *Culture in History: Essays in Honor of Paul Radin,* ed. by Stanley Diamond, pp. 713–31. Columbia University Press, New York.
- 1967 *The Evolution of Political Society.* Random House, New York.

FRIEDMAN, IRVING, AND CLIFFORD EVANS
- 1968 Obsidian Dating Revisited. *Science* 162:813.

GARCÍA PAYÓN, JOSÉ
- 1941 La Cerámica del Valle de Toluca. *Revista Mexicana de Estudios Antropológicos* 5:209–38.
- 1966 *Prehistoria de Mesoamérica: Excavaciones en Trapiche y Chalahuite, Veracruz, México, 1942, 1951 y 1959.* Cuadernos de la Facultad de Filosofía, Letras y Ciencias, no. 31. Universidad Veracruzana, Xalapa.
- 1971 Archaeology of Central Veracruz. *Handbook of Middle American Indians* 11:505–42.

GAY, CARLO T. E.
- 1966 Rock Carvings at Chalcacingo. *Natural History* 75:57–61.
- 1967 Oldest Paintings of the New World. *Natural History* 76:28–35.
- 1971 *Chalcacingo.* Akademische Druck- u. Verlagsanstalt, Graz.

1972 *Xochipala: The Beginnings of Olmec Art.* Art Museum and Princeton University Press, Princeton.

GORENSTEIN, SHIRLEY

1973 Some Observations on Mesoamerican Fortifications. Paper read at University Seminar on Primitive and Pre-Columbian Art, 7 December 1973, Columbia University, New York.

GREEN, DEE F., AND GARETH W. LOWE

1967 *Altamira and Padre Piedra: Early Preclassic Sites in Chiapas, Mexico.* New World Archaeological Foundation, Papers, vol. 20, Provo.

GREENGO, ROBERT E.

1967 Reconocimiento Arqueológico en el Noroeste de Guerrero. *Instituto Nacional de Antropología e Historia, Boletín,* no. 29, pp. 6–10, Mexico.

1970 The Preclassic in Guerrero, Mexico. Paper read at 35th Annual Meeting of the Society for American Archaeology, 30 April–2 May 1970, Museo Nacional de Antropología, Mexico.

GRENNES-RAVITZ, RONALD A.

1974 The Olmec Presence at Iglesia Vieja, Morelos. In *Mesoamerican Archaeology: New Approaches,* ed. by Norman Hammond, pp. 99–108. University of Texas Press, Austin.

GROVE, DAVID C.

1968a Chalcatzingo, Morelos, Mexico: A Reappraisal of the Olmec Rock Carvings. *American Antiquity 33:*486–91.

1968b "The Morelos Preclassic and the Highland Olmec Problem: An Archaeological Study." Ph.D. dissertation, Dept. of Anthropology, University of California, Los Angeles.

1968c The Preclassic Olmec in Central Mexico: Site Distribution and Inferences. In *Dumbarton Oaks Conference on the Olmec,* ed. by Elizabeth P. Benson, pp. 179–85. Dumbarton Oaks Research Library and Collection, Washington.

1970a The Morelos Formative: Cultural Stratigraphy and Implications. Paper read at 35th Annual Meeting of the Society for American Archaeology, 30 April–2 May 1970, Museo Nacional de Antropología, Mexico.

1970b *The Olmec Paintings of Oxtotitlan Cave, Guerrero, Mexico.* Dumbarton Oaks Studies in Pre-Columbian Art and Archaeology, no. 6, Washington.

1970c The San Pablo Pantheon Mound: A Middle Preclassic Site in Morelos, Mexico. *American Antiquity 35:*62–73.

1971 The Mesoamerican Formative and South American Influences. Paper read at Primer Simposio de Correlaciones Antropológicas Andino-Mesoamericano, July 1971, Salinas, Ecuador.

1972 Archaeological Investigations along the Río Cuautla, Morelos, 1969 and 1970. Informe submitted to the Instituto Nacional de Antropología e Historia, Mexico.

1973a Olmec Altars and Myths. *Archaeology 26:*128–35.

1973b Review of *Chalcacingo,* and *Xochipala: The Beginnings of Olmec Art,* by Carlo T. E. Gay. *American Anthropologist 75:*1138–40.

1974a The Highland Olmec Manifestation: A Consideration of What It Is and Isn't. In *Mesoamerican Archaeology: New Approaches,* ed. by Norman Hammond, pp. 109–28. University of Texas Press, Austin.

1974b *San Pablo, Nexpa, and the Early Formative Archaeology of Morelos, Mexico.* Vanderbilt University Publications in Anthropology, no. 12, Nashville.

REFERENCES

GROVE, DAVID C., AND LOUISE I. PARADIS
    1971   An Olmec Stela from San Miguel Amuco, Guerrero. *American Antiquity 36*: 95–102.

GROVE, DAVID C., KENNETH G. HIRTH, DAVID E. BUGÉ, AND ANN M. CYPHERS
    1976   Settlement and Cultural Development of Chalcatzingo. *Science 192*:1203–10.

GULLBERG, JONAS E.
    1959   Technical Notes on Concave Mirrors. In *Excavations at La Venta, Tabasco, 1955*, by Philip Drucker, Robert F. Heizer, and Robert J. Squier. Smithsonian Institution, Bureau of American Ethnology, Bulletin, no. 170, pp. 280–3, Washington.

GUZMÁN, EULALIA
    1934   *Los Relieves de las Rocas del Cerro de la Cantera, Jonacatepec, Mor.* Museo Nacional de Arqueología, Historia y Etnografía, Anales, época 5, vol. 1, pp. 237–51, Mexico.

HABERLAND, WOLFGANG
    1969   Current Research: Central America. *American Antiquity 34*:357–9.

HAMMOND, NORMAN
    1972   A Minor Criticism of the Type-Variety System of Ceramic Analysis. *American Antiquity 37*:450–2.
    1977   The Earliest Maya. *Scientific American 236*(3):116–33.

HARVEY, HERBERT R.
    1971   Ethnohistory of Guerrero. *Handbook of Middle American Indians 11*:603–18.

HEISER, CHARLES B., JR.
    1973   *Seed to Civilization: The Story of Man's Food.* Freeman, San Francisco.

HEIZER, ROBERT F.
    1967   Analysis of Two Low Relief Sculptures from La Venta. In *Studies in Olmec Archaeology*. University of California Archaeological Research Facility, Contributions, no. 3, pp. 25–55, Berkeley.
    1968   New Observations on La Venta. In *Dumbarton Oaks Conference on the Olmec*, ed. by Elizabeth P. Benson, pp. 9–40. Dumbarton Oaks Research Library and Collection, Washington.

HENDERSON, JOHN S.
    1974   "Preclassic Archaeology in the State of Guerrero, Mexico." Ph.D. dissertation, Dept. of Anthropology, Yale University, New Haven.

HENDRICHS PEREZ, PEDRO R.
    1940–1941   Datos Sobre la Técnica Minera Prehispánica. *El México Antiguo 5*:148–60, 179–94, 311–28.

HILL, JAMES N.
    1966   A Prehistoric Community in Eastern Arizona. *Southwestern Journal of Anthropology 22*:9–30.
    1970   *Broken K Pueblo: Prehistoric Social Organization in the American Southwest.* University of Arizona, Anthropological Papers, vol. 18, Tucson.

JACK, ROBERT N., AND ROBERT F. HEIZER
    1968   "Finger-Printing" of some Mesoamerican Obsidian Artifacts. In *Papers on Mesoamerican Archaeology*. University of California Archaeological Research Facility, Contributions, no. 5, pp. 81–100, Berkeley.

JACK, ROBERT N., THOMAS R. HESTER, AND ROBERT F. HEIZER
    1972   Geologic Sources of Archaeological Obsidian from Sites in Northern and

Central Veracruz, Mexico. In *Studies in the Archaeology of Mexico and Guatemala*. University of California Archaeological Research Facility, Contributions, no. 16, pp. 117–22, Berkeley.

JOHNSON, FREDERICK, AND RICHARD S. MACNEISH
1972   Chronometric Dating. In *The Prehistory of the Tehuacan Valley*, vol. 4, *Chronology and Irrigation*, ed. by Frederick Johnson, pp. 3–55. University of Texas Press, Austin.

JORALEMON, P. D.
1971   *A Study of Olmec Iconography*. Dumbarton Oaks Studies in Pre-Columbian Art and Archaeology, no. 7, Washington.

KIDDER, ALFRED V.
1965   Preclassic Pottery Figurines of the Guatemalan Highlands. *Handbook of Middle American Indians* 2:146–55.

KROEBER, A. L.
1944   *Peruvian Archaeology in 1942*. Viking Fund Publications in Anthropology, no. 4, New York.

LANNING, EDWARD P.
1967   *Peru before the Incas*. Prentice-Hall, Englewood Cliffs.

LEE, THOMAS A., JR.
1969   *The Artifacts of Chiapa de Corzo, Chiapas, Mexico*. New World Archaeological Foundation, Papers, vol. 26, Provo.

LISTER, ROBERT H.
1971   Archaeological Synthesis of Guerrero. *Handbook of Middle American Indians* 11:619–31.

LITVAK KING, JAIME
1971   *Cihuatlán y Tepecoacuilco: Provincias Tributarias de México en el Siglo XVI*. Instituto de Investigaciones Históricas, Sección de Antropología, Serie Antropológica, no. 12. Universidad Nacional Autónoma de México, Mexico.

LONGACRE, WILLIAM A.
1970   *Archaeology as Anthropology: A Case Study*. University of Arizona, Anthropological Papers, vol. 17, Tucson.

LORENZO, JOSÉ LUIS
1965   *Tlatilco: Los Artefactos (III)*. Serie Investigaciones, no. 7. Instituto Nacional de Antropología e Historia. Mexico.

LOWE, GARETH W.
1959   *Archaeological Exploration of the Upper Grijalva River, Chiapas, Mexico*. New World Archaeological Foundation, Papers, vol. 2, Provo.
1962   *Mound 5 and Minor Excavations, Chiapa de Corzo, Chiapas, Mexico*. New World Archaeological Foundation, Papers, vol. 12, Provo.
1971   The Civilizational Consequences of Varying Degrees of Agricultural and Ceramic Dependency Within the Basic Ecosystems of Mesoamerica. In *Observations on the Emergence of Civilization in Mesoamerica*. University of California Archaeological Research Facility, Contributions, no. 11, pp. 212–48, Berkeley.

LOWE, GARETH W., AND PIERRE AGRINIER
1960   *Mound 1, Chiapa de Corzo, Chiapas, Mexico*. New World Archaeological Foundation, Papers, vol. 8, Provo.

LOWE, GARETH W., AND J. ALDEN MASON
1965   Archaeological Survey of the Chiapas Coast, Highlands, and Upper Grijalva

REFERENCES

Basin. *Handbook of Middle American Indians* 2:195–236.

MACNEISH, RICHARD S.
- 1954 An Early Archaeological Site Near Panuco, Vera Cruz. American Philosophical Society, Transactions, vol. 44, pp. 539–641, Philadelphia.
- 1970 Social Implications of Changes in Population and Settlement Pattern of the 12,000 Years of Prehistory in the Tehuacán Valley of Mexico. In *Population and Economics*, ed. by P. Deprez, pp. 215–50. University of Manitoba Press, Winnipeg.
- 1972 The Evolution of Community Patterns in the Tehuacán Valley of Mexico and Speculations about the Cultural Processes. In *Man, Settlement and Urbanism*, ed. by Peter J. Ucko, Ruth Tringham, and G. W. Dimbleby, pp. 67–93. Duckworth, London.

MACNEISH, RICHARD S., AND FREDERICK A. PETERSON
- 1962 *The Santa Marta Rock Shelter, Ocozocoautla, Chiapas, Mexico*. New World Archaeological Foundation, Papers, vol. 14, Provo.

MACNEISH, RICHARD S., ANTOINETTE NELKEN-TERNER, AND IRMGARD W. JOHNSON
- 1967 *The Prehistory of the Tehuacan Valley*. Vol. 2, *Nonceramic Artifacts*. University of Texas Press, Austin.

MACNEISH, RICHARD S., FREDERICK A. PETERSON, AND KENT V. FLANNERY
- 1970 *The Prehistory of the Tehuacan Valley*. Vol. 3, *Ceramics*. University of Texas Press, Austin.

MEIGHAN, CLEMENT W.
- 1970 Obsidian Hydration Rates. *Science* 170:99–100.

MEIGHAN, CLEMENT W., LEONARD J. FOOTE, AND PAUL V. AIELLO
- 1968a Obsidian Dating in West Mexican Archeology. *Science* 160:1069–75.
- 1968b Obsidian Dating Revisited. *Science* 162:814.

MELLAART, JAMES
- 1967 *Çatal Hüyük: A Neolithic Town in Anatolia*. McGraw-Hill, New York.

MIRANDA, F.
- 1947 Rasgos de la Vegetación de la Cuenca del Río de las Balsas. *Revista de la Sociedad Mexicana de Historia Natural* 8:95–114.

MORRIS, CRAIG
- 1972 State Settlements in Tawantinsuyu: A Strategy of Compulsory Urbanism. In *Contemporary Archaeology: A Guide to Theory and Contributions*, ed. by Mark P. Leone, pp. 393–401. Southern Illinois University Press, Carbondale.

MORRIS, CRAIG, AND DONALD E. THOMPSON
- 1970 Huanuco Viejo: An Inca Administrative Center. *American Antiquity* 35:344–62.

MOSELEY, MICHAEL E.
- 1975 *The Maritime Foundations of Andean Civilization*. Cummings, Menlo Park.

MUMFORD, LEWIS
- 1960 University City and Concluding Address. In *City Invincible: A Symposium on Urbanization and Cultural Development in the Ancient Near East*, ed. by Carl H. Kraeling and Robert McC. Adams, pp. 5–19, 224–46. University of Chicago Press, Chicago.

MUNSELL COLOR CO., INC.
- 1954 *Munsell Soil Color Charts*. Baltimore.

MURRA, JOHN V.
- 1962 An Archaeological "Restudy" of an Andean Ethnohistorical Account. *American*

Antiquity 28:1-4.
1968   An Aymara Kingdom in 1567. *Ethnohistory* 15:115-51.
1972   El "Control Vertical" de un Máximo de Pisos Ecológicos en la Economía de las Sociedades Andinas. In *Visita de la Provincia de León de Huánuco (1562)*, vol. 2, pp. 429-76. Universidad Hermilio Valdizán, Huanuco.

NAVARRETE, CARLOS
1959   *A Brief Reconnaissance in the Region of Tonalá, Chiapas, Mexico.* New World Archaeological Foundation, Papers, vol. 4, Orinda.
1960   *Archaeological Explorations in the Region of the Frailesca, Chiapas, Mexico.* New World Archaeological Foundation, Papers, vol. 7, Provo.
1969   Los Relieves Olmecas de Pijijiapan, Chiapas. *Anales de Antropología* 6:183-95.
1971   Algunas Piezas Olmecas de Chiapas y Guatemala. *Anales de Antropología* 8:69-82.

NICHOLSON, HENRY B.
1971a   Major Sculpture in Pre-hispanic Central Mexico. *Handbook of Middle American Indians* 10:92-134.
1971b   Religion in Pre-hispanic Central Mexico. *Handbook of Middle American Indians* 10:395-446.

NOGUERA, EDUARDO
1965   *La Cerámica Arqueológica de Mesoamérica.* Instituto de Investigaciones Históricas, Primera Serie, no. 86. Universidad Nacional Autónoma de México, Mexico.

OCHOA CAMPOS, MOISES
1964   *Guerrero: Análisis de un Estado Problema.* Trillas, Mexico.

PADDOCK, JOHN
1968   Current Research: Western Mesoamerica. *American Antiquity* 33:122-8.

PARSONS, JEFFREY R.
1968   Teotihuacan, Mexico, and Its Impact on Regional Demography. *Science* 162:872-7.

PARSONS, LEE A., AND BARBARA J. PRICE
1971   Mesoamerican Trade and Its Role in the Emergence of Civilization. In *Observations on the Emergence of Civilization in Mesoamerica.* University of California Archaeological Research Facility, Contributions, no. 11, pp. 169-95, Berkeley.

PATTERSON, THOMAS C.
1971a   Chavín: An Interpretation of Its Spread and Influence. In *Dumbarton Oaks Conference on Chavín*, ed. by Elizabeth P. Benson, pp. 29-48. Dumbarton Oaks Research Library and Collection, Washington.
1971b   The Emergence of Food Production in Central Peru. In *Prehistoric Agriculture*, ed. by Stuart Struever, pp. 181-207. Natural History Press, Garden City.
1973   *America's Past: A New World Archaeology.* Scott, Foresman, Glenview.

PIÑA CHÁN, ROMÁN
1955a   *Chalcatzingo, Morelos.* Dirección de Monumentos Prehispánicos, Informes, no. 4. Instituto Nacional de Antropología e Historia, Mexico.
1955b   *Las Culturas Preclásicas de la Cuenca de México.* Fondo de Cultura Económica, Mexico.
1958a   *Tlatilco (I).* Serie Investigaciones, no. 1. Instituto Nacional de Antropología e Historia, Mexico.

REFERENCES

1958b *Tlatilco: A Través de su Cerámica (II)*. Serie Investigaciones, no. 2. Instituto Nacional de Antropología e Historia, Mexico.

1971 Preclassic or Formative Pottery and Minor Arts of the Valley of Mexico. *Handbook of Middle American Indians* 10:157-78.

PIÑA CHÁN, ROMÁN, AND VALENTÍN LÓPEZ G.
1952 Excavaciones en Atlihuayán, Morelos. *Tlatoani* 1:12.

PIRES-FERREIRA, JANE W.
1975 *Formative Mesoamerican Exchange Networks with Special Reference to the Valley of Oaxaca*. University of Michigan, Museum of Anthropology, Memoirs, vol. 7, Ann Arbor.

1976a Obsidian Exchange in Formative Mesoamerica. In *The Early Mesoamerican Village*, ed. by Kent V. Flannery, pp. 292-306. Academic Press, New York.

1976b Shell and Iron-Ore Mirror Exchange in Formative Mesoamerica, with Comments on Other Commodities. In *The Early Mesoamerican Village*, ed. by Kent V. Flannery, pp. 311-26. Academic Press, New York.

PORTER, MURIEL NOE
1953 *Tlatilco and the Preclassic Cultures of the New World*. Viking Fund Publications in Anthropology, no. 19, New York.

PROSKOURIAKOFF, TATIANA
1960 Historical Implications of a Pattern of Dates at Piedras Negras, Guatemala. *American Antiquity* 25:454-75.

1961 The Lords of the Maya Realm. *Expedition* 4(1):14-21.

1971 Early Architecture and Sculpture in Mesoamerica. In *Observations on the Emergence of Civilization in Mesoamerica*. University of California Archaeological Research Facility, Contributions, no. 11, pp. 141-56, Berkeley.

RECINOS, ADRIÁN
1950 *Popol Vuh: The Sacred Book of the Ancient Quiché Maya*, trans. by Delia Goetz and Sylvanus G. Morley. University of Oklahoma Press, Norman.

RENFREW, COLIN, J. E. DIXON, AND J. R. CANN
1966 Obsidian and Early Cultural Contact in the Near East. *Proceedings of the Prehistoric Society* 32:30-72.

ROUSE, IRVING
1954 On the Use of the Concept of Area Co-Tradition. *American Antiquity* 19:221-5.

1955 On the Correlation of Phases of Culture. *American Anthropologist* 57:713-22.

1960 The Classification of Artifacts in Archaeology. *American Antiquity* 25:313-23.

1972 *Introduction to Prehistory: A Systematic Approach*. McGraw-Hill, New York.

SABLOFF, JEREMY A., AND ROBERT E. SMITH
1969 The Importance of Both Analytic and Taxonomic Classification in the Type-Variety System. *American Antiquity* 34:278-85.

SAHAGÚN, FR. BERNARDINO DE
1959 *Florentine Codex: General History of the Things of New Spain*. Book 9, *The Merchants*, trans. by A. J. O. Anderson and Charles E. Dibble. School of American Research and University of Utah Press, Santa Fe.

SANDERS, WILLIAM T.
1961 *Ceramic Stratigraphy at Santa Cruz, Chiapas, Mexico*. New World Archaeological Foundation, Papers, vol. 13, Provo.

SANDERS, WILLIAM T., AND BARBARA J. PRICE
1968 *Mesoamerica: The Evolution of a Civilization*. Random House, New York.

REFERENCES

SEARS, WILLIAM H.
  1960 Ceramic Systems and Eastern Archaeology. *American Antiquity* 25:324–9.
SERVICE, ELMAN
  1962 *Primitive Social Organization: An Evolutionary Perspective*. Random House, New York.
SHARER, ROBERT J.
  1974 The Prehistory of the Southeastern Maya Periphery. *Current Anthropology* 15:165–87.
SHARER, ROBERT J., AND JAMES C. GIFFORD
  1970 Preclassic Ceramics from Chalchuapa, El Salvador, and Their Relationships with the Maya Lowlands. *American Antiquity* 35:441–62.
SHEPARD, ANNA O.
  1965 *Ceramics for the Archaeologist*. Carnegie Institution of Washington, Publication 609, Washington.
SHOOK, E. M.
  1965 Archaeological Survey of the Pacific Coast of Guatemala. *Handbook of Middle American Indians* 2:180–94.
SMITH, ROBERT E., GORDON R. WILLEY, AND JAMES C. GIFFORD
  1960 The Type-Variety Concept as a Basis for the Analysis of Maya Pottery. *American Antiquity* 25:330–40.
SORENSON, JOHN L.
  1956 *An Archaeological Reconnaissance of West-Central Chiapas, Mexico*. New World Archaeological Foundation, Publication 1, Orinda.
STEWARD, JULIAN H.
  1955 Some Implications of the Symposium. In *Irrigation Civilizations: A Comparative Study*, ed. by Julian H. Steward. Social Science Monographs, no. 1, Pan American Union, Washington.
STIRLING, MATTHEW W.
  1942 *An Initial Series from Tres Zapotes, Veracruz, Mexico*. Contributed Technical Papers, Mexican Archaeology Series, vol. 1, no. 1. National Geographic Society, Washington.
  1943 *Stone Monuments of Southern Mexico*. Smithsonian Institution, Bureau of American Ethnology, Bulletin, no. 138, Washington.
  1955 *Stone Monuments of the Rio Chiquito, Veracruz, Mexico*. Anthropological Papers, no. 43. Smithsonian Institution, Bureau of American Ethnology, Bulletin, no. 157, pp. 1–28. Washington.
  1964 The Olmecs: Artists in Jade. In *Essays in Precolumbian Art and Archaeology*, ed. by S. K. Lothrop, pp. 43–59. Harvard University Press, Cambridge.
  1968 Early History of the Olmec Problem. In *Dumbarton Oaks Conference on the Olmec*, ed. by Elizabeth P. Benson, pp. 1–8. Dumbarton Oaks Research Library and Collection, Washington.
STRONG, WILLIAM D., A. V. KIDDER, AND A. J. D. PAUL
  1938 *Preliminary Report on the Smithsonian Institution–Harvard University Archeological Expedition to Northwestern Honduras, 1936*. Smithsonian Miscellaneous Collections, vol. 97, no. 1, Washington.
STROSS, F. H., J. R. WEAVER, G. E. A. WYLD, R. F. HEIZER, AND J. A. GRAHAM
  1968 Analysis of American Obsidians by X-ray Fluorescence and Neutron Activation Analysis. In *Papers on Mesoamerican Archaeology*. University of California Archaeological Research Facility, Contributions, no. 5, pp. 59–75, Berkeley.

REFERENCES

STUART, L. C.
    1964   Fauna of Middle America. *Handbook of Middle American Indians* 1:316–62.

THOMPSON, J. E. S.
    1943   *Some Sculptures from Southeastern Quezaltenango, Guatemala.* Notes on Middle American Archaeology and Ethnology, no. 17. Carnegie Institution of Washington, Division of Historical Research, Cambridge.
    1956   *Notes on the Use of Cacao in Middle America.* Notes on Middle American Archaeology and Ethnology, no. 128. Carnegie Institution of Washington, Division of Historical Research, Cambridge.

TOLSTOY, PAUL
    1971a   Recent Research into the Early Preclassic of the Central Highlands. In *Observations on the Emergence of Civilization in Mesoamerica.* University of California Archaeological Research Facility, Contributions, no. 11, pp. 25–8, Berkeley.
    1971b   Utilitarian Artifacts of Central Mexico. *Handbook of Middle American Indians* 10:270–96.

TOLSTOY, PAUL, AND A. GUENETTE
    1965   Le Placement de Tlatilco dans le cadre du pré-classique du Bassin de Mexico. *Journal de la Société des Américanistes* 54:47–91.

TOLSTOY, PAUL, AND LOUISE I. PARADIS
    1970   Early and Middle Preclassic Culture in the Basin of Mexico. *Science* 167:344–51.

VAILLANT, GEORGE C.
    1930   *Excavations at Zacatenco.* American Museum of Natural History, Anthropological Papers, vol. 32, pt. 1, New York.
    1931   *Excavations at Ticoman.* American Museum of Natural History, Anthropological Papers, vol. 32, pt. 2, New York.
    1932   A Pre-Columbian Jade. *Natural History* 32:512–20.
    1935   *Excavations at El Arbolillo.* American Museum of Natural History, Anthropological Papers, vol. 35, pt. 2, New York.

VAILLANT, SUZANNAH B., AND GEORGE C. VAILLANT
    1934   *Excavations at Gualupita.* American Museum of Natural History, Anthropological Papers, vol. 35, pt. 1, New York.

VIVÓ ESCOTO, JORGE A.
    1964   Weather and Climate of Mexico and Central America. *Handbook of Middle American Indians* 1:187–215.

WAGNER, PHILIP L.
    1964   Natural Vegetation of Middle America. *Handbook of Middle American Indians* 1:216–64.

WARREN, BRUCE W.
    1961   The Archaeological Sequence at Chiapa de Corzo. In *Los Mayas del Sur y sus Relaciones con los Nahuas Meridionales,* pp. 75–83. Octava Mesa Redonda, Sociedad Mexicana de Antropología, Mexico.

WEAVER, MURIEL PORTER
    1967   *Tlapacoya Pottery in the Museum Collection.* Indian Notes and Monographs, Miscellaneous Series, no. 56. Museum of the American Indian, Heye Foundation, New York.
    1972   *The Aztecs, Maya and Their Predecessors: Archaeology of Mesoamerica.* Seminar Press, New York.

WEST, ROBERT C.
- 1964a The Natural Regions of Middle America. *Handbook of Middle American Indians* 1:363–83.
- 1964b Surface Configuration and Associated Geology of Middle America. *Handbook of Middle American Indians* 1:33–83.

WHEATLEY, P.
- 1971 *The Pivot of the Four Quarters: A Preliminary Enquiry into the Origins and Character of the Ancient Chinese City.* Aldine, Chicago.

WILLEY, GORDON R.
- 1945 Horizon Styles and Pottery Traditions in Peruvian Archaeology. *American Antiquity* 11:49–56.
- 1948 A Functional Analysis of "Horizon Styles" in Peruvian Archaeology. In *A Reappraisal of Peruvian Archaeology,* ed. by Wendell C. Bennett. Society for American Archaeology, Memoirs, vol. 4, pp. 8–15, Menasha.
- 1962 The Early Great Styles and the Rise of the Pre-Columbian Civilizations. *American Anthropologist* 64:1–14.
- 1970 Type Descriptions of the Ceramics of the Real Xe Complex, Seibal, Peten, Guatemala. In *Monographs and Papers in Maya Archaeology.* Peabody Museum of Archaeology and Ethnology, Papers, vol. 61, pp. 313–55, Cambridge.

WILLEY, GORDON R., AND PHILIP PHILLIPS
- 1958 *Method and Theory in American Archaeology.* University of Chicago Press, Chicago.

WILLEY, GORDON R., T. PATRICK CULBERT, AND RICHARD E. W. ADAMS, EDS.
- 1967 Maya Lowland Ceramics: A Report from the 1965 Guatemala City Conference. *American Antiquity* 32:289–315.

WITTFOGEL, KARL
- 1957 *Oriental Despotism: A Comparative Study of Total Power.* Yale University Press, New Haven.
- 1972 The Hydraulic Approach to Pre-Spanish Mesoamerica. In *The Prehistory of the Tehuacan Valley.* Vol. 4, *Chronology and Irrigation,* ed. by Frederick Johnson, pp. 59–80. University of Texas Press, Austin.